HANDBOOK FOR THE COMMON LECTIONARY

HANDBOOK FOR THE COMMON LECTIONARY

Edited by
Peter C. Bower

Developed by

The Office of Worship
of the
Presbyterian Church (U.S.A.)

Published by
The Geneva Press
Philadelphia

Book design by Christine Schueler

First edition

Published by The Geneva Press®
Philadelphia, Pennsylvania

PRINTED IN THE UNITED STATES OF AMERICA
2   4   6   8   9   7   5   3

Library of Congress Cataloging-in-Publication Data

Handbook for the Common lectionary.

   Bibliography: p.
   Includes indexes.
   1. Bible—Homiletical use. 2. Bible—Liturgical
lessons, English. 3. Lectionaries. 4. Bible—
Criticism, interpretation, etc. I. Bower, Peter C.
II. Common lectionary.
BS534.5.H36 1987   264′.34   86-31949
ISBN 0-664-24048-8 (pbk.)

TO
MOLLY MARGARET

One of Christ's grace-filled servants

"Wherever she was, there was Eden."
—Samuel Clemens

CONTENTS

ABBREVIATIONS

GG	The Gelineau Gradual
GP	Gradual Psalms
HB	The Hymnbook
HL	The Hymnal
LBW	Lutheran Book of Worship
LW	Lutheran Worship
MFT	Music from Taizé
MP&E	Morning Praise and Evensong
NHAS	New Hymns for All Seasons
NSC	New Songs for the Church
OEW	On Eagle's Wings
PFTD	The Psalmody for the Day
PP	Psalm Praise
PS	A Psalm Sampler
SOT&P	Songs of Thanks and Praise
WB	The Worshipbook
WII	Worship II
24P&1C	Twenty-four Psalms and a Canticle
30P&2C	Thirty Psalms and Two Canticles
(E)	Easy
(M)	Medium
(D)	Difficult

PREFACE

Since the beginnings of Christianity, the reading of scripture and its interpretation have been given special importance in Christian worship. Paul admonished early church leaders to devote particular attention to the public reading of the scriptures (1 Tim. 4:13). In scripture reading and sermon, the faithful are nurtured in the faith, guided in the life of discipleship, and bound together in the body of Christ.

The custom of reading a series of biblical lessons in worship is inherited from the ancient Jewish synagogue. Across the centuries, numerous lectionaries have been developed to ensure that the fullness of scripture is declared over a period of time. Lectionaries, by providing selected passages to be read in public worship throughout the church year, set forth a systematic and comprehensive approach to the use of scripture. A lectionary is therefore a helpful means of acquainting the faithful with the full range of scripture in all its richness and variety.

Presbyterians in the United States have had a lectionary since early in this century. In 1932 a brief lectionary was included in *The Book of Common Worship*. In 1946 the lectionary in use in the Church of Scotland was included in *The Book of Common Worship*. This lectionary was complete, appointing Old Testament, Epistle, and Gospel lessons and a psalm for each Sunday and festival for a two-year period. In 1964 a trial-use lectionary was introduced as part of a process to revise *The Book of Common Worship*. However, when the Catholic lectionary appeared, the committee responsible for revising *The Book of Common Worship* recognized the potential of the new lectionary and set aside the trial-use selections. After making appropriate changes for Presbyterian use, the Catholic lectionary was incorporated, in 1970, in *The Worshipbook*, the successor to *The Book of Common Worship*.

The Catholic lectionary was developed for use in the Roman Catholic Church as part of its post-Vatican II liturgical reformation. An ecumenical group of thirty biblical scholars assisted in its development, and it soon became an ecumenical lectionary. Other denominations and ecclesiastical bodies followed the Presbyterians in adopting it, making their own revisions. The result was five versions of the lectionary, even though nearly all the readings in each version were held in common.

In 1980, the Joint Office of Worship of the antecedent denominations of the Presbyterian Church (U.S.A.) developed *A Handbook for the Lectionary* (Geneva Press) to provide a resource to assist users of the lectionary in *The Worshipbook*. Horace T. Allen, Jr., was the author and editor. Dr. Allen included a provocative essay on understanding the lectionary. He also incorporated many practical helps organizing material that had previously been published in the journal *Reformed Liturgy & Music*, of which Dr. Allen had been editor. The book was well received by pastors, musicians, and worship committees.

With the appearance of the new Common Lectionary, however, the resource became largely out of date. The Common Lectionary is the work of an ecumenical body, the Consultation on Common Texts. In response to the appearance of five versions of the lectionary, the Consultation formed a committee to resolve the differences among the various versions and prepare a consensus lectionary to recommend to the churches. The committee was chaired by Dr. Lewis A. Briner, a Presbyterian pastor. Horace T. Allen, Jr., who was then chairperson of the Consultation on Common Texts, also played an important role in its development. The committee's work was published in 1983 as *Common Lectionary: The Lectionary Proposed by the Consultation on Common Texts* and is available from The Church Hymnal Corporation (800 Second Avenue, New York, NY 10017). In addition to resolving differences among the various versions, the Common Lectionary also represents efforts to overcome some of the weaknesses of the Catholic lectionary that became apparent through its use. Presbyterians and others soon incorporated the readings appointed in the Common Lectionary into their publications. For Presbyterians, the Common Lectionary has now largely replaced the one in *The Worshipbook*.

With the implementation of the Common Lectionary it was clear that a new resource, comparable to *A Handbook for the Lectionary*, was needed. The Office of Worship anticipated the need of such a resource and immediately began publishing in its journal, *Reformed Liturgy & Music*, practical suggestions for using the Common Lectionary. When the three-year cycle was completed, Peter C. Bower, editor of *Reformed Liturgy & Music*, was engaged to further edit the material that had been published and write an introductory essay on using lectionaries. This *Handbook for the Common Lectionary* is the result.

Like its predecessor, this handbook provides three scripture readings for each Lord's Day and each festival of the year in the three-year cycle, together with brief notations on each reading to help the reader to interpret the nature of the passage. Suggestions for musical settings for the psalm appointed for the day are listed. Hymns and anthems, based upon the readings or their themes, are also suggested. Pastors, musicians, and worship committees are thus given practical help in worship planning.

We commend the book to all who are concerned that scripture be given a central place in the worship of the church.

HAROLD M. DANIELS
Director of the Office of Worship
Presbyterian Church (U.S.A.)

INTRODUCTION

To use a lectionary or not to use a lectionary—that is *not* the question. A lectionary simply provides for a systematic reading of the scriptures. Or one could say, more eloquently, lectionaries are "orderly sequences of selections from Scripture to be read aloud at public worship by a religious community."[1] By either definition, lectionaries explicitly intend to allow a community of faith to hear the fullness of the Bible in an orderly manner.

Clearly, any system of selecting biblical texts for a community of faith will eventually create a lectionary—a table of readings in an orderly sequence. The selections need not be bound in book form, or printed ahead in table form, or used by more than one community of faith. Any compilation of an orderly sequence of selections from scripture for use within a congregation may be classified as a lectionary.

Technically speaking, of course, a lectionary is the actual book of lections ("scripture lessons") to be read according to a prescribed schedule during either Sunday worship or daily prayer. Some traditions (e.g., Roman Catholic) print the assigned scriptural texts in a single volume entitled *Lectionary.* Such a book eliminates the need for flipping pages when shifting from one reading to the next, marking beginnings and endings of pericopes, or even looking up the scheduled readings for the day. One simply opens the lectionary and reads the texts for the day as printed. Such user-friendly material is common nowadays. One variation is the weekly bulletin cover or insert that contains the actual text of the scripture readings for the day—as if each week you received a page from a book-length lectionary. By saving all the pages of the weekly lections for a whole year, you could assemble them into your very own twelve-month lectionary. Also, lectionary software will soon be widely available for computers. When that time arrives, options will abound: we will be able to print the assigned texts in the weekly order for worship, on bulletin inserts for further study after worship or as a preview for the following week, in church newsletters, for display on the narthex bulletin board, and so forth—all technological-age appropriations of the ancient lectionary.

The word "lectionary" is also commonly used to refer to a list of scheduled lections for a period of time. When preachers say they "preach from the lectionary," they are usually referring to a schedule of readings rather than an actual book. Such tables of readings are often printed in church service books or distributed in pamphlet form and will be available on computer software also.

Usually one thinks of a lectionary, either a book or a list, as an advance schedule of lections to be read. But one could possibly conceive of a lectionary as a record of lections already read over a period of time: a lectionary in retrospect. In that extended sense, a lectionary could look either forward to scheduled readings or backward to actual lections read over several months or even years. In both cases, one would discern an "orderly sequence of selections from Scripture"—the lectionary's essential ingredients.

The root of the word "lectionary" is the Latin *lectio* (lection, lesson, or selection), which denotes "a picking out or selecting, a reading." Preachers who choose their own readings and assign them to a day are, in effect, building their own sequence of biblical selections—a self-chosen lectionary-under-construction. If we compiled all these texts at the end of a year, we would have a twelve-month lectionary in retrospect. On the other hand, preachers who pick their biblical texts according to a commonly accepted set of readings are adhering to a previously ordered table of biblical selections. The sequence is known well in advance by all parties concerned.

Thus whether or not to use a lectionary is not the question, because everyone uses a lectionary of one form or another. The question is, Which kind of lectionary will we use? Or, more to the point, Who will select the texts, and on what basis will they be selected?

Two Basic Patterns for Text Selection

Over the past two thousand years, two basic systematic approaches to text selection have evolved: beeline, or *lectio continua*, and leapfrog, or *lectio selecta*.

Lectio continua

Lectio continua, the "continuous reading" of a biblical book, verse by verse, would mean in its purest form beginning at Genesis 1:1 and reading straight through to Revelation 22:21. This systematic approach to the orderly reading of scripture may derive from the centuries-old custom of continuous reading of the entire Torah (Pentateuch) in Jewish synagogues on a weekly basis throughout the year, a practice still continued today.

A close cousin to continuous reading is the method of "semi-continuous reading," which moves through a biblical book, section by section, but skips over passages regarded as less important (e.g., genealogies or lists of kings).

Lectio selecta

Lectio selecta, "selected reading," chooses a biblical text according to its relationship to time of year, first lesson, festival, theme, and so forth. The Jewish practice of selecting a second lesson called haftarah, a reading from the Prophets, demonstrates this ancient method of choosing a biblical text to coincide with the time of year or the lesson from the Torah. Some scholars[2] cite this pattern in Luke 4:16–30, the account of Jesus' sermon in his hometown synagogue at Nazareth. When he stood to read, Jesus was given the book of the prophet Isaiah and read what we know today as the first two verses of chapter 61—an example, perhaps, of a haftarah reading.

A multiple use of *lectio selecta* for a day would form a *cento* or combination of passages. Two ways[3] of creating this patchwork composition of verses from various parts of a biblical book or books are (1) "mosaic" type (cf. testimony books) and (2) "harmony," used especially with the Gospels (beloved from Tatian's time to modern conflates of "the History of the Passion").

Whether the text selectors are individuals or groups, people intrinsic or extrinsic to the life of a worshiping congregation, the biblical texts will be chosen according to either *lectio continua* or *lectio selecta* (the beeline or the leapfrog approach), or a combination of the two.

Caution: Any pattern for selecting biblical texts will inevitably result in "a canon within the Canon"—implying that the passages not included are of lesser value. This thought should give us pause before we succumb to the temptation to believe a faultless form of text selection exists, much less a perfect lectionary. Given such a caveat, the important question is the basis for selecting biblical texts. On what grounds were the specific biblical texts chosen for a particular congregation in a particular week in a particular place? Why were texts chosen throughout history?

Factors That Shaped the Organizing of Lectionaries

Luther Reed sums up some of the contributing forces[4] that shaped the organizing of lectionaries and resulted in an ongoing blending of both *lectio continua* and *lectio selecta*. (Neither method of text selection seems to dominate the other consistently.)

1. Early on, story and time—canon and calendar—were interrelated. Biblical books, on the basis of their contents, were naturally associated with certain seasons. For example, Job and Jonah were drawn to Good Friday—an early application of *lectio selecta*.

2. Biblical books were also often read in continuous fashion—*lectio continua*.

3. But the ordering of time also was interrelated with liturgical practice through a common calendar with its church festivals and seasons, which often interrupted such *lectio continua* sequences and set the mood for choices from scriptures.

4. Baptism and its preparation were powerful factors, particularly during the Lenten season when preparing for Easter baptisms.

5. Commemoration of saints accounts for other choices.

6. Sometimes a combination of themes and saint's days shaped a season.

7. "Station churches" in Rome, where the pope celebrated Mass on a set date, played a part.

8. Agricultural year determined some selections (e.g., parables of the Laborers in the Vineyard on Septuagesima and the Sower on Sexagesima reflected that this time of the year—February—was a season for preparing vineyards and fields in Italy).

9. Specific historical situations were a factor (e.g., Jesus weeping over Jerusalem, assigned to a Sunday near August 10, the traditional date for the fall of Jerusalem in 586 B.C.E. *and* 70 C.E.).

These factors that influenced the shaping of lectionaries over the centuries gave birth to a great variation in schemes for public reading of the Bible. To repeat, neither the *lectio continua* nor the *lectio selecta* pattern has consistently prevailed. There is an unlimited number of ways to compile a lectionary.

The Limitless Variety of Lectionaries

Not only are there a vast number of ways to organize a lectionary, but a lectionary is often intended for a particular group of readers. Lectionaries can be grouped by common language, geographical region, culture, history, liturgical rite, denominational or confessional family, tradition, worldwide ecumenical fellowship, continuity of centuries (time), biblical, theological, or social themes, or any combination of the above. Given such variety, one must ask: What principles of text selection will a lectionary adopt? What are the purposes of the lectionary? On what bases will it be constructed? To answer these questions, one must ask a number of others.

1. *What is the breadth of the canon included in the text selections?* What is the "official storybook" of the church, or at least the stories that will be told and retold through a lectionary?

2. *Who selected the texts?* Was it an individual, representatives of a group, the whole group, a commission, a committee? Who appointed the members of the commission or committee, an individual or a group?

3. *What length of time does the lectionary encompass?* A cluster of festivals, Sundays, or weekdays? Several weeks or months? A season, a year, two years, three years, six years?

4. *How many readings are there for each day?*

5. *Does each reading stand on its own,* or does it relate to other readings of the day, season, or year?

6. *What is the length of the readings?* A few verses or many? Sections of stories, or stories in their entirety? Does the lectionary allow the inclusion of an extraordinarily long story that has a number of movements woven through its narrative tale?[5]

7. *For whom is the lectionary intended?* An individual's private study and meditation, or a group's public reading and reflection, or a combination?

8. *For what type of service are the readings intended?* What is their intended liturgical use, eucharistic or daily prayer (matins/vespers)?

9. *Are there calendrical connections?* Any relationship between story and ordered time, canon and calendar? Are there appropriate times at which some stories should be told? For instance, do the Christmas and Easter stories coincide with their calendrical days of the year?

10. *Are there cultic conjunctions?* Any relationship between story and liturgical practice, canon and cult? Do any liturgical celebrations influence the selection of a particular text or vice versa? For example, do baptisms, historical situations, saint's days, or thematic days prompt the choosing of texts?

Any historical survey of lectionaries quickly reveals a multitude of responses to these questions. No two lectionaries are identical, for each was designed by different people at different times in different places and for different purposes. The diversity of lectionaries in format, length, purpose, and texture is as varied as the people of God who have used them. In the 1970s, American Lutheran revisers considered fifty-nine pericopic systems; in the 1960s, Roman Catholics analyzed Latin lectionaries from the sixth to twelfth centuries, checked fifteen Eastern rites, and surveyed dozens of Protestant lectionaries from the Reformation to the present.[6]

The Inseparable Link Between Story and Time

A primary factor in shaping the organizing of lectionaries has been the inseparable link between story and time, which has braided together *lectio continua* and *lectio selecta*. Story and time always have been connected. As far back as 15,000 years ago, Cro-Magnon humans lived and hunted in the Vézère River valley of southwestern France and painted on their cave walls pictures of hundreds of animals—deer, cows, horses, bison, boars, stags, ibex. They painted on top of their paintings and on top of past paintings for thousands of years, always expressing their recollections of past hunts as well as their hopes for future hunts—storytelling across time. Their everyday life, therefore, was informed and directed by past events providing future hopes.

We twentieth-century Americans find great affinity for such recollections and hopes across time. Any Fourth of July celebration exhibits recollections of the past and hopes for the future—storytelling across time. Our present-day life is informed and directed by past deeds providing future hopes.

Hearing the stories of God's past frees us to have faith in God's future and, therefore, live in the present. "Faith comes from what is heard," writes Paul (Rom. 10:17). By hearing the stories of God's faithful past and promised future, we know to whom we belong and to what we are called in the present, where God's unfinished story inexorably moves toward God's promised future. Recalling the events, covenants, and promises in the story of God-with-us enables us to appropriate them for the present moment and be continually transformed by them. These stories across time endlessly rewrite and redirect our past-present-future life.

That Jewish and Christian worship, therefore, instinctively linked story and time is really no surprise. It was the only way to wend through the record of time with any stability and direction. The foundational "Hebrew corporate-historical model of worship" delineated by David Buttrick[7] is ipso facto grounded in community *and* set in motion by a sense of narrative history or movement across time. God's purposeful design directs the people of God toward an end. Therefore, God's people are on the go, on the move with God.

Jews annually retell, in the context of a communal meal, the exodus story about God redeeming them from bondage. The Haggadah (narrative story) for the Seder (order of service) at Pesach (Passover) is an all-encompassing, identity-shaping, and direction-giving story across time about how God liberates them from slavery. By passionately telling their children year after year the story of the exodus from affliction, suffering, sorrow, and struggle, Jews articulate an alternative world that forms the heart of their people. The more they relive that story, the more permanent it becomes for their present and future lives. Without the exodus story there is no people called Israel.

Likewise, without the Paschal Vigil (or even a truncated Easter-morning celebration) and its life-shaping stories, there is no people called Christians. The great saving acts of the Lord not only recorded in scripture but read, contemplated, proclaimed, interpreted, and lived over and over again create an alternative world that forms the heart of Christ's church. If Christians were asked, "Where is your

God?" they would be apt to answer, "Well, the strangest thing happened to us on a hill outside Jerusalem. . . ."

Both Jewish and Christian worship include retelling the memory of God's faithful past (story—canon) and ritually enacting that past (cult—liturgical practice) in order to have hope in God's promised future and thereby live freely in the present. Telling the story of God-with-us and naming that presence on daily, weekly, monthly, seasonal, and annual cycles (ordered time) always have been and still are crucial to both Jewish and Christian worship. That is why lectionaries across the centuries have intentionally or unintentionally linked story and time and therefore always blended *lectio continua* and *lectio selecta*.

Four Commonly Voiced Disadvantages to Using a Lectionary

Many people use the word "lectionary" to refer only to "orderly sequences of selections from Scripture" chosen by people other than themselves. Most objections to the use of a lectionary, therefore, relate to the issue of text selection: criteria for selecting, who selects, the process by which texts are chosen, what is selected, when a text is selected, and so forth. Four distinct yet overlapping disadvantages are usually voiced by such opponents to use of a lectionary.

The freedom of the pulpit (or preacher) is hampered

A lectionary curtails, if not revokes, the freedom of the preacher to select the biblical text for public worship. This hindrance is often couched in language about "the freedom of the pulpit." If the pulpit is truly free, this argument goes, the pastor alone must choose the text(s) upon which the sermon will be based. A lectionary, therefore, drains the creativity of a preacher's freedom to choose and to think carefully about the appropriate text for the following Sunday's circumstances. Pastors who yield to a lectionary as the medium for selecting the weekly word of God surrender a significant theological decision. Result: the decline of the pastor as an active theologian.

Perhaps the underlying objection to this seeming abolition of clerical authority regarding text selection is, "I want to choose my own text; I don't like an external authority selecting the text for me." Or, more pointedly, "I don't like having someone else tell me on which biblical text to preach; conversely, I know best what God wants said on a given Sunday to the people I serve." That's understandable, because few people like being told what to do. One of the reasons many people stay away from churches in the first place is that they don't like Jesus' commandments: "Love one another as I have loved you" (John 15:12); "Love your enemies and pray for those who persecute you" (Matt. 5:44); "Sell your possessions, and give alms" (Luke 12:33). While we may allow Christ to issue orders to us, we hardly desire to succumb to a mere mortal, Paul, instructing us to "feed your enemies if they are hungry, and give them drink if they are thirsty" (Rom. 12:20), or "bear one another's burdens, and so fulfil the law of Christ" (Gal. 6:2).

Some questions regarding this disadvantage

1. To what extent is "freedom of the pulpit" a pastoral prerogative jealousy guarded within some traditions of the church?

2. To what extent does "freedom of the pulpit" regarding text selection risk becoming rampant individualism?

3. To what extent do we wish to be linked to others in the body of Christ?

4. To what extent do we seek commonalities of the faith? (Perhaps the same question could be asked regarding our use of eucharistic prayers, orders for worship, psalmody, hymnody, or other elements of corporate worship.)

5. At what point does the subjectivity of an individual's selections hinder the community of the faithful from hearing the fullness of the word of God?

6. What role does the subjectivity of the individual play in selecting weekly passages?

Time does not order scripture; scripture orders time

This disadvantage may be translated as "*lectio continua* supersedes *lectio selecta.*" These protestors believe that lectionary users (or, more specifically, *lectio selecta* users) submit themselves and make scripture beholden to the calendar of the church year. Thus, time orders scripture, for lessons are determined by themes from the liturgical calendar. Hughes Oliphant Old accurately depicts the development of this pattern of liturgical preaching:

> Leo the Great was the bishop of Rome from 440 to 461. . . . His preaching is not primarily a systematic attempt to interpret Scripture but rather a series of sermons based on the lectionary. Leo's sermons are based on the *lectio selecta*. His sermons are not intended to explain the Scripture lessons which have been read so much as to present the liturgical theme of the day. They are liturgical homilies rather than expositions of Scripture.[8]

Lectio selecta, therefore, simply lifts up timely themes to coincide with the seasons of the year. Time orders scripture. *Lectio continua*, on the other hand, calls us to the authority of scripture, which has its own order. Scripture, thus, orders time.

Some questions regarding this disadvantage

1. Does such a critique recognize that over 60 percent of the Sun-

days of the year occur during ordinary time—days that are not included under feasts and festivals of the church—when *lectio continua* takes precedence in text selections?

2. Should this concern be categorized under biblical preaching vs. topical preaching rather than biblical preaching vs. liturgical preaching?

3. May all lectionary preaching be fairly characterized as lifting up liturgical themes rather than biblical themes?

4. To what extent will preachers heed Hughes Oliphant Old's wise injunction on biblical preaching, "Great preaching takes time"?[9]

5. Would sole use of *lectio continua* uncouple story from time, unintentionally detach story from the flow of past-present-future time?

The world sets the agenda for text selection

Many people empirically proclaim that over the centuries those preachers who exercised the greatest impact upon their world were those who spoke to the needs and issues of their day.[10] It is no surprise, then, that those who favor the world (events) setting the agenda for the church object to using a lectionary. And with good reason: "For some people, the very idea of liturgical preaching conjures up an image of total irrelevance: priests dressed in outlandish clothes, who, after performing arcane rituals, address the initiates on such esoteric topics as Gelasian sacramentaries, Nicene Creeds, Whitsuntide, antependia, Gregorian chant, epicleses, and responsorial psalms."[11]

Who sets the agenda for preaching, a preplanned, rigid lectionary or the events of the world, near and far? Aspects of life should set the agenda for worship. Any events that impinge on our life together should be brought to worship, whether they be local or national elections, assassinations, gene-splicing, military invasions of one country by another, landmark judicial cases, or suicides. From near to far, local and cosmic events with overarching significance cry out for explanation.

Some questions regarding this disadvantage

1. To what extent should preachers heed Karl Barth's judicious counsel to prepare sermons with the Bible in one hand and the daily newspaper in the other so that preachers might perceive the interactive (rather than dominating) relationship between the two?

2. Are prophetic sermons on the issues of the day more relevant than lectionary preaching that speaks the word of God to concrete circumstances of the world in which we live?

3. To what extent are we to hear the scriptures as God's living Word for all people in all times and all places?

4. Is the weekly question for preachers, On what event(s) to preach a biblical word? Or, In what way(s) does the biblical text allow the preacher to speak to the event?

The needs of people set the agenda for text selection

There is an ongoing need for pastoral sensitivity to the needs of people. An impersonal system of text selection cannot respond to the daily struggles of life. Lectionary texts do not match what's happening to people. Therefore, lectionaries are out of sync with the daily events of life, whether they are crisis situations—such as natural disasters, shelter for the homeless, a fatal auto accident, domestic violence, grief, or marital difficulties—or events known in advance— such as abortion issues, state placement in the community of a group home for the mentally retarded, anxiety over an announced job promotion, construction of a freeway through the neighborhood, or alcoholism. Lectionaries do not allow for situational preaching.

Obviously, issues of the day within people's lives, the world, nation, state, city, or town may interrupt *any* systematic approach to selecting biblical texts. One hopes that preachers do not feel frozen in a system that prevents responding to issues of import for the community of faith that gathers to worship. At the same time, one hopes that preachers would first reexamine the lectionary passages for the day and open themselves to the possibility that one of the texts may speak precisely to the event at hand.

> If we are to believe that the lectionary and the liturgy can be a source of preaching that not only comforts but also challenges the faithful, it means, of course, that we begin with the conviction that the scriptures and the liturgy are *not*, in themselves, at odds with or out of touch with what is human. In fact, it means that we see in the scriptures a continual attempt to wrestle with the very meaning of human existence at the level of depth, and that we accept the New Testament's presentation of Jesus as the one in whom the deepest meaning of existence is revealed.[12]

The two preceding disadvantages both relate to concerns for pastoral sensitivity and subjectivity regarding the precedence of world events and people's personal needs. Can lectionary preaching speak to such needs?

We all gasped in horror on Tuesday, January 28, 1986, the day of the incredible, heart-stopping tragedy of the space shuttle *Challenger*'s explosion shortly after lift-off, killing all seven crew members, including the beloved New Hampshire teacher, Christa McAuliffe, whose bold words, "Reach for the stars," have become an epitaph for the ill-fated mission. What did the biblical texts of the Common Lectionary have to say on the following Sunday? Which would you have selected as an appropriate Word of God for the Lord's Day that week?

Jeremiah 1:4–10 Jeremiah's vision, in which Yahweh anoints him to be a "prophet to the nations." "But I do not know how to speak," laments Jeremiah. "Fear not," answers Yahweh, "I am with you. What I command, you shall speak." Yahweh then touches Jeremiah's mouth, saying, "I have put my words into your mouth so that you shall speak the double-edged word of judgment and salvation that uproots and smashes, and builds and plants."

1 Corinthians 13:1–13 What is love? Love is action, not a feeling. Love is self-giving, even unto death, in the manner of Christ's self-giving. Love maintains all faithfulness, all hope, all steadfastness. Love is eternal because it is the purpose and nature of God. Today we see that dimly, but someday we shall see clearly and understand fully.

Luke 4:21–30 Everyone is aglow the day the hometown boy, Joseph's son, returns to preach his inaugural sermon. All speak well of him and marvel at his words, until he speaks about the favoring of outsiders—Gentiles by name. Then the crowd's admiration turns to rejection, and they seek to execute vigilante justice on the brow of a hill outside the city. Yet Jesus passes through the midst of this frenzied crowd and goes away.

During Liberty Weekend, July 4–6, 1986, the dedication ceremonies of the refurbished Statue of Liberty dominated the mass media—newspapers, radio, television, and magazines. We were saturated with the pageantry of dancing and singing around the feet of Lady Liberty. Showering fireworks seemed to radiate from her torch of freedom to the tired, the poor, and the downtrodden. What did the Word of God, as selected by the Common Lectionary, have to say on the final day of that celebratory weekend? You could have taken your pick among three incredibly timely passages.

1 Kings 21:1–3, 17–21 In expropriating Naboth's vineyard, King Ahab and Queen Jezebel did everything right and nothing wrong, according to the law. But they did everything wrong and nothing right, according to God's ethics; they are guilty of insidious murder and acquisitive land-grabbing, announces Yahweh's speaker, Elijah. Now Ahab will have to live with the consequences of his killing and seizing—his dynasty will end.

Galatians 6:7–18 Paul's final words to the Galatians: "Don't kid yourselves; God is not mocked. You are accountable for what you do and say. What you sow, you shall reap. Remember, the only thing you may glory in is the cross—the sign of the powers of the old order who humiliated and seemingly defeated our Lord Jesus Christ. Yet by the cross Christ transforms those who constitute God's people into a new creation of mercy and peace."

Luke 10:1–12, 17–20 Jesus appoints seventy others to go out into the world and harvest a ripe crop before it spoils in the field. He sends them ahead of himself, as lambs in the midst of wolves, to announce that "the kingdom of God has come near to you." In the face of adversity, the Seventy discover the incredible power of their Lord's words, but their real joy is in learning that God embraces them forever.

Upbeat or downbeat, unplanned or planned, tragedy or celebration, it is amazingly providential (some people would say coincidental) how systematic approaches to the exposition of scriptures yield unfathomable riches for the people of God when we allow the Word of God to speak to us, rather than futilely attempting to select a passage to confirm what we want to say. When a preacher has a topic or event in mind and is searching for a text, the temptation is to eisegete biblical texts while searching for the appropriate one—a risky business, at best, and a failure to allow the abundant fruit of the Word of God to speak to us, at worst. We are to stand under the Word of God and listen, guided by the tradition of the church over the ages.

Likewise, pastors are "set under" a lectionary's lessons, then invited to listen to the texts—as Hughes Oliphant Old urges—through disciplined study, patient contemplation, and careful preparation. Agreed, pastors have not chosen the lessons for the day, but pastors are still subject to the individual integrity of each lectionary's lesson as well as its interrelationship with each of the other texts.

Advantages to Using the Common Lectionary

Clearly signifies the centrality of the Word for Christian worship

This increases possibilities not only for biblically based sermons (as opposed to topically based sermons) but for all of corporate worship. When worship planners begin with a biblical text, all elements of corporate worship—hymns, anthems, prayers, service music, as well as environment, movement, mood, dance, visual arts, sound, scent, and appropriate signs and symbolic acts—may arise from and complement both the scripture reading(s) and each other. Biblical texts then clearly shape the other elements of Christian worship, which means "worship can then have scriptural integrity and consistency."[13]

Manifests our underlying unity with other Christians and nurtures a communal ecclesiology

By hearing and reflecting on the same passages of scripture on the Lord's Day, we establish and maintain ecumenical links with Christians of many other persuasions. "Behind this lectionary lies an ecclesiology that is communal, organic, and sacramental."[14]

The value of preaching from the lectionary is that it gives us a catholic canon, even though imperfect, rather than a private canon. We preach not an individual faith but rather the faith of the church, which examines and licenses us, thereby authorizing us to speak for it in preaching the faith of the universal community of believers.[15]

Regularly rehearses the work of Christ

The liturgical year that evolved over the centuries is in essence a retelling of the redemptive work (not the life) of Christ: he taught; he was crucified; he was raised up; he has given the Spirit. The intermixing of story, time, and liturgical practice in such a regular, orderly rehearsal of the work of Christ has been central to the church's corporate worship since the first century. "The lectionary was to proclaim the passion, death, resurrection, and ascension of Christ, fully realized in him and being realized in us who, through faith and baptism, have been joined to him."[16]

Increases possibilities for reading and preaching the Bible in its fullness

The Presbyterian Directory for the Service of God states it this way:

The Scripture: Breadth of Readings
The minister shall have discretion in the choice and length of the passages of Scripture read. In making these selections the minister should exercise care, so that over a period of time the people shall hear the full message of Scripture. . . . It is appropriate that the readings follow, with such latitude as may be proper in varying situations, a set order or lectionary designed to assure that the fullness of God's Word is declared.[17]

Conversely, one could say a congregation increases its chances for freedom from a preacher's selecting texts suited to his or her subjective interests. Or, as Lewis Briner states it, "The congregation's best defense against clerical caprice."[18]

Engenders weekday ecumenical study and planning

Using the lectionary promotes more than simply a sense of unity or commonality on the Lord's Day. An unexpected benefit of the past two decades has been the weekly study groups of pastors, musicians, and worship planners from various traditions who discuss the scriptures for the coming Sunday or exchange musical ideas, eucharistic prayers, litanies, or other liturgical forms. "In some places, congregations of different denominations are jointly supporting the ministry of a church musician who, by working with the lectionary, may provide similar musical contributions to the liturgy of those churches."[19]

Provides a useful planning tool

The lectionary allows advance planning and preparing for corporate worship on the Lord's Day. This is especially valuable for musicians, other artists, and presumably preachers, who well know the care and time needed for planning, ordering materials, and practicing ahead of time. Advance notice of the scripture readings makes it possible to block out actual services months before their time.

Encourages shared planning and shared leadership

Advance planning often leads to shared planning (which should help eliminate unintentional duplication of biblical texts in multiple-staff churches) and shared planning often means shared leadership in corporate worship, especially regarding the inclusion of laypeople. Unfortunately, we often limit our definition of leadership in public worship to speaking roles "up there in front of everyone." Acting, reading, singing, dancing, playing an instrument, and miming are only some of the latent skills waiting to be tapped within any community of faith. Shared leadership can allow worship to become corporate.

Fosters an orderly discipline for scriptural study

The printed lectionary enables both laity and clergy to study privately as a means of preparation for the approaching Sunday's corporate worship. An ever-increasing number of resources have flooded bookstores and church publishing house catalogs. Printed aids in particular, both Protestant and Roman Catholic, offer assistance in exegetical study, sermon preparation, and service planning. (See Resources at the back of this book.)

Equalizes clergy and laity

The rise of the Common Lectionary allows all church members to begin at the same level, for advance notice of scripture texts provides clergy and laity alike with a common basis in the Word of God, reinforces parity, helps remove any game-playing regarding what the word will be this week, undercuts pretentious notions of superiority, and helps pastors to step down from congregation-imposed or self-constructed pedestals.

Encourages worshipers to prepare for corporate worship

A widely disseminated advance list of scripture readings allows people to read and to study the actual lessons for the day ahead of corporate worship, which may be one of the most valuable tools for enriching church members' experience of corporate worship on the Lord's Day. The Directory for the Service of God states it this way:

> *The Lord's Day: Preparation for Worship*
> The worship of God requires preparation by prayer, meditation, study of the Bible, and physical rest, so that body and mind may be alert to the privileges and responsibilities of the Lord's Day.

Preaching and Hearing: Hearing the Word
The worshipers also have a duty in preaching, because preaching calls
for hearing as well as speaking. . . . As the preacher has obligations in
sermon preparation, so the hearer must also prepare to listen responsibly.[20]

If hearers are to "prepare to listen responsibly," any guidance given—
such as an advance announcement of the scripture readings scheduled for public worship, or a group study of those texts—can only
help hearers in their preparation. Indeed, it may be one of the most
effective ways not only to permit but to encourage worshipers to
prepare for corporate worship.

Provides multiple lections

These lections, sometimes consonantal, sometimes dialectical, af-
ford the "richness of counterpoint and stereo, rather than just a thin
monaural melody line."[21] The underlying premise of a multiple lection system is the often-cited Reformation principle (quoting a maxim
of Augustine) that "the best interpreter of Scripture is Scripture itself."

The Singular Strength of the Common Lectionary:
Communal Ecclesiology

First, a note of pessimism. All the preceding advantages can be
abrogated by whimsical, irresponsible, lazy, ignorant clergy and laity.
Temptations to be successful abound. E. Glenn Hinson has observed
that the prevailing social model of North America, that of the business corporation, has imposed itself or been absorbed (without res-
ervation) by churches all across the land.[22] Constantly, we are
bombarded with management jargon that labels ministry as understanding church organizational behavior, establishing goals and objectives, setting budgets, managing fiscal affairs, recruiting members,
developing leaders, assessing personnel, sustaining professional
growth, enabling change, managing conflict, and administering pro-
grams—from brainstorming through prioritizing, impacting, pro-
gramming, and evaluating. Whatever happened to preaching and
teaching the good news?

In a time of decline in membership and influence of the church,
clergy and laity are understandably tempted to embrace these seemingly successful models of corporate management. Unfortunately,
the "goals and objectives" (if one dares to name them as such) of the
gospel are often obscured in the interests of the financial and numer-
ical success of the corporation church. In terms of lectionary use,
James F. White has remarked that the dominance of the "success
motive" in our culture often leads to the selection of user-friendly
biblical texts (or topics) upon which to preach. The name of that game

is "telling people what they want to hear—or already believe."

Therefore, in the name of success, every "advantage to lectionary use" can be mutilated into a disadvantage through eisegesis, lack of planning, self-preservation, closed-mindedness to fresh ideas or new theologies ("I know what I believe, don't confuse me with the facts" mentality), procrastination, endless novelty of gimmicks, lazy habits regarding reading and study, pastoral self-interest, subjectivity, ignorance, tendentious views, temptation to skip over difficult texts, shaping the word of God to our prejudices and limited vision, lack of pastoral relationship with the congregation, ad infinitum.

On the other hand, all but one of the preceding advantages may be reinforced by sensitive, intelligent, effective, conscientious biblical preachers. All but one advantage could be put to beneficial use by responsible clergy and laity who select their own "orderly sequence of selections from Scripture to be read aloud at public worship"—a lectionary in the broadest sense of the word.

But one advantage—the nurturing of communal ecclesiology—comes only with a widely used lectionary such as this one. Why? Because hidden in such a lectionary lies an ecclesiology that is communal. The determinative principle of this present lectionary, notes J. Irwin Trotter, is implied:

> Here is the clue to the fundamental organizing principle of the Lectionary: the central importance of the Eucharist in the worship of the church. Salvation is not something that happens individually, but it is incorporation into the whole. Preaching has the function of drawing persons into this Eucharistic fellowship. This is really the basic organizing principle behind the Lectionary.[23]

The reason this is such a paradoxically threatening and transforming advantage is that it grates against the entrenched individualism of the culture in which we live and are nourished daily, sometimes within the church itself, where we experience "very personalist and solitary ways of worshiping, 'telling your beads' alone in a corner, while the priest was whispering the Mass in Latin."[24] Individualism appears in every commonly voiced disadvantage to use of a lectionary.

The very fact that the Common Lectionary scripture texts are read and preached during the weekly Lord's Day corporate worship allows their mysterious bonding force to work its wonder among worshiping communities of Christians. "When in the history of the church Catholic and Reforming have we had such a potent instrument and symbol both of our unity in the Word and of our calling to mission?"[25]

The Formation of NACCL

"Nothing else in the past fifty years has made quite the ecumenical impact in the North American continent as has this Sunday after Sunday use of essentially the same scripture lessons at public worship by Christians of varying traditions."[26] Because of this widespread use among English-speaking churches on the North American continent, and in light of critical concerns for a commonly agreed upon table of readings as well as other improvements, "the (North American) Consultation on Common Texts (CCT) convened in Washington, D.C., a conference attended by representatives of thirteen churches in the United States and Canada, March 29–31, 1978. The purpose was to assess the usefulness of the Roman Lectionary and to determine what steps, if any, should be taken in terms of harmonization and revision."[27] The minutes of that conference state, "The representatives voted unanimously that they desired closer unity and as much consensus as possible with the three-year lectionary."[28]

In addition, the representatives attending this conference "agreed on a calendar, on the need for a commonly accepted schedule of psalmody, and on certain terminology. In particular they recommended to the Consultation on Common Texts that it set up a small working body to produce a consensus table of readings which would revise the present Old Testament selections in the Sunday cycle."[29]

A ten-member NACCL labored for four years and then submitted its work to the CCT for approval. The two articles that best describe further the process of the Consultation on Common Texts' ongoing "harmonization and revision" of the Roman Lectionary are Horace T. Allen, Jr., Introduction to *Common Lectionary: The Lectionary Proposed by the Consultation on Common Texts* and Lewis A. Briner, "A Look at New Proposals for the Lectionary."[30]

Briner also identifies nine "problem areas" in the Roman-ecumenical lectionary appropriated by North American churches:[31]

1. The most problematic area: simplistic use of prophecy-fulfillment themes in selecting Old Testament texts
2. Meager number of narrative Old Testament passages
3. Breaking up Old Testament books into short snippets
4. Lack of Old Testament passages illustrating the role of women in sacred history
5. For some churches, the inclusion of deuterocanonical (apocryphal) readings
6. Insufficient opportunity for continuous or semicontinuous reading
7. Omission of certain verses, producing gaps in the readings
8. Occasional inadequate scene setting because of omission of introductory verses that identify speaker or context
9. Varying methods of counting and naming days, particularly after Epiphany of the Lord and Day of Pentecost, creating differing liturgical calendars

Principles of Text Selection in the Common Lectionary

The impetus for all current lectionaries was provided by the Roman Catholic lectionary of 1969, adapted by numerous churches, especially in North America. *The Worshipbook—Services* (Presbyterian), published in 1970, became the ecumenical forerunner in offering a modification of that Roman Catholic lectionary. Alterations included inserting canonical lections for deuterocanonical texts, lengthening some pericopes, and plugging some gaps in the readings. Since the Common Lectionary is essentially a harmonization of denominational lectionaries begotten by this Roman Catholic parent, it is important to identify some generative principles underlying the creation of the 1969 Roman Catholic lectionary and still presupposed in the Common Lectionary.[32]

1. Finds thematic unity in the Paschal mystery, "which had been completed in Christ and is to be completed in us."[33] Coupled with the eucharistic context (no. 6 below), this principle produces the strong Christocentric focus of selected texts.

2. Reasserts the Christological base of the weekly festival (Lord's Day) for the annual cycles of incarnation and resurrection (Christmas and Easter).[34]

3. Provides three readings for each weekly Lord's Day Eucharist—one each from the Old Testament, Epistles, and Gospels.

4. Sets up a multiple-year cycle of three years' duration, primarily to permit a yearly focus on each of the Synoptic Gospels.

5. Uses both the "thematic harmony" and the "semicontinuous reading" methods of selecting texts. Often unnoticed by exegetes, preachers, and liturgy planners is this two-pronged principle of selecting texts according to both *lectio continua* and *lectio selecta* because there are two sets of Sundays: those in the Christmas and Easter cycles (which utilize the *lectio selecta* method), and those in ordinary time (which employ the ongoing story in a semicontinuous manner).

6. Presents the eucharistic service as the liturgical context of the readings. "The eucharistic context of this lectionary is clearly also the single most significant factor in the dominance of the Gospel lesson as the 'controlling' lesson."[35]

In addition, the ten questions posed earlier in this introduction, regarding the operative principles of any lectionary, require some response concerning the Common Lectionary.

1. *What is the breadth of the canon included in the text selections?* What is the "official storybook" of the church, or at least the stories that will be told and retold through a lectionary? Though a representative sampling of salvation-history narratives as well as other seminal stories are included, the Old Testament readings in the Roman-

ecumenical lectionaries are the most constant point of contention because of reliance on the prophecy-fulfillment theme for their selection. The Common Lectionary seeks to rectify this dilemma partially by including semicontinuous readings on the Sundays after Pentecost, as well as more readings from the Prophets and Wisdom literature. Concerning the New Testament, essentially all the Synoptic Gospels may be read, as well as substantial portions of John, Acts, Epistles, and Revelation.

2. *Who selected the texts?* More properly, one should ask, Who resolved the differences in the current lectionaries? A ten-member ecumenical committee—Roman Catholic, Episcopal, Presbyterian, Lutheran, and United Methodist pastors and scholars—set up by the Consultation on Common Texts (CCT).

3. *What length of time does the lectionary encompass?* A three-year cycle, primarily to permit a yearly focus on one of the Synoptic Gospels.

4. *How many readings are there for each day?* Three readings at each weekly Lord's Day service—one each from the Old Testament, Epistles, and Gospels.

5. *Does each reading stand on its own,* or does it relate to other readings of the day, season, or year? Both; it depends on whether it is a Sunday of a liturgical season or a Sunday in ordinary time; also, whether the reading has been selected according to the principle of thematic harmony or semicontinuous reading.

6. *What is the length of the readings?* A few verses or many? Sections of stories, or stories in their entirety? Does the lectionary allow the inclusion of an extraordinarily long story that has a number of movements woven through its narrative tale? Yes and no. Sometimes pericopes seem to include several stories and sometimes cut them off too soon. One must exercise care in altering any texts.

7. *For whom is the lectionary intended?* A group's public reading and reflection.

8. *For what type of service are the readings intended?* What is their intended liturgical use? A eucharistic context that includes the liturgy of the Word.

9. *Are there calendrical connections?* Any relationship between story and ordered time, canon and calendar? The inseparable link between story and time clearly comes into focus here as well as in numerous other aspects. For instance, incarnation (Christmas) and death-resurrection (Easter) stories do coincide with their calendrical days of the year.

10. *Are there cultic conjunctions?* Any relationship between story and liturgical practice, canon and cult? Liturgical celebrations do influence the selection of pericopes. For example, the eucharistic context prompts the Christocentric focus of texts.

CCT's Proposed Revisions to the Roman-Ecumenical Lectionary

"This CCT proposal is basically a *harmonization* of existing denominational tables and an *adaptation* of the Old Testament pericopes for the Sundays which follow Pentecost, to accord with a certain broadly defined typological principle and also to include semicontinuous reading of the Hebrew Bible."[36] Yet to be resolved is the concern that simplistic use of the prophecy-fulfillment theme seems to govern the choice of Old Testament readings; for some people this "invariable practice of choosing the Old Testament lesson to cohere with the gospel is hermeneutically indefensible and limiting."[37] Thus we face what Horace Allen calls "the complex issue of the Christian church's relation to Israel: to what extent must the Hebrew scriptures be 'christianized' in order to be scripture?"[38]

James Sanders presents a fivefold caution regarding various deficiencies:[39]

1. Dominance of calendar over canon; the subservience of the canon to the calendar

2. Dominance of New Testament over Old Testament

3. Dominance of Christocentric over theocentric approach

4. Dominance of early first-century salvation-history over preceding and succeeding centuries

5. Dominance of *lectio selecta* over *lectio continua*

To which Horace Allen responds that this lectionary's assumed "context is the un-Protestant (though not un-Reformed) weekly union of Word and Sacrament. This raises the Christological issue in a new way. However we might debate the need for more theocentric-Christocentric alternation as a theological matter, the cultic context of the Sacrament of Holy Communion . . . does emphatically affect the discussion. . . . Both the calendar and the cult of the church are emphatically Christological."[40]

1. In response to the lack of Old Testament stories, the following alterations attempt to increase that number through the inclusion of semicontinuous reading of Old Testament narrative passages (scheduled on the Sundays after Pentecost):

Year A—20 Pentateuchal stories (from the call of Abraham to the death of Moses), and 3 Sundays each of Ruth and prophetic eschatological texts

Year B—14 weeks of the Davidic Narrative, and 4 Sundays of Wisdom literature

Year C—Solomon's prayer (1 Kings 8) and 9 stories from the Elijah and Elisha cycles, and 15 weeks of writings from the Prophets

2. Additional Old Testament passages illustrate the role of women in sacred history.

Year A, Sundays between October 16 and November 5 (Propers 24, 25, 26), three successive readings:
Ruth 1:1–19a   Ruth's unilateral pledge to Naomi
Ruth 2:1–13   Ruth takes the initiative to provide food for Naomi
Ruth 4:7–17   Naomi's emptiness transformed into fullness through Ruth's faithful "steadfast love"
Year C, Sunday between July 17 and July 23 (Proper 11):
2 Kings 4:8–17   The woman of Shunem's hospitality for Elisha

3. There are alternatives to deuterocanonical texts.

2nd Sunday of Advent (C)	Baruch 5:1–9 *or* Mal. 3:1–4
1st Sunday after Christmas (C)	Ecclus. 3:3–7, 14–17 *or* 1 Sam. 2:18–20, 26
2nd Sunday after Christmas (ABC)	Ecclus. 24:1–4, 12–16 *or* Jer. 31:7–14
6th Sunday after the Epiphany (A)	Ecclus. 15:15–20 *or* Deut. 30:15–20
8th Sunday after the Epiphany (C)	Ecclus. 27:4–7 *or* Isa. 55:10–13

4. Some gaps in the readings are plugged.

Day	1970 Presbyterian Worshipbook Lectionary	1983 Common Lectionary
5th Sunday after the Epiphany (B)	1 Cor. 9:16–19, 22–23	1 Cor. 9:16–23
7th Sunday after the Epiphany (C)	1 Cor. 15:42–50	1 Cor. 15:35–38, 42–50
3rd Sunday in Lent (A)	John 4:5–15, 19–26	John 4:5–26, (27–42)
3rd Sunday in Lent (B)	Ex. 20:1–3, 7–8, 12–17	Ex. 20:1–17
5th Sunday in Lent (A)	John 11:1–4, 17, 34–44	John 11:(1–16), 17–45

5. Text lengthening and minor textual rearrangement includes contextual material, apostolic and personal greetings, and local ecclesial issues and accommodates churches reading from a Bible rather than a lectionary of readings.

Day	1970 Presbyterian Worshipbook Lectionary	1983 Common Lectionary
2nd Sunday of Advent (A)	Rom. 15:4–9	Rom. 15:4–13
2nd Sunday of Advent (B)	2 Peter 3:8–14	2 Peter 3:8–15a
Epiphany (ABC)	Eph. 3:1–6	Eph. 3:1–12
2nd Sunday after the Epiphany (A)	Isa. 49:3–6	Isa. 49:1–7
2nd Sunday after the Epiphany (C)	Isa. 62:2–5	Isa. 62:1–5
4th Sunday after the Epiphany (C)	Luke 4:22–30	Luke 4:21–30
5th Sunday after the Epiphany (A)	1 Cor. 2:1–5	1 Cor. 2:1–11
1st Sunday in Lent (B)	Mark 1:12–15	Mark 1:9–15
4th Sunday in Lent (A)	John 9:1–11	John 9:1–41
4th Sunday in Lent (B)	2 Chron. 36:14–21	2 Chron. 36:14–23
5th Sunday in Lent (A)	Ezek. 37:11–14	Ezek. 37:1–14

6. In order to synchronize all churches' methods of counting Sundays in ordinary time, the CCT has adopted a combination of the "Episcopalian method" of counting the weeks "backward" from the First Sunday of Advent and the "Methodist system" of identifying the actual dates between which a Sunday may occur. Therefore:

Proper 29 will always fall on the last Sunday after Pentecost (Christ the King), which will always occur between November 20 and 26.
Proper 28 will always occur between November 13 and 19.
Proper 27 will always occur between November 6 and 12.
Proper 26 will always occur between October 30 and November 5, and so forth, until you arrive at:
Proper 7 will always occur between June 19 and 25.
Proper 6 will always occur between June 12 and 18.
Proper 5 will always occur between June 5 and 11.
Proper 4 will always occur between May 29 and June 4.

7. In the event of a "late" Pentecost, scripture readings not needed in a particular year are omitted in the Sundays at the *beginning* of the post-Pentecost period. For example, in 1987:

Pentecost (June 7) will be followed by
Trinity Sunday (June 14), and then
Proper 7 (Sunday, June 21, which occurs between June 19 and 25).
In 1988:
Pentecost (May 22) will be followed by
Trinity Sunday (May 29), and then
Proper 5 (Sunday, June 5, which occurs between June 5 and 11).

Methods of Singing the Psalms

All the psalm settings, with the exception of those sung to Anglican chant, involve congregational participation. Except for the metrical and paraphrased psalms, most of the settings are responsorial—that is, an antiphon (refrain) sung by the congregation and the verses sung by a cantor, a choir, or both. Six types of psalmody are represented in the suggested psalm list.

1. *Metrical and paraphrased:* The texts of all the verses are in the same meter.

2. *Gelineau:* This method was created by Father Joseph Gelineau, a French Jesuit. The text to the psalm is chanted with accented words and syllables falling on a constant pulse throughout. The antiphon is usually metrical.

3. *Gregorian psalm tone:* The text is chanted on a reciting note, making use of a mediant cadence in the middle of the psalm verse and a final cadence at the end of the verse. An intonation is used to sing the first few syllables of each verse following the antiphon.

4. *Cantillation:* The verses are sung by a cantor with free improvisation on the text.

5. *Anglican:* The psalm is sung in harmony in speech rhythm.

6. *Mixed medium:* The rhythm is a combination of metrical and Gelineau styles of psalmody.

Contributors to This Handbook

The notes on the scripture readings, and the suggested psalm settings, hymns, and anthems were printed first in issues of *Reformed Liturgy & Music,* a quarterly journal of the Presbyterian Church (U.S.A.). *RL&M,* as it is commonly known, is published by the church's Office of Worship (Harold M. Daniels, Director) and has been designated by the Presbyterian Association of Musicians as its official journal.

Published under the ongoing title of "Practical Aids to Lectionary Use," these lectionary notes and musical suggestions were printed in *RL&M* from the Summer 1983 issue (vol. 17, no. 3), through the Spring 1986 issue (vol. 20, no. 2), with the following authors contributing the indicated material:

Lectionary Notes (Years A, B, C)

Peter C. Bower, Pastor of the Drayton Avenue Presbyterian Church, Ferndale, Michigan, and Editor of *Reformed Liturgy & Music*

Suggested Psalm Settings (Years A, B, C)

Hal H. Hopson, Resident Composer and Associate Professor—Church Music, Scarritt College, Nashville

Suggested Hymns and Anthems

Year A—Betty L. Peek and Richard M. Peek, Co-Directors of Music, Covenant Presbyterian Church, Charlotte, North Carolina

Year B—Lucile L. Hair, Director of Music, University Presbyterian Church, Baton Rouge, Louisiana

Year C—Robert Fort, Professor of Music, School of Music, Stetson
University, DeLand, Florida, and Organist–Choir Director of First
Presbyterian Church, DeLand, Florida

All these writers have used and continue to use the Common Lectionary on a regular basis in their ministries and hope their contributions
in this volume will further such use among many other communities
of faith in their corporate worship. May these notes and suggestions
prove, indeed, to be "practical aids to lectionary use."

PETER C. BOWER

NOTES

1. John Reumann, "A History of Lectionaries: From the Synagogue at Nazareth to Post-Vatican II," *Interpretation: A Journal of Bible and Theology*, vol. 3, no. 2 (April 1977), p. 116.
 2. Adolf Büchler, "The Reading of the Law and Prophets in a Triennial Cycle," *Jewish Quarterly Review*, vol. 6 (1894), p. 11; Hughes Oliphant Old, "The Ministry of the Word," *Worship: That Is Reformed According to Scripture*, in John H. Leith and John W. Kuykendall, series eds., *Guides to the Reformed Tradition* (Atlanta: John Knox Press, 1984), p. 60.
 3. Reumann, "A History of Lectionaries," p. 124.
 4. Luther D. Reed, *The Lutheran Liturgy*, rev. ed. (Philadelphia: Muhlenberg Press, 1960), pp. 460–462.
 5. Two examples of very long stories are 2 Kings 5, "Naaman, Elisha, and Gehazi: A Story of a Cleansed Leper and an Avaricious Servant, Linked by a Bold Confession of Faith and Two Mysterious Mule Loads of Earth," and John 9, "The Blind Man Who Sees More Clearly at Each Stage of Interrogation About His Healing."
 6. Reumann, "A History of Lectionaries," p. 127, n. 55.
 7. See David G. Buttrick, "A Sketchbook: Preaching and Worship," *Reformed Liturgy & Music*, vol. 16, no. 1 (Winter 1982), pp. 34, 35.
 8. Old, "The Ministry of the Word," *Worship: That Is Reformed According to Scripture*, pp. 66–67.
 9. Hughes Oliphant Old, book review of *A Handbook for the Lectionary*, by Horace T. Allen, Jr., *Worship*, vol. 56, no. 1 (January 1982), pp. 85, 86.
 10. Clyde E. Fant, Jr., and William M. Pinson, Jr., eds., *Twenty Centuries of Great Preaching*, vol. 1: *Biblical Sermons to Savonarola* (Waco: Word Books, 1971), p. v.
 11. William Skudlarek, "The Pastoral Use of the Lectionary," *The Word in Worship: Preaching in a Liturgical Context* (Nashville: Abingdon Press, 1981), p. 45.
 12. Ibid., p. 48.
 13. Lewis A. Briner, "Using the Lectionary," *Reformed Liturgy & Music*, vol. 9, no. 4 (Fall 1975), p. 14.
 14. J. Irwin Trotter, "Are We Preaching a 'Subversive' Lectionary?" *School of Theology at Claremont Bulletin: Occasional Paper Number 7*, vol. 28, no. 2 (December 1985), p. 1.
 15. James F. White, *Introduction to Christian Worship* (Nashville: Abingdon Press, 1980), pp. 138–139.
 16. William Skudlarek, "The Structure and Use of the Lectionary," *The Word in Worship: Preaching in a Liturgical Context*, pp. 33–34.
 17. Directory for the Service of God, *The Constitution of the Presbyterian Church (U.S.A.), Part II: Book of Order*, 1986–87 (New York and Atlanta: The

Office of the General Assembly of the Presbyterian Church (U.S.A.), 1986), S-2.0500.

18. Briner, "Using the Lectionary," p. 14.

19. Horace T. Allen, Jr., Introduction to *Common Lectionary: The Lectionary Proposed by the Consultation on Common Texts* (New York: Church Hymnal Corp., 1983), pp. 8–9.

20. Directory for the Service of God, *Book of Order*, 1986–87, S-2.0300; S-2.0600.

21. Briner, "Using the Lectionary," p. 15.

22. E. Glenn Hinson, "The Lima Text as a Pointer to the Future: A Baptist Perspective," pp. 9–10; an address to the Tenth International Congress of Societas Liturgica, meeting at Boston University, Boston, Massachusetts, August 1–6, 1986.

23. Trotter, "Are We Preaching a 'Subversive' Lectionary?" p. 2.

24. Ibid., p. 1.

25. Horace T. Allen, Jr., "Using the Consensus Lectionary: A Response," in *Social Themes of the Christian Year: A Commentary on the Lectionary*, ed. Dieter T. Hessel (Philadelphia: Geneva Press, 1983), p. 268.

26. Lewis A. Briner, "A Look at New Proposals for the Lectionary," *Worship*, vol. 3, no. 2 (1983), p. 83.

27. Allen, Introduction to *Common Lectionary*, p. 9.

28. Minutes of the Consultation on Common Texts (Washington, D.C., March 28–31, 1978).

29. Allen, Introduction to *Common Lectionary*, p. 9.

30. Allen, Introduction to *Common Lectionary*, pp. 7–27 (see note 19); Briner, "A Look at New Proposals for the Lectionary" (see note 26).

31. Briner, "A Look at New Proposals for the Lectionary," p. 84.

32. Horace T. Allen, Jr., describes in detail and comments on numerous principles and assumptions upon which the Roman Catholic and Common lectionaries have been constructed: Introduction to *Common Lectionary: The Lectionary Proposed by the Consultation on Common Texts*, pp. 10–19; "Understanding the Lectionary," *A Handbook for the Lectionary* (Philadelphia: Geneva Press, 1980), pp. 34–38; and "Using the Consensus Lectionary: A Response," in *Social Themes of the Christian Year: A Commentary on the Lectionary*, ed. Hessel, pp. 264–268. An additional summary of the primary principles upon which the 1969 Roman Catholic lectionary is built is in Skudlarek, "The Structure and Use of the Lectionary," *The Word in Worship: Preaching in a Liturgical Context*, pp. 32–37.

33. Skudlarek, "The Structure and Use of the Lectionary," p. 33, in which he cites Godfrey Diekmann, "Labores coetuum a studiis: De Lectionibus in Missa," *Notitiae* 1 (November 1975), pp. 33–37.

34. See Allen, Introduction to *Common Lectionary*, pp. 10–11.

35. Ibid., p. 16.

36. Ibid., p. 10.

37. Ibid., p. 18.

38. Allen, Introduction to *Common Lectionary*, p. 19.

39. James A. Sanders, "Canon and Calendar: An Alternative Lectionary Proposal," in *Social Themes of the Christian Year: A Commentary on the Lectionary*, ed. Hessel, pp. 258–260.

40. Allen, "Using the Consensus Lectionary: A Response," *Social Themes of the Christian Year*, p. 267.

FIRST SUNDAY OF ADVENT (A)

Isaiah 2:1-5 A vision of the coming Day of Yahweh, when all nations gather at the holiest of places, Mt. Zion, for Yahweh's teaching on the true way. Result: universal peace reigns; weapons and soldiers are passé because Yahweh judges all disputes.

Romans 13:11-14 The hour *(kairos)* of the Second Coming of the Lord *is* dawning. So awake, all believers, and be dressed; "put on Christ" and live as the people of light.

Matthew 24:36-44 All time is in God's hands. No one knows the day and the hour of the Second Coming when the remnant will be "taken" (welcomed). So, people of God, discard your everyday hustle-bustle and be vigilant, be prepared, and wait anxiously for the joy and excitement of the Lord's unknown return.

Psalm 122
1. Metrical psalm, *With Joy I Heard My Friends Exclaim,* from *The Psalter,* 1912, HB 439, tune: Morning Hymn
2. Gelineau, *I Rejoiced When I Heard Them Say,* GG, p. 155
3. Gregorian psalm tone, *GP,* Lent 4 B

Hymns for the Day	HL	HB	WB
Creator of the Stars of Night	–	–	348
Watchman, Tell Us of the Night	109	149	617
O God of Every Nation	–	–	498
O God of Earth and Altar	419	511	497
Wake, Awake, for Night Is Flying	–	–	614
Hark, What a Sound!	110	150	–
Hark! the Glad Sound, the Savior Comes	–	–	410

Anthems for the Day
Isa. 2:1-5 *And It Shall Come to Pass,* Jean Berger (Augsburg); SATB (D)

Rom. 13:11-14 *O Day Full of Grace,* Weyse—David Johnson (Augsburg); SAB (E)

Matt. 24:36-44 *Hosanna to the Son of David,* T. L. da Vittoria (Concordia); SATB (ME)

Ps. 122 *I Was Glad,* Peter Hallock (Walton); 2-part choir, congregation (E)

SECOND SUNDAY OF ADVENT (A)

Isaiah 11:1-10 A vision of a time of justice and of peace. From the stump of the tree of Jesse shall grow a new branch, a new ruler upon whom the Spirit of the Lord rests. Then wolves and lambs shall live together, and a little child shall lead them.

Romans 15:4-13 Christ Jesus is the fulfillment of the Old Testament hope and promise (e.g., Isa. 11:10). So in the same manner of Christ, care for one another and thus live in unity and harmony, glorifying God.

Matthew 3:1-12 From out of nowhere comes John the Baptist (an Elijah-like forerunner to Jesus), who preaches, "The time of 'the age to come' has drawn near; so turn yourselves to the new age." And all Jerusalem and Judea reorient their lives through baptism, confessing their sins. Now they are all charged with the awesome responsibility of bearing fruit that matches their reorientation to the new age.

Psalm 72:1-8
1. Metrical psalm, *Hail to the Lord's Anointed*, James Montgomery, *LBW* 87, tune: *Freut euch, ihr lieben*
2. Gelineau, *O God, Give Your Judgement*, *30P&2C*, p. 22
3. Gregorian psalm tone, *GP*, Advent 2 A

Hymns for the Day	HL	HB	WB
O Come, O Come, Emmanuel	108	147	489,490
Come, Thou Long-expected Jesus	113	151	342
Comfort, Comfort You My People	–	–	347
O Word of God Incarnate	215	251	532
Descend, O Spirit, Purging Flame	–	–	353
Love Divine, All Loves Excelling	308	399	471
Lo, How a Rose E'er Blooming	–	162	455

Anthems for the Day
Isa. 11:1-10 *O Come, O Come, Emmanuel*, arr. George Lynn (Mercury); 2-part mixed voices, organ (E)
Rom. 15:4-13 *Lord, Keep Us Steadfast*, Luther-Distler (Augsburg); SAB (E)
Matt. 3:1-12 *Comfort, Comfort Ye My People*, Claude Goudimel (*A First Motet Book,* Concordia); SATB (ME)
Ps. 72:1-8 *Psalm for Epiphany*, C. Alexander Peloquin (G.I.A.); SATB, congregation (M)

THIRD SUNDAY OF ADVENT (A)

Isaiah 35:1-10 The barren desert is going to bloom; therefore, strengthen your weak knees, stand up, and say, "God is coming to save you!" The blind, the deaf, the lame, the dumb—all shall be transformed.

James 5:7-10 In the same way that farmers await the harvest of their crops, cultivate patience as you await the coming of the Lord. Yes, the prophets were ill-treated for their proclamations but they patiently persisted. So faithfully and patiently continue your witness.

Matthew 11:2-11 Is Jesus of Nazareth the One who is to come, or should we look for another? "What do you hear and see?" replies Jesus. "The blind, the lame, lepers, the deaf, the poor, and the dead all live as if in the new age. What kind of person did you expect to see—a pietist hobnobbing with the king, or a radical social activist?"

Psalm 146:5-10
1. Psalm paraphrase, *Praise We Our Maker While We've Breath*, Isaac Watts, WB 558
2. Gelineau, *It Is He Who Keeps Faith For Ever*, GG, p. 7
3. Gregorian psalm tone, *GP*, Advent 3 A
4. *PS*, p. 36

Hymns for the Day	HL	HB	WB
Hail to the Brightness	391	505	–
Break Forth, O Beauteous Heavenly Light	–	–	314
Break Forth, O Living Light of God	–	–	316
Come, You Thankful People, Come	460	525	346
Christ Is the World's True Light	–	492	326
The Morning Light Is Breaking	389	499	–
Thy Kingdom Come, O Lord	425	488	–
Jesus Shall Reign	377	496	443

Anthems for the Day

Isa. 35:1-10 *Like as the Hart*, Giovanni Palestrina (*First Concord Anthem Book*, E. C. Schirmer; also available separately); SATB (M)

James 5:7-10 *Thou Knowest, Lord, the Secrets*, Henry Purcell (Novello); SATB (M)

Matt. 11:2-11 *Go and Tell John*, Lloyd Pfautsch (Hope); SATB (E)

Ps. 146:5-10 *With All My Whole Heart, O God*, Le Jeune–Couper (Mercury); SATB (ME)

FOURTH SUNDAY OF ADVENT (A)

Isaiah 7:10-16 Isaiah offers the disbelieving King Ahaz of Judah a sign of God's care, but the king piously refuses to test the Lord for a sign. "Well, then," says Isaiah, "the Lord will give you a sign: a young woman shall conceive and bear a son, and shall call his name Immanuel, for God is with his people."

Romans 1:1-7 Paul identifies himself as a slave of Jesus Christ and as one who has been entrusted and set apart by Christ to proclaim the gospel. Those whom Paul addresses are also called to belong to Christ and to proclaim the good news.

Matthew 1:18-25 Jesus' conception and birth is fulfillment of Isaiah's prophecy. This Son of David and Son of God, begotten through the Holy Spirit, is named Emmanuel, for God is with his people.

Psalm 24
1. Psalm paraphrase, *Lift Up Your Heads, Ye Mighty Gates,* George Weissel, trans. Catherine Winkworth, *HB* 152, *WB* 454, tune: Truro
2. Gelineau, *O Gates, Lift High Your Heads, GG,* p. 156
3. Gregorian psalm tone, *GP,* Advent 4 A
4. Mixed medium, *Psalm 24,* Arthur Wills (G. Schirmer)
5. *PS,* p. 16

Hymns for the Day	HL	HB	WB
Lift Up Your Heads, O Mighty Gates	114	152	454
Savior of the Nations, Come	–	–	565
O for a Thousand Tongues	199	141	493
O How Shall We Receive You	–	–	506
God Himself Is with Us	51	13	384

Anthems for the Day
Isa. 7:10-16 *Behold, a Virgin Shall Conceive* (recitative) and *O Thou That Tellest Good Tidings to Zion* (air and chorus), G. F. Handel (*Messiah,* ed. Watkins Shaw, Novello); alto solo and choir SATB (M)

Rom. 1:1-7 *Hosanna to the Son of David,* Gesius-Thomas (Concordia); SATB (E)

Matt. 1:18-25 *A Dove Flew Down from Heaven,* Hermann Schroeder (Concordia); SATB, flute, 2 violins (MD)

Ps. 24 *God Is My Strong Salvation,* Halsey Stevens (Mark Foster); SATB (E)

CHRISTMAS EVE/DAY (ABC)

Isaiah 9:2-7 Darkness reigns everywhere, yet people have seen a great light: the presence of God. All rejoice, as with joy at the harvest, for the rule of darkness will be lifted. A child shall reign as God's representative on earth, and God's light shall shine without end.

Titus 2:11-14 Jesus, the grace of God, has appeared for the salvation of all and taught us a new way of life. Because we now live in the light of his Second Coming, we can celebrate his first coming when he gave himself for us and set us free from all wickedness.

Luke 2:1-20 The birth of Jesus in the "city of David," Bethlehem, and the angelic proclamation to shepherds in the same area where David was a shepherd. *Gloria in excelsis!* The shepherds go to Bethlehem. As they return to their fields, they glorify and praise God "for all they had heard and seen." Their listeners are astonished. Mary treasures all these things.

Psalm 96
1. Metrical psalm, *O Sing a New Song to the Lord*, from the *Scottish Psalter*, 1650, *HB* 37, *WB* 525, tune: Song 67
2. Free paraphrase, *Earth and All Stars*, Herbert Brokering, *WB* 354, tune: Earth and All Stars
3. Gelineau, *O Sing a New Song to the Lord*, *GG*, p. 126
4. Gregorian psalm tone, *GP*, Christmas Day ABC
5. Anglican chant, *O Come, Let Us Sing*, William Boyce, *HB* 586
6. *PS*, p. 28

Hymns for the Day	HL	HB	WB
Ah, Dearest Jesus, Holy Child	118	173	279
All My Heart This Night Rejoices	125	172	287
Angels, from the Realms of Glory	124	168	298
Angels We Have Heard on High	–	158	299
Away in a Manger	126	157	–
The True Light That Enlightens Man	–	–	598
It Came Upon the Midnight Clear	127	160	438
Deck Yourself, My Soul (for Communion)	–	–	351
Silent Night	132	154	567
Hark! the Herald Angels Sing	117	163	411
What Child Is This	–	159	630

Anthems for the Day
Isa. 9:2-7 *For Unto Us a Child Is Born*, G. F. Handel (*Messiah*, ed. Watkins Shaw, Novello); (D)

Titus 2:11-14 *Of the Father's Love Begotten*, Richard Peek (C. Fischer); SATB (ME)

Luke 2:1-20 *In Excelsis Gloria*, Flor Peeters (Augsburg); SATB (E)

Ps. 96 *Psalm 96*, J. P. Sweelinck (Mercury); SATB (M)

CHRISTMAS DAY: ADDITIONAL LECTIONS 1 (ABC)

Isaiah 62:6-7, 10-12 Remind Yahweh of his promises and plead unceasingly for their fulfillment. Prepare the way, clear it of any obstacles, for Yahweh keeps his promises. "Behold, your salvation comes."

Titus 3:4-7 God our Savior has appeared and has saved us by God's mercy (and not because of any good deeds on our part). Through Jesus Christ our Savior, God has poured out the Holy Spirit on us and transformed us and given us new life in the waters of baptism.

Luke 2:8-20 Jesus is born in the "city of David," Bethlehem, and the angels tell the shepherds in the same area where David was a shepherd. *Gloria in excelsis!* The shepherds go to Bethlehem. As they return to their fields, they glorify and praise God "for all they had heard and seen." Their listeners are astonished. Mary treasures all these things.

Psalm 97
1. Metrical psalm, *The Lord Is King!*, Christopher Idle; *PP*, no. 112, contemporary musical setting by Norman Warren
2. Gelineau, *The Lord Is King*, GG, p. 163
3. Gregorian psalm tone, *GP*, Christmas Day 2 ABC

Hymns for the Day	HL	HB	WB
Joy to the World!	122	161	444
Born in the Night, Mary's Child	–	–	312
O Sing a Song of Bethlehem	138	177	526
O Little Town of Bethlehem	121	171	511
Once in Royal David's City	454	462	539
On This Day Earth Shall Ring	–	–	538
O Come, All Ye Faithful	116	170	486
What Child Is This	–	159	630

Anthems for the Day
Isa. 62:6-7, 10-12 *Zion Hears Her Watchman's Voices*, J. S. Bach (*Cantata 41, Sleepers, Wake!*, Belwin-Mills); unison male voices, violin, organ (E)

Titus 3:4-7 *Love Came Down at Christmas*, Joseph Goodman (A. Broude); 2-part chorus, organ (M)

Luke 2:8-20 *The Word Became Flesh*, George Brandon (E. C. Kirby); unison (E)

Ps. 97 *The Lord Is King O'er Land and Sea*, Heinrich Schütz (*Four Psalms*, Mercury) (CE)

CHRISTMAS DAY: ADDITIONAL LECTIONS 2 (ABC)

Isaiah 52:7-10 A messenger is coming across the mountains. Ascending and descending from one hill to the next, he joyously cries out, "Your God reigns!" Let everyone sing together of the "salvation of God."

Hebrews 1:1-12 God has spoken to us through the prophets; now God speaks uniquely to us through the Son, the descending-ascending savior of all. The true image of God is Christ, whose throne is forever and ever. He is of the same flesh and blood as we are, yet greater than all the angels. God's Son is the risen exalted Christ.

John 1:1-14 "In the beginning was the Word, and the Word was with God." All things were made through the Word, and in the Word were life and light. The Word came into the world and to God's people, but the world rejected the Word, as did God's people. Yet those who received and believed in the Word were given power to announce and to bear witness, as John (the Baptizer) did, to the coming of the Word among us, full of grace and truth.

Psalm 98
1. Metrical psalm, *New Songs of Celebration Render*, Erik Routley, *SOT&P*, p. 2, tune: *Rendez à Dieu*
2. Psalm paraphrase, *Sing a New Song to the Lord*, Timothy Dudley-Smith, *WII* p. 245, tune: *Cantate Domino* by David G. Wilson, contemporary setting
3. Gelineau, *Sing a New Song to the Lord, GG*, p. 15
4. Gregorian psalm tone, *GP*, Christmas Day 3 ABC

Hymns for the Day	HL	HB	WB
Book of Books	–	248	–
Christ for the World We Sing	–	489	–
Christ Is the World's Redeemer	–	136	–
Every Star Shall Sing a Carol	–	–	359
Father, We Greet You	–	285	364
God Has Spoken—by His Prophets	–	–	382
Joy to the World!	122	161	444
Light of the World, We Hail Thee	422	138	–
Of the Father's Love Begotten	–	7	534

Anthems for the Day
Isa. 52:7-10 *How Beautiful Are the Feet of Him*, G. F. Handel (E. C. Schirmer); SATB (E)
Heb. 1:1-12 *Let All the Angels of God Worship Him*, G. F. Handel (*Messiah*, ed. Watkins Shaw, Novello); SATB (M)
John 1:1-14 *Verbum caro factum est*, Hans Leo Hassler (A. Broude); SSATTB or SSATBB (MD)
Ps. 98 *O Sing Unto the Lord*, Hans Leo Hassler (E. C. Schirmer); SATB (M)

FIRST SUNDAY AFTER CHRISTMAS (A)

Isaiah 63:7-9 In the context of a lament, these words of thanksgiving recount the Lord's *hesed* (steadfast love). God made covenant with Israel and was her deliverer in Israel's exodus. God redeemed Israel through steadfast love. God was present with the people.

Hebrews 2:10-18 Jesus was of the same flesh and blood as all human beings. He experienced all that we experience: human existence, temptation, suffering, death. In fact, by suffering and dying he was "made perfect" (brought to completion) as one who totally shared humanity. Thus he became the pioneer of salvation and deliverer of all who fear death.

Matthew 2:13-15, 19-23 Rejection and persecution of Jesus by those in authority begins at birth. But God delivers Jesus through Joseph's obedience to divine commands. When the earthly rulers' clamor for Jesus' death subsides, Joseph again faithfully obeys divine commands and brings the child to the land of Israel, to the district of Galilee, in a city called Nazareth.

Psalm 111
1. Gregorian psalm tome *GP*, Epiphany 4 B
2. Cantillation (also tones are given for a simpler rendition), Arlo Duba, unpublished

Hymns for the Day	HL	HB	WB
All Beautiful the March of Days	471	96	281
Born in the Night, Mary's Child	–	–	312
Look, Ye Saints, the Sight Is Glorious	201	133	–
Lord, Bless and Pity Us	–	493	456
Love Divine, All Loves Excelling	308	399	471
My Faith Looks Up to Thee	285	378	–
Open Now the Gates of Beauty	–	40	544
Son of God, Eternal Savior	–	–	573
The Head That Once Was Crowned with Thorns	195	211	589

Anthems for the Day

Isa. 63:7-9 *For God So Loved the World*, Heinrich Schütz (*A Second Motet Book*, Concordia); SATB (M)

Heb. 2:10-18 *I Know Not How*, anonymous American hymn, tune arr. George Brandon (Art Masters); SATB (E)

Matt. 2:13-15, 19-23 *Coventry Carol*, arr. Martin Shaw (*Carols for Choirs*, Book I, Oxford); 2 versions: SAB original and SATB (E)

Ps. 111 *My Heart Is Full Today*, Richard Proulx (Augsburg); high and low voices (M)

THE NAME OF JESUS [January 1] (ABC)

Numbers 6:22-27 The well-known Aaronic blessing: three simple poetic lines, each petitioning Yahweh to move toward his people through the presence of his protection, favor, and peace. And where the name of Yahweh is put upon his people, he is present in blessing.

Galatians 4:4-7 When the right time had come, God sent his Son, fully human, to release all those under the law so they might be God's children. Then God sent the Spirit of his Son, who empowered these adopted children to name God as "*Abba*, Father."

or **Philippians 2:9-13** Part of a primitive Christological hymn; the name bestowed by God upon Jesus is the name "Lord." At the name of Jesus, may all confess him as Lord and live as his people, for God will support us.

Luke 2:15-21 Shepherds see what the angel of the Lord announced and thus glorify and praise God for all they have heard and seen. After eight days, the infant is circumcised and named "Jesus" in fulfillment of the angel's command at the annunciation.

Psalm 67
1. Metrical psalm, *Lord, Bless and Pity Us*, from *The Psalter*, 1912, HB 493, WB 456, tune: St. Michael
2. Gelineau, *O God, Be Gracious and Bless Us*, GG, p. 17
3. Gregorian psalm tone, *GP*, Proper 15 A
4. Mixed medium, *Psalm 67*, Arthur Wills (G. Schirmer)
5. *PS*, p. 21

Hymns for the Day	HL	HB	WB
All Hail the Power of Jesus' Name!	192	132	285
At the Name of Jesus	–	143	303
Born in the Night, Mary's Child	–	–	312
Creator of the Stars of Night	–	–	348
Gentle Mary Laid Her Child	453	167	375
Lord, Dismiss Us with Your Blessing	54	79	458
O Come, All Ye Faithful	116	170	486
While Shepherds Watched Their Flocks	120	169	643
We Gather Together	–	18	624

Anthems for the Day
Num. 6:22-27 *The Lord Bless You*, J. S. Bach (Concordia); SA or TB (M)
Gal. 4:4-7 or **Phil. 2:9-13** *At the Name of Jesus*, R. Vaughan Williams (Oxford); SATB with congregation (E)
Luke 2:15-21 *Magnificat*, R. Vaughan Williams (G. Schirmer); SATB or SAB or unison (E)
Ps. 67 *Psalm 67*, Regina Fryxell (H. W. Gray); unison with optional second part (ME)

JANUARY 1 [When observed as New Year] (A)

Deuteronomy 8:1-10 Moses exhorts the Israelites to obey the commandments: Remember all that Yahweh did for you as you wandered through the wilderness: Yahweh guided, clothed, nourished, sustained, taught, disciplined you. Live in his commandments.

Revelation 21:1-6a Visions of a new heaven and a new earth are seen. The new Jerusalem descends from God and joins the transformed earth where chaotic waters, tears, mourning, crying, death have all disappeared. Human beings will see God and live in holy fellowship together. Shouts the great voice from the throne, "I make all things new."

Matthew 25:31-46 A terrifying picture: Christ the judge, seated on a throne, separates the wicked from the righteous. All are judged by Christ's call to love endlessly: feed the hungry and the thirsty, welcome strangers, clothe the naked, visit the sick and the imprisoned. The wicked are shocked at their designation, for they did not see the face of Christ in their neighbors, particularly the lowly. Ironically, the righteous are just as surprised, for all they saw was human need and so responded with love.

Psalm 117
1. Psalm paraphrase, *From All That Dwell Below the Skies,* Isaac Watts, HB 33, WB 373, tune: *Lasst uns erfreuen*
2. Gelineau, *O Praise the Lord, 24P&1C,* p. 28
3. Taizé, *Laudate Dominum* (Praise the Lord, All You Peoples), *MFT* (vocal edition), p. 10

Hymns for the Day	HL	HB	WB
Ah, Dearest Jesus, Holy Child	118	173	279
God Is Working His Purpose Out	–	500	389
God of Our Life	88	108	395
Great God, We Sing That Mighty Hand	470	527	408
If You Will Only Let God Guide You	–	344	431
Jesus, Lead the Way	–	334	441
Our God, Our Help in Ages Past	77	111	549
O Holy City, Seen of John	409	508	505
Open Now the Gates of Beauty	–	40	544

Anthems for the Day
Deut. 8:1-10 *Lead Us, O Lord,* Thomas Bateson (Ars Nova [Brodt]); SATB (ME)
Rev. 21:1-6a *The Old Year Now Away Is Fled,* Richard Peek (H. W. Gray); SATB (E)
Matt. 25:31-46 *Enter Not Into Judgement,* Thomas Attwood (H. W. Gray); SATB (E)
Ps. 117 *Psalm 117,* Normand Lockwood (Kjos); SATB (MD)

SECOND SUNDAY AFTER CHRISTMAS (ABC)

Jeremiah 31:7-14 Shout for joy because the Lord has graciously delivered Israel from bondage. The Lord will gather the people (including those dependent upon others) from the ends of the earth and will shepherd them to flowing streams and reveal a father's love for his firstborn. Declare to the world, "The Lord has repurchased his flock; he will comfort them and bless them with abundant life."

Ephesians 1:3-6, 15-18 Thanks be to you, O God, for blessing our union with Christ by bestowing the gift of the Spirit, and for choosing us as your servants for the purpose of praising your glorious free grace. May the God of our Lord Jesus Christ continually give us discernment regarding our calling and rich inheritance.

John 1:1-18 "In the beginning was the Word, and the Word was with God." All things were made through the Word, and in the Word were life and light. The Word came into the world and to God's people, but the world rejected the Word, as did God's people. Yet those who received and believed in the Word were given power to announce and to bear witness, as John (the Baptizer) did, to the coming of the Word among us, full of grace and truth.

Psalm 147:12-20
1. Metrical psalm, *O Praise Your God, O Zion*, from *The Psalter*, 1912, *MP&E*, p. 69
2. Gregorian psalm tone, *GP*, Christmas 1 ABC

Hymns for the Day	HL	HB	WB
Break Forth, O Beauteous Heavenly Light	–	–	314
Joy to the World!	122	161	444
My Shepherd Will Supply My Need	–	–	477
O Word of God Incarnate	215	251	532
Praise to God, Immortal Praise	–	–	556
Praise Ye the Lord, for It Is Good	–	36	–
The King of Love My Shepherd Is	99	106	590
The Lord's My Shepherd	97	104	592
The True Light That Enlightens Man	–	–	598

Anthems for the Day
Jer. 31:7-14 *My Shepherd Will Supply My Need*, arr. Virgil Thomson (H. W. Gray); SATB (E)
Eph. 1:3-6, 15-18 *Benedictus*, David McK. Williams (H. W. Gray); unison (E)
John 1:1-18 *O Magnum Mysterium*, Ludovico da Vittoria (G. Schirmer); SATB (MD)
Ps. 147:12-20 *I Will Greatly Rejoice in the Lord*, Jean Berger (Augsburg); SATB (MD)

THE EPIPHANY OF THE LORD (ABC)

Isaiah 60:1-6 Awake, light has overcome the darkness! The glory of the Lord's presence will be reflected in Jerusalem's arising to rebuild the city. Open your eyes and see the caravans from all the nations that shall come of their own free will to your light. Rejoice, for they bring your sons and daughters as well as a multitude of treasures and herds of animals.

Ephesians 3:1-12 Paul's vocation is the privilege of making known to the Gentiles God's plan of salvation. And his gospel message is that through the sheer grace of God, the Gentiles have been included in God's people. Now all the people of God, Jews and Gentiles, share the same promises revealed in Jesus Christ and receive his Spirit to proclaim God's plan of salvation.

Matthew 2:1-12 Magi from the East come to Jerusalem in search of the King of the Jews. King Herod, out of fear, also wants to know where this threatening challenger can be found. Herod offers the magi a deal they can't refuse. But when the magi arrive in the presence of the child, they fall down on their knees and worship him and give him everything they have. They return home another way, other than through Herod's palace.

Psalm 72:1-14
1. Metrical psalm, *Hail to the Lord's Anointed,* James Montgomery, *LBW* 87, tune: *Freut euch, ihr lieben*
2. Gelineau, *O God, Give Your Judgement, 30P&2C,* p. 22
3. Gregorian psalm tone, *GP,* Advent 2 A

Hymns for the Day	HL	HB	WB
As with Gladness Men of Old	135	174	302
Brightest and Best	136	175	318
O Morning Star, How Fair and Bright	321	415	521
O One with God the Father	137	–	–
Savior of the Nations, Come	–	–	565
We Three Kings	–	176	–
What Star Is This	–	–	632

Anthems for the Day
Isa. 60:1-6 *For Behold, Darkness Shall Cover the Earth,* G. F. Handel (*Messiah,* ed. Watkins Shaw, Novello); bass solo (M)
Eph. 3:1-12 *Saw You Never in the Twilight,* Wilbur Held (Augsburg); unison (E)
Matt. 2:1-12 *The Three Kings,* Peter Cornelius, arr. Ivor Atkins (*Carols for Choirs,* Book I, Oxford); mezzo-soprano solo, SSAATTBB (M)
Ps. 72:1-14 *Psalm for Epiphany,* C. Alexander Peloquin (G.I.A.); SATB, congregation (M)

BAPTISM OF THE LORD
[First Sunday After the Epiphany] (A)

Isaiah 42:1-9 Yahweh officially presents his chosen servant, upon whom he has put his Spirit, who is to perform the task of bringing forth *mishpat* (justice) to the nations by his own suffering. Yahweh gives his servant as a light to the people who live in darkness.

Acts 10:34-43 In his speech to Gentile "God-fearers" at Cornelius' house in Caesarea, Peter recounts how his own life has been transformed by the power of the risen Lord, and that everyone else (Jews and Gentiles) also can be transformed by that power. God's desire is that all people be joined to Christ, for all have been acquitted.

Matthew 3:13-17 Jesus is baptized by John the Baptist. Why? According to Jesus' first words in Matthew's Gospel, to fulfill God's will and therefore begin to put God's plan into action. And as Jesus emerges from the water, God's Spirit descends upon him like a dove, and a voice from heaven says, "This is my beloved Son, with whom I am well pleased."

Psalm 29
1. Free paraphrase, *God the Omnipotent!*, Henry F. Chorley and John Ellerton, HB 487, tune: Russian Hymn
2. Gelineau, *O Give the Lord, You Sons of God*, 24P&1C, p. 10

Hymns for the Day	HL	HB	WB
As with Gladness Men of Old	135	174	302
Brightest and Best	136	175	318
Christ Shall Have Dominion	–	502	–
God Has Spoken—by His Prophets	–	–	382
Light of the World, We Hail Thee	422	138	–
What Star Is This	–	–	632

Anthems for the Day

Isa. 42:1-9 *But the Lord from the North*, Felix Mendelssohn (*Elijah*, no. 41, G. Schirmer); SATB (MD)

Acts 10:34-43 *At the Name of Jesus*, Jacobus Gallus (Concordia); SATB (ME)

Matt. 3:13-17 *The Lone, Wild Bird* (WB 591); unison or SATB (E)

Ps. 29 *Give to Jehovah*, Heinrich Schütz (*Morning Star Choir Book*, vol. 2, Concordia); unison (M)

SECOND SUNDAY AFTER THE EPIPHANY (A)

Isaiah 49:1-7 Yahweh's chosen servant summons the nations to hear Yahweh's word. The servant publicly announces his prenatal call and his subsequent despondency about performing the task in vain. But now Yahweh has expanded the call to be a light to all the nations (Gentiles), in order that "salvation may reach the ends of the earth."

1 Corinthians 1:1-9 The opening greeting and thanksgiving in which Paul thanks God for grace given through Christ Jesus. Therefore, we are enriched by spiritual gifts, particularly in "all speech and all knowledge." God has given us everything we need and will sustain us to the day of the Lord which brings judgment.

John 1:29-34 John (the Baptizer) identifies Jesus as the "Lamb of God" and the preexistent one. John bears this witness because he was given a divine revelation on how to recognize this one. So when John was baptizing with water, he saw the Spirit descend on Jesus like a dove from heaven and therefore bears witness that this Jesus is the "Son of God."

Psalm 40:1-11
1. Metrical psalm, *I Waited for the Lord My God,* from *The Psalter,* 1912, HB 413, tune: Arbridge
2. Gelineau, *I Waited, I Waited for the Lord,* GG, p. 107
3. Gregorian psalm tone, *GP,* Good Friday ABC

Hymns for the Day	HL	HB	WB
Behold the Lamb of God!	153	–	307
Christ, Whose Glory Fills the Skies	26	47	332
He Did Not Want to Be Far	–	–	412
O God, Our Faithful God	–	–	500
O Love, How Deep, How Broad, How High!	139	–	518
O Morning Star, How Fair and Bright	321	415	521
Spirit of God, Descend Upon My Heart	204	236	575

Anthems for the Day

Isa. 49:1-7 *Adam Lay Ybounden,* Philip Ledger (Oxford); (ME)

1 Cor. 1:1-9 *Almighty and Everlasting God,* Orlando Gibbons (Oxford); SATB (MD)

John 1:29-34 *Agnus Dei,* Gabriel Fauré, arr. Stevens (AMSI); SATB (M)

Ps. 40:1-11 *I Waited for the Lord,* Felix Mendelssohn (G. Schirmer); 2 soprano soloists and SATB (M)

THIRD SUNDAY AFTER THE EPIPHANY (A)

Isaiah 9:1-4 Darkness is everywhere, yet people have seen a great light—the presence of God. All rejoice, as with joy at the harvest, for the rule of darkness will be lifted.

1 Corinthians 1:10-17 Discussion, quarreling, disunity reign in the Corinthian church. Rival groups of people line up behind their favorite leader and rely on their own wisdom rather than the power of the cross. This church's life denies the gospel of Jesus Christ in which they all believe. "Thank God," says Paul, "that I am not your Savior."

Matthew 4:12-23 Jesus begins his public ministry in fulfillment of the prophecy according to Isaiah 9:1-2. He preaches that the kingdom of heaven is at hand, so turn around and recognize, cooperate with, and celebrate the age to come. Then Jesus begins the process of selecting "disciples." As he casually passes by a lake, Jesus almost randomly issues a call to whomever he sees. No job interview, prior experience, or credentials of any kind are needed—he simply calls them. Result: two pairs of brothers abandon everything and follow immediately.

Psalm 27:1-6
1. Psalm paraphrase, *God Is Our Strong Salvation*, James Montgomery, *HB* 347, tune: *Mein Leben*
2. Psalm paraphrase, *God Is Our Strong Salvation*, James Montgomery, *WB* 388, tune: Wedlock
3. Gelineau, *The Lord Is My Light and My Help*, *GG*, p. 59
4. Folk setting, *The Lord Is Near*, Michael Joncas, *OEW*, p. 66 (guitar chords included)

Hymns for the Day	HL	HB	WB
God Is Our Strong Salvation	92	347	388
Light of the World (tune: Munich)	–	138	–
O Morning Star, How Fair and Bright	321	415	521
Through the Night (tune: Ebenezer)	345	475	–
Veiled in Darkness Judah Lay	–	–	613
We Are One in the Spirit	–	–	619

Anthems for the Day
Isa. 9:1-4 *Creator of the Stars of Night*, Howard Boatwright (E. C. Schirmer); SATB (MD)
or *Creator of the Stars of Night* (WB 348); unison (E)
1 Cor. 1:10-17 *Blessed Jesus, at Thy Word*, arr. Theophil Rothenburg (*SAB Choral Book*, Concordia); (M)
Matt. 4:12-23 *Brightest and Best*, John Gardner (No. 1 of *Five Hymns in Popular Style*, Oxford); SATB (MD)
Ps. 27:1-6 *God Is My Strong Salvation*, Robert Powell (Associated); SAB (M)

FOURTH SUNDAY AFTER THE EPIPHANY (A)

Micah 6:1-8 Yahweh summons unfaithful Israel to trial, where all creation serves as witnesses. "Where did I fail you?" pleads Yahweh, who then recites all his saving deeds in fulfillment of his promises to Israel. The penitent though still misguided defendant seeks to atone for wrongdoing: "What kind of offering will please you: a burnt one, calves, rams, oil, first-born?" But Yahweh requires only an offering of ourselves: to do justly, love mercy, and walk humbly with God.

1 Corinthians 1:18-31 The gospel always seems to turn our world upside down. Here worldly wisdom and strength are characterized as foolish and weak, and the nonsense and weakness of the crucifixion are labeled as wise and strong. The epitome of God's love for us is revealed in the offensiveness of the cross.

Matthew 5:1-12 Jesus teaches his disciples the Beatitudes as he begins the Sermon on the Mount.

Psalm 37:1-11
1. Psalm paraphrase, *The Steps of Those Whom He Approves*, from *The Psalter*, 1912, *HB* 422, tune: Downs
2. Psalm paraphrase, *Give to the Winds Your Fears*, Paul Gerhardt (trans. John Wesley), tune: St. Bride, *HB* 364, *WB* 377
3. Gregorian psalm tone, *GP*, Epiphany 4 A

Hymns for the Day	HL	HB	WB
Blest Are the Pure in Heart	–	226	–
God's Word Is like a Flaming Sword	–	–	405
How Shall the Young Direct Their Way?	–	258	–
In the Cross of Christ I Glory	154	195	437
Jesus, I My Cross Have Taken	274	–	–
The Steps of Those Whom He Approves	–	422	–
When I Survey the Wondrous Cross	152	198	635

Anthems for the Day
Micah 6:1-8 *Cantata 45*, no. 1, J. S. Bach (Breitkopf & Härtel); SATB (D)
1 Cor. 1:18-31 *When Christ Comes to Die on Calvary*, Richard Hillert (*WB* 634); unison (E)
Matt. 5:1-12 *A German Requiem*, no. 1, Johannes Brahms (G. Schirmer); SATB (MD)
Ps. 37:1-11 "O Rest in the Lord" (air), Felix Mendelssohn (*Elijah*, no. 31, G. Schirmer); alto solo (E)
"Fret Not," Jean Pasquet (Elkan-Vogel); SATB (M)

FIFTH SUNDAY AFTER THE EPIPHANY (A)

Isaiah 58:3-9a Israel has strictly followed the law regarding fasting, but Yahweh seems not to take notice. Why? "Because you pursue your own interests," admonishes Yahweh. "You make a show of your fasting, you call attention to it while continuing to quarrel and fight and oppress others. You think I approve of that? Give aid to the hungry, the homeless, the naked— liberate others—and then you will see my favor shine like the dawning of the sun's light."

1 Corinthians 2:1-11 Paul contrasts the wisdom of human speeches and the message of the cross. His own oratorical skills, Paul says, are modest and unpersuasive. But the proclamation of Jesus Christ crucified and the power of the Spirit are what convert hearers to belief, trust, and obedience. If the wisdom of the world had known this, "wise" rulers would not have crucified the Lord.

Matthew 5:13-16 "You are the salt of the earth." You are a light amid the darkness of the world. Let your light shine before all. How? By good works and deeds of justice so the world will praise the heavenly Father.

Psalm 112:4-9
1. Gelineau, *He Is a Light in the Darkness, GG*, p. 71
2. Gregorian psalm tone, *GP*, Proper 8 B

Hymns for the Day	HL	HB	WB
Come, Labor On	366	287	–
Hope of the World	–	291	423
O Lord of Life, to Thee We Lift	–	256	–
O Morning Star, How Fair and Bright	321	415	521
Spread, O Spread the Mighty Word	–	–	577
When I Survey the Wondrous Cross	152	198	635

Anthems for the Day
Isa. 58:3-9a *Surge Illuminare*, William Byrd (Novello); SATB (MD)
1 Cor. 2:1-11 *How Excellent Thy Name*, Howard Hanson (C. Fischer); SATB, divisi (MD)
Matt. 5:13-16 *The Three Kings*, Peter Cornelius, arr. Ivor Atkins (*Carols for Choirs*, Book I, Oxford); mezzo-soprano solo, SSAATTBB (M)
Ps. 112:4-9 *Blessed Are the Men Who Fear Him*, Felix Mendelssohn (*Elijah*, no. 9, G. Schirmer); SATB (M)

SIXTH SUNDAY AFTER THE EPIPHANY
(Proper 1) (A)

Deuteronomy 30:15-20 Yahweh loves Israel; he desires well-being for his people. The question is, Will Israel love Yahweh as a child loves a parent? Every day Israel must decide if she will love Yahweh by faithfully obeying his commandments, which leads to prosperity in the good land, or if she will turn away from Yahweh and therefore lose the land and die.

1 Corinthians 3:1-9 Jealousy and strife are signs of immature faith or, perhaps, inability or resistance to hearing the gospel: living as people of the flesh. Living as people of the Spirit means all human servants perform God's work together in the vineyard, each according to his or her specific function. God alone gives growth.

Matthew 5:17-26 Jesus has not come to abolish the Law but to fulfill it. Anyone (including scribes and Pharisees) who sets aside or obscures even the least of these commandments will be named by Yahweh as "least in the kingdom of heaven." So we must reconcile with our brother or sister before we offer anything to God in public worship.

Psalm 119:1-8
1. Psalm paraphrase, *How I Love Thy Law, O Lord!*, from *The Psalter*, 1912, HB 253, tune: Spanish Hymn
2. Gelineau, *They Are Happy Whose Life Is Blameless*, GG, p. 74
3. Gregorian psalm tone, *GP*, Proper 26 B

Hymns for the Day	HL	HB	WB
How I Love Thy Law, O Lord!	–	253	–
Jesus, Priceless Treasure	–	414	442
O God of Light, Your Word	–	247	499
O Let My Supplicating Cry	–	323	–
O Master, Let Me Walk with Thee	364	304	520
Praise to the Lord, the Almighty	6	1	557
Whate'er Our God Ordains Is Right	291	366	633

Anthems for the Day
Deut. 30:15-20 *Blessed Is the Man*, Corelli-Stone (Boston Music); SAB (ME)
1 Cor. 3:1-9 *Ye Are Not in the Flesh*, J. S. Bach (*Motet III, Jesu, Meine Freude*, Peters); SSATB (D)
Matt. 5:17-26 *If Ye Love Me*, Thomas Tallis (*Church Anthem Book*, p. 179, Oxford); SSATB (M)
Ps. 119:1-8 *Teach Me, O Lord*, Thomas Attwood (*First Concord Anthem Book*, p. 144, E. C. Schirmer); SATB (E)

SEVENTH SUNDAY AFTER THE EPIPHANY
(Proper 2) (A)

Isaiah 49:8-13 Yahweh speaks to exiled Israel, who laments that Yahweh has forgotten her. To the contrary, Yahweh has brought an end to Israel's suffering—in fact, the restoration is already occurring—and is bringing those who sit in darkness out into the light. It is impossible for Yahweh to forget his people because his love for them far exceeds that of a mother's love for her suckling child. A picture of the restored Israel is inscribed on Yahweh's hands. Yahweh keeps his promises.

1 Corinthians 3:10-11, 16-23 Christ is the sole foundation of the church. Church leaders are but his servants who are all building upon this unchangeable foundation. The raw material used in constructing this temple is the people of God. This will sound foolish to the world, but it is God's wisdom. So all the church leaders and everything in the church belong to the people who belong to Christ who belongs to God.

Matthew 5:27-37 Three signs of fractured human relationships are adultery, divorce, and oath taking. Jesus calls us to trust the promises of God, to become one in love, and to speak the simple truth, as signs of the age to come.

Psalm 62:5-12
1. Metrical psalm, *My Soul with Expectation*, from the *Scottish Psalter*, 1650, *HB* 113, tune: St. Flavian
2. Metrical psalm, *In Silence My Soul Is Waiting*, Michael Saward, *PP*, no. 99, music by Christian Strover. An attractive contemporary setting
3. Gelineau, *In God Alone Is My Soul at Rest*, *GG*, p. 89
4. Gregorian psalm tone, *GP*, Epiphany 8 A

Hymns for the Day	HL	HB	WB
Christ Is Made the Sure Foundation	336	433	325
Glorious Things of You Are Spoken	339	434	379
Open Now the Gates of Beauty	–	40	544
The Church's One Foundation	333	437	582
We Dedicate This Temple	–	519	–
Where High the Heavenly Temple	–	389	–

Anthems for the Day
Isa. 49:8-13 *Sing, O Ye Heavens*, Johann Friedrich Peter (H. W. Gray); SSATTB (M)
1 Cor. 3:10-11, 16-23 *O Love, How Deep, How Broad, How High*, Richard Peek (C. Fischer); SATB (ME)
Matt. 5:27-37 *Create in Me, O God, a Clean Heart*, Johannes Brahms (G. Schirmer); SATBB (M)
Ps. 62:5-12 *Thee Will I Love, O Lord*, Arthur Honegger (*King David*, E. C. Schirmer); SATB (MD)

EIGHTH SUNDAY AFTER THE EPIPHANY
(Proper 3) (A)

Leviticus 19:1-2, 9-18 A part of the "Holiness Code" mandates that Israel is not to clean up gleanings in fields and vineyards (leave them for the poor), not to use words to deceive others, not to do injustice against neighbors, and not to hate "brothers" or take revenge against her own people. "I am the Lord your God who makes holy," and you are to reflect in word and deed what has been made holy. Therefore, love your neighbor as your own kin.

1 Corinthians 4:1-5 Paul is apparently the target of some hate mail from Corinthian church members who condemn him and his teaching. But all church leaders, writes Paul, are but "servants of Christ and stewards of the mysteries of God." So any judging that takes place is in the hands of Christ. No need then to worry about others judging you. Paul says, "I don't even judge myself because it is the Lord alone who will judge your faithfulness."

Matthew 5:38-48 Mosaic law on retribution restricts excess revenge or compensation. Jesus fulfills and surpasses this law by introducing a new principle: Do not take any action against those who seek to do physical violence to you, insult you, file litigation against you, extract forced labor from you, or make demands for gifts and loans. But love and serve your enemies (even to the extent of accepting a cross) and pray for them as a sign of the age to come.

Psalm 119:33-40
1. Metrical psalm, *How Shall the Young Direct Their Way?*, from *The Psalter,* 1912, *HB* 258, tune: Preston (Doane)
2. Gregorian psalm tone, *GP*, Proper 18 A

Hymns for the Day	HL	HB	WB
All People That on Earth Do Dwell	1	24	288
Give to the Winds Your Fears	294	364	377
Holy, Holy, Holy!	57	11	421
If You Will Only Let God Guide You	105	344	431
O God of Light, Your Word	–	247	499
The Lord Will Come	185	230	–
This Is My Father's World	70	101	602

Anthems for the Day
Lev. 19:1-2, 9-18 *O Lord God, Unto Whom Vengeance Belongeth*, Robert Baker (H. W. Gray); SSATTB (MD)
1 Cor. 4:1-5 *The Lord Will Come and Not Be Slow*, Richard Peek (H. W. Gray), 2-part mixed (E)
Matt. 5:38-48 *Strengthen for Service*, Austin Lovelace (E. C. Kirby); unison (E)
Ps. 119:33-40 *Teach Me, O Lord*, Benjamin Rogers–Wienandt (Flammer); SATB (ME)

TRANSFIGURATION OF THE LORD
[Last Sunday After the Epiphany] (A)

Exodus 24:12-18 Yahweh summons Moses to the top of the mountain at Sinai in order that he may receive the tables of stone Yahweh has inscribed. A cloud envelops the mountain for a six-day period of preparation, but on the seventh day Yahweh calls Moses to enter the cloud. Fire and light ("the glory of the Lord") suddenly burst through the cloud in full view of the people. Moses remains on the mountain forty days in order to receive all the instructions from Yahweh.

2 Peter 1:16-21 The writer directly confronts some opponents of the gospel by keeping alive Peter's testimony, which is based not on devised fables but on a historical event of the life of Jesus. Specifically, Peter was an eyewitness of the transfiguration and personally heard the voice confirm Christ's divine sonship. Thus the Old Testament's prophecy of the coming of the Messiah has been certified by God, and therefore all would do well to pay attention to scripture with the aid of the Spirit.

Matthew 17:1-9 Before the eyes of the disciples, the ordinary man named Jesus shines with the dazzling brilliance of the light of God. Peter wants to preserve this mountaintop high by stopping the action and living there. But a cloud overshadows them and a hidden voice speaks the same words spoken at the baptism of Jesus: "This is my beloved Son, with whom I am well pleased; listen to him." The glow and the cloud disappear, and the disciples only see the ordinary man named Jesus, who is walking down the mountain toward Jerusalem to die on a cross.

Psalm 2:6-11
1. Gregorian psalm tone, *PFTD*, Series A, p. 27

Hymns for the Day	*HL*	*HB*	*WB*
Blessing and Honor and Glory and Power	196	137	311
Hills of the North, Rejoice	–	478	–
I to the Hills Will Lift My Eyes	–	377	430
O God of Light, Your Word	–	247	499
O Morning Star, How Fair and Bright	321	415	521
Of the Father's Love Begotten	–	7	534
The God of Abraham Praise	8	89	587

Anthems for the Day

Ex. 24:12-18 *I Will Lift Up My Eyes*, Leo Sowerby (Boston Music); alto solo with SATB (E)

2 Peter 1:16-21 *Worthy Art Thou, O Lord God*, Anton Bruckner (Augsburg); SSAATTBB (MD)

Matt. 17:1-9 *Jesu, Joy of Man's Desiring*, J. S. Bach–Dunn (E. C. Schirmer); SATB (E)

Ps. 2:6-11 *Thou Shalt Break Them*, G. F. Handel (*Messiah*, ed. Watkins Shaw, Novello); tenor solo (M)

ASH WEDNESDAY (ABC)

Joel 2:1-2, 12-17a Blow the trumpet, for the Day of Yahweh is coming! Yahweh's judgment is near! Turn back to Yahweh with all your heart. Fast, weep, mourn. Return to Yahweh who manifests *hesed* (steadfast love). Perhaps Yahweh will forgive you and bless you. Gather together all the people and turn back to Yahweh.

2 Corinthians 5:20b–6:2 (3-10) Do you remember what God in Christ has done for you all? Then accept the reconciliation that God offers you in Christ. Let God transform you! Christ shared our human estrangement from God so that we sinners might be joined with Christ and reconciled with God. So work with God today, for the day of salvation is now.

Matthew 6:1-6, 16-21 Three acts of personal piety (charity, private prayer, and fasting) and a note on treasuring God's will—all are signs of the age to come. Don't broadcast your acts of personal piety to the world. God sees what you do and therefore will give to you from the future. What you value in life is where you will devote your time, energy, emotional commitment, everything.

Psalm 51:1-12
1. Metrical, *God, Be Merciful to Me*, from *The Psalter*, 1912, HB 282, tune: Redhead, No. 76
2. Gelineau, *Have Mercy on Me, God*, GG, p. 34
3. Gregorian psalm tone, *GP*, Lent 5 B
4. David Isele, *Have Mercy on Me, O God, Praise God in Song*, p. 28
5. *PS*, p. 18

Hymns for the Day	HL	HB	WB
God of Compassion, in Mercy Befriend Us	290	122	392
I'm So Glad Troubles Don't Last Always	–	–	432
Lord, from the Depths to You I Cry	240	277	459
Lord, Who Throughout These Forty Days	144	181	470
The Church's One Foundation	333	437	582

Anthems for the Day
Joel 2:1-2, 12-17a *Ye People, Rend Your Hearts* and *If with All Your Hearts*, Felix Mendelssohn (*Elijah*, G. Schirmer); tenor solo
2 Cor. 5:20b–6:2 (3-10) *Grant Us Thy Peace*, Felix Mendelssohn (Boosey & Hawkes); SATB (E)
Matt. 6:1-6, 16-21 *Two Men Betook Themselves to Pray in the Temple*, Heinrich Schütz (Concordia); SATB, SATB soli (M)
Ps. 51:1-12 *Wash Me Thoroughly from My Wickedness*, S. S. Wesley (*Church Anthem Book*, Oxford); SATB (ME)

FIRST SUNDAY IN LENT (A)

Genesis 2:4b-9, 15-17, 25–3:7 Yahweh forms a creature from the clay of the earth and breathes life into the earth creature. Then Yahweh plants a garden as a good place for the earth creature and gives the earth creature a specific job, freedom, and boundaries in which to live. Enter the serpent with a new agenda. Result: The set boundaries are seen as an option and then violated. Human freedom is perverted and the specific job given by Yahweh is neglected. Humans now focus on themselves and therefore see their own nakedness.

Romans 5:12-19 Paul asserts that sin and death became part of our human experience "through one man," yet "all sinned." All humanity reenacts what this "one man" introduced: aspiring to become like God. But, in Christ, God's free gift of grace for all humanity was deliberately introduced. This one righteous act sets free all humanity and gives life to all.

Matthew 4:1-11 Jesus has just been called and "ordained" in baptism. Now he is tempted to become three different kinds of messiah: prosperity giver, miracle worker, or political leader. But Jesus repudiates each temptation with a quote from Deuteronomy and says he will let God define his ministry.

Psalm 130
1. Metrical, *Lord, from the Depths to Thee I Cried*, from the *Scottish Psalter*, 1650, *HB* 277, tune: Song 67 (Gibbons)
2. Gelineau, *Out of the Depths I Cry to You, O Lord*, GG, p. 33
3. Gregorian psalm tone, *GP*, Holy Saturday ABC
4. *PS*, p. 33

Hymns for the Day	HL	HB	WB
Call Jehovah Your Salvation	292	123	322
Cast Your Burden on the Lord	288	–	323
O Worship the King	2	26	533
Lord, from the Depths to You I Cry	240	277	459
Lord, Who Throughout These Forty Days	144	181	470
When We Are Tempted to Deny Your Son	–	–	640

Anthems for the Day
Gen. 2:4b-9, 15-17, 25–3:7 *O God, Be Merciful*, Christopher Tye (Oxford); SATB (M)
Rom. 5:12-19 *Since by Man Came Death*, G. F. Handel *(Messiah)*; SATB (M)
Matt. 4:1-11 *Father, with All Your Gospel's Power*, harm. J. S. Bach *(Westminster Praise*, Hinshaw); SATB (E)
Ps. 130 *Out of the Deep*, Henry Purcell *(Sing Joyfully*, vol. 3, Walton); SAB (M)

SECOND SUNDAY IN LENT (A)

Genesis 12:1-4a (4b-8) Yahweh chooses a barren, landless, futureless couple and promises descendants, land, and a future in which their name will be magnified. Abram faithfully embraces Yahweh's promises and begins his pilgrimage of eternal wandering in the new land.

Romans 4:1-5 (6-12), 13-17 For working hard or performing good deeds, people earn wages or rewards and therefore can boast of their achievements. For trusting the promises of God who justifies the impious and the irreligious, people receive God's free gift of grace. Look at Abraham, who was justified not by works but by grace through faith.

John 3:1-17 By day, Nicodemus is everything you could want to be; by night, he comes secretly in search of Jesus. By day, Nicodemus controls the affairs of his kingdom; by night, he comes looking for the kingdom of God. Replies Jesus, "Unless one is born of water and the Spirit, he cannot enter the kingdom of God." "How can this be?" asks Nicodemus.

or **Matthew 17:1-9** The transfiguration of Jesus

Psalm 33:18-22
1. Gelineau, *Ring Out Your Joy to the Lord*, GG, p. 105
2. Gregorian psalm tone, *GP*, Lent 2 A

Hymns for the Day	HL	HB	WB
If You Will Only Let God Guide You	–	344	431
I'm Not Ashamed to Own My Lord	–	292	–
O Wondrous Type, O Vision Fair	142	182	531
Strong Son of God, Immortal Love	175	228	578
The God of Abraham Praise	8	89	587
Where Cross the Crowded Ways of Life	410	507	642

Anthems for the Day
Gen. 12:1-4a (4b-8) *If Thou but Suffer God to Guide Thee*, Jody Lindh (Concordia); SATB (E)
Rom. 4:1-5 (6-12), 13-17 *To Abraham the Promise Came* (WB 608); SATB (E)
John 3:1-17 *For God So Loved the World*, Heinrich Schütz (*A Second Motet Book*, Concordia); SATB (M)
or **Matt. 17:1-9** *This Is My Beloved Son*, Knut Nystedt (Concordia); SATB (E)
Ps. 33:18-22 *O Be Joyful*, R. Vaughan Williams (Stainer & Bell); SATB (MD)

THIRD SUNDAY IN LENT (A)

Exodus 17:3-7 The Israelites "contend with" and "test" Yahweh as they trek through the desert, for they are about to perish for lack of water. At Yahweh's instructions, Moses strikes a rock with his rod and Yahweh miraculously produces living water as a sign of the life which Yahweh pours forth upon his people.

Romans 5:1-11 Since we are justified by faith, we are at peace with God. So let's stand up straight and rejoice, for "God has poured out his love into our hearts through the Holy Spirit." While we were sinning against God by resisting and seeking to destroy his Son, God reconciled us to himself through the death of his Son. At the cross, we are drenched by the incredible depth of God's love for us.

John 4:5-26 (27-42) Jesus sits down by Jacob's well for conversation with a Samaritan (despised) woman (second-class citizen). The metaphor of water permeates their strange dialogue and recalls for hearers the multitude of images of water in both John's Gospel and throughout the Bible.

Psalm 95
1. Metrical, *O Come and Sing Unto the Lord*, from *The Psalter*, 1912, *HB* 29, tune: Irish
2. Metrical, *To God with Gladness Sing*, *MP&E*, tune: Darwall's 148th
3. Gelineau, *Come, Ring Out Our Joy to the Lord*, *24P&1C*, p. 22
4. Gregorian psalm tone, *GP*, Lent 3 A
5. *PS*, pp. 25, 26

Hymns for the Day	*HL*	*HB*	*WB*
Come, Holy Ghost, Our Souls Inspire	–	237	335
God Himself Is with Us	51	13	384
Guide Me, O Thou Great Jehovah	104	339	409
I to the Hills Will Lift My Eyes	–	377	430
If You Will Only Let God Guide You	105	344	431
O Come and Sing Unto the Lord	–	29	488
O Love of God Most Full	84	118	–
Sinner, Please Don't Let This Harvest Pass	–	–	570
You, Holy Father, We Adore	–	–	644

Anthems for the Day
Ex. 17:3-7 *O Come, Every One That Thirsteth*, Felix Mendelssohn (*Elijah*, G. Schirmer); SATB (M)
Rom. 5:1-11 *O Jesus, Grant Me Hope and Comfort*, Franck-Stein (Schmitt, Hall & McCreary); SATB (M)
John 4:5-26 (27-42) *God Is a Spirit*, Alexander Kopylov (*First Concord Anthem Book*, E. C. Schirmer); SATB (E)
Ps. 95 *O Come, Let Us Sing Unto the Lord*, William Byrd (Concordia); SATB (M)

FOURTH SUNDAY IN LENT (A)

1 Samuel 16:1-13 Yahweh commands Samuel to offer a sacrifice at Bethlehem as a ruse to anointing the one whom Yahweh has chosen as king. At the sacrifice, Samuel surveys seven sons of Jesse who are present, but Yahweh selects none of these. The youngest, most inexperienced, least likely son is taking care of the sheep. And Yahweh says, "Arise, anoint him; for this is he."

Ephesians 5:8-14 Jesus Christ is the victorious, transforming light in person. Living "in Christ" is living "in the light." So you who are the Lord's people, live as creatures of the light, give witness to the light, and the light will transform all darkness into light.

John 9:1-41 The first seven verses recount a sight-giving miracle in which Jesus heals a blind man. Now the real action: neighbors, Pharisees, Jewish leaders interrogate the blind man and his parents on the credentials and techniques of the healer. Ironically, each conversation shows the blind man seeing more clearly—"The man called Jesus," "He is a prophet," "Lord, I believe"—and those who walk by their own light are increasingly blinded. "I am the light of the world," says Jesus; "I give sight to those in darkness."

Psalm 23
1. Metrical, *The Lord's My Shepherd*, from the *Scottish Psalter*, 1650, HB 104, tune: Crimond
2. Gelineau, *The Lord Is My Shepherd*, GG, p. 136
3. Gregorian psalm tone, *GP*, Proper 23 A
4. Frank Quinn, *The Lord Is My Shepherd*, MP&E, p. 196
5. *PS*, p. 14

Hymns for the Day	HL	HB	WB
Christ Is the World's True Light	–	492	326
Hail to the Lord's Anointed	111	146	–
Light of Light, Enlighten Me	–	73	–
Light of the World, We Hail Thee	422	138	–
The King of Love My Shepherd Is	99	106	590
The Lord's My Shepherd	97	104	592
The True Light That Enlightens Man	–	–	598
Wake, Awake, for Night Is Flying	–	–	614

Anthems for the Day
1 Sam. 16:1-13 *The Last Words of David*, Randall Thompson (E. C. Schirmer); SATB (MD)
Eph. 5:8-14 *O Mighty God, Our Lord*, Heinrich Schütz (Mercury); 2-part (E)
John 9:1-41 *By Cool Siloam's Shady Rill*, Louie White (Galaxy); SATB (MD)
Ps. 23 *Psalm 23*, Heinz Werner Zimmermann (Augsburg); SATB (ME)

FIFTH SUNDAY IN LENT (A)

Ezekiel 37:1-14 The vision of the valley of dry bones. Asks Yahweh, "Can these bones live?" "Perhaps you know," replies Ezekiel. "Preach to the dry bones," commands Yahweh, "that they shall live." So Ezekiel does as commanded. And astonishingly the bones come together and breath comes into them, all by the power of the Word of God.

Romans 8:6-11 According to Paul, our human situation leads to self-destruction or to striking out against others (including God) who frustrate our desires. The way of our human world leads to sin and death. The way of the Spirit frees us from our world of sin and death and leads us to life—a world where all are servants.

John 11: (1-16) 17-45 Lazarus dies and Jesus goes to "awake" him. On the way, Jesus encounters Martha and Mary. He arrives at Lazarus' tomb and miraculously restores him to life. "I am the resurrection and the life," says Jesus; "whoever lives and believes in me shall never die."

Psalm 116:1-9
1. Metrical, *How Full of Kindness Is the Lord*, NHAS, p. 84, tune: Stracathro
2. Gelineau, *I Love the Lord for He Has Heard the Cry of My Appeal*, 24P&1C, p. 25
3. Gregorian psalm tone, *GP*, Friday in Easter Week ABC

Hymns for the Day	HL	HB	WB
All Praise Be Yours	–	–	290
God Has Spoken—by His Prophets	–	–	382
Hope of the World	–	291	423
O Jesus Christ, to You May Hymns Be Rising	–	–	509
Spirit Divine, Attend Our Prayers	212	243	574
The Son of God Goes Forth to War	271	354	–
Whate'er Our God Ordains Is Right	291	366	633
When Jesus Wept	–	–	636

Anthems for the Day
Ezek. 37:1-14 *Ezekiel Saw the Wheel*, Spiritual, arr. Gilbert Martin (Hinshaw); SATB (M)
Rom. 8:6-11 *The Fruit of the Spirit Is Love*, Johann Geisler (Boosey & Hawkes); SATB, flute (MD)
John 11:(1-16) 17-45 *I Know that My Redeemer Lives*, Johann Michael Bach (*Church Anthem Book*, Oxford); SATBB (M)
Ps. 116:1-9 *What Have I to Do with Thee*, Felix Mendelssohn (*Elijah* no. 8, G. Schirmer); soprano and bass soli, may be followed by chorus, *Blessed Are the Men Who Fear Him* (no. 9); SATB (M)

PASSION SUNDAY [Sixth Sunday in Lent] (A)

Isaiah 50:4-9a The third of the four Songs of the Servant of Yahweh: Each day Yahweh wakens me and opens my ears to his word which sustains me. Though I have suffered ridicule, insults, hostility, and physical abuse, I have not turned from my task. I trust Yahweh's help; Yahweh will vindicate me. So who will declare me guilty?

Philippians 2:5-11 A primitive Christological hymn about the descent and ascent of a divine savior. By divesting himself of divine glory, he voluntarily assumed the form of a human servant who impoverished himself and "became obedient unto death, even death on a cross." That's why God raised him up and gave him the name above every other name: Lord.

Matthew 26:14–27:66 The passion narrative according to Matthew.

or **Matthew 27:11-54** The Roman governor Pilate questions a silent Jesus about his alleged kingship. A frenzied crowd demands that Pilate set free Barabbas and crucify Jesus. Whipped, mocked, and spat upon, Jesus the "King of the Jews" is crucified. "If you are the Son of God," taunt the people, "come down from the cross." The lonely, suffering Jesus cries out only despair—"My God, my God . . ."—and dies. Behold, the Temple curtain is torn in two, the earth shakes, tombs are opened, and soldiers at the cross confess Jesus as the Son of God.

Psalm 31:9-16
1. Gelineau, *In You, O Lord, I Take Refuge, GG,* p. 37

Hymns for the Day	HL	HB	WB
Ah, Holy Jesus	158	191	280
All Praise Be Yours	–	–	290
Beneath the Cross of Jesus	162	190	308
Every Star Shall Sing a Carol	–	–	359
In the Cross of Christ I Glory	154	195	437
Throned Upon the Awful Tree	–	197	605
When I Survey the Wondrous Cross	152	198	635
When Jesus Wept	–	–	636

Anthems for the Day

Isa. 50:4-9a *He Was Despised,* G. F. Handel (*Messiah,* ed. Watkins Shaw, Novello); alto solo (M)

Phil. 2:5-11 *Let This Mind Be in You,* Lee Hoiby (Presser); SATB (MD)

Matt. 26:14–27:66 or **Matt. 27:11-54** *The Royal Banners Forward Go,* Anton Bruckner (Concordia); SATB (ME)

Ps. 31:9-16 *In Thee, O Lord, Have I Trusted,* G. F. Handel (Mercury); SAB (E)

PALM SUNDAY [Sixth Sunday in Lent] (A)

Isaiah 50:4-9a The third of the four Songs of the Servant of Yahweh: Each day Yahweh wakens me and opens my ears to his word which sustains me. Though I have suffered ridicule, insults, hostility, physical abuse, I have not turned from my task. I trust Yahweh's help; Yahweh will vindicate me. So who will declare me guilty?

Philippians 2:5-11 A primitive Christological hymn about the descent and ascent of a divine savior. By divesting himself of divine glory, he voluntarily assumed the form of a human servant who impoverished himself and "became obedient unto death, even death on a cross." That's why God raised him up and gave him the name above every other name: Lord.

Matthew 21:1-11 Jesus instructs his disciples to prepare for the entry into Jerusalem. All is done in deliberate fulfillment of Zechariah's prophecy (Zech. 9:9), even to the extent of providing an ass and a colt, so that Jesus may enter as a humble kingly figure. Most of the crowd spread their garments or branches upon the road for this solemn, majestic procession and shout "Hosanna!" Upon entering Jerusalem, the people ask, "Who is this?" And the crowd replies, "This is the prophet Jesus from Nazareth of Galilee."

Psalm 118:19-29
1. Metrical, *The Glorious Gates of Righteousness, HB* 71, tune: Zerah
2. Gelineau, *Give Thanks to the Lord for He Is Good, GG,* p. 46
3. Gregorian psalm tone, *GP,* Passion (Palm) Sunday ABC

Hymns for the Day	HL	HB	WB
All Glory, Laud, and Honor	146	187	284
At the Name of Jesus	–	143	303
Hosanna, Loud Hosanna	147	185	424
O How Shall We Receive You	–	–	506
Lift Up Your Heads, O Mighty Gates	114	152	454
Ride On! Ride On in Majesty!	150	188	563
So Lowly Does the Savior Ride	–	–	571

Anthems for the Day

Isa. 50:4-9a *Surely He Hath Borne Our Griefs,* Heinrich Graun (Concordia); SATB (M)

Phil. 2:5-11 *Let This Mind Be in You,* Mrs. H. H. A. Beach (Presser); SATB with soprano, baritone soli (ME)

Matt. 21:1-11 *Come, Faithful People, Come Away,* Richard Peek (Hope); 2-part (E)

Ps. 118:19-29 *This Is the Day the Lord Hath Made,* Anon. English (*A Sixteenth-Century Anthem Book,* Oxford); SATB (E)

MONDAY OF HOLY WEEK (ABC)

Isaiah 42:1-9 The first of the four Songs of the Servant of Yahweh (vs. 1-4) and the response to it (vs. 5-9). Yahweh officially presents his chosen servant, upon whom he has put his Spirit, who is to perform the task of bringing forth *mishpat* (justice) to the nations by his own suffering. Yahweh gives his servant as a light to the people who live in darkness. Verses 8-9 affirm that Yahweh will give no glory or praise to any idol, and that Yahweh declares in advance new things of the future.

Hebrews 9:11-15 Christ enters not the earthly Holy of Holies, offering a ritual sacrifice, but he enters once for all the holy dwelling place of God, offering a sacrifice of himself—his own life-giving blood. In his sacrifice Christ attains what none other ever could—eternal redemption for his people. Christ is truly the high priest of the "good things that have come."

John 12:1-11 Irrepressible Mary gets carried away at dinner and shocks everyone by pouring thousands of dollars' worth of perfume on Jesus' feet. "An extravagant waste," cries the morally upright Judas, "the money could have been given to the poor." Replies Jesus, "You'll always have the opportunity to serve the poor; so leave her alone, for you'll not always have me. She has saved her perfume for my burial." Mary anointed her only Lord and Savior.

Psalm 36:5-10
1. Metrical, *Thy Mercy and Thy Truth, O Lord*, HB 82, tune: Dundee
2. Gregorian psalm tone, *GP*, Monday of Holy Week ABC

Hymns for the Day	HL	HB	WB
Come, Thou Almighty King	52	244	343
Cross of Jesus, Cross of Sorrow	155	196	–
God Is Working His Purpose Out	–	500	389
In the Cross of Christ I Glory	154	195	437
Thy Mercy and Thy Truth, O Lord	–	82	–
When I Survey the Wondrous Cross	152	198	635

Anthems for the Day
Isa. 42:1-9 *Behold, My Servant*, Jack Boyd (Boston Music); SATB (M)
Heb. 9:11-15 *O Spotless Lamb*, J. S. Bach–Thoburn (Augsburg); (M)
John 12:1-11 *Master, No Offering Costly and Sweet* (*HB* 299)
Ps. 36:5-10 *Awake, My Soul*, S. Drummond Wolff (Concordia); SAB (ME)

TUESDAY OF HOLY WEEK (ABC)

Isaiah 49:1-7 The second of the four Songs of the Servant of Yahweh. Yahweh's chosen servant summons the nations to hear Yahweh's word. The servant publicly announces his prenatal call and his subsequent despondency about performing the task in vain. But now Yahweh has expanded the call to be a light to all the nations (Gentiles) in order that "salvation may reach the ends of the earth."

1 Corinthians 1:18-31 The gospel always seems to turn our world upside down. Here wordly wisdom and strength are characterized as foolish and weak, and the nonsense and weakness of the crucifixion are labeled as wise and strong. The epitome of God's love for us is revealed in the offensiveness of the cross.

John 12:20-36 Some Gentiles seek to see Jesus. "The hour has come . . . ," says Jesus, "for when a single grain of wheat falls into the earth and dies, it produces many grains." Jesus then wrestles with the full import of "the hour" and decides to submit obediently to the Father's will. An affirming voice from heaven accepts the Son's obedience and promises the Son his own glorification. In fact, Jesus' decision to die will open the possibility for others to be liberated from the ruler of this world. Jesus' hour of glory, his death, brings forth life for Jesus and for all those who follow him and serve him.

Psalm 71:1-12
1. Metrical, *O Gracious God, Forsake Me Not*, HB 396, tune: Martyrdom
2. Gelineau, *In You, O Lord, I Take Refuge*, GG, p. 159
3. Gregorian psalm tone, *GP*, Tuesday of Holy Week ABC

Hymns for the Day	HL	HB	WB
A Mighty Fortress Is Our God	266	91	274
Christ Is the World's True Light	–	492	326
O Jesus, I Have Promised	268	307	–
O Jesus, Joy of Loving Hearts	354	215	510
O Jesus, We Adore Thee	156	200	–
Who Trusts in God, a Strong Abode	–	375	–

Anthems for the Day
Isa. 49:1-7 *And with His Stripes We Are Healed*, G. F. Handel (*Messiah*, ed. Watkins Shaw, Novello); SATB (M)
1 Cor. 1:18-31 *Faithful Cross*, Leland Sateren (Augsburg); SATB (E)
John 12:20-36 *Yet a Little While*, Knut Nystedt (Summy-Birchard); SSATBB (M)
Ps. 71:1-12 *A Mighty Fortress Is Our God*, Hans Leo Hassler (Concordia); SATB (M)

WEDNESDAY OF HOLY WEEK (ABC)

Isaiah 50:4-9a The third of the four Songs of the Servant of Yahweh: Each day Yahweh wakens me and opens my ears to his word which sustains me. Though I have suffered ridicule, insults, hostility, physical abuse, I have not turned from my task. I trust Yahweh's help; Yahweh will vindicate me. So who will declare me guilty?

Hebrews 12:1-3 A lifelong marathon race: that's what you're in for when you join the crowd trying to keep pace with Jesus. So strip off your warm-up suit, throw away your pride, scrap your blueprints for success and any other sins that weigh you down. To endure in this race, you've got to be lean. And you've got to be determined and tenacious in keeping your eyes fixed on Jesus. He didn't become discouraged or give up because of hostility from sinners or even death on the cross. So persevere in following the pacesetter Jesus. And remember, you're not alone—all the racers from the past are cheering you on.

John 13:21-30 Following the act of footwashing, Jesus announces that one who is present will betray him. Such a disclosure perks up the disciples' conversation and introduces the unknown Beloved Disciple. Jesus then dips some bread in the sauce and gives it to Judas, presumably to indicate him as the betrayer. Then, at Jesus' request, Judas leaves "to do what he has to do."

Psalm 70
1. Gelineau, *O God, Make Haste to My Rescue, 30P&2C*, p. 21
2. Gregorian psalm tone, *GP*, Proper 27 A

Hymns for the Day	HL	HB	WB
Christ, Above All Glory Seated	–	–	324
For All the Saints	429	425	369
O Christ, Whose Love Has Sought Us Out	–	–	485
O Love, How Deep, How Broad, How High!	139	–	518
O What Their Joy and Their Glory Must Be	430	424	–

Anthems for the Day
Isa. 50:4-9a *He Was Despised*, G. F. Handel *(Messiah)*; contralto solo (ME)
Heb. 12:1-3 *He Who Would Valiant Be*, arr. Gerald Near (Augsburg); SATB (E)
John 13:21-30 *Ecce Quomodo Moritur Justus*, Georg Reutter *(Sing Joyfully*, vol. 4, Walton); SATB (E)
Ps. 70 *Haste Thee, O God*, Adrian Batten *(Anthems for Choirs*, vol. 1, Oxford); SATB (M)

MAUNDY THURSDAY (A)

Exodus 12:1-14 The P account of the preparation and celebration of the Passover. Though conducted within each family (or group of families able to consume a whole lamb), this meal is the time at which all Israel thanks God for having redeemed them and made them a people, and renews their hope in the coming salvation.

1 Corinthians 11:23-26 The tradition Paul received "from the Lord" he now passes on to others: that the Lord Jesus took bread, gave thanks, broke it, and distributed it, and in the same manner the cup. Christ gave himself away, his own body and blood. So if anyone eats the bread or drinks the cup in a way that contradicts the self-giving body of Christ, the true nature of the church, then those persons eat and drink judgment upon themselves. Wait for one another so you may serve others as the reconciled body of Christ.

John 13:1-15 Jesus kneels to scrub dirt from the feet of his disciples. Appalled by such an undignified act, Peter exclaims, "You'll never wash my feet, ever." "Unless you let me wash you," replies Jesus, "then you'll have no share in my life." "In that case then," says Peter, "wash me all over." "Don't you understand what I have done for you?" asks Jesus. "If I, your Lord and Teacher, have washed your feet, you also ought to wash one another's feet. Serve, forgive, give as I have."

Psalm 89:20-21, 24, 26
1. Gregorian psalm tone, *GP*, Epiphany 1 ABC
2. Howard Hughes, *Forever I Will Sing—The Son of David* (G.I.A.)

Hymns for the Day	HL	HB	WB
Ancient of Days	58	246	297
Deck Yourself, My Soul	–	–	351
O God of Bethel, by Whose Hand	98	342	496
O Love, How Deep, How Broad, How High!	139	–	518
One Table Spread	–	–	541
'Twas on That Night	360	448	–

Anthems for the Day
Ex. 12:1-14 *Thanks Be to Thee*, G. F. Handel (E. C. Schirmer); unison (E)
1 Cor. 11:23-26 *When Our Lord Was Betrayed*, Heinrich Schütz (Hanssler); SATB (M)
John 13:1-15 *Drop, Drop, Slow Tears*, Kenneth Leighton (Novello); SAATTBB (MD)
Ps. 89:20-21, 24, 26 *Thee Will I Love, O Lord*, Arthur Honegger (*King David*, E. C. Schirmer); SATB (MD)

GOOD FRIDAY (ABC)*

Isaiah 52:13–53:12 The fourth of the four Songs of the Servant of Yahweh. Yahweh promises the coming vindication of his servant. Thus many are shocked to see an afflicted, disfigured, marred servant. Has God smitten him for past sins? No, the servant has participated in our human brokenness. He has "borne our griefs and carried our sorrows" according to God's will. This humiliated servant is the one whom Yahweh will vindicate.

Hebrews 4:14-16; 5:7-9 We have a great high priest to represent us to God, a simple human being named Jesus who lived in the same kind of power-hungry, achievement-oriented, complacently religious, me-first world. But this Jesus was sinless. He is the perfect one who is the source of salvation and now reigns with God.

John 18:1–19:42 The passion narrative according to John.

or **John 19:17-30** The crucifixion and death of Jesus.

Psalm 22:1-18
1. Gelineau, *My God, My God, Why Have You Forsaken Me?*, *30P&2C*, p. 5
2. Gregorian psalm tone, *GP*, Good Friday ABC
3. Howard Hughes, *My God, My God, Why Have You Abandoned Me?* (G.I.A.)

Hymns for the Day	HL	HB	WB
Ah, Holy Jesus	158	191	280
Alone You Journey Forth, O Lord	–	–	294
Go to Dark Gethsemane	–	193	–
O Sacred Head, Now Wounded	151	194	524
The Son of God Goes Forth to War	271	354	–
There Is a Green Hill Far Away	157	202	–
Throned Upon the Awful Tree	–	197	605
Were You There When They Crucified My Lord?	–	201	–

Anthems for the Day
Isa. 52:13–53:12 *Behold the Lamb of God*, Healey Willan (Concordia); 2-part mixed (E)
Heb. 4:14-16; 5:7-9 *God So Loved the World*, Hugo Distler (Concordia); SAB (M)
John 18:1–19:42 or **19:17-30** *O Vos Omnes* (O Ye People), Pablo Casals (A. Broude); SATB, divisi (MD)
Ps. 22:1-18 *He Trusted in God*, G. F. Handel (*Messiah*, ed. Watkins Shaw, Novello); SATB (M)

---

*NOTE: Easter Vigil will be found in Year C, pp. 221–224.

EASTER DAY (A)

Acts 10:34-43 At Cornelius' house in Caesarea, Peter recounts how his own life has been transformed by the power of the risen Lord, and everyone else (Jews and Gentiles) also can be transformed by that power.

or **Jeremiah 31:1-6** Yahweh promises to rebuild and renew *all* Israel—the object of Yahweh's *hesed.*

Colossians 3:1-4 In our baptism in Christ, we were given the gift of resurrection with Christ and therefore called to new life through the eyes of resurrection faith.

or **Acts 10:34-43** *See above.*

John 20:1-18 Peter and the Beloved Disciple seek the truth about the empty tomb. Mary engages the "gardener" in conversation, who says, "Tell them I am ascending."

or **Matthew 28:1-10** Two women at Jesus' tomb encounter God's power in the form of an earthquake and an angel. They hurriedly leave the tomb in fear and great joy.

Psalm 118:14-24
1. Metrical, *This Is the Day the Lord Hath Made,* HB 69, tune: Arlington
2. Gelineau, *This Is the Day the Lord Has Made,* GG, p. 46
3. Gregorian psalm tone, *GP,* Easter Day ABC
4. Richard Proulx, *Processional Psalm for a Festival* (G.I.A.)

Hymns for the Day	HL	HB	WB
"Christ the Lord Is Risen Today"	165	–	330
Come, You Faithful, Raise the Strain	168	205	344
Guide Me, O Thou Great Jehovah	104	339	409
Jesus Christ Is Risen Today	163	204	440
The Head That Once Was Crowned with Thorns	195	211	589

Anthems for the Day
Acts 10:34-43 *Today Is Risen Christ the Lord,* Melchior Vulpius (Concordia); SATB, brass (M)
or Jer. 31:1-6 *Sound the Cymbal,* Franz Schubert (*Rare Choral Masterpieces,* Schmitt, Hall & McCreary); SATB (E)
Col. 3:1-4 *Jesus Christ Is Risen Today,* Alan Hovhaness (Associated); SATB (ME)
or Acts 10:34-43 *(See above)*
John 20:1-18 *Alleluia! for Christ the Lord Is Risen,* J. S. Bach (Concordia); (ME)
or Matt. 28:1-10 *Mary Magdalene,* Johannes Brahms (H. W. Gray); SATB (E)
Ps. 118:14-24 *This Is the Day Which the Lord Hath Made,* Flor Peeters (Augsburg); SATB (MD)

EASTER EVENING (ABC)

Acts 5:29-32 The apostles' response to the Sanhedrin's prohibition of teaching "in the name of Jesus": we must obey God rather than men in giving witness to God's raising of Jesus from death.

or Daniel 12:1-3 A vision of the archangel Michael ushering in the day of resurrection for Israel and consummating God's plan for all of creation.

1 Corinthians 5:6-8 You are the new people of God by God's gracious act of salvation through the sacrifice of his Son, the true paschal lamb.

or Acts 5:29-32 *See above.*

Luke 24:13-49 Two of Jesus' followers walking from Jerusalem to Emmaus are joined by the risen Jesus, but they fail to recognize him. Astounded at his unawareness of events in Jerusalem, the two travelers relate their hopes concerning Jesus of Nazareth, whom they thought was the one to redeem Israel, and their disillusionment upon his death on the cross. Jesus responds to their despair by interpreting the scriptures to them. Then they go into a home where, at the table, "Jesus took the bread and blessed, and broke it, and gave it to them. And their eyes were opened and they recognized him." The travelers immediately return to Jerusalem to tell others that "the Lord has risen." Then Jesus suddenly appears to his disciples. They are terrified. He shows them his hands and feet, eats some fish, and opens their minds about how the scriptures have been fulfilled.

Psalm 150
1. Metrical, *Praise the Lord, His Glories Show, HB* 4, tune: Llanfair
2. Metrical, *Bless'd Be the Lord Our God!, P&E*, tune: Diademata
3. Gregorian psalm tone, *GP*, Trinity Sunday A
4. *PS*, pp. 39, 40

Hymns for the Day	HL	HB	WB
All Praise to God in Highest Heaven	–	–	291
Christ Jesus Lay in Death's Strong Bands	–	–	327
Come, You Faithful, Raise the Strain	168	205	344
Earth and All Stars	–	–	354
Praise to the Lord, the Almighty	6	1	557

Anthems for the Day
Acts 5:29-32 *Christ the Lord Is Risen Again*, Walter Pelz (Augsburg); SATB (M)
or **Dan. 12:1-3** *Stars of the Morning*, Richard Peek (cantata, *St. Stephen*, Brodt); SSATTBB (M)
1 Cor. 5:6-8 *Christ Our Passover*, Alec Wyton (H. W. Gray); SAATB with brass quartet, timpani (or organ) (M)
or **Acts 5:29-32** *(See above)*
Luke 24:13-49 *Hearts and Voices Raise*, Carlton Young (Augsburg); SATB, triangle, tambourine (E)
Ps. 150 *Praise the Lord Who Reigns Above*, Halsey Stevens (Mark Foster); 4-part canon (E)

SECOND SUNDAY OF EASTER (A)

Acts 2:14a, 22-32 A portion of Peter's Pentecost speech: God performed signs and wonders through Jesus' life and ministry to certify his divinity. Yet the lawless crucified Jesus (in the name of the law). But God freed him from death and raised him up. David himself said God would not abandon his faithful servant in death (see Ps. 16:8-11).

1 Peter 1:3-9 By God's mercy we who are baptized in Christ are born again to a living hope—that God protects for us—through Christ's resurrection. Though you may suffer some trials now that test your faith, rejoice because God has brought about your rebirth. Let the genuineness of your faith praise and honor Jesus, in whom you believe without even seeing.

John 20:19-31 Verses 19-23 are a series of symbolic episodes. The risen Jesus appears to his frightened disciples and says, "Peace." Then he shows them his hands and his side (which fills the disciples with joy) and again says, "Peace." He gives them the Holy Spirit by breathing on them and concludes with an eschatological saying about resisting forgiveness. In verses 24-31, Thomas says he must see with his eyes before he will believe. So again Jesus appears. He tells Thomas to touch his side. Thomas confesses. Blessed are those who believe solely on the basis of the word alone.

Psalm 16:5-11
1. Metrical, *When in the Night I Meditate*, HB 68, tune: Dundee
2. Gregorian psalm tone, *GP*, Proper 16 B

Hymns for the Day	HL	HB	WB
All Who Love and Serve Your City	–	–	293
At the Name of Jesus	–	143	–
Fairest Lord Jesus	194	135	360
He Did Not Want to Be Far	–	–	412
Here, O Lord, Your Servants Gather	–	–	417
O Sons and Daughters, Let Us Sing!	167	206	527
The Day of Resurrection!	166	208	584
Thine Is the Glory	–	209	–

Anthems for the Day
Acts 2:14a, 22-32 *Since by Man Came Death*, G. F. Handel (*Messiah* ed. Watkins Shaw, Novello); SATB (M)
1 Peter 1:3-9 *Easter Anthem*, William Billings (G. Schirmer); SATB (ME)
John 20:19-31 *O that I Knew Where I Might Find Him!* W. Sterndale Bennett (*Church Anthem Book*, Oxford); SATB (ME)
Ps. 16:5-11 *But Thou Didst Not Leave His Soul in Hell*, G. F. Handel (*Messiah*, ed. Watkins Shaw, Novello); tenor solo (M)

THIRD SUNDAY OF EASTER (A)

Acts 2:14a, 36-41 The concluding segment of Peter's Pentecost speech: This Jesus whom you crucified is the one whom God raised from the dead and made Lord. "What shall we do?" cries the guilt-stricken crowd. Repent, and be baptized in the name of Christ for the forgiveness of your sins, and you shall receive the gift of the Holy Spirit.

1 Peter 1:17-23 Conduct yourselves in awe of the holy God, the impartial judge. For you know that Christ's death has ransomed you from your worthless ways and that his incarnation marked the beginning of the last days according to God's eternal plan now manifested in Christ's resurrection.

Luke 24:13-35 Two of Jesus' followers walk from Jerusalem to a small village. They are joined by the risen Jesus, but their eyes prevent them from recognizing him. Astounded at his unawareness regarding recent events in Jerusalem, the two travelers relate their hopes concerning Jesus of Nazareth, whom they thought was the one to redeem Israel, and their disillusionment upon his death on the cross. Jesus responds to their despair by interpreting the scriptures to them. Then they go into a home where, at the table, "Jesus took the bread and blessed, and broke it, and gave it to them. And their eyes were opened and they recognized him." The travelers immediately return to Jerusalem to tell others that "the Lord has risen."

Psalm 116:12-19
1. Metrical, *What Shall I Render to the Lord*, HB 32, tune: Lambeth
2. Gelineau, *I Trusted Even When I Said*, GG, p. 25
3. Gregorian psalm tone, *GP*, Easter 3 B

Hymns for the Day	HL	HB	WB
Behold the Lamb of God!	153	–	307
"Christ the Lord Is Risen Today"	165	–	330
Come, Christians, Join to Sing	191	131	333
O Sons and Daughters, Let Us Sing!	167	206	527
That Easter Day with Joy Was Bright	–	–	581

Anthems for the Day
Acts 2:14a, 36-41 *Brethren, We Have Met to Worship*, arr. Randolph Currie (Choristers Guild); 2-part mixed (E)
1 Peter 1:17-23 *Blessed Be the God and Father*, S. S. Wesley (*Church Anthem Book*, Oxford); SATB, soprano solo (ME)
Luke 24:13-35 *And They Drew Nigh*, Leo Sowerby (H. W. Gray); SATB (ME)
Ps. 116:12-19 *Whate'er Our God Ordains Is Right* (WB 633)

FOURTH SUNDAY OF EASTER (A)

Acts 2:42-47 Luke's well-known idealized picture of the fourfold marks of apostolic church life—devoted study, fellowship, bread-breaking, and praying together—sounds like what we do today. But wait, there's a fifth mark: They sold all their possessions, redistributed their money according to human need, and shared everything in common. Result: The Lord daily added to their community those who were being saved.

1 Peter 2:19-25 You will be blessed for your innocent suffering on behalf of your faith. After all, the shepherd Christ himself suffered unjustly for you— he bore your sins in his body on the cross and gave his life for all lost sheep which made possible new life.

John 10:1-10 The first six verses depict Jesus as the single gate to the sheep-fold. Through this one gate is the only proper way for the sheep to enter. The last four verses depict Jesus both as the true shepherd whose voice the sheep will obey and as the sole gate leading to salvation for all sheep.

Psalm 23
1. Metrical, *The Lord's My Shepherd*, from the *Scottish Psalter*, 1650, HB 104, tune: Crimond
2. Gelineau, *The Lord Is My Shepherd*, GG, p. 136
3. Gregorian psalm tone, GP, Proper 23 A
4. Frank Quinn, *The Lord Is My Shepherd*, MP&E, p. 196
5. *PS*, p. 14

Hymns for the Day	HL	HB	WB
God, Be Merciful to Me	–	282	–
Saviour, Like a Shepherd Lead Us	458	380	–
Saviour, Who Thy Flock Art Feeding	348	–	–
The King of Love My Shepherd Is	99	106	590
The Lord's My Shepherd	97	104	592
There's a Wideness in God's Mercy	93	110	601
You Servants of God, Your Master Proclaim	198	27	645

Anthems for the Day
Acts 2:42-47 *I Will Pour Out My Spirit*, arr. Robert Leaf (Augsburg); SATB, narrative, optional congregation (ME)

1 Peter 2:19-25 *Greater Love Hath No Man*, John Ireland (Galaxy); SATB with soprano, bass soli (M)

John 10:1-10 *I Am the Good Shepherd*, Thomas Matthews (Presser); 2-part treble (E)

Ps. 23 *The God of Love My Shepherd Is*, Richard Peek (E. C. Kirby); SATB or SA or TB (E)

FIFTH SUNDAY OF EASTER (A)

Acts 7:55-60 Obeying Christ and unconcerned about building his own successful ministry, Stephen faithfully preaches the Word of God. His listeners respond to the Word of God by becoming enraged, shaking their fists and hurling verbal epithets as well as stones and rocks, after checking their hats and coats with Saul. But Stephen, faithful to the end, dies as a servant of Christ, forgiving his stoners for they know not what they do.

1 Peter 2:2-10 Once you were nobodies, but God has called you out of darkness into his own marvelous light. Why? To declare, to witness about his mercy revealed in Jesus Christ, the keystone that holds all together yet is a stumbling block for the world.

John 14:1-14 Jesus' departure means his return to the Father. "But where are you going?" asks Peter. "To prepare a place for you all," replies Jesus, "where there are enough rooms for everyone. Be not afraid, I'll return to take you all." Thomas quickly speaks out: "But we don't know the way." "I am the way to the Father," says Jesus. "Then show us," Philip pleads. "Whoever has seen me has seen the Father," says Jesus.

Psalm 31:1-8
1. Metrical, *In You, Lord, I Have Put My Trust*, LW p. 406, tune: *In dich hab' ich gehoffet*
2. Gelineau, *In You, O Lord, I Take Refuge*, GG, p. 81
3. Gregorian psalm tone, *GP*, Holy Saturday ABC

Hymns for the Day	HL	HB	WB
Blessing and Honor and Glory and Power	196	137	311
Built on the Rock	–	432	320
Christ Is Made the Sure Foundation	336	433	325
He Is the Way	–	–	413
Lead On, O King Eternal	371	332	448
Sing Praise to God, Who Reigns Above	–	15	568
Thou Art the Way	254	221	–
When Stephen, Full of Power and Grace	–	–	638

Anthems for the Day

Acts 7:55-60 *When Stephen, Full of Power and Grace*, Richard Peek (H. W. Gray); SATB (E)

1 Peter 2:2-10 *Christ: Foundation, Head, and Cornerstone*, Lloyd Pfautsch (Lawson-Gould); SATB (M)

John 14:1-14 *Come, My Way, My Truth, My Life*, Philip Dietterich (H. W. Gray); SATB (ME)

Ps. 31:1-8 *Incline Thine Ear, Oh, Lord*, A. Arkhangelsky (M. Witmark & Sons); SATB (ME)

SIXTH SUNDAY OF EASTER (A)

Acts 17:22-31 Paul preaches the gospel to some Athenians. Appealing first to the common ground of human yearning to worship God, Paul defines who their unknown God is. God is Creator of all, who lives not in any human-made shrines nor needs anything his creatures can make, since God is the giver of all life and breath. The way to know God is through Jesus Christ who was crucified but raised from death.

1 Peter 3:13-22 A rhetorical question begins this text: Would anyone harm a righteous person? No? Well that's precisely why the readers of this letter are suffering. Maybe suffering for your faith is a possibility. So be fearless, be prepared, maintain the right relationship with God, and the world will be put to shame and God will be glorified. For Christ himself suffered—he died for your sins—but he was resurrected and exalted.

John 14:15-21 "Whoever loves me keeps my commandments," says Jesus. How do you do that in a world without Jesus to tell us what to do? Tell his teachings to one another, interpret his teachings for our own age, live out his teachings in relation to one another. Amazingly, that's just what the Holy Spirit prompts in us, and that's why Jesus promised to send us another "companion interpreter."

Psalm 66:8-20
1. Metrical, *Come, Ye That Fear the Lord, HB* 296, tune: Forest Green
2. Gelineau, *Cry Out with Joy to God, All the Earth, GG,* p. 55

Hymns for the Day	HL	HB	WB
Come Down, O Love Divine	–	–	334
Come, Ye That Fear the Lord	–	296	–
Holy Spirit, Truth Divine	208	240	422
I Sing as I Arise Today	–	–	428
O Spirit of the Living God	207	242	528
Rejoice, the Lord Is King	193	140	562

Anthems for the Day
Acts 17:22-31 *God's Time Is Best,* J. S. Bach (*Cantata 106,* Kalmus); first chorus, SATB (MD)
1 Peter 3:13-22 *Worthy Art Thou, O Lord God,* Anton Bruckner (Augsburg); SATB with divisi, 3 trombones (optional) (MD)
John 14:15-21 *If Ye Love Me, Keep My Commandments,* Thomas Tallis (G. Schirmer); SATB (M)
Ps. 66:8-20 *O Come Hither,* Maurice Greene (*Anthems for Choirs,* vol. 2, Oxford); SATB (ME)

THE ASCENSION OF OUR LORD (ABC)

Acts 1:1-11 Jesus charges the apostles to wait in Jerusalem for "the promise of the Father" which is the gift of the Holy Spirit. The apostles ask the risen Jesus if he will now restore the kingdom to Israel. "That's not your worry but God's," replies Jesus. "You'll receive power when the Holy Spirit comes, and then you shall be my witnesses proclaiming the gospel everywhere." Then Jesus is lifted up and departs on a cloud.

Ephesians 1:15-23 May God give you the Spirit who will make you wise and understanding in the knowledge of Christ. In this way you will know the hope to which Christ has called you (the kind of New Age that is coming) and recognize God's power among us, especially his power in raising Christ to a position above all earthly powers.

Luke 24:46-53 Jesus preaches a kerygmatic sermon on Christ as Lord and the message of repentance and forgiveness. He then constitutes his disciples as the New Israel, promises them the gift of the Spirit, and ascends.

or **Mark 16:9-16, 19-20** Jesus appears to Mary Magdalene, two disciples, and then to eleven disciples: "Go and preach the gospel!" He then ascends to the right hand of God.

Psalm 47
1. Metrical, *O Clap Your Hands, All Ye People, NSC,* p. 5, tune by Eric Reid
2. Gelineau, *All Peoples, Clap Your Hands, GG,* p. 58
3. Gregorian psalm tone, *GP,* Ascension Day ABC

Hymns for the Day	*HL*	*HB*	*WB*
All Hail the Power of Jesus' Name!	192	132	285
Christ, Above All Glory Seated	–	–	324
Christ, Whose Glory Fills the Skies	26	47	332
Crown Him with Many Crowns	190	213	349
Jesus Shall Reign	377	496	443
Light of Light, Enlighten Me	21	73	–
The Lord Ascendeth Up on High	172	212	–

Anthems for the Day
Acts 1:1-11 *At the Name of Jesus,* R. Vaughan Williams (Oxford); SATB (ME)
Eph. 1:15-23 *Alleluia! Sing to Jesus,* Hal Hopson (Augsburg); 2-part (E)
Luke 24:46-53 *Now Glad of Heart Be Everyone!,* Richard Peek (E. C. Kirby); SATB (E)
or **Mark 16:9-16, 19-20** *The Lord Is King O'er Land and Sea,* Heinrich Schütz (*Four Psalms,* Mercury); SATB (E)
Ps. 47 *O Clap Your Hands,* R. Vaughan Williams (Stainer & Bell); SATB with divisi, brass, timpani (MD)

SEVENTH SUNDAY OF EASTER (A)

Acts 1:6-14 In verses 6-11, the apostles ask the risen Jesus if he will now restore the kingdom to Israel. "That's not your worry but God's," replies Jesus. "You'll receive power when the Holy Spirit comes, and then you shall be my witnesses proclaiming the gospel everywhere." Then Jesus is lifted up and departs on a cloud while the apostles stand gazing at the sky. "Why are you apostles standing there looking at the sky?" ask two angels. "Jesus will return the same way he departed. So get on with your ministry here and now." In verses 12-14, the apostles return to Jerusalem and gather in the upper room.

1 Peter 4:12-14; 5:6-11 Rejoice in your sufferings as a Christian. You shouldn't be surprised at this test of your faith, for suffering belongs to Christ, whose way you are called to follow. So when you suffer for your faith, you know that's a sign of God's blessing. Be alert, be firm in your faith because enemies are seeking to devour you, but after your suffering God will bring all to perfection.

John 17:1-11 Jesus reveals to us not only God but God's will for us. Christ is gone now, but the church is here to show the world what God's will is. No wonder Christ prays for the church. If the church is to show God's will, then the church must be unified and faithful.

Psalm 68:1-10
1. Gelineau, *But the Just Shall Rejoice at the Presence of God, GG,* p. 111
2. Gregorian psalm tone, *GP,* Easter 7 ABC

Hymns for the Day	HL	HB	WB
A Hymn of Glory Let Us Sing	–	–	273
All Hail the Power of Jesus' Name!	192	132	285
Crown Him with Many Crowns	190	213	349
Glorious Is Your Name, Most Holy	–	–	378
Glory Be to God the Father	60	–	–
Jesus Shall Reign	377	496	443
The Friends of Christ Together	–	–	586
The Lord Ascendeth Up on High	172	212	–

Anthems for the Day
Acts 1:6-14 *God Is Gone Up,* Gerald Finzi (Boosey & Hawkes); SATB with divisi (MD)
1 Peter 4:12-14; 5:6-11 *God Is Ever Sun and Shield,* J. S. Bach (*Third Morning Star Choir Book,* Concordia); unison with oboe or flute (M)
John 17:1-11 *Tibi Laus,* Orlando Lassus (*Rare Choral Masterpieces,* Schmitt, Hall & McCreary); SATB (ME)
Ps. 68:1-10 *The Lord Gave the Word,* G. F. Handel (*Messiah,* ed. Watkins Shaw, Novello); SATB (M)

THE DAY OF PENTECOST (A)

Acts 2:1-21 Wind and tongues of fire—the Holy Spirit—spread among all the believers. Are they drunk? "No," says Peter, "it's only nine in the morning. But while I have your attention, let me tell you about Jesus Christ."

or **Isaiah 44:1-8** Yahweh promises to pour out his Spirit on his people, who will then experience re-creation.

1 Corinthians 12:3b-13 The Spirit bestows different gifts to each person, but all are from one and the same Spirit.

or **Acts 2:1-21** *See above.*

John 20:19-23 A series of symbolic episodes: The risen Jesus appears to his frightened disciples and says, "Peace." Then he shows them his hands and his side (which fills the disciples with joy) and again says, "Peace." He gives them the Holy Spirit by breathing on them and concludes with an eschatological saying about resisting forgiveness.

or **John 7:37-39** Jesus stands up in the Temple court and proclaims that he is the source of living water.

Psalm 104:24-34
1. Metrical, *O Worship the King All Glorious Above*, HB 26, tune: Lyons
2. Gelineau, *Bless the Lord, My Soul!*, GG, p. 63
3. Gregorian psalm tone, *GP*, Pentecost ABC

Hymns for the Day	HL	HB	WB
Come, Holy Ghost, Our Souls Inspire	–	237	335
Come, Holy Spirit, God and Lord!	–	–	336
O Spirit of the Living God	207	242	528
Spirit Divine, Attend Our Prayers	212	243	574
The Day of Pentecost Arrived	–	–	583

Anthems for the Day
Acts 2:1-21 *Dum Complerentu Dies*, T. L. da Vittoria (*Renaissance Singer*, E. C. Schirmer); SSATB (M)
Isa. 44:1-8 *Be Not Afraid*, Felix Mendelssohn (*Elijah*, no. 22, G. Schirmer); SATB, chorus (M)
1 Cor. 12:3b-13 *Come, Holy Ghost*, Orlando Gibbons (A. Broude); SATB (ME)
or **Acts 2:1-21** *(See above)*
John 20:19-23 *Come, Then, O Holy Breath of God*, Palestrina-Malin (Edward B. Marks); SSATB (MD)
or **John 7:37-39** *Come, O Creator Spirit, Come*, Josquin Desprez (Concordia); SATB (E)
Ps. 104:24-34 *The Eyes of All*, Richard Feliciano (E. C. Schirmer); SATB (M)

TRINITY SUNDAY
[First Sunday After Pentecost] (A)

Deuteronomy 4:32-40 Look at the unprecedented, miraculous "signs" and "wonders" of Yahweh on behalf of his chosen people, Israel: speaking to them from a fire, liberating them from oppression, covenanting with them from a mountaintop, instructing them from heaven, freely choosing them as his people, leading them to the promised land, showing them that Yahweh alone is God, for there is no other.

2 Corinthians 13:5-14 An appeal to the Corinthians to examine themselves: Consider whether you are truly Christians. Presumably the response is affirmative; therefore, pray to God for ongoing maturation of your faith that you may live faithfully. A series of pastoral charges to the community of faith and the well-known and often used triadic liturgical formula conclude this letter.

Matthew 28:16-20 An account of the Great Commission in which the exalted Jesus appears to his followers on a mountaintop and, in his lordly authority, charges them to "make disciples of all nations, baptizing them and . . . teaching them all I have commanded you." The fulfillment of this mission depends not on human authority or ingenuity, but on the promised continuing presence of the Lord.

Psalm 33:1-12
1. Metrical, *Praise the Lord, Rejoice, Believers*, by Janie Alford (manuscript)
2. Gelineau, *For the Lord of the Lord Is Faithful*, GG, p. 24
3. Gregorian psalm tone, *GP*, Easter 3 C

Hymns for the Day	HL	HB	WB
All Creatures of Our God and King	–	100	282
Glory Be to God the Father	60	–	–
Holy God, We Praise Your Name	–	–	420
Holy, Holy, Holy!	57	11	421
I Sing as I Arise Today	–	–	428
O Trinity of Blessed Light	59	245	–
The Apostles' Creed	–	–	259

Anthems for the Day
Deut. 4:32-40 *Is Not His Word Like a Fire?*, Felix Mendelssohn (*Elijah*, no. 17, G. Schirmer); baritone solo (MD)
2 Cor. 13:5-14 *Thou Wilt Keep Him in Perfect Peace*, S. S. Wesley (H. W. Gray); SATTB (ME)
Matt. 28:16-20 *Lo, I Am with You*, Daniel Moe (Augsburg); SATB (MD)
Ps. 33:1-12 *O Fear the Lord, Ye His Saints*, Dale Wood (Augsburg); SATB (E)

SUNDAY BETWEEN MAY 29 AND JUNE 4
(Proper 4) (A) [use only if after Trinity Sunday]*

Genesis 12:1-9 Yahweh chooses a barren, landless, futureless couple and promises descendants, land, and a future in which their name will be magnified. Abram faithfully embraces Yahweh's promises and begins his pilgrimage of eternal wandering in the new land.

Romans 3:21-28 Sometimes the good news can be bad news. For those living under the illusion that good deeds and obedience to the law can gain and preserve God's acceptance, Paul's words are offensive. He says we are all sinners, but by the free gift of God's grace all gain God's acceptance through Christ Jesus. You can rely only on the mercy and graciousness of God offered to all through Christ. Such news may be frightening because we can no longer boast about being righteous. God is the righteous one who justifies us by his love for us.

Matthew 7:21-29 Evildoers who do mighty works and faith healings in the name of Christ shall not enter the kingdom of heaven because Christ never knew them. Those who hear and obey Christ's words are like those who build stone houses on a rock base, and those who do not hear and obey are like those who build mud houses in an arroyo. The crowds were astonished at Jesus' teaching, for he taught with authority.

Psalm 33:12-22
1. Gelineau, *The Lord Looks on Those Who Revere Him, GG,* p. 24
2. Gregorian psalm tone, GP, Lent 2 A

Hymns for the Day	HL	HB	WB
Built on the Rock	–	432	320
God Bless Our Native Land	413	514	–
In Christ There Is No East or West	341	479	435
O God, Beneath Your Guiding Hand	462	523	495
O God of Bethel, by Whose Hand	98	342	496
O Where Are Kings and Empires Now	334	431	530

Anthems for the Day
Gen. 12:1-9 *Benedictus,* David McK. Williams (H. W. Gray); unison (E)
Rom. 3:21-28 *Greater Love Hath No Man,* John Ireland (Galaxy); SATB with soprano, bass soli (M)
Matt. 7:21-29 *Hosanna! Me Build a House,* West Indian Folk Tune, arr. Peek (Flammer); SA (E)
Ps. 33:12-22 *Look Down, O Lord,* William Byrd (E. C. Schirmer); SATB (ME)

---

*NOTE: If the Sunday between May 24 and May 28 follows Trinity Sunday, use the Eighth Sunday after the Epiphany on that day.

SUNDAY BETWEEN JUNE 5 AND JUNE 11
(Proper 5) (A) [use only if after Trinity Sunday]

Genesis 22:1-18 God tests Abraham in order to find out whether Abraham trusts only God's promise. "Give up your only son," summons God—a repugnant, disturbing test—yet Abraham faithfully obeys. Asks Isaac, "Where is the lamb?" "God will provide," replies Abraham, and an angel of the Lord cries out, "Now I know you trust only God's promise because you have not withheld from God that which is most precious to you." Miraculously, God provides a ram for the offering and again blesses Abraham.

Romans 4:13-18 For trusting the promises of God, who justifies the impious and the irreligious, people receive God's free gift of grace. Look at Abraham, who was justified not by works but by grace through faith.

Matthew 9:9-13 Jesus not only calls a tax collector (i.e., racketeer) to follow him but sits down to a meal with a host of outcasts and sinners. Why does Jesus eat with such disreputable, immoral people? "Because," replies Jesus, "I have not come to call the respectable, righteous people, but sinners." Imagine that! There's room at Christ's table for all who hear Christ's words and know they can let go of their self-righteousness and enter as forgiven sinners.

Psalm 13
1. Metrical, *Forgotten for Eternity*, PP, p. 69
2. Gregorian psalm tone, *GP*, Proper 25 B

Hymns for the Day	HL	HB	WB
Come, Let Us to the Lord Our God	–	125	–
Faith of Our Fathers!	267	348	361
Jesus Calls Us	223	269	439
Somebody's Knocking at Your Door	–	–	572
Whate'er Our God Ordains Is Right	291	366	633

Anthems for the Day
Gen. 22:1-18 *On God and Not on Human Trust*, Johann Pachelbel (Concordia); SATB (M)
Rom. 4:13-18 *O Lord, Increase My Faith*, Orlando Gibbons (H. W. Gray); SATB (M)
Matt. 9:9-13 *We Hurry with Tired, Unfaltering Footsteps*, J. S. Bach (Galaxy); SA (M)
Ps. 13 *Psalm XIII*, Johannes Brahms (G. Schirmer); SSA (M)

SUNDAY BETWEEN JUNE 12 AND JUNE 18
(Proper 6) (A) [use only if after Trinity Sunday]

Genesis 25:19-34 Yahweh blesses barren Rebecca and old Isaac with the gift of twin sons, who struggle with each other in Rebecca's womb (as well as throughout the rest of their lives). Why this conflict? Because Yahweh scandalously inverted the conventional order by choosing the elder to serve the younger, the last to become first. Amazingly, Yahweh's divine purposes are fulfilled in the human exchange of the birthright.

Romans 5:6-11 Since we are justified by faith, we are at peace with God. So let's stand up straight and rejoice, for "God has poured out his love into our hearts through the Holy Spirit." While we were sinning against God by resisting and seeking to destroy his Son, God reconciled us to himself through the death of his Son. At the cross, we are drenched by the incredible depth of God's love for us.

Matthew 9:35–10:8 Verse 35 concludes a series of miracle stories with Jesus visiting "all the cities and villages," teaching, preaching, and healing. What Jesus experiences are helpless people, sheep without a shepherd, a bountiful harvest without enough reapers. So Jesus invites his disciples to pray for laborers to bring in the harvest, and then he commissions the Twelve with his authority to preach the same message he preaches (*see* Matt. 4:17) to the lost sheep of Israel, and to perform the same signs of the kingdom that he performs.

Psalm 46
1. Metrical, *A Mighty Fortress Is Our God* (found in most hymnals)
2. Contemporary setting, *Psalm 46* from *Three Psalms of Celebration*, Arthur Wills (Royal School of Church Music, 1980)
3. Gregorian psalm tone, *GP*, Easter Vigil, Proper 29 C

Hymns for the Day	HL	HB	WB
A Mighty Fortress Is Our God	266	91	274
All Glory Be to God On High	–	–	283
God of the Ages, by Whose Hand	–	–	396
Heralds of Christ	379	498	416
O God of Bethel, by Whose Hand	98	342	496

Anthems for the Day
Gen. 25:19-34 *Draw Near, All Ye People*, Felix Mendelssohn (*Elijah*, no. 14, G. Schirmer); baritone solo

Rom. 5:6-11 *Reconciliation*, Lloyd Pfautsch (Augsburg); SATB (ME)

Matt. 9:35–10:8 *The Lord Gave the Word*, G. F. Handel (*Messiah*, ed. Watkins Shaw, Novello); SATB (M)

Ps. 46 *A Mighty Fortress Is Our God*, Hans Leo Hassler (Concordia); SATB (M)

SUNDAY BETWEEN JUNE 19 AND JUNE 25
(Proper 7) (A) [use only if after Trinity Sunday]

Genesis 28:10-17 See the fugitive Jacob, the slick con man, cowardly fleeing for his life from an enraged Esau bent on revenge. The clever cheat, a common crook, runs until, weary in the dark, he curls up against a stone and sleeps. At daybreak, Jacob awakes and exclaims, "Surely Yahweh was in this place." Ostensibly, Yahweh gave this dreaming purloiner the same unconditional, guaranteed promise made to Abraham and Isaac. Yahweh seems unfair or, worse, immoral. Of all the people in the world to pick, Yahweh chooses Jacob, a coward and a crook.

Romans 5:12-19 Paul asserts that sin and death became part of our human experience "through one man," yet "all sinned." All humanity reenacts what this "one man" introduced: aspiring to become like God. But in Christ, God's free gift of grace for all humanity was deliberately introduced. This one righteous act sets free all humanity and gives life to all.

Matthew 10:24-33 Disciples, expect to receive the same response and treatment as your master. There is nothing to fear—the worst they can do is to kill you. So shout what I whisper to you and boldly face the consequences, knowing you are ultimately under God's care.

Psalm 91:1-10
1. Metrical, *Call Jehovah Thy Salvation, HB* 123, tune: Hyfrydol
2. Gelineau, *He Who Dwells in the Shelter of the Most High, GG,* p. 23
3. Gregorian psalm tone, *GP,* Lent 1 C
4. *PS,* p. 24

Hymns for the Day	HL	HB	WB
Call Jehovah Your Salvation	292	123	322
God's Word Is like a Flaming Sword	–	–	405
Lord, from the Depths to You I Cry	240	277	459
Lord Jesus, Think on Me	239	270	–
Thou Whose Purpose Is to Kindle	–	–	603

Anthems for the Day
Gen. 28:10-17 *The Gate of Heaven,* Randall Thompson (E. C. Schirmer); SATB (M)
Rom. 5:12-19 *Wash Me Thoroughly from My Wickedness,* S. S. Wesley (*Church Anthem Book,* Oxford); SATB (ME)
Matt. 10:24-33 *Thou Shalt Break Them,* G. F. Handel (*Messiah,* ed. Watkins Shaw, Novello); tenor solo
Ps. 91:1-10 *Be Not Afraid,* Felix Mendelssohn (*Elijah,* no. 22, G. Schirmer); SATB (M)

SUNDAY BETWEEN JUNE 26 AND JULY 2
(Proper 8) (A)

Genesis 32:22-32 An all-night wrestling match between the swindler Jacob and a mysterious opponent seems to be a draw until the enigmatic rival cripples Jacob's hip and requests release because day is breaking. The trickster Jacob, however, seeks a blessing, but receives a new name. When he asks the name of the inscrutable stranger, he receives a blessing. "I have seen God face to face," exclaims Jacob, "and yet my life is preserved."

Romans 6:3-11 Why not continue in sin so God's grace and glory may overflow? Responds Paul, "How can we who died to sin still live in it? When we were baptized into union with Christ, we became one with him in death and were set free from the power of sin, and then we were raised with Christ to new life. So our old being is dead to sin, and we now have a new life in Christ."

Matthew 10:34-42 Some tough, discomforting words of Jesus: "Those who love their family, race, denomination, country, or anyone else more than me are not worthy to be my disciple. . . . And those who seek to save their life by their own plans will surely lose it." The way of the cross is not in question, rather our willingness to follow it. Whoever hospitably receives Christ's representatives or messengers or disciples, even if only by a cup of water, also receives Christ and will therefore be rewarded by God in the age to come.

Psalm 17:1-7, 15
1. Metrical, *Come, My Soul, You Must Be Waking* (loose paraphrase), WB 337
2. Gelineau, *Lord, Hear a Cause That Is Just, GG,* p. 133
3. Gregorian psalm tone, *GP,* Proper 27 C

Hymns for the Day	HL	HB	WB
At the Name of Jesus	–	143	303
Beneath the Cross of Jesus	162	190	308
In the Cross of Christ I Glory	154	195	437
The Day of Resurrection!	166	208	584
The Strife Is O'er, the Battle Done	164	203	597

Anthems for the Day
Gen. 32:22-32 *Blessed Is the Man,* Maurice Greene (*Sing Joyfully,* vol. 2, Walton); SA or TB (E)
Rom. 6:3-11 *God's Son Has Made Me Free,* Edvard Grieg, arr. Overby (Augsburg); SATB (MD)
Matt. 10:34-42 *The King's Highway,* David McK. Williams (H. W. Gray); SATB (ME)
Ps. 17:1-7, 15 *Give Ear Unto Me,* Benedetto Marcello (H. W. Gray); SA (E)

SUNDAY BETWEEN JULY 3 AND JULY 9
(Proper 9) (A)

Exodus 1:6-14,22–2:10 Joseph's generation all died while in Egypt, but the descendants amazingly increased. "Too many and too mighty," complains the new king of Egypt. So the Israelites are enslaved and subjected to taskmasters. But the more the Israelites are oppressed, the more they multiply. So Pharaoh commands that all male Hebrew babies are to be thrown into the Nile. A Hebrew couple give birth to a son who is set adrift on the Nile's edge. Ironically, Pharaoh's daughter draws the infant out of the water, approves the infant's mother as nurse, and gives the Hebrew boy an Egyptian name, Moses.

Romans 7:14-25a Paul's personal confession about the universal human condition: "Somehow I make a bumbling mess out of all my good intentions and end up doing evil. The power of sin imprisons me. Who shall liberate me from this vicious cycle? Thanks be to God, who does this through Jesus Christ!"

Matthew 11:25-30 The masters of the law seem to be the most confused or obstinate about Jesus' message of grace. Thanks be to God, then, for his revelation to the unlearned and the foolish. Yet you are still invited to trade your yoke of law for the yoke of grace, which paradoxically demands more from you yet will give you rest.

Psalm 124
1. Metrical, *Now Israel May Say*, HB 357, tune: Old 124th

Hymns for the Day	HL	HB	WB
God of Compassion, in Mercy Befriend Us	–	122	392
God of Pity, God of Grace	252	–	–
God Who Made the Earth	–	466	–
If You Will Only Let God Guide You	105	344	431
Jesus, Lead the Way	–	334	441
Jesus, Lover of My Soul	233	216	–
Lord, Bless and Pity Us	–	493	456
Now Israel May Say	–	357	–

Anthems for the Day
Ex. 1:6-14, 22–2:10 *O Shepherd of Israel*, Christian Gregor (Brodt); SA (E)
Rom. 7:14-25a *Have Mercy, Lord*, Cristobal Morales (Concordia); SATB (E)
Matt. 11:25-30 *He Shall Feed His Flock*, G. F. Handel (*Messiah*, ed. Watkins Shaw, Novello); alto and soprano solos
Ps. 124 *Thee Will I Love, O Lord*, Arthur Honegger (*King David*, E. C. Schirmer); SATB (MD)

SUNDAY BETWEEN JULY 10 AND JULY 16
(Proper 10) (A)

Exodus 2:11-22 Moses looks with sympathy on the burdensome toil of his own kin, and in secrecy and stealth he impetuously murders an Egyptian to avenge the flogging of a Hebrew brother. Returning the next day as triumphant self-appointed savior of his people, Moses is unexpectedly rejected by his own kin—"Who made you ruler and judge over us?"—and has to flee for his life. Into the desert he runs until he comes upon a well where romance flourishes. The Hebrew fugitive daringly rescues seven women from a band of thugs, marries a non-Israelite woman, and finds a home amid foreigners.

Romans 8:9-17 If God's Spirit dwells among you, then you live according to the Spirit and therefore are heirs with Christ—provided you suffer with him—of all the blessings of God.

Matthew 13:1-9, 18-23 A foolish farmer indiscriminately sows seeds along the highway, in thornbushes, on rock piles, all about his fields. Yet, there's going to be a harvest—thirty, sixty, a hundredfold. God keeps his word! So preach the gospel and trust God.

Psalm 69:6-15
1. Metrical, *Thy Loving-kindness, Lord, Is Good and Free,* HB 393, tune: Ellers
2. Gelineau, *It Is for You that I Suffer Taunts,* GG, p. 87
3. Gregorian psalm tone, *GP,* Wednesday of Holy Week ABC

Hymns for the Day	HL	HB	WB
"Am I My Brother's Keeper?"	–	–	295
Christ for the World We Sing	378	489	–
Come, Thou Almighty King	52	244	343
God Is Working His Purpose Out	–	500	389
Jesus, Priceless Treasure	–	414	442
Lord, from the Depths to You I Cry	240	277	459
Lord of the Strong, When Earth You Trod	–	–	466

Anthems for the Day

Ex. 2:11-22 *Man, That Is Born of a Woman,* John Cole (*Sing Joyfully,* vol. 4, Walton); SATB (E)

Rom. 8:9-17 *Ye Are Not in the Flesh,* J. S. Bach (Motet III, *Jesu, Meine Freude,* Peters); SSATB (D)

Matt. 13:1-19, 18-23 *The Word of God,* Jean Berger (Augsburg); SATB, optional instruments (D)

Ps. 69:6-15 *Improperium,* Gaudenzio Battistini (*Sing Joyfully,* vol. 4, Walton); SATB (E)

SUNDAY BETWEEN JULY 17 AND JULY 23
(Proper 11) (A)

Exodus 3:1-12 Yahweh freely chooses to reveal himself to Moses in a burning bush in the desert. Out of nowhere, Yahweh bursts into Moses' tranquil life: "I have witnessed the oppression and suffering of my people, therefore, I will save them by sending you to lead them out of Egypt." "But," protests Moses, "I am a nobody." So God gives Moses a sign: "When you lead my people out of Egypt, you shall serve God upon this mountain."

Romans 8:18-25 Our sufferings pale in light of the glory that will be revealed to us. Yet all creation groans, as do we who have the firstfruits of the Spirit, for redemption. But we have an advantage: the gift of the Spirit supports our confident hope that we shall be saved.

Matthew 13:24-30, 36-43 What to do about the presence of weeds amid growing crops? Usually you yank out the weeds lest they choke the crops, but here you are counseled to wait until harvesttime. Strange. Ah, but then you remember Jesus' words in Matthew 7:1.

Psalm 103:1-13
1. Metrical, *Bless, O My Soul! the Living God*, HB 8, tune: Park Street
2. Gelineau, *My Soul, Give Thanks to the Lord*, GG, p. 77
3. Gregorian psalm tone, *GP*, Lent 3 C

Hymns for the Day	HL	HB	WB
Amazing Grace!	–	275	296
Bless, O My Soul! the Living God	–	8	–
Come, Thou Almighty King	52	244	343
Hope of the World	–	291	423
The God of Abraham Praise	8	89	587
The King Shall Come When Morning Dawns	187	232	–
When Stephen, Full of Power and Grace	–	–	638

Anthems for the Day

Ex. 3:1-12 *Go Down, Moses*, Spiritual, arr. Roger Wagner (Lawson-Gould); SATB (M)

Rom. 8:18-25 *Perfect Through Suffering*, Seth Bingham (Peters); SATB (M)

Matt. 13:24-30, 36-43 *Then Shall the Righteous Shine Forth*, Felix Mendelssohn (*Elijah*, no. 39, G. Schirmer); tenor solo (M)

Ps. 103:1-13 *Bless Thou the Lord, O My Soul*, Austin Lovelace (E. C. Kirby); SATB (E)

SUNDAY BETWEEN JULY 24 AND JULY 30
(Proper 12) (A)

Exodus 3:13-20 "Whom shall I tell the Israelites sent me?" asks Moses. "I AM WHO I AM," replies God. "Tell them *YHWH*, the God of Abraham, Isaac, and Jacob, has sent you. Because I have heard my people's groanings and cries, I shall bring them out of the affliction of Egypt to a land flowing with milk and honey. Go, assemble the leaders of Israel and entreat Pharaoh to allow you all to travel in the wilderness for three days. Pharaoh will deny you permission, but I shall convince him with mighty wonders."

Romans 8:26-30 We do not know how to pray, yet the Spirit transforms our weak groanings into prayer. The Spirit pleads with God on our behalf so we may share in the glory which God prepares for those who love him.

Matthew 13:44-52 Without even searching, a man unexpectedly stumbles upon a pot of gold at the beginning of the rainbow. The treasure is simply a free gift he cannot possess, but receive only in joy. A man, upon finding a great pearl, discovers its purchase price will cost him everything, including himself. A net, all by itself, gathers fish of every kind—the good, the bad, and the ugly—which are sorted only when the net is full. "Do you understand all this?" asks Jesus. "Yes," respond his disciples. "Good, then you will find your identity in God's will and live according to the treasures of the kingdom."

Psalm 105:1-11
1. Gregorian psalm tone, *GP*, Wednesday of Easter Week ABC

Hymns for the Day	HL	HB	WB
Guide Me, O Thou Great Jehovah	104	339	409
Jesus, Priceless Treasure	–	414	442
O Spirit of the Living God	207	242	–
O What Their Joy and Their Glory Must Be	430	424	–
The God of Abraham Praise	8	89	587
The Lord Will Come and Not Be Slow	185	230	–
Whate'er Our God Ordains Is Right	291	366	633

Anthems for the Day
Ex. 3:13-20 *Thanks Be to Thee, O Lord*, G. F. Handel (E. C. Schirmer); SATB with alto solo (E)
Rom. 8:26-30 *Come, O Creator Spirit, Come*, Josquin Desprez (Concordia); SATB (E)
Matt. 13:44-52 *Jesu, Priceless Treasure*, J. S. Bach (Augsburg); SATB (E)
Ps. 105:1-11 *Sing Ye Praises to Our King*, Aaron Copland (Boosey & Hawkes); SATB (M)

SUNDAY BETWEEN JULY 31 AND AUGUST 6
(Proper 13) (A)

Exodus 12:1-14 Instructions on celebrating the paschal sacrifice which will take on new meaning as the Passover festival—the family meal at which Israel thanks God for redeeming them and making them a people, and at which the people renew their hope in the salvation to come.

Romans 8:31-39 Who can be against us? Nobody, for God spared his own son for us all. Who dares accuse us? Nobody, for God has acquitted us; Christ stands before us. Who can separate us from the love of Christ? Nobody, for God has hold over us in Christ, and God's hold on us is inexorable.

Matthew 14:13-21 One of the multitude of remembered meals involving God-with-us. Jesus takes five loaves and two fish and, after giving thanks to God, breaks the bread and gives all to the disciples to distribute among 5,000-plus people. Miraculously, in the midst of this human meal of eating and drinking, God's grace is sufficient to feed all the hungry.

Psalm 143:1-10
1. Metrical, *When Morning Lights the Eastern Skies*, HB 49, tune: St. Stephen
2. Gregorian psalm tone, *GP*, Easter Vigil ABC

Hymns for the Day	HL	HB	WB
Be Known to Us in Breaking Bread	356	446	–
Be Still, My Soul	281	374	–
Become to Us the Living Bread	–	–	305
Come, You Faithful, Raise the Strain	168	205	344
Give to the Winds Your Fears	294	364	377
Let Us Break Bread Together	–	447	452
When Morning Lights the Eastern Skies	–	49	–

Anthems for the Day

Ex. 12:1-14 *Christ, Our Passover*, Willis Bodine (H. W. Gray); SATB with brass quartet, timpani, and organ (MD)

Rom. 8:31-39 *Who Shall Separate Us*, Heinrich Schütz (Chantry); SATB (M)

Matt. 14:13-21 *After the People Had Seen*, Melchior Vulpius (Concordia); SATB (M)

Ps. 143:1-10 *Enter Not Into Judgement*, Thomas Attwood (H. W. Gray); SATB (E)

SUNDAY BETWEEN AUGUST 7 AND AUGUST 13
(Proper 14) (A)

Exodus 14:19-31 Moses' prebattle, motivational speech to the Israelites: "Fear not, stand firm, keep still, for Yahweh will fight for you." Yahweh commands Moses to raise his walking stick over the waters so they will divide. An angel of God and the pillar of cloud move to the rear of the Israelites and veil them from the Egyptians. And all comes to fulfillment according to the word of God. Yahweh drives back the sea by a strong east wind, throws the Egyptians into panic, causes their wheels to become mired in mud, and tosses them into the sea. Thus Yahweh saves Israel from the Egyptians, and Israel believes in Yahweh and his servant Moses.

Romans 9:1-5 Paul mourns for his Jewish brothers and sisters who are God's people—recipients of the glory, covenants, law, and promises of God. Before them come the patriarchs, and from them comes Christ, who assures them salvation. For these people, his own flesh and blood, Paul would surrender his own salvation.

Matthew 14:22-33 The disciples are in a boat, a northeaster flinging them from wave to wave. Jesus is off praying, yet here he comes toward the disciples, "walking on the water"—wouldn't you be afraid? "Have no fear," says Jesus, "it is I." "If it is you, Lord," yells Peter, "then bid me to come to you on the water." "Come," says Jesus. So Peter leaves the security of the boat and walks on the water toward Jesus, but suddenly in the face of wind and rain and storm, Peter's faith ebbs and, afraid, he begins to sink. Jesus immediately rescues him, and the disciples confess Jesus as the "Son of God."

Psalm 106:4-12
1. Gregorian psalm tone, *GP*, Lent 2 B

Hymns for the Day	HL	HB	WB
Faith of Our Fathers!	267	348	361
Give to the Winds Your Fears	294	364	377
O Come and Sing Unto the Lord	49	29	488
Strong Son of God, Immortal Love	175	228	578
They Cast Their Nets in Galilee	–	421	–

Anthems for the Day
Ex. 14:19-31 *Sing to the Lord*, Edward Bairstow (H. W. Gray); SATB (M)
Rom. 9:1-5 *Benedictus*, William Barnard (H. W. Gray); unison (ME)
Matt. 14:22-33 *The God of Glory Thundereth*, Alan Hovhaness (Peters); SATB (M)
Ps. 106:4-12 *Strike the Cymbal*, Franz Schubert, arr. Lovelace (Choristers Guild); 2-part (E)

SUNDAY BETWEEN AUGUST 14 AND AUGUST 20
(Proper 15) (A)

Exodus 16:2-15 The Israelites find themselves in the desert without food and water. Literally starving to death, they begin complaining; some want to rebel and some want to return to Egypt. Aaron asks, "What do you want?" "We want bread!" shout the people. Aaron shockingly replies, "Good, you will see the glory." Yahweh then miraculously rains down manna (which means "What is it?") from heaven which the people are invited to share with one another. The people then turn their back on Egypt and its power and face the wilderness and its uncertainty, where they amazingly see the glory.

Romans 11:13-16, 29-32 Ironically, the Jews' disobedience (hardness of heart) provides the disobedient Gentiles an opportunity: when the first disciples are rebuffed by their own people, they turn to the Gentiles and preach the good news revealed in Jesus Christ. Doubly ironic it is that the Jews' disobedience (unbelief) is also a necessary stage for their return to faith. For both Jew and Gentile, the journey to God's mercy leads through disobedience. Imagine the joy when all are reconciled—it will be life from the dead!

Matthew 15:21-28 A Canaanite woman cries out to Jesus about her daughter's trouble, saying, "Lord, help me." Despite his disciples' protestations, Jesus responds to this non-Israelite woman's faith and to her wit (about undeserving dogs eating crumbs from the master's table).

Psalm 78:1-3, 10-20
1. Metrical, *O Come, My People, to My Law*, HB 255, tune: Heber (Kingsley)
2. Gelineau, *The Things We Have*, GG, p. 103
3. Gregorian psalm tone, *GP*, Proper 13 A

Hymns for the Day	HL	HB	WB
All People That on Earth Do Dwell	1	24	288
At Even, When the Sun Was Set	43	55	–
Before the Lord Jehovah's Throne	63	81	306
O for a Thousand Tongues	199	141	493
The King of Love My Shepherd Is	99	106	590

Anthems for the Day

Ex.16:2-15 *Panis Angelicus*, Manuel Cardoso (*Rare Choral Masterpieces*, p. 10, Schmitt, Hall & McCreary); SSAT (E)

Rom. 11:13-16, 29-32 *The Lord Will Suffer God to Guide Thee*, J. S. Bach (C. Fischer); SATB (M)

Matt. 15:21-28 *Great and Glorious*, F. J. Haydn (Mills); SATB (M)

Ps.78:1-3, 10-20 *Let My Complaint Come Before Thee*, Adrian Batten (*A Sixteenth-Century Anthem Book*, Oxford); SATB (ME)

SUNDAY BETWEEN AUGUST 21 AND AUGUST 27
(Proper 16) (A)

Exodus 17:1-7 On their journey through the wilderness, the Israelites lack water. Parched tongues waggle, complain, quarrel, find fault, contend against Moses. "What am I to do?" cries Moses. "Surely they'll stone me." Once again Yahweh miraculously provides for his testing, trying, challenging people. From a rock, life-giving water pours forth as a sign of his glory to his unbelieving, resistant people.

Romans 11:33-36 Life is a mystery, but a mystery into which Christians peer and announce, "God! God in all, above all, under all, through all things." Yet who can comprehend God? God's ways are not our ways. God's wisdom defies human understanding. God is inscrutable, unsearchable, unknowable. P.S.: A cross, a tomb, and an Easter morning offer a key to unlocking the mystery. Glory! Hallelujah!

Matthew 16:13-20 Through God's revelation Peter confesses Jesus as the Christ, though he doesn't understand his own words. Yet upon this follower, a rock of a disciple, Jesus promises to build his church and bestow the kingdom's keys.

Psalm 95
1. Metrical, *O Come and Sing Unto the Lord*, from *The Psalter*, 1912, *HB* 29, tune: Irish
2. Metrical, *To God with Gladness Sing*, *MP&E*, tune: Darwall's 148th.; also in *SOT&P*, p. 1
3. Gelineau, *Come, Ring Out Our Joy to the Lord*, *GG*, p. 27
4. Gregorian psalm tone, *GP*, Proper 29 A
5. *PS*, pp. 25, 26

Hymns for the Day	HL	HB	WB
Built on the Rock	–	432	320
God Himself Is with Us	51	13	384
Let All the World in Every Corner Sing	9	22	–
O Come and Sing Unto the Lord	49	29	488
O Where Are Kings and Empires Now	334	431	530
O Word of God Incarnate	215	251	532

Anthems for the Day
Ex. 17:1-7 *Sitientes Venite ad Aquas* (Come to the Waters), T. L. da Vittoria (Ricordi); SATB (M)

Rom. 11:33-36 *Achieved Is the Glorious Work*, F. J. Haydn (second chorus on this text from *The Creation*, G. Schirmer); SATB (M)

Matt. 16:13-20 *Built on a Rock*, Lindeman-Brandon (Augsburg); SAB (E)

Ps. 95 *O Come, Let Us Sing Unto the Lord*, William Byrd (Concordia); SATB (M)

SUNDAY BETWEEN AUGUST 28 AND SEPTEMBER 3
(Proper 17) (A)

Exodus 19:1-9 Yahweh has brought Israel to Sinai (as promised to Moses in Ex. 3:12), bearing the people on eagles' wings. Moses recites the story of Yahweh's saving deeds on behalf of Israel. And now Yahweh invites them to keep a covenant by which Israel will be Yahweh's own people, a kingdom of priests, and a holy nation—covenant blessings described in terms of a further call to service. And all the people answered together, "All that Yahweh has spoken we will do."

Romans 12:1-13 Present your bodies as a living sacrifice, for that is spiritual worship. Sacrifice, though, is precisely the opposite of our self-fulfillment culture. But don't conform to the way this world thinks and values. Be transformed. So how do you present your body? Use your gifts according to the grace given you: preach, serve, teach, give away your cash, encourage others, love one another, practice hospitality, share your belongings with others, serve the Lord—that's spiritual worship.

Matthew 16:21-28 Jesus speaks of his impending death and resurrection. Peter, who seeks a triumphant Messiah, misunderstands, whereupon Jesus rebukes him and teaches about discipleship.

Psalm 114
1. Gregorian psalm tone, *GP*, Proper 12 B

Hymns for the Day	HL	HB	WB
Christ Is Made the Sure Foundation	336	433	325
Jesus Calls Us	223	269	439
O Love, How Deep, How Broad, How High!	139	–	518
O Love That Wilt Not Let Me Go	307	400	519
Take My Life, and Let It Be Consecrated	242	310	–
"Take Up Thy Cross," the Saviour Said	–	293	–
The Church's One Foundation	333	437	582

Anthems for the Day

Ex. 19:1-9 *O Sing Joyfully*, Adrian Batten (*A Sixteenth-Century Anthem Book*, Oxford); SATB (ME)

Rom. 12:1-13 *To Do God's Will*, Jean Berger (Augsburg); SATB (M)

Matt. 16:21-28 *Let All the Angels of God Worship Him*, G. F. Handel (*Messiah*, ed. Watkins Shaw, Novello); SATB (M)

Ps. 114 *Clouds and Darkness Are Round About Him*, Antonín Dvořák (vocal solo, *Biblical Songs*, Book 1, no. 1, Simrock); high- or low-voice editions

SUNDAY BETWEEN SEPTEMBER 4 AND SEPTEMBER 10 (Proper 18) (A)

Exodus 19:16-24 Events at Mt. Sinai escalate to a fever pitch. After two days of ritual preparations by the people, Yahweh prepares to speak. Booming thunder and fulminating smoke and fire envelop the mountaintop, sending a shudder through the people, but Moses leads them out to the foot of the mountain. While shofars blast, Yahweh speaks with Moses, legitimating his special office as mediator. But wait, Yahweh summons Moses up the mountain for yet further instructions on ritual preparations before Yahweh will deliver his words.

Romans 13:1-10 Believe it or not, the authority of government comes from God, and its purpose is to order society ethically, meting out punishment and rewards. For many Christians this is a perplexing text, but take heart, for it must also be exasperating to God, who raised up Jesus Christ and continues to rule his creation above and in spite of governments as well as mysteriously through them.

Matthew 18:15-20 Personal offenses must be disciplined, for they affect the life of the whole community. First, strive for reconciliation privately; second, seek the counsel of others; third, the church must discipline its members, even if that means excommunication. In all three ways Christ will be present in the community, for church members who cannot fight openly with each other cannot love each other.

Psalm 115:1-11
1. Gelineau, *I Love the Lord for He Has Heard*, GG, p. 115

Hymns for the Day	HL	HB	WB
God Is Love: Let Heaven Adore Him	–	–	386
God Is Our Strong Salvation	92	347	388
Guide Me, O Thou Great Jehovah	104	339	409
Joyful, Joyful, We Adore Thee	5	21	446
Lord of All Being, Throned Afar	87	87	463
Love Divine, All Loves Excelling	308	399	471

Anthems for the Day
Ex.19:16-24 *God Is Our Refuge and Our Strength*, Alan Hovhaness (A. Broude); SATB (M)
Rom. 13:1-10 *O Jesus Christ, to Thee May Hymns Be Rising*, Daniel Moe (Augsburg); SATB (M)
Matt. 18:15-20 *Ubi Duo Vel Tres* (Wherever Two or Three), Claudio Monteverdi (*Sing Joyfully*, vol. 3, Walton); SAB (E)
Ps. 115:1-11 *We Seek Not, God, Our Lord, for Glory*, F. J. Haydn (Concordia); SATB (ME)

SUNDAY BETWEEN SEPTEMBER 11 AND SEPTEMBER 17 (Proper 19) (A)

Exodus 20:1-20 Yahweh spoke to Moses at Mt. Sinai concerning Israel's relationship with Yahweh and with neighbors. This Mosaic covenant is one of human obligation which prohibits Israel from violating the exclusive claims of the divine Lord who liberated them from bondage in Egypt. Conversely, these words distinctively assert the sovereignty of Yahweh and the exclusivity of the Yahweh-Israel bond. In addition, this covenant protects the fundamental rights of all free Israelite citizens.

Romans 14:5-12 Often we are fastidious about peripheral concerns such as virtuous diets, principled religious observances, and righteous Christian lifestyle. We are, however, to serve not ideologies, rules, laws, or principles, but God revealed in Jesus Christ, who lived and died for us that we might belong to him in life and death.

Matthew 18:21-35 A servant pleads for "a little more time" to repay his multimillion-dollar debt, while absurdly demanding immediate repayment of a twenty-dollar debt from another servant. Would you behave this way if you were really gripped by the stupendous forgiveness of God in Jesus Christ?

Psalm 19:7-14
1. Metrical, *Most Perfect Is the Law of God*, from *The Psalter*, 1912, *HB* 257, tune: Glasgow
2. Gelineau, *The Law of the Lord Is Perfect*, *GG*, p. 121
3. Gregorian psalm tone, *GP*, Proper 21 B

Hymns for the Day	HL	HB	WB
At the Name of Jesus	–	143	303
God Be in My Head	–	395	–
God, That Madest Earth and Heaven	41	58	404
How Gentle God's Commands	279	105	–
Most Perfect Is the Law of God	–	257	–
O Jesus Christ, to You May Hymns Be Rising	–	–	509
O Love Divine, That Stooped to Share	–	116	–
The Spirit Breathes Upon the Word	–	260	–

Anthems for the Day
Ex. 20:1-20 *The Holy Ten Commandments*, F. J. Haydn (Mercury); canons for 3-5 equal voices (ME)
Rom. 14:5-12 *At the Name of Jesus*, R. Vaughan Williams (Oxford); SATB with congregation (ME)
Matt. 18:21-35 *Thy Kingdom Come*, Gardner Evans (C. Fischer); SATB (M)
Ps. 19:7-14 *Blessed Are All They That Fear the Lord*, Leo Sowerby (H. W. Gray); SATB (M)

SUNDAY BETWEEN SEPTEMBER 18 AND SEPTEMBER 24 (Proper 20) (A)

Exodus 32:1-14 Moses has been on the mountain "forty days and forty nights" receiving instructions from Yahweh. At the foot of the mountain, a commotion brews among the people. Desiring a sign of the divine presence, the people impatiently, impulsively, truculently demand of Aaron, "Up, make us *elohim* (gods)!" How quickly Israel reneges on her covenant promise. Aaron complies and the "golden calf" is produced, an imitation of what Yahweh is about to give them (see Ex. 25:1-9). Says Yahweh to Moses, "Let me at these stiff-necked calf worshipers, *your* people—I'll wipe them out and start over with you." But Moses boldly intercedes for his wayward people. "Why does your anger burn hot against your people? You will be laughed at by the Egyptians if these Israelites fail to survive. You made promises to our ancestors; do you intend to keep your promises?"

Philippians 1:21-27 An imprisoned Paul writes to the threatened and therefore fearful Philippians, "If you die, you will be with Christ. If you live, you can bear witness to Christ. So don't fear death; be obedient to Christ."

Matthew 20:1-16 Some laborers grumble because they toiled all day in the scorching heat for a fair wage, but received the same pay as those who worked only an hour. Apparently God's free grace contravenes our sense of fairness.

Psalm 106:7-8, 19-23
None known to be available

Hymns for the Day	HL	HB	WB
Christ Is the World's Redeemer	–	136	–
Christ, of All My Hopes the Ground	316	314	–
Father Eternal, Ruler of Creation	–	486	362
Father, We Greet You	–	285	364
Guide Me, O Thou Great Jehovah	104	339	409
Jesus, Thy Boundless Love to Me	314	404	–
Judge Eternal, Throned in Splendor	417	517	447

Anthems for the Day

Ex. 32:1-14 *Miserere Mei, Domine* (Show Your Mercy on Me, Lord), Antonio Caldara (*Sing Joyfully*, vol. 3, Walton); SAB (E)

Phil. 1:21-27 *Thy Word with Me Shall Always Stay*, Jean Berger (Augsburg); SATB (M)

Matt. 20:1-16 *Nimm Was Dein Ist, und Gehe Hin* (Take That Thine Is, and Go Thy Way), J. S. Bach (Chorus I in *Cantata 144*, Kalmus); SATB (MD)

Ps. 106:7-8, 19-23 *Fathers and Brethren, Hearken*, Richard Peek (Cantata, *St. Stephen*, Brodt); baritone solo (M)

SUNDAY BETWEEN SEPTEMBER 25 AND OCTOBER 1 (Proper 21) (A)

Exodus 33:12-23 Will Yahweh accompany his stiff-necked, sinful, covenant-breaking people? Thus, Moses prays for the restoration of Yahweh's presence denied in Exodus 33:3, 5. He pleads, "Since I have a special relationship with you, show me your character and purposes and reaffirm that these sinful people are still yours." Yahweh consents partially by responding, "My presence will go." So Moses resumes his plea: "If I and your people do not have your presence with us, then do not take us up from here." To this plea, Yahweh grants full concession. But maybe this restoration of Yahweh's presence will lead to the destruction of Israel, so Moses further pleads for a revelation of Yahweh's gracious and merciful nature. Now Yahweh takes the initiative in "passing by" Moses and therefore revealing an overpowering glimpse of the divine character and purposes.

Philippians 2:1-13 A primitive Christological hymn about the descent and ascent of a divine savior. By divesting himself of divine glory, he voluntarily assumed the form of a human servant who impoverished himself and "became obedient unto death, even death on a cross." That's why God raised him up and gave him the name above every other name: Lord.

Matthew 21:28-32 A father tells two sons to work in the vineyard. "I won't," says one son, but he does. "I will," says the other son, but he doesn't. Actions do speak louder than words. Do we do God's will? The first action demanded is repentance.

Psalm 99
1. Gregorian psalm tone, *GP*, Epiphany A
2. Pointed in *LBW* for psalm tone, p. 262

Hymns for the Day	HL	HB	WB
All Hail the Power of Jesus' Name	192	132	285
Every Star Shall Sing a Carol	–	–	359
God the Omnipotent!	420	487	–
Judge Eternal, Throned in Splendor	417	517	447

Anthems for the Day
Ex. 33:12-23 *Psalm XCVII*, Heinrich Schütz (*Four Psalms*, Mercury); SATB (E)
Phil. 2:1-13 *At the Name of Jesus*, Jacobus Gallus (Concordia); SATB (ME)
Matt. 21:28-32 *Lead Us, O Lord*, Thomas Bateson (Ars Nova [Brodt]); SATB (ME)
Ps. 99 *Glory and Worship Are Before Him*, Henry Purcell (*First Concord Anthem Book*, E. C. Schirmer); SATB (E)

SUNDAY BETWEEN OCTOBER 2 AND OCTOBER 8 (Proper 22) (A)

Numbers 27:12-23 Yahweh commands Moses to ascend the "mountain of Abarim" in order to see the land promised to the Israelites, a land that Moses shall not enter because of his disobedience at Meribah. Prays Moses, "Let Yahweh appoint someone to command, lead, shepherd Israel." And Yahweh replies to Moses' request, "Take Joshua, son of Nun, and before the chief priest and the whole community, lay your hand upon his head and install him as your successor, and give him some of your authority so that the congregation of Israel will obey him." "And Moses did as Yahweh commanded him."

Philippians 3:12-21 Paul exhorts the Christians in Philippi to imitate him in pressing on toward the goal of true righteousness which God has already given in Christ. Lay aside your achievements and credentials and seek to share Christ's sufferings and death and hopes for resurrection from the dead, for your worthiness comes only from God and is received by faith.

Matthew 21:33-43 A self-incriminating parable about the human world's rejection of God's invitation to the kingdom. "Therefore, the kingdom will be given to a nation producing the fruits of it." Praise God for this second chance.

Psalm 81:1-10
1. Gelineau, *Raise a Song and Sound the Timbrel*, GG, p. 82
2. Gregorian psalm tone, *GP*, Proper 4 A

Hymns for the Day	HL	HB	WB
Be Thou My Vision	325	303	304
Christ Is Made the Sure Foundation	336	433	325
God of the Prophets!	481	520	398
God Our Father, You Our Maker	–	–	399
How Firm a Foundation	283	369	425
The Lord's My Shepherd	97	104	593

Anthems for the Day
Num. 27:12-23 *S'e Il Signore Mio Pastore* (God the Lord, He Is My Shepherd), Benedetto Marcello (*Sing Joyfully*, vol. 2, Walton); SA, TB, or 2-part mixed (E)
Phil. 3:12-21 *Vinea Mea* (You Are My Vineyard), Michael Haydn (*Sing Joyfully*, vol. 4, Walton); SATB (E)
Matt. 21:33-43 *Christ Is Made the Sure Foundation*, Lloyd Pfautsch (Lawson-Gould); SSAATTBB (MD)
Ps. 81:1-10 *O Sing Joyfully*, Adrian Batten (*A Sixteenth-Century Anthem Book*, Oxford); SATB (ME)

SUNDAY BETWEEN OCTOBER 9 AND OCTOBER 15 (Proper 23) (A)

Deuteronomy 34:1-12 Imagine the following: A Hebrew baby is rescued from a watery death by the daughter of Pharaoh, who then gives the Hebrew child an Egyptian name; when the child grows up he impetuously murders a man and flees as a fugitive from justice; while slinking through the wilderness he marries a non-Hebrew woman and, at a mountain, experiences a call from Yahweh. Of all people, this man is chosen by God as the prophet without equal. Having served as mediator and intercessor for Israel, Moses now must turn over leadership to Joshua. So Moses views the promised land from afar—because of his wayward people's sin, he must remain outside the land—and is buried in an unknown location in order to prevent any grave cult. He was the first and the greatest of the prophets.

Philippians 4:1-9 Paul exhorts the Philippian community to seek unity, harmony, agreement in the Lord. And, above all, he urges them to rejoice. Even in their common suffering, Paul and the Philippians can rejoice because the Lord is at hand and will consummate the work of salvation begun in them.

Matthew 22:1-14 A king invites many guests to a wedding feast, but they all are too busy to come so they offer polite excuses. The king becomes very angry and invites other guests. They all come, good and bad alike, so that the wedding hall is filled. The king enters and shockingly tosses out a guest with soiled clothes. We are appalled! But then again, the least we can do is to attire ourselves appropriately for the messianic banquet. Be transformed!

Psalm 135:1-14
1. Pointed in *LBW* for psalm tone, p. 282

Hymns for the Day	HL	HB	WB
Give to the Winds Your Fears	–	364	377
Of the Father's Love Begotten	–	7	534
Now Thank We All Our God	459	9	481
Rejoice, O Pure in Heart	297	407	561
Rejoice, the Lord Is King	193	140	562
They Cast Their Nets in Galilee	–	421	–

Anthems for the Day
Deut. 34:1-12 Choral Concertato, *God of the Prophets*, Paul Bunjes (Concordia); SATB, congregation, trumpet (E)
Phil. 4:1-9 *Rejoice in the Lord Always*, Anonymous 16th c. (*A Sixteenth-Century Anthem Book*, Oxford); SATB (M)
Matt. 22:1-14 *Tell Thou Them*, Jan Bender (Concordia); SATB (M)
Ps. 135:1-14 *Praise Ye the Lord*, W. A. Mozart (Presser); SATB with soprano solo (E)

SUNDAY BETWEEN OCTOBER 16 AND OCTOBER 22 (Proper 24) (A)

Ruth 1:1-19a An Israelite woman, Naomi, feels that the Lord has turned against her. Why? Because she has endured stark famine in her homeland and fled as a refugee with her family to a strange land where her husband died and her two sons married foreigners. Later her two sons die, leaving no male heir and making their widowed mother a dependent. What to do? Upon hearing that "Yahweh had visited his people and given them food," Naomi sets out for home, determined to travel life's journey alone because she bitterly believes "the hand of the Lord is against her." But one of her foreign-born daughters-in-law, Ruth, unilaterally pledges unmerited loyalty and fidelity to Naomi and thereby embodies the elusive but attainable *hesed* (covenant love) which Yahweh wills for human relationships.

1 Thessalonians 1:1-10 The life and faith of the Thessalonians, despite their suffering, is a sign that God has chosen them. They are an example to all believers.

Matthew 22:15-22 The Pharisees deviously seek to trap Jesus by asking him, "Is it right for Jews to pay taxes to the Roman government?" Jesus deftly replies, "Give Caesar his things, and give God his things." His response is really a question—What things do not belong to God?

Psalm 146
1. Metrical, *O Praise the Lord, My Soul!*, MP&E, p. 39, tune: St. Thomas (A. Williams)
2. Gelineau, *It Is He Who Keeps Faith For Ever*, GG, p. 7
3. Gregorian psalm tone, *GP*, Proper 18 B
4. Gregorian psalm tone, *PFTD*, p. 11
5. *PS*, p. 36

Hymns for the Day	HL	HB	WB
Faith of Our Fathers!	267	348	361
O God, Our Faithful God	–	–	500
Praise to God, Immortal Praise	–	–	556
Praise to the Lord, the Almighty	6	1	557
Praise We Our Maker While We've Breath	–	–	558

Anthems for the Day
Ruth 1:1-19a *Whither Thou Goest*, Flor Peeters (Peters); vocal solo, high or low (M)
1 Thess. 1:1-10 *The Lord Is a Mighty God*, Felix Mendelssohn (Kjos); SATB (E)
Matt. 22:15-22 *Jesus and the Pharisees*, Melchior Franck (Concordia); SATB (ME)
Ps. 146 *I Will Give Thanks with All My Heart*, Normand Lockwood (Augsburg); SATB (MD)

SUNDAY BETWEEN OCTOBER 23 AND OCTOBER 29 (Proper 25) (A)

Ruth 2:1-13 Ruth takes the initiative to provide food for her mother-in-law, Naomi, and for herself (an act of *hesed*?). As Ruth was gleaning the harvest fields, "it so happened" (is this coincidence or providence?) that Ruth entered Boaz' land. Enter Boaz, a "covenant brother" of Naomi, a "man of substance," who is willing, able, and determined to care for widows and orphans. Ruth and Boaz meet in his fields, where Boaz assists this woman of poverty (an act of *hesed*?). "Why," asks Ruth, "are you so kind to me, a foreigner?" "Because," replies Boaz, "I have heard about what you have done for your mother-in-law, Naomi."

1 Thessalonians 2:1-8 Paul repudiates trumped-up charges by his opponents. "You know yourself," says Paul, "that in no way did we seek any personal gain. Rather, because of our motherly love for you, God gave us the strength to preach the gospel and devote ourselves to you."

Matthew 22:34-46 The Pharisees try to trap Jesus by asking him a trick question about the "greatest commandment." So Jesus quotes Deuteronomy: "Love God with all your heart, soul, and mind." Then Jesus unexpectedly adds, "Love neighbors as your own kin." You cannot love God without loving your neighbor, nor vice versa. Then Jesus questions the Pharisees about the Messiah. Reply the Pharisees, "He is the son of David." "Then how can David call him Lord?" responds Jesus. The Pharisees answer with silence and ask no more questions.

Psalm 128
1. Gelineau, *O Blessed Are Those Who Fear the Lord*, GG, p. 16
2. Gregorian psalm tone, *GP*, Proper 22 B

Hymns for the Day	HL	HB	WB
For the Beauty of the Earth	71	2	372
Lord of the Strong, When Earth You Trod	–	–	466
O God, Beneath Your Guiding Hand	462	523	495
O Lord, Our Lord, in All the Earth	–	95	515
Take Thou Our Minds, Dear Lord	245	306	579

Anthems for the Day
Ruth 2:1-13 *May God Smile on You*, J. S. Bach (*Wedding Cantata 196*, Peters); tenor and baritone duet (ME)
1 Thess. 2:1-8 *Like as a Father*, Luigi Cherubini (Summy-Birchard); canon for 3 equal voices (E)
Matt. 22:34-46 *Du Sollst Gott, Deinen Herrn, Lieben* (Thou Shalt Love the Lord Thy God), J. S. Bach (*Cantata 77*, Chorus I, Kalmus or Breitkopf & Härtel); SATB (M)
Ps. 128 *Psalm 128*, Robert Wetzler (Augsburg); SATB (E)

SUNDAY BETWEEN OCTOBER 30 AND NOVEMBER 5 (Proper 26) (A)

Ruth 4:7-17 Boaz knows a good package deal when he sees one. So he shrewdly arranges for the proper men of authority to be present at the city gate when he maneuvers an ancient public ceremony of the seller (an anonymous relative) giving his sandal to the buyer (Boaz) to confirm the real estate transaction. Then Boaz speaks about buying Naomi's land and Ruth as his wife in order to perpetuate the male name of the dead. And the people affirm, "We are witnesses. May Yahweh bless this family." And Yahweh does so, bestowing the gift of new life through the union of Ruth and Boaz. Then the women praise Yahweh for transforming Naomi's emptiness into fullness through Ruth's faithful *hesed*, and name the newborn Obed, who became the father of Jesse, who became the father of David.

1 Thessalonians 2:9-13, 17-20 Paul obviously is not seeking to be a people-pleasing preacher, because both he and the Thessalonians have suffered as a result of giving witness to God's gospel. For those who welcomed God's word, thanks be to God.

Matthew 23:1-12 Don't do as the scribes and Pharisees do, for they are poor examples to follow. They are vainly preoccupied with fulfilling the jots and tittles of the law which has made the law into a burden. Also, do not make claims for yourself. You are all one in Christ. Your greatness is revealed by your service to neighbors.

Psalm 127
1. Gelineau, *If the Lord Does Not Build the House*, 24P&1C, p. 34
2. Pointed in *LBW* for psalm tone, p. 280

Hymns for the Day	HL	HB	WB
Built on the Rock	–	432	320
City of God	338	436	–
Come, Thou Long-expected Jesus	113	151	342
O Day of God, Draw Nigh	–	–	492
O Lord, Our God, Most Earnestly	–	–	514
Wake, Awake, for Night Is Flying	–	–	614
Watchman, Tell Us of the Night	109	149	617

Anthems for the Day
Ruth 4:7-17 *O God, Thou Art My God,* Henry Purcell (Novello); SATB (M)

1 Thess. 2:9-13, 17-20 *Blessed Is the Man*, Arcangelo Corelli (Boston Music); SAB (M)

Matt. 23:1-12 *Wer Sich Selbst Erhoehet, Der Soll Erniedriget Werden* (He That Exalteth Himself Shall Be Abased, and He That Humbleth Himself Shall Be Exalted), J. S. Bach (*Cantata 47*, Kalmus or Breitkopf & Härtel); SATB (MD)

Ps. 127 *Audivi Vocem de Coelo* (I Heard a Voice from Heaven), Thomas Tallis (Oxford); SATB (D)

SUNDAY BETWEEN NOVEMBER 6 AND NOVEMBER 12 (Proper 27) (A)

Amos 5:18-24 Why do you pseudo-pietistic people yearn for the Day of Yahweh? You have escaped one evil only to fall prey to another. Your so-called place of security is in reality a snake's den. You have invoked your own destruction, for when the Day of Yahweh arrives it will be the day of wrath for you. Yahweh hates your irrelevant festivals, selfish offerings, and meaningless songs of praise, for they are all disconnected from your daily life. Let justice and righteousness cascade like floods that engulf all of you and all that you do.

1 Thessalonians 4:13-18 When the Lord comes again, will those believers who have already died still share in the resurrection? Yes! In fact, they shall rise first and then come with the Parousia to meet the living.

Matthew 25:1-13 Ten young women in a bridal party await the coming of the bridegroom. Five of them (the wise ones) take full containers of oil for their lamps so they will be ready at a moment's notice. The other five (the foolish ones) take no oil for their lamps and are unprepared when the delayed bridegroom finally arrives. Be prepared! March with burning torches—keep them blazing. You never know the day or the hour you will be asked to stand loyal and bold for Christ. And when he arrives, surely you don't want to miss the grand messianic feast.

Psalm 50:7-15
1. Gregorian psalm tone, *GP*, Proper 5 A
2. Pointed in *LBW* for psalm tone, p. 238

Hymns for the Day	*HL*	*HB*	*WB*
All Praise to God in Highest Heaven	–	–	291
Be Still, My Soul	281	374	–
God of the Living, in Whose Eyes	–	–	397
Praise the Lord, for He Is Good	–	115	–
Rejoice, Rejoice, Believers	115	231	–
The Strife Is O'er, the Battle Done	164	203	–
Wake, Awake, for Night Is Flying	–	–	614

Anthems for the Day

Amos 5:18-24 *Woe Unto Them That Draw Iniquity with Cords of Vanity*, Randall Thompson (*Peaceable Kingdom*, no. II, E. C. Schirmer); SATB (MD)

1 Thess. 4:13-18 *If We Believe That Jesus Died*, John Goss (A. Broude); SATB (ME)

Matt. 25:1-13 Cantata, *Therefore Watch That Ye Be Ready*, Andreas Hammerschmidt (Concordia); SSATB with strings (M)

Ps. 50:7-15 *Offer Unto God*, F. Melius Christiansen (*Psalm 50*, Augsburg); SATB (M)

SUNDAY BETWEEN NOVEMBER 13 AND NOVEMBER 19 (Proper 28) (A)

Zephaniah 1:7, 12-18 Listen! The Day of Yahweh is near. At that time, Yahweh will punish those who have succumbed to the temptation to deny that Yahweh can intervene in the world's affairs, or the temptation to embrace patchwork religious practices, or the temptation to live indifferently and complacently. Such persons are bringing terrible consequences upon themselves when the Day of Yahweh arrives. None of their wealth or achievements can save them.

1 Thessalonians 5:1-11 You already know the Day of the Lord will arrive like a thief in the night. So be prepared, stay awake, be vigilant. Put on the armor of faith, hope, and love and look forward to life with Christ.

Matthew 25:14-30 Three servants are charged with the responsibility of managing a master's property. Two of the servants risk their share of the property by investing it, and they double their money. They are good and faithful servants who deserve a reward. The third servant plays it safe by hiding his share and thereby preserving it for the hard master. He is an evil, lazy worker. A simple parable until you remember that God is *not* a ruthless, hard boss, but God is love. So how do we live in God's free-grace world? Play it safe? Invest ourselves in order to please a tyrannical master? Neither?

Psalm 76
None known to be available

Hymns for the Day	HL	HB	WB
God Moves in a Mysterious Way	103	112	391
God the Omnipotent!	420	487	–
O Day of God, Draw Nigh	–	–	492
O What Their Joy and Their Glory Must Be	430	424	–
The Lord Will Come and Not Be Slow	185	230	–
Thou Whose Purpose Is to Kindle	–	–	603
We Are Living, We Are Dwelling	374	356	618

Anthems for the Day

Zeph. 1:7, 12-18 *Howl Ye; For the Day of the Lord Is at Hand,* Randall Thompson (*Peaceable Kingdom,* no. IV, E. C. Schirmer); SATB-SATB (D)

1 Thess. 5:1-11 *Lord, Thou Hast Been Our Refuge,* R. Vaughan Williams (G. Schirmer); SATB (D)

Matt. 25:14-30 *Create in Me, O God,* Johannes Brahms (G. Schirmer); SATBB (E)

Ps. 76 *Let My Complaint Come Before Thee,* Adrian Batten (*A Sixteenth-Century Anthem Book,* Oxford); SATB (E)

CHRIST THE KING
[Sunday Between November 20 and November 26]
(Proper 29) (A)

Ezekiel 34:11-16, 20-24 Israel's shepherds—political and religious leaders—took care of themselves and allowed their sheep to be deported to foreign lands. So now Yahweh will serve as shepherd of Israel. He will gather his scattered sheep and return them to their own land, where he will guide, heal, reconcile, feed, rebuke, and punish them with justice. Then he will establish one shepherd as his servant, a descendant of David, who will faithfully feed and care for his sheep.

1 Corinthians 15:20-28 The end of physical life is death, nonexistence, nonbeing. Christ died, as will all humans, but Christ was raised up, as all those joined to Christ will be, by the power of God. Yet the last enemy, death, still rages throughout creation until Christ destroys "every rule and every authority and power." Then he will deliver the kingdom to God, including himself as a subject under God's rule.

Matthew 25:31-46 Christ the judge is seated on a throne, separating the wicked from the righteous. All are judged by Christ's call to love endlessly: feed the hungry and the thirsty, welcome strangers, clothe the naked, visit the sick and the imprisoned. The wicked are shocked at their designation, for they did not see the face of Christ in their neighbors, particularly the lowly. Ironically, the righteous are just as surprised, for all they saw was human need and so responded with love.

Psalm 23
1. Metrical, *The Lord's My Shepherd*, from the *Scottish Psalter*, 1650, *HB* 104, tune: Crimond
2. Gelineau, *The Lord Is My Shepherd, GG*, p. 136
3. Gregorian psalm tone, *GP*, Proper 23 A
4. Frank Quinn, *The Lord Is My Shepherd, MP&E*, p. 196
5. PS, p. 14

Hymns for the Day

	HL	HB	WB
Mine Eyes Have Seen the Glory	–	–	474
My Shepherd Will Supply My Need	–	–	477
Sinner, Please Don't Let This Harvest Pass	–	–	570
The King of Love My Shepherd Is	99	106	590
Where Cross the Crowded Ways of Life	410	507	642

Anthems for the Day
Ezek. 34:11-16, 20-24 *Jubilate Deo*, Robert Roth (E. C. Kirby); SA, TB or 2-part mixed (E)

1 Cor. 15:20-28 *Since by Man Came Death*, G. F. Handel (*Messiah*, ed. Watkins Shaw, Novello); SATB (M)

Matt. 25:31-46 *If I Can Stop One Heart from Breaking*, Jean Berger (Kjos); SATB (E)

Ps. 23 *The Lord's My Shepherd*, S. S. Wesley (*Church Anthem Book*, Oxford); SATB (ME)

ALL SAINTS' DAY
[November 1 or First Sunday in November] (A)

Revelation 7:9-17 A vision of the glory and joy of the faithful in the New Age. A countless multitude comprised of all peoples, tongues, nations, races, and tribes stands before the throne and before the Lamb. Clothed in white robes (because they have been washed in the blood of the Lamb) and waving palm branches in their hands, the numberless throng and angels sing and shout acclamations. They serve God day and night. They experience the life of salvation where there is no more hunger, no more thirst, no more enervating heat, no more tears, no more pain, for Christ their shepherd guides them to springs of eternal living water.

1 John 3:1-3 What we shall be ultimately has not been fully revealed. But we do know that when Christ appears at the Parousia, we shall see him as he is and we shall be like him, conformed to him, transformed by him. We may be unfinished people during our journey, but we are God's children. The world may not know who we are because it did not recognize Christ, but we are God's children right now. Look at the love God has already bestowed upon us, that we should be called children of God. And so we are!

Matthew 5:1-12 Jesus teaches his disciples the Beatitudes as he begins the Sermon on the Mount.

Psalm 34:1-10
1. Metrical, *The Lord I Will at All Times Bless*, HB 412, tune: Ames
2. Gelineau, *I Will Bless the Lord at All Times*, GG, p. 104
3. Gregorian psalm tone, *GP*, Proper 14 B

Hymns for the Day	HL	HB	WB
For All the Saints	429	425	369
Give to the Winds Your Fears	294	364	377
O Lord of Life, Where'er They Be	–	–	513
O What Their Joy and Their Glory Must Be	430	424	–
The Lord I Will at All Times Bless	–	412	–
You Servants of God, Your Master Proclaim	198	27	645

Anthems for the Day
Rev. 7:9-17 *Worthy Is the Lamb That Was Slain*, G. F. Handel (*Messiah*, ed. Watkins Shaw, Novello); SATB (MD)
1 John 3:1-3 *God So Loved the World*, John Goss (*Church Anthem Book*, Oxford); SATB (E)
Matt. 5:1-12 *Blessed Are They That Mourn*, Johannes Brahms (*A German Requiem*, Chorus I, G. Schirmer); SATB (M)
Ps. 34:1-10 *O Taste and See*, R. Vaughan Williams (Oxford); SATB (E)

THANKSGIVING DAY (A)*

Deuteronomy 8:7-18 Always remember who redeemed you all from bondage, who led you through the perilous wilderness, who brought you water out of solid rock, who fed you in the barren desert, for it is the same one who promises you the land where all your needs will be supplied. You will never go hungry. So don't think you have pulled yourself up by your own boot-straps, but give all the thanks to Yahweh, who has done all this for you in the past and promises you an abundant future.

2 Corinthians 9:6-15 God is the giver of all good gifts. If you are wiling to give away your God-given gifts, then God will make sure you always have gifts to give others. After all, God loves cheerful givers who enrich God's creation and who, in turn, are enriched themselves. Truly, the essence of thanksgiving is a life of giving in response to the undeserved grace of God in Christ.

Luke 17:11-19 Ten lepers cry out to Jesus for pity. "Go!" commands Jesus (no comfort here), "Show yourselves to the priests." They obey. They do what Jesus tells them to do—that's faith—and they are healed. But one leper, a despised outsider, turns back to give thanks, glorifying God. He obeys and worships. No wonder Jesus says to him, "Your faith has made you whole."

Psalm 65
1. Metrical, *Thy Might Sets Fast the Mountains*, HB 99, tune: Webb
2. Gelineau, *You Care for the Earth*, GG, p. 94

Hymns for the Day	HL	HB	WB
Come, You Thankful People, Come	460	525	346
Now Thank We All Our God	459	9	481
O God, Beneath Your Guiding Hand	462	523	495
Sing to the Lord of Harvest	–	–	569
Sinner, Please Don't Let This Harvest Pass	–	–	570
We Gather Together	–	18	624
We Plow the Fields and Scatter	464	524	–

Anthems for the Day
Deut. 8:7-18 *Sing to the Lord of Harvest*, Healey Willan (Concordia); SATB (E)
2 Cor. 9:6-15 *O Sing the Glories of Our Lord*, H. K. Andrews (Oxford); SATB (E)
Luke 17:11-19 *Now Thank We All Our God*, J. S. Bach (Concordia); SATB with 2 trumpets, timpani, optional cello or bassoon (ME)
Ps. 65 *Thou Visitest the Earth*, Maurice Greene (*Church Anthem Book*, Oxford); SATB (E)

---

*NOTE: Readings for Thanksgiving Day are not strictly tied to Year A, B, or C.

FIRST SUNDAY OF ADVENT (B)

Isaiah 63:16–64:8 Yahweh, you are our Father and our Redeemer from of old. Return to us your people. Be present among us. Make your name known to your adversaries as you did in liberating us from bondage in Egypt. Yes, we have sinned. All of us wandered from your way and are blown about by the wind of our desires. None of us calls upon your name, for your absence has exacerbated our iniquities. But, Yahweh, we are the clay and you are our potter. Therefore, mold us!

1 Corinthians 1:3-9 In the opening greeting and thanksgiving, Paul thanks God for his grace given through Christ Jesus. Therefore, we are enriched by spiritual gifts, particularly in all "speech and knowledge." God has given us everything we need and will sustain us to the Day of the Lord which brings judgment.

Mark 13:32-37 Some people believe they can predict the actual apocalyptic ending of the world. But does anybody know this? Neither angels nor the Son of Man knows. So don't pay any attention to soothsayers. Rather, look alive, keep alert, be responsible all the time, keeping your eye out for the Lord, who is coming from the joyous messianic banquet. This is a word for everybody.

Psalm 80-1-7
1. Gelineau, *O Shepherd of Israel*, 30P&2C, p. 23
2. Gregorian psalm tone, *GP*, Advent 1 B

Hymns for the Day	HL	HB	WB
Watchman, Tell Us of the Night	109	149	617
O God of Every Nation	–	–	498
O Come, O Come, Emmanuel	108	147	489
Wake, Awake, for Night Is Flying	–	–	614
O God of Earth and Altar	419	511	497

Anthems for the Day
Isa. 63:16–64:8 *Collect*, Leslie Bassett (World Library); SATB with electronic tape (D)
1 Cor. 1:3-9 *O Mighty God, Our Lord*, Heinrich Schütz (Mercury); 2-part (ME)
Mark 13:32-37 *Wake, Awake*, John Horman (Hinshaw); 3-part (E)
Ps. 80:1-7 *Advent Anthem*, Richard Proulx (Augsburg); SATB (M)

SECOND SUNDAY OF ADVENT (B)

Isaiah 40:1-11 God announces to a vice-president, "Let Israel know her struggles are ended. Reassure my people." The vice-president shouts to a line manager, "Build the roadway! God is going to Mt. Zion and will pick up his captive people on the way." The line manager replies, "All grass withers, so what shall I cry to these people? They're in bad shape and won't believe." Answer: Get up on a high place and preach, "Behold, your God comes!"

2 Peter 3:8-15a The human world will end when God says so. Until such time, God is incredibly patient in yearning and hoping that all his children will repent before the Day of the Lord arrives. How shall you live now? Expect, anticipate, look forward to the coming of "new heavens and a new earth in which righteousness dwells," and prepare yourselves and the human world to be ready and fit for God's new order.

Mark 1:1-8 In the wilderness, the prophet-like John the Baptizer—dressed like Elijah in 2 Kings 1:8—proclaims the advent of the Lord: "Prepare the way! The mighty one who will baptize you with the Holy Spirit is coming." How shall we prepare? Turn away from your sins of pride, guilt, vanity, bigotry, or self-esteem. Strip off anything weighing you down. Look at "all the country of Judea, and all the people of Jerusalem who were baptized, confessing their sins."

Psalm 85:8-13
1. Gelineau, *I Will Hear What the Lord God Has to Say*, GG, p. 5
2. Gregorian psalm tone, *GP*, Advent 2 B

Hymns for the Day	HL	HB	WB
Heralds of Christ	379	498	416
Comfort, Comfort You My People	–	–	347
Come, Thou Long-expected Jesus	113	151	342
The Lord Will Come and Not Be Slow	185	230	–
Hark, What a Sound	110	150	–

Anthems for the Day
Isa. 40:1-11 *Comfort All Ye My People*, Gabriel Fauré (C. Fischer); SATB (ME)
2 Peter 3:8-15a *The Lord Will Come and Not Be Slow*, Henry Ley (*Oxford Easy Anthem Book*, Oxford); SATB (E)
Mark 1:1-8 *Prepare Ye the Way*, Allen Pote (C. Fischer); 2-part (E)
Ps. 85:8-13 No setting suggested

THIRD SUNDAY OF ADVENT (B)

Isaiah 61:1-4, 8-11 The prophet announces his calling through God's Spirit. He has been anointed to proclaim the season of Yahweh's favor when the afflicted, the disenfranchised, the oppressed, the tormented, the grieving, the imprisoned shall be restored. Says Yahweh, "I despise injustice; so I will restore Israel as a sign of my purposes of salvation." As surely as seeds sprout and grow, the season of Yahweh's favor will burgeon and all will praise him.

1 Thessalonians 5:16-24 Some final admonitions by Paul at the close of one of his earliest letters: Rejoice, pray, give thanks constantly in all that you do. Open yourselves to the unbelievable work of the Holy Spirit, but always test such professed actions to see if they match the proclamation of God's will as revealed by Christ—if they don't, then avoid; if they do, then follow. May the God of peace sanctify the whole of your life. And, above all, rejoice always, for God—the faithful one, the one who keeps covenant—will sanctify you so that you are ready for the coming of our Lord Jesus Christ.

John 1:6-8, 19-28 The rulers send some priests and Levites to interrogate John (the Baptizer) about his identity. Are you the Christ? No! Are you Elijah? No! Are you the prophet? No! (He isn't anyone important.) Then why do you baptize? Because among you stands one whom you don't know, but he is the one. And before him, I am nothing.

Luke 1:46b-55 (The Song of Mary)
1. Metrical, *O Praise, My Soul, the Lord, NHAS,* p. 48, tune: Edwin
2. Gelineau, *My Soul Glorifies the Lord, 24P&1C,* p. 41
3. Gregorian psalm tone, *GP,* Advent 3 B

Hymns for the Day	*HL*	*HB*	*WB*
Let All Mortal Flesh Keep Silence	112	148	449
Rejoice, Rejoice, Believers	115	231	–
Hark! the Glad Sound, the Savior Comes	–	–	410
Light of the World, We Hail Thee	422	138	–
Joyful, Joyful, We Adore Thee	–	21	446

Anthems for the Day
Isa. 61:1-4, 8-11 *Good Tidings to the Meek,* Randall Thompson (E. C. Schirmer); SATB (M)
1 Thess. 5:16-24 *Rejoice in the Lord Always,* Henry Purcell (C. Fischer); SATB-ATB soli (ME)
John 1:6-8, 19-28 *Lo, I Am the Voice of One Crying in the Wilderness,* Heinrich Schütz (G. Schirmer); SSATBB (MD)
Luke 1:46b-55 *Magnificat,* R. Vaughan Williams (G. Schirmer); SATB (M)

FOURTH SUNDAY OF ADVENT (B)

2 Samuel 7:8-16 David aspires to build Yahweh a house (temple). Now Yahweh delivers his reply to David through the mouth of the prophet Nathan: "I took you from the sheep pastures; I chose you as ruler of my people; I have been with you wherever you went; I have made for you a great name; I have given you rest from all your enemies; I will build you a house (dynasty) that will last forever, for my steadfast love will be always with your descendants."

Romans 16:25-27 Glory to the one who can strengthen you in faith according to the good news of Jesus Christ, according to the revelation of the mystery now made known to all, and according to the command of God who brings about obedience of faith. "To the only wise God be glory for evermore through Jesus Christ!"

Luke 1:26-38 The angel Gabriel announces to an ordinary peasant girl that she will be impregnated by the invisible power of God and give birth to a son who "will be called the Son of the Most High; and of his kingdom there will be no end." "Preposterous!" you say. Consider this: From the beginning of time God has been at work in bringing forth Jesus Christ so he could be one with his people. Now in this final annunciation story in the Bible, God's purpose will be fulfilled. God will act to save his people. This child is to be born to this woman for the saving of the world. We join our voices with Mary in saying, "Let it be according to your word; let it happen through our lives."

Psalm 89:1-4, 19-24
1. Metrical, *My Song Forever Shall Record*, HB 516, tune: St. Petersburg
2. Gelineau, *With My Chosen One I Have Made a Covenant*, GG, p. 12
3. Gregorian psalm tone, *GP*, Proper 8 A

Hymns for the Day	*HL*	*HB*	*WB*
Son of God, Eternal Savior	393	–	573
Hail to the Lord's Anointed	111	146	–
Lo, How a Rose E'er Blooming	–	162	455
Come, Thou Long-expected Jesus	113	151	342
O How Shall We Receive You	–	–	506

Anthems for the Day
2 Sam. 7:8-16 *And the Father Will Dance*, Mark Hayes (Hinshaw); SATB (E)
Rom. 16:25-27 *Blessing*, Natalie Sleeth (Choristers Guild); unison and flute (E)
Luke 1:26-38 *A Dove Flew Down from Heaven*, Hermann Schroeder (Concordia); SATB, flute, 2 violins (MD)
Ps. 89:1-4, 19-24 No setting suggested

CHRISTMAS/EVE DAY (ABC)

Isaiah 9:2-7 Darkness reigns everywhere, yet people have seen a great light: the presence of God. All rejoice, as with joy at the harvest, for the rule of darkness will be lifted. A child shall reign as God's representative on earth, and God's light shall shine without end.

Titus 2:11-14 Jesus, the grace of God, has appeared for the salvation of all and taught us a new way of life. Because we now live in the light of his second coming, we can celebrate his first coming when he gave himself for us and set us free from all wickedness.

Luke 2:1-20 The birth of Jesus in the "city of David," Bethlehem, and the angelic proclamation to shepherds in the same area where David was a shepherd. *Gloria in excelsis!* The shepherds go to Bethlehem. As they return to their fields, they glorify and praise God "for all they had heard and seen." Their listeners are astonished. Mary treasures all these things.

Psalm 96
1. Metrical psalm, *O Sing a New Song to the Lord*, from the *Scottish Psalter*, 1650, *HB* 37, *WB* 525, tune: Song 67
2. Free paraphrase, *Earth and All Stars*, Herbert Brokering, *WB* 354, tune: Earth and All Stars
3. Gelineau, *O Sing a New Song to the Lord*, *GG*, p. 126
4. Gregorian psalm tone, *GP*, Christmas Day ABC
5. Anglican chant, *O Come, Let Us Sing*, William Boyce, *HB* 586
6. *PS*, p. 28

Hymns for the Day	HL	HB	WB
Joy to the World!	122	161	444
O Little Town of Bethlehem	121	171	511
Once in Royal David's City	454	462	539
What Child Is This	–	159	630
Angels, from the Realms of Glory	124	168	298

Anthems for the Day
Isa. 9:2-7 *The People That Walked in Darkness*, Houston Bright (Shawnee); SATB (MD)

Titus 2:11-14 *Salvation Has Come to Us*, J. S. Bach–Buszin arr. (Schmitt, Hall & McCreary); SATB (ME)

Luke 2:1-20 *Birthday Carol*, David Willcocks (Oxford); SATB (ME)

Ps. 96 *Sing to the Lord a New Song*, Johann Staden (Concordia); SATB, 2 flutes (MD)

CHRISTMAS DAY: ADDITIONAL LECTIONS 1
(ABC)

Isaiah 62:6-7, 10-12 Remind Yahweh of his promises and plead unceasingly for their fulfillment. Prepare the way, clear it of any obstacles, for Yahweh keeps his promises. "Behold, your salvation comes."

Titus 3:4-7 God our Savior has appeared and has saved us by God's mercy (and not because of any good deeds on our part). Through Jesus Christ our Savior, God has poured out the Holy Spirit on us and transformed us and given us new life in the waters of baptism.

Luke 2:8-20 Jesus is born in the "city of David," Bethlehem, and the angels tell the shepherds in the same area where David was a shepherd. *Gloria in excelsis!* The shepherds go to Bethlehem. As they return to their fields, they glorify and praise God "for all they had heard and seen." Their listeners are astonished. Mary treasures all these things.

Psalm 97
1. Metrical psalm, *The Lord Is King!*, Christopher Idle; *PP*, no. 112, contemporary musical setting by Norman Warren
2. Gelineau, *The Lord Is King*, *GG*, p. 163
3. Gregorian psalm tone, *GP*, Christmas Day 2 ABC

Hymns for the Day	HL	HB	WB
Joy to the World!	122	161	444
Born in the Night, Mary's Child	–	–	312
O Sing a Song of Bethlehem	138	177	526
O Little Town of Bethlehem	121	171	511
Once in Royal David's City	454	462	539
On This Day Earth Shall Ring	–	–	538
O Come, All Ye Faithful	116	170	486
What Child Is This	–	159	630

Anthems for the Day
Isa. 62:6-7, 10-12 *Daughters of Zion*, G. F. Handel–Buszin arr. (Schmitt, Hall & McCreary); SATB (ME)
Titus 3:4-7 *A Boy Was Born*, Lewis Kirby (J. Fischer); SATB (ME)
Luke 2:8-20 *Infant Holy, Infant Lowly*, Gerre Hancock (H. W. Gray); SATB (M)
Ps. 97 *Sing to the Lord a New Song*, J. Pachelbel–Ehret (Hinshaw); SATB, double chorus or organ (M)

CHRISTMAS DAY: ADDITIONAL LECTIONS 2
(ABC)

Isaiah 52:7-10 A messenger is coming across the mountains. Ascending and descending from one hill to the next he joyously cries out, "Your God reigns!" Let everyone sing together of the "salvation of God."

Hebrews 1:1-12 God has spoken to us through the prophets; now God speaks uniquely to us through the Son, the descending-ascending savior of all. The true image of God is Christ, whose throne is forever and ever. He is of the same flesh and blood as we are, yet greater than all the angels. God's Son is the risen exalted Christ.

John 1:1-14 "In the beginning was the Word, and the Word was with God." All things were made through the Word, and in the Word were life and light. The Word came into the world and to God's own people, but the world rejected the Word, as did God's own people. Yet those who received and believed in the Word were given power to announce and to bear witness, as John (the Baptizer) did, to the coming of the Word among us, full of grace and truth.

Psalm 98
1. Metrical psalm, *New Songs of Celebration Render*, Erik Routley, *SOT&P*, p. 2, tune: *Rendez à Dieu*
2. Psalm paraphrase, *Sing a New Song to the Lord*, Timothy Dudley-Smith, *WII*, p. 245, tune: *Cantate Domino* by David G. Wilson, fresh, contemporary setting
3. Gelineau, *Sing a New Song to the Lord*, *GG*, p. 15
4. Gregorian psalm tone, *GP*, Christmas Day 3 ABC

Hymns for the Day	HL	HB	WB
Book of Books	–	248	–
Christ for the World We Sing	–	489	–
Christ Is the World's Redeemer	–	136	–
Every Star Shall Sing a Carol	–	–	359
Father, We Greet You	–	285	364
God Has Spoken—by His Prophets	–	–	382
Joy to the World!	122	161	444
Light of the World, We Hail Thee	422	138	–
Of the Father's Love Begotten	–	7	534

Anthems for the Day
Isa. 52:7-10 *How Beautiful Upon the Mountains*, John Carter (Hinshaw); 2-part (E)

Heb. 1:1-12 *Of the Father's Love Begotten*, Richard Peek (C. Fischer); SATB (ME)

John 1:1-14 *In the Beginning Was the Word*, W. J. Reynolds (Kjos); SATB, divisi (D)

Ps. 98 *Sing to the Lord a New Song*, Samuel Adler (*Ecumenical Praise*, no. 10, Agape); SATB, congregation (E)

FIRST SUNDAY AFTER CHRISTMAS (B)

Isaiah 61:10–62:3 Is the land renewed each year so new crops can sprout? Is the Lord God going to restore his people? You know the answer, so rejoice and exult in Yahweh. Announce this good news until Yahweh's glory and power in saving Jerusalem illuminates all the nations. Israel shall shed her old name and ragged clothes, and be renamed and arrayed in festive clothes and sparkling jewels. Yahweh's salvation shall bring complete transformation.

Galatians 4:4-7 When God decided the right time had come, he sent his Son, fully human, to release all those under the law so they might be God's children. Then God sent the Spirit of his Son, who empowered these adopted children to name God as *"Abba,* Father."

Luke 2:22-40 Parents who fulfill the law and prophets who break into song and utterances of thanksgiving frame this narrative of the presentation of Jesus. Simeon the watchman has now seen the Lord's salvation, a light to the nations, and Anna begins telling everyone that the redemption of Jerusalem is at hand. Ironically, the birth and the presentation of the child who is "God with us" will eventually demand his own death as the way to purify and restore life to his people.

Psalm 111
1. Gregorian psalm tone, *GP*, Epiphany 4 B
2. Cantillation (also tones are given for a simpler rendition), Arlo Duba, unpublished

Hymns for the Day	HL	HB	WB
Lord, Dismiss Us with Your Blessing	54	79	458
Now Thank We All Our God	459	9	481
Once in Royal David's City	454	462	539
Let All Mortal Flesh Keep Silence	112	148	449
O Sing a Song of Bethlehem	–	177	526

Anthems for the Day
Isa. 61:10–62:3 *I Will Greatly Rejoice,* Donald Rotermund (Concordia); SATB (M)
Gal. 4:4-7 *Evergreen,* Daniel Pinkham (E. C. Schirmer); unison with electronic tape (E)
Luke 2:22-40 *Nunc Dimittis,* R. Vaughan Williams (G. Schirmer); SATB (ME)
Ps. 111 *My Heart Is Full Today,* Richard Proulx (Associated); 2-part (M)

THE NAME OF JESUS [January 1] (ABC)

Numbers 6:22-27 The well-known Aaronic blessing: three simple poetic lines, each petitioning Yahweh to move toward his people through the presence of his protection, favor, and peace. And where the name of Yahweh is "put upon his people," he is present in blessing.

Galatians 4:4-7 When the right time had come, God sent his Son, fully human, to release all those under the law so they might be God's children. Then God sent the Spirit of his Son, who empowered these adopted children to name God as *"Abba,* Father."

or **Philippians 2:9-13** Part of a primitive Christological hymn, the name bestowed by God upon Jesus is the name "Lord." At the name of Jesus, may all confess him as Lord and live as his people, for God will support us.

Luke 2:15-21 Shepherds see what the angel of the Lord announced and thus glorify and praise God for all they have heard and seen. After eight days, the infant is circumcised and named "Jesus" in fulfillment of the angel's command at the annunciation.

Psalm 67
1. Metrical psalm, *Lord, Bless and Pity Us,* from *The Psalter,* 1912, HB 493, WB 456, tune: St. Michael
2. Gelineau, *O God, Be Gracious and Bless Us, GG,* p. 17
3. Gregorian psalm tone, *GP,* Proper 15 A
4. Mixed medium, *Psalm 67,* Arthur Wills (G. Schirmer)
5. *PS,* p. 21

Hymns for the Day	HL	HB	WB
All Hail the Power of Jesus' Name!	192	132	285–286
At the Name of Jesus	–	143	303
Born in the Night, Mary's Child	–	–	312
Creator of the Stars of Night	–	–	348
Gentle Mary Laid Her Child	453	167	375
Lord, Dismiss Us with Your Blessing	54	79	458
O Come, All Ye Faithful	116	170	486
While Shepherds Watched Their Flocks	120	169	643
We Gather Together	–	18	624

Anthems for the Day
Num. 6:22-27 *The Lord Bless You,* J. S. Bach (Concordia); SA or TB (M)
Gal. 4:4-7 or **Phil. 2:9-13** *At the Name of Jesus,* R. Vaughan Williams (Oxford); SATB with congregation (E)
Luke 2:15-21 *Magnificat,* R. Vaughan Williams (G. Schirmer); SATB or SAB or unison (E)
Ps. 67 *Psalm 67,* Regina Fryxell (H. W. Gray); unison with optional second part (ME)

JANUARY 1 [When observed as New Year] (B)

Ecclesiastes 3:1-13 All time is in God's hands. From birth to death, all humans are in God's hands. No one can discern, much less control, the mysterious purposes of God. So relax and enjoy the gift of life, regardless of how mundane it may seem at times. Abandon your vain search for God, and simply trust God's wisdom.

Colossians 2:1-7 Alluring, charming, persuasive, entertaining teachers and preachers abound. All will mislead you, so ignore them. Build and shape your life in conformity to Christ. Remain firm in the faith (just as you were taught), be filled with thanksgiving, and live in union with Christ, who reveals all the treasures of God's wisdom and knowledge.

Matthew 9:14-17 Followers of John the Baptist ask Jesus, "Why don't your disciples fast as do we and the Pharisees?" Answers Jesus, "Do you mourn at a wedding feast? Do you patch a shrunken garment with an unshrunken patch? Do you use old wineskins for new wine?" It is impossible to combine such things. Likewise, it is impossible to mix old religious ways with new life in Christ.

Psalm 8
1. Metrical, *O Lord, Our Lord, in All the Earth, HB* 95, tune: Dunfermline
2. Metrical, *O Lord, Our Lord, in All the Earth, MP&E*, p. 5, tune: St. Bernard
3. Gelineau, *When I See the Heavens, GG*, p. 14
4. Gregorian psalm tone, *GP*, Holy Name ABC

Hymns for the Day	*HL*	*HB*	*WB*
O God, You Are the Father	–	93	504
Ring Out, Wild Bells	466	–	–
Great God, We Sing That Mighty Hand	470	527	408
God of Our Life	88	108	395
Ring Out the Old, Ring In the New	–	526	–

Anthems for the Day
Eccl. 3:1-13 *A Time for All Things*, Douglas Wagner (Sacred Music); SATB (E)
Col. 2:1-7 *This Is the Day*, Daniel Moe (*Ecumenical Praise*, no. 109, Agape); SATB or unison (ME)
Matt. 9:14-17 *Be a New and Different Person*, Paul Christiansen (Schmitt, Hall & McCreary); SATB (ME)
Ps. 8 *How Excellent Thy Name*, Howard Hansen (C. Fischer); SATB (MD)

SECOND SUNDAY AFTER CHRISTMAS (ABC)

Jeremiah 31:7-14 Shout for joy because the Lord has graciously delivered Israel from bondage. The Lord will gather the people (including those dependent upon others) from the ends of the earth and will shepherd them to flowing streams and reveal a father's love for his firstborn. Declare to the world: "The Lord has repurchased his flock; he will comfort them and bless them with abundant life."

Ephesians 1:3-6, 15-18 Thanks be to you, O God, for blessing our union with Christ by bestowing the gift of the Spirit, and for choosing us as your servants for the purpose of praising your glorious free grace. May the God of our Lord Jesus Christ continually give us discernment regarding our calling and rich inheritance.

John 1:1-18 "In the beginning was the Word, and the Word was with God." All things were made through the Word, and in the Word were life and light. The Word came into the world and to God's own people, but the world rejected the Word as did God's own people. Yet those who received and believed in the Word were given power to announce and to bear witness, as John (the Baptizer) did, to the coming of the Word among us, full of grace and truth.

Psalm 147:12-20
1. Metrical psalm, *O Praise Your God, O Zion*, from *The Psalter*, 1912, *MP&E*, p. 69
2. Gregorian psalm tone, *GP*, Christmas 1 ABC

Hymns for the Day	HL	HB	WB
Break Forth, O Beauteous Heavenly Light	–	–	314
Joy to the World!	122	161	444
My Shepherd Will Supply My Need	–	–	477
O Word of God Incarnate	215	251	532
Praise to God, Immortal Praise	–	–	556
Praise Ye the Lord, for It Is Good	–	36	–
The King of Love My Shepherd Is	99	106	590
The Lord's My Shepherd	97	104	592
The True Light That Enlightens Man	–	–	598

Anthems for the Day

Jer. 31:7-14 *My Shepherd Will Supply My Need*, arr. Virgil Thomson (H. W. Gray); SATB (E)

Eph. 1:3-6, 15-18 *Benedictus*, David McK. Williams (H. W. Gray); unison (E)

John 1:1-18 *O Magnum Mysterium*, Ludovico da Vittoria (G. Schirmer); SATB (MD)

Ps. 147:12-20 *I Will Greatly Rejoice in the Lord*, Jean Berger (Augsburg); SATB (MD)

THE EPIPHANY OF THE LORD (ABC)

Isaiah 60:1-6 Awake, light has overcome the darkness! The glory of the Lord's presence will be reflected in Jerusalem's arising to rebuild the city. Open your eyes and see the caravans from all the nations that shall come of their own free will to your light. Rejoice, for they bring your sons and daughters as well as a multitude of treasures and herds of animals.

Ephesians 3:1-12 Paul's vocation is the privilege of making known to the Gentiles God's plan of salvation. And his gospel message is that through the sheer grace of God, the Gentiles have been included in God's people. Now all the people of God, Jews and Gentiles, share the same promises revealed in Jesus Christ and receive his Spirit to proclaim God's plan of salvation.

Matthew 2:1-12 Magi from the East come to Jerusalem in search of the King of the Jews. King Herod, out of fear, also wants to know where this threatening challenger can be found. So Herod offers the magi a deal they can't refuse. But when the magi arrive in the presence of the child, they fall down on their knees and worship him and give him everything they have. They return home another way, other than through Herod's palace.

Psalm 72:1-14
1. Metrical psalm, *Hail to the Lord's Anointed*, James Montgomery, *LBW* 87, tune: *Freut euch, ihr lieben*
2. Gelineau, *O God, Give Your Judgement*, *30P&2C*, p. 22
3. Gregorian psalm tone, *GP*, Advent 2 A

Hymns for the Day	HL	HB	WB
We Three Kings	–	176	–
Brightest and Best	136	175	318
Light of the World, We Hail Thee (tune: Lancashire)	422	138	–
Christ Is the World's True Light	–	492	326
Christ, Whose Glory Fills the Skies	26	47	332

Anthems for the Day
Isa. 60:1-6 *Surge, Illuminare*, Ned Rorem (Boosey & Hawkes) in English; SATB (MD)
Eph. 3:1-12 *For Your Light Has Come*, Ronald A. Nelson (Augsburg); SATB (E)
Matt. 2:1-12 *Epiphany Alleluias*, John Weaver (Boosey & Hawkes); SATB (ME)
Ps. 72:1-14 *Psalm for Epiphany*, Alexander Peloquin (G.I.A.); SATB (M)

BAPTISM OF THE LORD
[First Sunday After the Epiphany] (B)

Genesis 1:1-5 All was dark upon the formless, chaotic, unordered waters of creation. God spoke: "Let there be light." And there was light, for when God speaks, action occurs. Then God separated the light from the darkness and named the light "day." Chaos is transformed into cosmos by God's order and differentiation. "And God saw that the light was good. . . . And there was evening and there was morning, one day."

Acts 19:1-7 Paul encounters in Ephesus about a dozen disciples of John and asks them if they received the Holy Spirit. "Never heard about, much less received it," they reply; "we were baptized by John." Paul responds, "That's an incomplete baptism of repentance only; even John told you to believe in the one coming after him." So they had themselves baptized in the name of the Lord Jesus, accompanied by Paul's laying his hands on them. Now the Holy Spirit came upon them and they spoke in tongues and prophesied.

Mark 1:4-11 In the wilderness, the prophet-like John the Baptizer proclaims the advent of the Lord: "Prepare the way! The mighty one who will baptize you with the Holy Spirit is coming." How shall we prepare? Turn away from your sins of pride, guilt, vanity, bigotry, or self-esteem. Look at "all the country of Judea, and all the people of Jerusalem who were baptized, confessing their sins." John then baptizes Jesus of Nazareth in the muddy Jordan. As Jesus emerges from the water, he sees the heavens open and is confirmed by the gift of the Spirit and a voice repeating words reminiscent of a coronation (Ps. 2:7), "You are my beloved Son." The New Age has arrived in the person of Jesus Christ.

Psalm 29
1. Free paraphrase, *God the Omnipotent!*, Henry F. Chorley and John Ellerton, HB 487, tune: Russian Hymn
2. Gelineau, *O Give the Lord, You Sons of God*, 24P&1C, p. 10

Hymns for the Day	HL	HB	WB
Hail to the Lord's Anointed	111	146	–
Come, O Come, Great Quickening Spirit	–	–	338
Descend, O Spirit, Purging Flame	–	–	353
Thou Whose Purpose Is to Kindle	–	–	603
O Day of Rest and Gladness	–	70	–
Morning Has Broken	–	464	–

Anthems for the Day
Gen. 1:1-5 *Tell Man [All] of God*, Buryl Red (Broadman); 2-part or SATB (E)
Acts 19:1-7 *We Know That Christ Is Raised*, C. V. Stanford (*Ecumenical Praise*, no. 111, Agape); unison (E)
Mark 1:4-11 *Carol of the Baptism*, George Brandon (Concordia); SAB (ME)
Ps. 29 *Bring to Jehovah*, Heinrich Schütz (*Sing Joyfully*, Walton); unison (E)

SECOND SUNDAY AFTER THE EPIPHANY (B)

1 Samuel 3:1-10 (11-20) Injustice, infidelity, and corruption permeated temple life at Shiloh. Worse, "the word of Yahweh was rare." Yet Yahweh persistently calls to the boy Samuel during his sleep so he may deliver the word of Yahweh. A suspenseful and dramatic call unfolds four times, reaching its climax when Samuel finally hears Yahweh's revelation: Samuel must deliver Yahweh's word of judgment upon the whole house of Eli. Amazingly, Eli accepts that word. More amazingly, that word comes true precisely as proclaimed by Samuel, who is then "established as a prophet of Yahweh."

1 Corinthians 6:12-20 For some people, freedom is license to "do your own thing." They pursue affairs of the body such as gluttony or sexual promiscuity, "as long as they don't harm anyone." But such "freedom" is really another form of enslavement to, among other things, the currently popular narcissistic hedonism. Of course, writes Paul, we are free, but at a staggering cost. We are free from the vicious cycle of endlessly seeking social approval so that we may live in the Spirit, serving the Lord and neighbors. We are free from the Platonic dualism of separating body and spirit so that our total self may be joined to Christ and used not for our pleasure but in service to him.

John 1:35-42 Two of John's disciples heard Jesus was "the Lamb of God," so they hesitantly followed him. "For what are you seeking?" Jesus asks all prospective disciples. They answer, "Where are you staying?" "Come and see," invites Jesus. They go where he goes. They follow where he leads. They stay where he stays. Result: Andrew announces to his brother, Simon Peter, "We have found the Messiah," and brings him to Jesus, who changes Simon's name to Cephas, giving him a new name, a new role, a new self, a new life.

Psalm 63:1-8
1. Metrical, *O Lord, Our God, Most Earnestly, HB* 327, tune: Stracathro; *WB* 514
2. Gelineau, *O God, You Are My God, GG,* p. 132
3. Gregorian psalm tone, *GP,* Epiphany 2 B
4. *PS,* p. 20

Hymns for the Day	*HL*	*HB*	*WB*
Jesus Calls Us	223	269	439
We Are One in the Spirit	–	–	619
God Himself Is with Us	51	13	384
Built on the Rock (vs. 3, 4)	–	432	320

Anthems for the Day
1 Sam. 3:1-10 (11-20) *Here Am I, Send Me,* Erik Routley (*Eternal Light,* C. Fischer); SATB or unison (E)

1 Cor. 6:12-20 *Temples of God,* Ronald A. Nelson (Augsburg); 2-part mixed or children (E)

John 1:35-42 *Lamb of God, I Look to Thee,* W. Bengson (H. W. Gray); children or unison (E)

Ps. 63:1-8 *O Lord, Our God, Most Earnestly* (*WB* 514)

THIRD SUNDAY AFTER THE EPIPHANY (B)

Jonah 3:1-5, 10 Corrupt, wicked, and sinful Nineveh deserves nothing less than total destruction, which is precisely what Yahweh intends for this monstrous city. But reluctant and resistant Jonah, Yahweh's designated speaker, has to be prodded a second time to proclaim this message of doom. Nevertheless, Jonah obeys and warns Nineveh that the end is in sight for them. Nineveh, however, believes the word of God and does a 180-degree turnaround from her iniquitous past. When God saw this, God too repented. Immortal, invisible, unchanging God changed his mind and did not punish Nineveh.

1 Corinthians 7:29-31 (32-35) "The form of this world is passing away." So live "as though you were not" *of* this world even though you live *in* this world. Depend not upon this world's institutions or values but solely upon God, by giving yourself totally to the Lord's service.

Mark 1:14-20 The *kairos* (time) has been fulfilled because, after John was imprisoned, the intruding sovereignty of God invaded our world in Galilee when Jesus began proclaiming "the gospel of God." Declared Jesus, "The kingdom of God has drawn near; turn around and see and believe the good news." After announcing the kingdom, Jesus calls four everyday people, Simon and Andrew and James and John, who leave behind everything and immediately follow.

Psalm 62:5-12
1. Metrical psalm, *My Soul with Expectation*, from the *Scottish Psalter*, 1650, HB 113, tune: St. Flavian
2. Metrical psalm, *In Silence My Soul Is Waiting*, Michael Saward, PP, no. 99, music by Christian Strover
3. Gelineau, *In God Alone Is My Soul at Rest*, GG, p. 89
4. Gregorian psalm tone, *GP*, Epiphany 8 A

Hymns for the Day	HL	HB	WB
Take Thou Our Minds, Dear Lord	245	306	579
They Cast Their Nets in Galilee	–	421	–
The Light of God Is Falling	400	482	–
God Has Spoken—by His Prophets	–	–	382
"Thy Kingdom Come"	363	484	–

Anthems for the Day
Jonah 3:1-5, 10 *Jonah*, Dale Wood (C. Fischer); any combination of voices (E)
1 Cor. 7:29-31 (32-35) *The Kingdom of God*, Austin Lovelace (Hope); SATB (E)
Mark 1:14-20 *They Cast Their Nets in Galilee*, Michael McCabe (C. Fischer); 2-part (E)
Ps. 62:5-12 *Truly My Soul*, William Billings (Boston Music); SAB (E)

FOURTH SUNDAY AFTER THE EPIPHANY (B)

Deuteronomy 18:15-20 The Israelites could not bear the fiery presence or voice of Yahweh at Horeb. Yahweh says to Moses, "Tell them I shall raise up a prophet like you, someone from among your own people, whom everyone shall obey. The prophet I raise up shall speak my words and reveal my will. Anyone who dares to refuse my words, I shall punish. Anyone who dares to speak in my name without authority, or in the name of other gods, shall die."

1 Corinthians 8:1-13 It's wonderful that you know "there is no God but one . . . from whom are all things and for whom we exist." You may legitimately be "puffed up" by rightness, but deflate your ego, swollen by correct belief, and subordinate your rightness to concern for others. It is *agape* (love) that "builds up" the community of faith. Flaunting your "knowledge" can become a stumbling block to some and consequently destroy the community.

Mark 1:21-28 Jesus enters a synagogue in Capernaum and teaches not as the scribes but with authority. All are astonished. Suddenly a man with an evil spirit enters and screams, "I know who you are, Jesus of Nazareth. You are the Holy One of God. Have you come to destroy us?" Jesus rebukes him simply: "Be quiet." The man shudders and the spirit comes out of him. All are astonished, saying, "What is this? He commands evil spirits with authority, and they obey him." News about Jesus spread quickly throughout Galilee.

Psalm 111
1. Gregorian psalm tone, *GP*, Epiphany 4 B
2. Cantillation (also tones are given for a simpler rendition), Arlo Duba, unpublished

Hymns for the Day	HL	HB	WB
Rejoice, the Lord Is King	193	140	562
How Sweet the Name of Jesus Sounds	310	130	–
God of the Prophets!	481	520	398
The Light of God Is Falling	400	482	–
Eternal God, Whose Power Upholds	–	485	357

Anthems for the Day
Deut. 18:15-20 *The Lord Gave the Word* and *How Beautiful Are the Feet*, G. F. Handel (*Messiah*, any edition); SATB (D) and soprano solo (ME)
1 Cor. 8:1-13 *Neighbors*, arr. Austin Lovelace (H. W. Gray); SATB (E)
Mark 1:21-28 *Good News*, Jane Marshall (C. Fischer); SATB, baritone solo (ME)
Ps. 111 *My Heart Is Full Today*, Richard Proulx (Augsburg); 2-part (M)

FIFTH SUNDAY AFTER THE EPIPHANY (B)

Job 7:1-7 Job wants an answer from God about the oppressive burden of life. At least slaves look forward to evening rest, and laborers anticipate a daily pay envelope. But for Job, nights of misery follow days of suffering which equal months of agony and emptiness. No design emerges from the weaver's tapestry of life—the shuttle tediously passes back and forth from nowhere to nowhere. God, life is short enough as it is; why must it be racked with pain?

1 Corinthians 9:16-23 Why does Paul preach the gospel? Simply because he is compelled to preach out of necessity. He has been chosen and divinely commissioned by God. Having no use for personal financial gain from preaching because it reaps its own rewards of joy, Paul voluntarily submits himself as a slave to all. No special interest groups own him. He is totally free from all other claims upon his life. True, he is bound to Christ, but he is completely free to experience the joys and sorrows of others and to speak their language as he preaches the gospel.

Mark 1:29-39 Jesus touches Simon's mother-in-law and the fever leaves her. She responds by serving. Jesus then heals many others of various diseases and expels numerous demons who know who Jesus is, but he does not allow them to reveal the "messianic secret." The next morning Simon and others intrude upon Jesus while he is praying, but Jesus responds to their pleas by announcing he must proclaim the gospel in neighboring towns—that is the purpose of his mission.

Psalm 147:1-11
1. Metrical, *Come, Sing Your Alleluias! MP&E*, p. 54
2. Gelineau, *Praise the Lord for He Is Good, GG*, p. 72
3. Gregorian psalm tone, *GP*, Proper 15 B

Hymns for the Day	HL	HB	WB
Sing Praise to God	–	15	568
At Even, When the Sun Was Set	43	55	–
I Look to Thee in Every Need	79	114	–
Praise We Our Maker While We've Breath	–	–	558
We Would See Jesus (vs. 4, 5)	–	183	–

Anthems for the Day
Job 7:1-7 *Have Mercy on Us, O My Lord*, Aaron Copland (Boosey & Hawkes); SATB (MD)
1 Cor. 9:16-23 *Seek to Serve*, Lloyd Pfautsch (Agape); 2-part (E)
Mark 1:29-39 *At Even, When the Sun Was Set* (*HB* 55); SATB or unison (E)
Ps. 147:1-11 *Sing to the Lord with Thanksgiving*, George Brandon (Concordia); SATB (ME)

SIXTH SUNDAY AFTER THE EPIPHANY
(Proper 1) (B)

2 Kings 5:1-14 Naaman, a Syrian military commander, suffers from leprosy. Hearing that healing is possible in Israel, he packs his bags and travels to see the king. But the only thing he receives from the king of Israel is the royal runaround—the king is unable to heal Naaman and knows it. But Elisha, the simple man of God, instructs Naaman to wash himself in the Jordan. This makes no sense to Naaman, for he could have done that back home; so he goes away in a rage. At the insistence of his servants, however, Naaman does wash and miraculously is made clean. He almost missed this experience because of his preconceived expectations of God's healing word.

1 Corinthians 9:24-27 Paul's image recurs, that of training for the race, straining toward the goal, and winning the prize. Perhaps a disciplined life of discipleship (prayer, study, and almsgiving?) is what's needed in a "do as you please" culture.

Mark 1:40-45 A leper, an untouchable outcast, approaches Jesus and says, "If you will, you can make me clean." Jesus' pity or anger (depending on which text you accept) galvanizes him to touch the leper and proclaim him clean. Then he charges the leper to fulfill the laws for ritual purification and to remain silent about Jesus' action and words so that others will not misunderstand who Jesus is. But the man promptly proclaims Jesus' saving words and deeds to everyone he meets. People then come to Jesus from all directions.

Psalm 32
1. Metrical, *How Blest Is He Whose Trespass, HB* 281, tune: Rutherford
2. Gelineau, *Happy the Man Whose Offence Is Forgiven, GG,* p. 86
3. Gregorian psalm tone, *GP,* Epiphany 7 B

Hymns for the Day	HL	HB	WB
Give to the Winds Your Fears	294	364	377
Lord Jesus, Think on Me	239	270	–
Amazing Grace!	–	275	296
Sometimes a Light Surprises	296	418	–
Love Divine, All Loves Excelling	308	399	471

Anthems for the Day
2 Kings 5:1-14 *Descend, O Spirit, Purging Flame* (WB 353); SATB (E)
1 Cor. 9:24-27 *Rise, My Soul, and Stretch Thy Wings* (HB 330); (E)
Mark 1:40-45 *Sometimes a Light Surprises,* Jane Marshall (*Ecumenical Praise,* no. 42, Agape); unison (E)
Ps. 32 *Give Thanks to the Lord,* Erik Satie, arr. Zanelli (Walton); SATB (M)

SEVENTH SUNDAY AFTER THE EPIPHANY
(Proper 2) (B)

Isaiah 43:18-25 "Behold, I am doing a new thing," proclaims Yahweh. Yes, the exodus from Egypt was dramatic and formative for Israel's existence, but now Yahweh is bringing about a new exodus—"a way in the wilderness and rivers in the desert." Of course, Israel brought this exile on herself. Instead of offering herself to Yahweh, she made Yahweh into a servant who had to bear the burden of Israel's sins. But because Yahweh is the forgiver without equal, Israel's sins will be blotted out by Yahweh, who will also bring about a new future for Israel.

2 Corinthians 1:18-22 As surely as God is faithful, the word we preach is Jesus Christ, who was constantly faithful in his obedience to the will of God. As God says "Yes" in Christ, we also shout "Amen," for all God's promises find fulfillment in Christ. And it is in Christ that God "establishes us," "commissions us," "puts his seal upon us," and "gives us his Spirit."

Mark 2:1-12 Four people carry a paralytic to Jesus, who is preaching the word to an overflow crowd at a home. Unable to get near Jesus, the four dig through the roof and lower the paralytic into the home. He comes to be healed, but Jesus unexpectedly forgives his sins. Controversy ensues for Jesus discerns that the scribes are charging him with blasphemy because they believe only God can forgive sins. So Jesus pronounces healing words, and the paralytic rises and walks as evidence that "the Son of man has authority on earth to forgive sins." It's an illogical deduction, but all are astonished and glorify God because they have never seen anything like this.

Psalm 41
1. Gelineau, *Happy the Man Who Considers the Poor*, GG, p. 78

Hymns for the Day	HL	HB	WB
Spirit Divine, Attend Our Prayers	212	243	574
Where Cross the Crowded Ways	410	507	642
Praise We Our Maker While We've Breath	–	–	558
New Every Morning Is the Love	31	45	–
O Jesus Christ, to You May Hymns Be Rising	–	–	509

Anthems for the Day
Isa. 43:18-25 *Rejoice in the Lord, Alleluia!*, Lani Smith (Sacred Music); SATB, handbells (E)

2 Cor. 1:18-22 *I Thank You, God*, Lloyd Pfautsch (G. Schirmer); SATB (M)

Mark 2:1-12 *Jesus Christ Has Come Into Capernaum*, Juhani Forsberg (*Ecumenical Praise*, no. 14, Agape); (E)

Ps. 41 *Be Merciful Unto Me, O God*, Stanley Glarum (Augsburg); SSAB or SATB (E)

EIGHTH SUNDAY AFTER THE EPIPHANY
(Proper 3) (B)

Hosea 2:14-20 Yahweh's bride, Israel, has been having an adulterous affair with the Baal gods, and Yahweh is fed up with her infidelity. But Yahweh strangely promises to start over again with her. Yahweh is going to lure Israel back to the wilderness (sometimes you have to go backward in order to go forward), and renew the covenant with her. Yahweh intends to reestablish a faithful relationship and thus offers Israel gifts of "righteousness, justice, steadfast love, and mercy." This is an offer Israel cannot refuse, can she?

2 Corinthians 3:1-6 Paul's credentials for ministry seem suspect: no transcript, no ordination exams, not even a letter of recommendation. But, Paul asserts that his ultimate letter of recommendation is the Corinthian church. They are the flesh-and-blood testimony, written by the Spirit of the living God, of his authority as an apostle. It is God alone who calls Paul and empowers him to serve.

Mark 2:18-22 Controversy ferments over the propriety of fasting. Righteous people, such as Pharisees or disciples of John the Baptist, are fasting, and Jesus' disciples are not. Why not? "When you're a guest at a wedding feast," says Jesus, "do you fast? As long as you have the bridegroom with you, you cannot fast. Rejoice now, the days for fasting will come when the bridegroom is taken away." New life in Christ cannot be hemmed to our old comfortable clothing; neither can it be poured into old predictable molds.

Psalm 103:1-13
1. Metrical, *Bless, O My Soul! the Living God*, HB 8, tune: Park Street
2. Gelineau, *My Soul, Give Thanks to the Lord*, GG, p. 77
3. Gregorian psalm tone, *GP*, Lent 3 C

Hymns for the Day	HL	HB	WB
There's a Wideness in God's Mercy	93	110	601
Praise to the Lord, the Almighty	6	1	557
Praise, My Soul, the King of Heaven	14	31	551
We Are One in the Spirit	–	–	619
Walk Tall, Christian	–	–	616

Anthems for the Day
Hos. 2:14-20 *My Song Is Love Unknown*, Carl Schalk (Concordia); 2-part (E)
2 Cor. 3:16 *The Fruit of the Spirit Is Love*, Johann Geisler (Boosey & Hawkes); SATB, flute (MD)
Mark 2:18-22 *Be a New and Different Person*, Paul Christiansen (Schmitt, Hall & McCreary); SATB (ME)
Ps. 103:1-13 *Bless the Lord, O My Soul*, Ippolitov-Ivanov (Boston Music); SATB (M)

TRANSFIGURATION OF THE LORD
[Last Sunday After the Epiphany] (B)

2 Kings 2:1-12a Elijah, on his last journey, tests his disciple Elisha three times concerning his loyalty, but each time Elisha vows lifelong commitment. Even the prophets' guilds fail to deter Elisha from following Elijah to the very end. Upon reaching the Jordan River, Elijah parts the waters with his mantle in Moses-like fashion. After crossing to dry ground, Elijah says to Elisha, "What shall I do for you, before I am taken from you?" Elisha asks for a "double share of your *ruach*" (spirit, wind). He asks for the creative power of Yahweh, which liberates. Then fire and wind whisk away Elijah while Elisha laments. But then he takes up the mantle of Elijah and parts the Jordan in Moses-like fashion.

2 Corinthians 4:3-6 It is not ourselves or our denomination that we preach, but Jesus Christ as Lord. We are called to preach, regardless of whether anyone listens, the light of the gospel, the glory of God shining in the face of Jesus Christ which radiates love, mercy, anger, compassion, pain, forgiveness. That's the glory of God it is our job to preach.

Mark 9:2-9 Peter and James and John see Jesus transfigured before them: his garments glisten intensely white. Though they are frightened and confused, Peter briefly perceives the transcendent reality of the blinding light and wants to preserve it right there. But a voice from a cloud utters words that recall Jesus' baptism and anticipate the centurion's proclamation: "This is my beloved Son; listen to him." Jesus then commands the disciples to keep silent about what they have seen, "until the Son of man should have risen from the dead." Then you will understand who Jesus is.

Psalm 50:1-6
1. Gregorian psalm tone, *GP*, Proper 5 A
2. Pointed in *LBW* for psalm tone, p. 238

Hymns for the Day	HL	HB	WB
Fairest Lord Jesus	194	135	360
O Wondrous Type, O Vision Fair	142	182	531
Christ, Whose Glory Fills the Skies	26	47	332
All Hail the Power of Jesus' Name!	192	132	285
At the Name of Jesus	–	143	303

Anthems for the Day
2 Kings 2:1-12a *Then Did Elijah*, Felix Mendelssohn (*Elijah*, G. Schirmer); SATB (D)

2 Cor. 4:3-6 *Christ, Upon the Mountain Peak*, Peter Cutts (*Ecumenical Praise*, no. 67, Agape); unison (E)

Mark 9:2-9 *This Is My Beloved Son*, Knut Nystedt (Concordia); SATB (E)

Ps. 50:1-6 *Psalm 50*, F. Melius Christiansen (Augsburg); SATB (D)

ASH WEDNESDAY (ABC)

Joel 2:1-2, 12-17a Blow the trumpet, for the Day of Yahweh is coming! Yahweh's judgment is near! Turn back to Yahweh with all your heart. Fast, weep, mourn. Return to Yahweh who manifests *hesed* (steadfast love). Perhaps Yahweh will forgive you and bless you. Gather together all the people and turn back to Yahweh.

2 Corinthians 5:20b–6:2 (3-10) Do you remember what God in Christ has done for you all? Then accept the reconciliation that God offers you in Christ. Let God transform you! Christ shared our human estrangement from God so that we sinners might be joined with Christ and reconciled with God. So work with God today, for the day of salvation is now.

Matthew 6:1-6, 16-21 Three acts of personal piety (charity, private prayer, and fasting) and a note on treasuring God's will—all are signs of the age to come. Don't broadcast your acts of personal piety to the world. God sees what you do and therefore will give to you from the future. What you value in life is where you will devote your time, energy, emotional commitment, everything.

Psalm 51:1-12
1. Metrical, *God, Be Merciful to Me*, from *The Psalter*, 1912, HB 282, tune: Redhead, No. 76
2. Gelineau, *Have Mercy on Me, God*, GG, p. 34
3. Gregorian psalm tone, *GP*, Lent 5 B
4. David Isele, *Have Mercy on Me, O God, Praise God in Song*, p. 28
5. *PS*, p. 18

Hymns for the Day	HL	HB	WB
Lord, Who Throughout These Forty Days	144	181	470
Jesus, Thy Boundless Love to Me	314	404	–
God, Be Merciful to Me	–	282	–
Be Thou My Vision	325	303	304
Have Thine Own Way, Lord	–	302	–
Amazing Grace!	–	275	296

Anthems for the Day
Joel 2:1-2, 12-17a *Ye People, Rend Your Hearts* and *If with All Your Hearts*, Felix Mendelssohn (*Elijah*, any edition); tenor solo (M)
2 Cor. 5:20b–6:2 (3-10) *Grant Us Thy Peace*, Felix Mendelssohn (Boosey & Hawkes); SATB (E)
Matt. 6:1-6, 16-21 *When Thou Prayest*, Carl Mueller (C. Fischer); SATB (M)
Ps. 51:1-12 *Create in Me, O God*, Johannes Brahms (G. Schirmer); SATB (MD)

FIRST SUNDAY IN LENT (B)

Genesis 9:8-17 God unilaterally establishes a covenant with Noah and his descendants—in fact, all creation. Never again shall all flesh, or the earth, be destroyed by floodwaters. Immutable God has changed his relationship with creation from destructive ire to free grace. As a sign of his covenant, God lays down his bow (his weapon of destruction) in the cloud, which will remind God of his everlasting covenant with creation.

1 Peter 3:18-22 Christ the righteous suffered and died undeservedly for us the unrighteous (even those who drowned during the "days of Noah"), in order to bring us all to God. The salvific waters of the Flood revealed long ago the faithful love of God now promised to us in the salvific waters of baptism. So the resurrected and exalted Christ, who sits at the right hand of God, rules over all creation and seeks the salvation of all people.

Mark 1:9-15 John baptizes Jesus of Nazareth in the muddy Jordan. As Jesus emerges from the water, he sees the heavens open and is confirmed by the gift of the Spirit and a voice repeating words reminiscent of a coronation (Ps. 2:7), "You are my beloved Son." The New Age has arrived in the person of Jesus Christ. Then the Spirit immediately drives Jesus into the desert where he is tested by Satan and ministered to by angels for forty days. The *kairos* (time) has been fulfilled because, after John is imprisoned, Jesus comes into Galilee proclaiming "the gospel of God."

Psalm 25:1-10
1. Metrical, *Grace and Truth Shall Mark the Way*, HB 372, tune: Holley
2. Gelineau, *Lord, Make Me Know Your Ways*, GG, p. 22
3. Taizé, *Miserere mei*, MFT, p. 18

Hymns for the Day	*HL*	*HB*	*WB*
Lord, Who Throughout These Forty Days	144	181	470
A Mighty Fortress Is Our God	266	91	274
Lord, from the Depths to You I Cry	240	277	459
Ah, Holy Jesus	–	191	280
When We Are Tempted to Deny Your Son	–	–	640

Anthems for the Day
Gen. 9:8-17 *Love the Lord, for His Rainbow and His Promise*, Walter Horsley (*100% Chance of Rain*, Choristers Guild); 2-part (E)
1 Peter 3:18-22 *We Know That Christ Is Raised*, C. V. Stanford (*Ecumenical Praise*, no. 111, Agape); unison (E)
Mark 1:9-15 *Dove Over Jordan*, Malcolm Williamson (*Dove Chorales*, Agape); unison or SATB (E)
Ps. 25:1-10 *To Thee, O Lord*, S. Rachmaninoff (Oxford); SATB, soprano solo (M)

SECOND SUNDAY IN LENT (B)

Genesis 17:1-10, 15-19 The Priestly account of God's solemn call of Abraham and the covenant God established with him. God's covenant is everlasting, for it is also established with Abraham's descendants who will receive the land of Canaan and be God's people. The sign of acceptance of this covenant is for Abraham and his descendants to circumcise every male among them. When God promises a son to aged, barren Sarah, Abraham responds with doubting laughter.

Romans 4:16-25 God's promise to Abraham and all his descendants is guaranteed solely by God's free grace. There is absolutely no way you can earn God's promise, especially by good works or adherence to the law. Abraham trusted God to do what he promised. That's faith.

Mark 8:31-38 Jesus' first passion prediction: the Son of Man must suffer, be rejected, be killed, and rise again. Peter remonstrates, "We don't want a convicted criminal for our leader. We'll never succeed if you do that." Jesus censures Peter: "You're demonically inspired." Jesus tells the multitude, "If you want to follow me, then deny yourself and take up your cross. You must be willing to lose your life in this world."

or **Mark 9:1-9** The transfiguration of Jesus.

Psalm 105:1-11
1. Gregorian psalm tone, *GP*, Wednesday of Easter Week ABC

Hymns for the Day	HL	HB	WB
Jesus, Lead the Way	–	334	441
Give to the Winds Your Fears	294	364	377
"Take Up Thy Cross," the Saviour Said	–	293	–
When I Survey the Wondrous Cross	152	198	635
My Faith Looks Up to Thee	285	378	–

Anthems for the Day

Gen. 17:1-10, 15-19 *Faith While Trees Are Still in Blossom*, Alec Wyton (*Ecumenical Praise*, no. 74, Agape); unison (E)

Rom. 4:16-25 *O Lord, Increase My Faith*, Orlando Gibbons (H. W. Gray); SATB (M)

Mark 8:31-38 *I'm Not Ashamed to Own My Lord* (*HB* 292); SATB (E)

or **Mark 9:1-9** *This Is My Beloved Son*, Knut Nystedt (Concordia); SAB (E)

Ps. 105:1-11 No setting suggested

THIRD SUNDAY IN LENT (B)

Exodus 20:1-17 The words Yahweh spoke to Moses at Mt. Sinai concerning Israel's relationship with Yahweh and with neighbors, the Mosaic covenant, is one of human obligation which prohibits Israel from violating the exclusive claims of the divine Lord who liberated them from bondage in Egypt. Conversely, these words distinctively assert the sovereignty of Yahweh and the exclusivity of the Yahweh-Israel bond. In addition, this covenant protects the fundamental rights of all free Israelite citizens.

1 Corinthians 1:22-25 What the world labels wise and strong, says Paul, is really foolish and weak. And what the world claims is the foolishness of the cross is really the power and wisdom of God. That is one reason we are called to show God's love for the world through such foolish things as loving enemies, handing out food to the hungry, giving away our possessions, or standing with the oppressed.

John 2:13-22 When Jesus enters the Temple he walks into a tumultuous hubbub of financial greed at its worst. The whole enterprise takes place in the court of the Gentiles. Sanctimonious Jewish aristocrats conspired to provide "separate but equal" facilities for Jews and Gentiles, thus giving false legitimacy to prejudice and segregation. Such entrenched evil causes Jesus to drive out everyone and everything, saying, "Destroy this Temple, and in three days I will raise up a new temple-church-people." And he does.

Psalm 19:7-14
1. Metrical, *Most Perfect Is the Law of God*, from *The Psalter*, 1912, HB 257, tune: Glasgow
2. Gelineau, *The Law of the Lord Is Perfect*, GG, p. 121
3. Gregorian psalm tone, *GP*, Proper 21 B

Hymns for the Day	HL	HB	WB
Judge Eternal, Throned in Splendor	417	517	447
O God, You Are the Father	–	93	504
God Moves in a Mysterious Way	103	112	391
Be Thou My Vision	325	303	304

Anthems for the Day
Ex. 20:1-17 *The Ten Commandments*, Jan Bender (*Sing to the Lord a New Song*, Concordia); 3-part canon (E)
1 Cor. 1:22-25 *Be Thou My Vision*, Alice Parker (Hinshaw); SATB or 2-part (E)
John 2:13-22 *God, Bring Thy Sword Over Pulpit and Pew*, Ron Nelson (Boosey & Hawkes); SATB (MD)
Ps. 19:7-14 *May the Words of My Mouth*, Ernest Bloch (A. Broude); SAATB (M)

FOURTH SUNDAY IN LENT (B)

2 Chronicles 36:14-23 King Zedekiah, the priests, and the people followed the idolatrous ways of the nations and, thereby, polluted the sacred house of Yahweh. Out of compassion for his people and his sacred house, Yahweh persisently sent messengers to proclaim his word, but the people refused to listen to them. So Yahweh brought the king of the Chaldeans, a merciless killer, to attack Zedekiah and the people in the sacred house of Yahweh, which was then burned to the ground. Any survivors were hauled off to exile. Yet in the midst of this terrible judgment, good news is announced: Yahweh's plan for his people is still intact, and the faithfulness of Yahweh is still present, for this judgment is but a painful cleansing in fulfillment of the prophets.

Ephesians 2:4-10 God is love—in fact, so abundantly full of love that God chooses to shower it on us so we will know how extraordinary his love for us is. Though we were spiritually dead, God gave us new life by raising us up with Christ. Always remember, our new life is a pure gift of God's grace. We are not self-made people but God's handiwork, created in Christ Jesus for good works.

John 3:14-21 God sent his Son into the world in order that the world might be saved through him. Yet, many people reject the light of salvation and choose the darkness of judgment. How odd that we think we can conceal our evil deeds from others and, worse, from ourselves, which results in bringing judgment upon ourselves. Look up and see the crucified Lord—our Savior—and behold the eternal light of life.

Psalm 137:1-6
1. Metrical, *By the Babylonian Rivers*, WB 321, tune: Latvian melody
2. Gelineau, *By the Rivers of Babylon*, GG, p. 31

Hymns for the Day	HL	HB	WB
Amazing Grace!	–	275	296
Come, Thou Fount of Every Blessing	235	379	341
Let Us with a Gladsome Mind	64	28	453
God Is Love; His Mercy Brightens	80	103	–
Depth of Mercy!	–	273	–

Anthems for the Day
2 Chron. 36:14-23 *Have Mercy on Us, O My Lord*, Aaron Copland (Boosey & Hawkes); SATB (MD)
Eph. 2:4-10 *God of Mercy, God of Grace*, J. S. Bach–McCurdy arr. (Boosey & Hawkes); SATB (ME)
John 3:14-21 *God So Loved the World*, Jan Bender (*Sing to the Lord a New Song*, Concordia); 2-part (E)
Ps. 137:1-6 *By the Babylonian Rivers* (WB 321)

FIFTH SUNDAY IN LENT (B)

Jeremiah 31:31-34 Yahweh is going to make a new covenant with his people. This new covenant will not be like the old Sinai one which his people adulterated, even though he was their faithful husband, but this time Yahweh will cut his new covenant into his people's hearts, minds, and wills. They will be his people; he will be their God. Everyone will know Yahweh— no need to teach one another about Yahweh—for he will forgive their iniquity and no longer remember their sin.

Hebrews 5:7-10 Often we forget that Jesus was fully human and therefore experienced all that we can ever face—pain, suffering, temptation to sell out God and make a fast buck, fear, loss, every part of the fleshly life we know so well. And in loud cries and tears, Jesus offered his prayers to God, but with a difference. He obeyed God's will and walked faithfully the path chosen for him by God. You can see why Hebrews call Jesus a great high priest, for he is the one who represents the world before God. He is the one whom God appointed to comfort and forgive us because he is the eternal source of salvation.

John 12:20-33 Some Greeks (Gentiles) "wish to see Jesus." Answered Jesus, "The hour has come for the Son of man to be glorified"—that is, his crucifixion will reveal the presence and power of God. So if you wish to see Jesus, look at Jesus lifted up on the cross and you will see Jesus for who he is—divine love drawing all to himself. Whoever wants to serve Jesus must be where he is, accept his way, and follow him, even to the cross.

Psalm 51:10-17
1. Metrical, *God, Be Merciful to Me*, from *The Psalter*, 1912, HB 282, tune: Redhead, No. 76
2. Gelineau, *Have Mercy on Me, God, GG*, p. 34
3. Gregorian psalm tone, *GP*, p. 34
4. *PS*, p. 18

Hymns for the Day	HL	HB	WB
Throned Upon the Awful Tree	–	197	605
The Head That Once Was Crowned with Thorns	195	211	589
Jesus Shall Reign	377	496	443
Beneath the Cross of Jesus	162	190	308
Go to Dark Gethsemane (vs. 1-3)	–	193	–

Anthems for the Day
Jer. 31:31-34 *This Is the Covenant*, Jean Berger (Augsburg); SATB (M)
Heb. 5:7-10 *Ah, Holy Jesus*, Roger Petrich (Oxford); SATB (ME)
John 12:20-33 *Go to Dark Gethsemane*, T. T. Noble (H. W. Gray); SATB (M)
Ps. 51:10-17 *Restore Unto Me*, J. Lully, arr. Nelson (Augsburg); 2-part with 2 C instruments (ME)

PASSION SUNDAY [Sixth Sunday in Lent] (B)

Isaiah 50:4-9a The third of the four Songs of the Servant of Yahweh: Each day Yahweh wakens me and opens my ears to his word which sustains me. Though I have suffered ridicule, insults, hostility, and physical abuse, I have not turned from my task. I trust Yahweh's help; Yahweh will vindicate me. So who will declare me guilty?

Philippians 2:5-11 A primitive Christological hymn about the descent and ascent of a divine savior. By divesting himself of divine glory, he voluntarily assumed the form of a human servant who impoverished himself and "became obedient unto death, even death on a cross." That's why God raised him up and gave him the name above every other name: Lord.

Mark 14:1-15:47 The passion narrative according to Mark.

or **Mark 15:1-39** Religious leaders deliver a bound Jesus to the civil authorities—namely, Pilate—for interrogation. "Are you the king of the Jews?" Jesus laconically replies, "You have said so." The mindless crowd, manipulated by the religious leaders, then twice rejects Jesus as king and calls for his death. So the people-pleasing Pilate releases the resistance-movement rebel, Barabbas, and sentences Jesus to be flogged and executed. Soldiers crown Jesus as king, spit on him, mock him, strip him, and crucify him. "My God, my God . . . ," cries Jesus and then dies, as does the whole world, inaugurating the New Age. Confesses a Roman soldier, "This man was the Son of God!"

Psalm 31:9-16
1. Gelineau, *In You, O Lord, I Take Refuge*, GG, p. 37

Hymns for the Day	HL	HB	WB
At the Name of Jesus	–	143	303
Hosanna, Loud Hosanna	147	185	424
All Glory, Laud, and Honor	146	187	284
When I Survey the Wondrous Cross	152	198	635
There Is a Green Hill Far Away	157	202	–

Anthems for the Day

Isa. 50:4-9a *He Was Despised*, G. F. Handel (*Messiah*, any edition); alto solo or unison women (ME)

Phil. 2:5-11 *Let This Mind Be in You*, John Yarrington (Chantry); SATB (M)

Mark 14:1-15:47 *O Come and Mourn with Me*, Hal Hopson (Agape); 2-part mixed, optional C instrument (M)

or Mark 15:1-39 *Behold the Saviour of Mankind*, S. Drummond Wolff (Concordia); SATB (ME)

Ps. 31:9-16 *In Thee, O Lord, Have I Put My Trust*, Halsey Stevens (Peters); SATB (MD)

PALM SUNDAY [Sixth Sunday in Lent] (B)

Isaiah 50:4-9a The third of the four Songs of the Servant of Yahweh: Each day Yahweh wakens me and opens my ears to his word which sustains me. Though I have suffered ridicule, insults, hostility, physical abuse, I have not turned from my task. I trust Yahweh's help; Yahweh will vindicate me. So who will declare me guilty?

Philippians 2:5-11 A primitive Christological hymn about the descent and ascent of a divine savior. By divesting himself of divine glory, he voluntarily assumed the form of a human servant who impoverished himself and "became obedient unto death, even death on a cross." That's why God raised him up and gave him the name above every other name: Lord.

Mark 11:1-11 Jesus instructs two of his disciples to fetch a colt on which no one has sat. If anyone asks why, simply say, "The Lord needs it" (an unacceptable reason to any owner). The two disciples do everything according to Jesus' plan, and all goes well. Jesus then sits upon the colt, and many people spread either their garments or branches on the road and cry out, "Hosanna! Blessed is the one who comes in the name of the Lord" (Ps. 118:26). In this manner, a lowly Jesus silently enters Jerusalem (the place he has thrice predicted where he will suffer and die), goes into the Temple, looks around at everything, and then returns to Bethany with the Twelve.

Psalm 118:19-29
1. Metrical, *The Glorious Gates of Righteousness*, HB 71, tune: Zerah
2. Gelineau, *Give Thanks to the Lord for He is Good*, GG, p. 46
3. Gregorian psalm tone, *GP*, Passion (Palm) Sunday ABC

Hymns for the Day	HL	HB	WB
All Glory, Laud, and Honor	146	187	284
At the Name of Jesus	–	143	303
Hosanna, Loud Hosanna	147	185	424
O How Shall We Receive You	–	–	506
Lift Up Your Heads, O Mighty Gates	114	152	454
O Jesus Christ, to You May Hymns Be Rising	–	–	509
Ride On! Ride On in Majesty!	150	188	563
So Lowly Does the Savior Ride	–	–	571

Anthems for the Day
Isa. 50:4-9a *Surely He Hath Borne Our Griefs*, Heinrich Graun (Concordia); SATB (M)
Phil. 2:5-11 *Let This Mind Be in You*, Mrs. H. H. A. Beach (Presser); SATB with soprano, baritone soli (ME)
Mark 11:1-11 *Procession of Palms*, Malcolm Williamson (G. Schirmer); SATB (M)
Ps. 118:19-29 *Open Wide the Gates of Justice*, Dietrich Buxtehude (Concordia); SAB, 2 violins (M)

MONDAY OF HOLY WEEK (ABC)

Isaiah 42:1-9 The first of the four Songs of the Servant of Yahweh (vs. 1-4) and the response to it (vs. 5-9). Yahweh officially presents his chosen servant, upon whom he has put his Spirit, who is to perform the task of bringing forth *mishpat* (justice) to the nations by his own suffering. Yahweh gives his servant as a light to the people who live in darkness. Verses 8-9 affirm that Yahweh will give no glory or praise to any idol, and that Yahweh declares in advance new things of the future.

Hebrews 9:11-15 Christ enters not the earthly Holy of Holies offering a ritual sacrifice, but he enters once for all the holy dwelling place of God, offering a sacrifice of himself—his own life-giving blood. In his sacrifice Christ attains what none other ever could—eternal redemption for his people. Christ is truly the high priest of the "good things that have come."

John 12:1-11 Irrepressible Mary gets carried away at dinner and shocks everyone by pouring thousands of dollars' worth of perfume on Jesus' feet. "An extravagant waste," cries the morally upright Judas, "the money could have been given to the poor." Replies Jesus, "You'll always have the opportunity to serve the poor; so leave her alone, for you'll not always have me. She has saved her perfume for my burial." Mary anointed her only Lord and Savior.

Psalm 36:5-10
1. Metrical, *Thy Mercy and Thy Truth, O Lord*, HB 82, tune: Dundee
2. Gregorian psalm tone, *GP*, Monday of Holy Week ABC

Hymns for the Day	HL	HB	WB
Hail to the Lord's Anointed	111	146	–
God Is Working His Purpose Out	–	500	389
Hark! the Glad Sound the Savior Comes	–	–	410
Thy Mercy and Thy Truth, O Lord	–	82	–
O Master, Let Me Walk with Thee	364	304	520

Anthems for the Day

Isa. 42:1-9 *Hail to the Lord's Anointed*, Malcolm Williamson (*Dove Chorales*, Agape); unison (E)

Heb. 9:11-15 *The Promise of Eternal Inheritance*, Rudolf Moser (Concordia); unison (E)

John 12:1-11 *The Best of Rooms*, Randall Thompson (E. C. Schirmer); SATB (MD)

Ps. 36:5-10 *O How Precious*, Raymond Haan (Hinshaw); 2-part (E)

TUESDAY OF HOLY WEEK (ABC)

Isaiah 49:1-7 The second of the four Songs of the Servant of Yahweh. Yahweh's chosen servant summons the nations to hear Yahweh's word. The servant publicly announces his prenatal call and his subsequent despondency about performing the task in vain. But now Yahweh has expanded the call to be a light to all the nations (Gentiles) in order that "salvation may reach the ends of the earth."

1 Corinthians 1:18-31 The gospel always seems to turn our world upside down. Here worldly wisdom and strength are characterized as foolish and weak, and the nonsense and weakness of the crucifixion are labeled as wise and strong. The epitome of God's love for us is revealed in the offensiveness of the cross.

John 12:20-36 Some Gentiles seek to see Jesus. "The hour has come . . . ," says Jesus, "for when a single grain of wheat falls into the earth and dies, it produces many grains." Jesus then wrestles with the full import of "the hour" and decides to submit obediently to the Father's will. An affirming voice from heaven accepts the Son's obedience and promises the Son his own glorification. In fact, Jesus' decision to die will open the possibility for others to be liberated from the ruler of this world. Jesus' hour of glory, his death, brings forth life for Jesus and for all those who follow him and serve him.

Psalm 71:1-12
1. Metrical, *O Gracious God, Forsake Me Not, HB* 396, tune: Martyrdom
2. Gelineau, *In You, O Lord, I Take Refuge, GG*, p. 159
3. Gregorian psalm tone, *GP*, Tuesday of Holy Week ABC

Hymns for the Day	HL	HB	WB
Whate'er Our God Ordains Is Right	291	366	633
O Love, How Deep, How Broad, How High!	139	–	518
Break Forth, O Living Light of God	–	–	316
Beneath the Cross of Jesus	162	190	308
Rock of Ages	237	271	–

Anthems for the Day
Isa. 49:1-7 *Canticle of Trust,* Richard Purvis (Sacred Music); SATB (ME)
1 Cor. 1:18-31 *'Tis the Gift to Be Simple* (WB 606)
John 12:20-36 *Christ Is the World's Light,* Hungarian carol (*Ecumenical Praise,* no. 66, Agape); SATB (E)
Ps. 71:1-12 *In Thee, O Lord,* Jane Marshall (Augsburg); SATB (E)

WEDNESDAY OF HOLY WEEK (ABC)

Isaiah 50:4-9a The third of the four Songs of the Servant of Yahweh: Each day Yahweh wakens me and opens my ears to his word which sustains me. Though I have suffered ridicule, insults, hostility, physical abuse, I have not turned from my task. I trust Yahweh's help; Yahweh will vindicate me. So who will declare me guilty?

Hebrews 12:1-3 A lifelong marathon race: that's what you're in for when you join the crowd trying to keep pace with Jesus. So strip off your warm-up suit, throw away your pride, scrap your blueprints for success and any other sins that weigh you down. To endure in this race, you've got to be lean. And you've got to be determined and tenacious in keeping your eyes fixed on Jesus. He didn't become discouraged or give up because of hostility from sinners or even death on the cross. So persevere in following the pacesetter Jesus. And remember, you're not alone—all the racers from the past are cheering you on.

John 13:21-30 Following the act of footwashing, Jesus announces that one who is present will betray him. Such a disclosure perks up the disciples' conversation and introduces the unknown Beloved Disciple. Jesus then dips some bread in the sauce and gives it to Judas, presumably to indicate him as the betrayer. Then, at Jesus' request, Judas leaves "to do what he has to do."

Psalm 70
1. Gelineau, *O God, Make Haste to My Rescue*, 30P&2C, p. 21
2. Gregorian psalm tone, *GP*, Proper 27 A

Hymns for the Day	*HL*	*HB*	*WB*
Awake, My Soul, Stretch Every Nerve	278	346	–
Fight the Good Fight	270	359	–
Ah, Holy Jesus	158	191	280
Alone You Journey Forth, O Lord	–	–	294
Alas! and Did My Saviour Bleed	249	199	–

Anthems for the Day
Isa. 50:4-9a *He Was Despised*, G. F. Handel (*Messiah*, any edition); contralto solo (ME)
Heb. 12:1-3 *Fight the Good Fight*, John Gardner (Oxford); SATB (ME)
John 13:21-30 *I Caused Thy Grief*, Paul Manz (Augsburg); SATB (M)
Ps. 70 *Thou, Lord, the Refuge of the Meek*, Josquin Desprez (J. Fischer); SAB (ME)

MAUNDY THURSDAY (B)

Exodus 24:3-8 Moses proclaims the words of the covenant, and the people accept. So Moses records Yahweh's words and builds an altar for sacrifices of offerings at the place where Israel and Yahweh will seal the covenant. Moses takes half of the blood (the sign of life) and sprinkles it on the altar. He then takes the book of the covenant and reads it aloud, and again the people give their spoken consent. So Moses takes the other half of the blood and splashes it on the people. Thus the covenant is sealed and the people now belong to Yahweh and to each other in one community.

1 Corinthians 10:16-17 When we participate in the body (bread) and blood (cup) of Christ, we are made one with him and with each other in one community. Moreover, the Christ to whom we are joined is the humiliated, rejected, crucified Savior who saves through suffering. The God revealed in Jesus Christ has experienced our human brokenness, yet still binds himself to us when we break bread and drink the cup that Christ drank.

Mark 14:12-26 Jesus and the Twelve are at table eating, when Jesus says, "One of you will betray me; one who is dipping bread in the same dish with me." Misunderstanding, betrayal, denial, and desertion are Mark's key watchwords in characterizing the Twelve throughout his Gospel. Yet, here at table, just before the disciples' ultimate defection, Jesus took bread, blessed it, broke it, and gave it to them, saying, "This is my body—for you." At the moment they turn against him, Jesus turns toward them and announces the new covenant, binding himself to them forever.

Psalm 116:12-19
1. Metrical, *What Shall I Render to the Lord, HB* 32, tune: Lambeth
2. Gelineau, *I Trusted Even When I Said, GG*, p. 25
3. Gregorian psalm tone, *GP*, Easter 3 B

Hymns for the Day	*HL*	*HB*	*WB*
Become to Us the Living Bread	–	–	305
Bread of the World	353	445	–
Bread of Heaven	–	–	313
According to Thy Gracious Word	358	444	–

Anthems for the Day
Ex. 24:3-8 *Lo, God Is Here,* Francis Jackson (Oxford); SATB (MD)
1 Cor. 10:16-17 *One Bread, One Body,* John Foley (*Glory and Praise,* vol. 11, National Institute of Liturgy); unison or 2-part (E)
Mark 14:12-26 *Bread of the World,* Stephen Paulus (Hinshaw); 2-part mixed (E)
Ps. 116:12-19 *What Shall I Render to My God,* Austin Lovelace (Canyon); SATB (E)

GOOD FRIDAY (ABC)*

Isaiah 52:13–53:12 The fourth of the four Songs of the Servant of Yahweh. Yahweh promises the coming vindication of his servant. Thus many are shocked to see an afflicted, disfigured, marred servant. Has God smitten him for past sins? No, the servant has participated in our human brokenness. He has "borne our griefs and carried our sorrows" according to God's will. This humiliated servant is the one whom Yahweh will vindicate.

Hebrews 4:14-16; 5:7-9 We have a great high priest to represent us to God, a simple human being named Jesus who lived in the same kind of power-hungry, achievement-oriented, complacently religious, me-first world. But this Jesus was sinless. He is the perfect one who is the source of salvation and now reigns with God.

John 18:1–19:42 The passion narrative according to John.

or **John 19:17-30** The crucifixion and death of Jesus.

Psalm 22:1-18
1. Gelineau, *My God, My God, Why Have You Forsaken Me?*, 30P&2C, p. 5
2. Gregorian psalm tone, *GP*, Good Friday ABC
3. Howard Hughes, *My God, My God, Why Have You Abandoned Me?* (G.I.A.)

Hymns for the Day	*HL*	*HB*	*WB*
When I Survey the Wondrous Cross	152	198	635
Were You There When They Crucified My Lord?	–	201	–
Behold the Lamb of God!	153	–	307
O Sacred Head, Now Wounded	151	194	524
Cross of Jesus, Cross of Sorrow	155	196	–

Anthems for the Day
Isa. 52:13–53:12 *O Vos Omnes* (O Ye People), Pablo Casals (A. Broude); SATB (D)
Heb. 4:14-16; 5:7-9 *I Caused Thy Grief*, Paul Manz (Augsburg); SATB (M)
John 18:1–19:42 *Wondrous Love*, arr. Douglas Wagner (Flammer); SATB (E)
or **John 19:17-30** *And God Looked Down at God That Day*, John Stanley (New Music); SATB (M)
Ps. 22:1-18 *My God, My God, Look Upon Me*, Maurice Greene (A. Broude); SSATB, tenor solo (M)

---

*NOTE: Easter Vigil will be found in Year C, pp. 221–224.

EASTER DAY (B)

Acts 10:34-43 At Cornelius' house in Caesarea, Peter recounts how his own life has been transformed by the power of the risen Lord and everyone else (Jews and Gentiles) also can be transformed by that power.

or Isaiah 25:6-9 One day the Lord of Hosts will make for all peoples a grand feast. The cloud of sorrow and troubles and death will vanish so that all tears shall succumb to laughter and joy, for Yahweh has spoken.

1 Corinthians 15:1-11 This is the good news in which we stand: Christ died for our sins according to the scriptures, was buried, raised on the third day, and appeared to Peter, to the Twelve, and to many faithful witnesses. Finally, he appeared to me, Paul, the least of all apostles.

or Acts 10:34-43 *See above.*

John 20:1-18 Peter and the Beloved Disciple seek the truth about the empty tomb. Mary engages the "gardener" in conversation, who says, "Tell them I am ascending."

or Mark 16:1-8 Three women go to Jesus' tomb to anoint his body. A young man in a white robe says, "Jesus has risen. Go, tell his disciples that he is going before you to Galilee." The women flee from the tomb, for they are afraid.

Psalm 118:14-24
1. Metrical, *This Is the Day the Lord Hath Made, HB* 69, tune: Arlington
2. Gelineau, *This Is the Day the Lord Has Made, GG,* p. 46
3. Gregorian psalm tone, *GP,* Easter Day ABC
4. Richard Proulx, *Processional Psalm for a Festival* (G.I.A.)

Hymns for the Day	*HL*	*HB*	*WB*
Jesus Christ Is Risen Today	163	204	440
Christ the Lord Is Risen Today	165	–	330
Come, You Faithful, Raise the Strain	168	205	344
The Day of Resurrection!	166	208	584
O Sons and Daughters, Let Us Sing	167	206	527

Anthems for the Day
Acts 10:34-43 *Dear Christians, One and All, Rejoice,* Hugo Distler (Concordia); SATB (M)
or Isa. 25:6-9 *This Is the Feast,* Daniel Moe (*Ecumenical Praise,* no. 13, Agape); unison (E)
1 Cor. 15:1-11 *This Is the Good News* (*WB* 263); unison (E)
or Acts 10:34-43 *(See above)*
or Mark 16:1-8 *An Easter Processional,* Gerald Near (H. W. Gray); 2-part mixed (ME)
John 20:1-18 *I Have Seen the Lord,* Alan Hovhaness (C. F. Peters); SATB (M)
Ps. 118:14-24 *Easter Antiphon,* Robert J. Powell (Augsburg); any two parts (E)

EASTER EVENING (ABC)

Acts 5:29-32 The apostles' response to the Sanhedrin's prohibition of teaching "in the name of Jesus": we must obey God rather than men in giving witness to God's raising of Jesus from death.

or **Daniel 12:1-3** A vision of the archangel Michael ushering in the day of resurrection for Israel and consummating God's plan for all of creation.

1 Corinthians 5:6-8 You are the new people of God by God's gracious act of salvation through the sacrifice of his Son, the true paschal lamb.

or **Acts 5:29-32** *See above.*

Luke 24:13-49 Two of Jesus' followers walking from Jerusalem to Emmaus are joined by the risen Jesus, but they fail to recognize him. Astounded at his unawareness of events in Jerusalem, the two travelers relate their hopes concerning Jesus of Nazareth, whom they thought was the one to redeem Israel, and their disillusionment upon his death on the cross. Jesus responds to their despair by interpreting the scriptures to them. Then they go into a home where, at the table, "Jesus took the bread and blessed, and broke it, and gave it to them. And their eyes were opened and they recognized him." The travelers immediately return to Jerusalem to tell others that "the Lord has risen." Then Jesus suddenly appears to his disciples. They are terrified. He shows them his hands and feet, eats some fish, and opens their minds about how the scriptures have been fulfilled.

Psalm 150
1. Metrical, *Praise the Lord, His Glories Show, HB* 4, tune: Llanfair
2. Metrical, *Bless'd Be the Lord Our God!, P&E*, tune: Diademata
3. Gregorian psalm tone, *GP*, Trinity Sunday A
4. *PS*, pp. 39, 40

Hymns for the Day	HL	HB	WB
Be Known to Us in Breaking Bread	356	446	–
All Glory Be to God on High	–	–	283
That Easter Day with Joy Was Bright	–	–	581
The Strife Is O'er, the Battle Done	164	203	597

Anthems for the Day
Acts 5:29-32 *Christ the Lord Is Risen Again*, Walter Pelz (Augsburg); choir and congregation, brass (E)
or **Dan. 12:1-3** *The Trumpet Shall Sound*, G. F. Handel (*Messiah*, any edition); bass solo
1 Cor. 5:6-8 *This Is the Feast of Victory*, Daniel Moe (*Ecumenical Praise*, no. 13, Agape); unison (E)
or **Acts 5:29-32** (*See above*)
Luke 24:13-49 *'Twas in the Breaking of the Bread*, Austin Lovelace (Hope); SATB (E)
Ps. 150 *Psalm 150*, Benjamin Britten (Boosey & Hawkes); 2-part and 4-part canon (M)

SECOND SUNDAY OF EASTER (B)

Acts 4:32-35 Since the community of believers in the risen Christ were of one heart and soul, they shared all their possessions in common and gave testimony to the resurrection of the Lord Jesus. As a result of this commitment to economic sharing, not a single needy person lived among them, for distribution of goods was made to each as any had need.

1 John 1:1–2:2 That which was from the beginning, the Word of life, was made manifest, and we have heard, seen, and even touched with our hands. This is the message we have heard from him and proclaim with great joy to you: God is light. How do we know if we are living in the light? When we live in fellowship with one another, we are living in fellowship with God (light). Paradoxically, we all continue to sin (so don't deceive yourselves by saying you have no sin), yet we have an advocate; for when we confess our sins, Christ faithfully forgives us and cleanses us.

John 20:19-31 Verses 19-23 are a series of symbolic episodes: The risen Jesus appears to his frightened disciples and says, "Peace." Then he shows them his hands and his side (which fills the disciples with joy) and again says, "Peace." He gives them the Holy Spirit by breathing on them and concludes with an eschatological saying about resisting forgiveness. In verses 24-31, Thomas says he must see with his eyes before he will believe. So again Jesus appears. He tells Thomas to touch his side. Thomas confesses. Blessed are those who believe solely on the basis of the word alone.

Psalm 133
1. Pointed in *LBW* for psalm tone, p. 282

Hymns for the Day	HL	HB	WB
O Sons and Daughters, Let Us Sing!	167	206	527
Thine Is the Glory	–	209	–
Strong Son of God, Immortal Love	175	228	578
Hark! the Glad Sound, the Savior Comes	–	–	410
Eternal Ruler of the Ceaseless Round	406	–	358

Anthems for the Day
Acts 4:32-35 *Neighbors,* arr. Austin Lovelace (H. W. Gray); SATB (E)
1 John 1:1–2:2 *The Joy of Us All,* Harriet Ziegenhals (Hope); SATB (E)
John 20:19-31 *We Have Seen the Lord,* Robert Wetzler (Augsburg); SATB, soprano solo (M)
Ps. 133 *Together in Unity,* Malcolm Williamson (*Carols of King David,* Boosey & Hawkes); unison (E)

THIRD SUNDAY OF EASTER (B)

Acts 3:12-19 Following the healing of a man lame from birth, Peter preaches to his fellow Israelites to repent.

1 John 3:1-7 What we shall be ultimately has not been fully revealed. But we do know that when Christ appears at the Parousia, we shall see him as he is and that we shall be like him, conformed to him, transformed by him. We may be unfinished people during our journey, but we are God's children. The world may not know who we are because it did not recognize Christ, but we are God's children right now. Look at the love God has already bestowed upon us, that we should be called children of God. But know also that there are children of the devil who break the bond of fellowship with Christ and therefore with one another. Little children, let them not deceive you, for they break God's law by their sinful acts of unrecognized racism, imperialism, sexism, ageism, consumerism, nationalism, and so on. But all who abide in Christ do not continue in sin, for he appeared to take away sins and to bind us to himself in fellowship.

Luke 24:35-48 The risen Jesus suddenly appears to his disciples. They are terrified. So Jesus shows them his hands and feet, eats some fish, and opens their minds about how the scriptures have been fulfilled.

Psalm 4
1. Gelineau, *When I Call, Answer Me, O God*, GG, p. 49
2. *When I Call, Answer Me, O God*, MP&E, p. 194
3. James Aylward, *God Who Can Make Me More than I Am* (G.I.A.)
4. *PS*, p. 12

Hymns for the Day	HL	HB	WB
The Strife Is O'er, the Battle Done	164	203	597
Hail, Thou Once Despised Jesus	–	210	–
On the Good and Faithful	–	52	–
Where Charity and Love Prevail	–	–	641
The Friends of Christ Together	–	–	586

Anthems for the Day
Acts 3:12-19 *Turn Ye, Turn Ye*, Charles Ives (Mercury); SATB (D)
1 John 3:1-7 *My Song Is Love Unknown*, Carl Schalk (Concordia); 2-part (E)
Luke 24:35-48 *He Is Risen*, Walter Pelz (Augsburg); unison with optional descant (E)
Ps. 4 *Give Ear, O Lord*, Heinrich Schütz (Mercury); (ME)

FOURTH SUNDAY OF EASTER (B)

Acts 4:8-12 Peter and John are on trial before the Sanhedrin for healing and preaching. "By what power or name did you do this?" inquire the prose-cutors. Filled with the Holy Spirit, Peter seizes the opportunity to bear testimony: "By the name of Jesus, whom you crucified, but whom God raised from the dead. God's power is, ironically, revealed in the crucifixion of his suffering servant, Jesus. And there is no other name in whom there is salvation. 'The stone which the builders rejected has become the head of the corner' [Ps. 118:22]."

1 John 3:18-24 Here's what God commands of us: "Believe in the name of his Son Jesus Christ and love one another." That means you ignore the tempting but unreliable tugs of your heart saying "do this" or "do that," and you unequivocally reject your conscience when it accuses you, for you live confidently in God's presence which is greater than these. Rather, love in deed and in truth, for "all who keep his commandments abide in him, and he in them."

John 10:11-18 "I am the good shepherd," says Jesus, "who chooses to lay down his life for his sheep that they may live—and not just the sheep you know or see, but also for all the sheep in other folds who belong to me. I am the good shepherd who intimately knows and cares for and loves all his sheep as one flock."

Psalm 23
1. Metrical, *The Lord's My Shepherd*, from the *Scottish Psalter*, 1650, *HB* 104, tune: Crimond
2. Gelineau, *The Lord Is My Shepherd*, *GG*, p. 136
3. Gregorian psalm tone, *GP*, Proper 23 A
4. Frank Quinn, *The Lord Is My Shepherd*, *MP&E*, p. 196
5. *PS*, p. 14

Hymns for the Day	HL	HB	WB
O Jesus, We Adore Thee	156	200	–
Christ Is Made the Sure Foundation	336	433	325
The King of Love My Shepherd Is	99	106	590
Take Thou Our Minds, Dear Lord	245	306	579
The Glorious Gates of Righteousness (v. 3)	–	71	–

Anthems for the Day
Acts 4:8-12 *Christ Is Made the Sure Foundation*, Dale Wood (Sacred Music); SATB (E)
1 John 3:18-24 *Where Charity and Love Prevail* (WB 641)
John 10:11-18 *I Am the Good Shepherd*, Dale Wood (Augsburg); unison (E)
Ps. 23 *The Lord Is My Shepherd*, John Rutter (Oxford); SATB (M)

FIFTH SUNDAY OF EASTER (B)

Acts 8:26-40 The familiar story of Philip and the baptism of the Ethiopian finance official. Make no mistake about God's role from beginning to end. An angel of the Lord instigated Philip's journey to the south of Jerusalem. And behold, Philip just happened to see an Ethiopian reading Isaiah 53:7-8 (about the Suffering Servant). Guided by the Spirit, Philip asked, "Do you understand what you're reading?" And at the Ethiopian's invitation, Philip began to proclaim the good news of Jesus which led to the baptism of the Ethiopian. Truly, God's grace always precedes any human profession of faith.

1 John 4:7-12 God is love! Love belongs to God! How do we know that? Because the ultimate revelation of love is God's sending his only Son into the world. And through Jesus' life and death God shows us what love is: not our loving God, but Jesus' laying down his life for us as an act of love so we might have new life. Now we know how to love one another.

John 15:1-8 Branches that bear no fruit are pruned so they may produce a crop. As Jesus says, you are already pruned clean by the word I have spoken to you, so remain in me, and I in you. Branches that try to produce fruit on their own will wither and be cut off. Apart from me, the true vine, you can do nothing. If you remain in me, and my words remain in you, then you shall bear much fruit, glorify my Father, and prove to be my disciples.

Psalm 22:25-31
1. Gelineau, *I Will Praise You, Lord, GG*, p. 53
2. Gregorian psalm tone, *GP*, Proper 11 B

Hymns for the Day	HL	HB	WB
In Heavenly Love Abiding	284	417	–
Where Charity and Love Prevail	–	–	641
Eternal God, Whose Power Upholds	–	485	357
Father Eternal, Ruler of Creation	–	486	362
O Holy Saviour, Friend Unseen (v. 2)	–	214	–

Anthems for the Day
Acts 8:26-40 *O Word of God Incarnate* (*WB* 532)
1 John 4:7-12 *Neighbors,* arr. Austin Lovelace (H. W. Gray); SATB (E)
John 15:1-8 *I Am the Vine,* Allen Pote (Sacred Music); unison or 2-part (E)
Ps. 22:25-31 No setting suggested

SIXTH SUNDAY OF EASTER (B)

Acts 10:44-48 While Peter is preaching in Cornelius' home, the Spirit falls on all the hearers. The Jewish Christians are amazed that the Spirit has been poured out even on the Gentiles. But the God revealed in the good news of Jesus Christ is a God who favors no nation, race, class, gender, occupation, or social status, because God intends his Spirit-empowered mission for *all* people.

1 John 5:1-6 If you believe "Jesus is the Christ," you are by definition a child of God and therefore love God as well as all other children of God. When you love God's children, you love God and obey his commandments. After all, our belief in Jesus as the Son of God is the conquering power because the salvific and life-giving water and blood flowed from Jesus Christ.

John 15:9-17 If you keep Jesus' commandments, you will remain in his love, just as he has kept his Father's commandments and remained in his love. Jesus' commandment to us and all his friends is to bear fruit that endures by loving one another as he has loved us.

Psalm 98
1. Metrical psalm, *New Songs of Celebration Render*, Erik Routley, *SOT&P*, p. 2, tune: *Rendez à Dieu*
2. Psalm paraphrase, *Sing a New Song to the Lord*, Timothy Dudley-Smith, *WII*, p. 245, tune: *Cantate Domino* by David G. Wilson, fresh, contemporary setting
3. Gelineau, *Sing a New Song to the Lord*, *GG*, p. 15
4. Gregorian psalm tone, *GP*, Christmas Day 3 ABC

Hymns for the Day	HL	HB	WB
In Christ There Is No East or West	341	479	435
We Are One in the Spirit	–	–	619
O Zion, Haste	382	491	–
Son of God, Eternal Savior	393	–	573
Love Divine, All Loves Excelling	308	399	471

Anthems for the Day
Acts 10:44-48 *Spirit, All Holy*, Finn Videro (Augsburg); SAT, tenor solo (ME)

1 John 5:1-6 *Love God with Your Heart*, folk song (*Three Peace and Brotherhood Canons*, Choristers Guild); (E)

John 15:9-17 *If Ye Love Me, Keep My Commandments*, Thomas Tallis (G. Schirmer); SATB (M)

Ps. 98 *With Songs of Rejoicing*, J. S. Bach, arr. Hal Hopson (C. Fischer); 2-part mixed (ME)

THE ASCENSION OF OUR LORD (ABC)

Acts 1:1-11 Jesus charges the apostles to wait in Jerusalem for "the promise of the Father" which is the gift of the Holy Spirit. The apostles ask the risen Jesus if he will now restore the kingdom to Israel. "That's not your worry but God's," replies Jesus. "You'll receive power when the Holy Spirit comes, and then you shall be my witnesses proclaiming the gospel everywhere." Then Jesus is lifted up and departs on a cloud.

Ephesians 1:15-23 May God give you the Spirit who will make you wise and understanding in the knowledge of Christ. In this way you will know the hope to which Christ has called you (the kind of New Age that is coming), and to recognize God's power among us, especially his power in raising Christ to a position above all earthly powers.

Luke 24:46-53 Jesus preaches a kerygmatic sermon on Christ as Lord and the message of repentance and forgiveness. He then constitutes his disciples as the New Israel, promises them the gift of the Spirit, and ascends.

or **Mark 16:9-16, 19-20** Jesus appears to Mary Magdalene, two disciples, and then to eleven disciples: "Go and preach the gospel!" He then ascends to the right hand of God.

Psalm 47
1. Metrical, *O Clap Your Hands, All Ye People, NSC*, p. 5, tune by Eric Reid
2. Gelineau, *All Peoples, Clap Your Hands, GG*, p. 58
3. Gregorian psalm tone, *GP*, Ascension Day ABC

Hymns for the Day	HL	HB	WB
A Hymn of Glory, Let Us Sing	–	–	273
The Lord Ascendeth Up on High	172	212	–
Christ, Above All Glory Seated	–	–	324
Christ, Whose Glory Fills the Skies	26	47	332
Crown Him with Many Crowns	190	213	349

Anthems for the Day
Acts 1:1-11 *Christ Is Alive*, Alastair Cassels-Brown (*Ecumenical Praise*, no. 68, Agape); SATB (ME)
Eph. 1:15-23 *Sing We Triumphant Hymns of Praise*, Erik Routley (Hinshaw); SATB, congregation and brass (ME)
Luke 24:46-53 *The Friends of Christ Together* (WB 586)
or **Mark 16:9-16, 19-20** *Go Ye Into All the World*, Robert Wetzler (Augsburg); 2-part mixed (E)
Ps. 47 *God Has Gone Up*, Jack Goode (H. W. Gray); SATB (M)

SEVENTH SUNDAY OF EASTER (B)

Acts 1:15-17, 21-26 Peter announces to a company of about 120 brethren that someone must be chosen to replace Judas as fulfillment of Psalm 109:8. Not just anyone could be chosen; only "one of those who accompanied us during all the time the Lord Jesus went in and out among us." So two names are presented and offered to the Lord in prayer, who then chooses Matthias through the casting of lots.

1 John 5:9-13 God's testimony is that he "gave us eternal life, and this life is in his Son." Those who belong to the Son have eternal life because the Son belongs to God, who gave eternal life to the Son. Conversely, those who do not belong to the Son do not have eternal life.

John 17:11b-19 Jesus' prayer for his disciples (in every age), which concludes the "Farewell Discourses." "Holy Father: keep them in the power of your name and your word. While I was with them I kept them safe by the power of your name, and I gave them your word so that none was lost. But now I am coming to you and they will be all alone, so protect them, especially from the evil [one]. As you sent me into the hostile world which rejected me, so also I have sent them into the same world. So sanctify, consecrate, set them apart with your word and in your name so they may carry out your mission to the world."

Psalm 1
1. Metrical, *That Man Hath Perfect Blessedness*, MP&E, p. 182, tune: Dunfermline
2. Metrical, *That Man Is Ever Blessed*, LW, p. 388, tune: St. Michael
3. Gelineau, *Happy Indeed Is the Man*, GG, p. 76
4. Gregorian psalm tone, GP, Epiphany 6 C

Hymns for the Day	HL	HB	WB
Jesus Shall Reign	377	496	443
God Has Spoken—by His Prophets	–	–	382
God of the Prophets!	481	520	398
Hope of the World	–	291	423
Christ Is the World's True Light	–	492	326

Anthems for the Day
Acts 1:15-17, 21-26 *Strengthen for Service, Lord*, Austin Lovelace (Canyon); unison (E)
1 John 5:9-13 *O Quench Us with Thy Goodness*, J. S. Bach (*Eight Extended Bach Chorales*, Hinshaw); SATB (M)
John 17:11b-19 *Divided Our Pathways*, Christopher Coelho, arr. Routley (*Ecumenical Praise*, no. 59, Agape); unison, cantor (E)
Ps. 1 *Blessed Is the Man*, Jane Marshall (Hinshaw); SATB (M)

THE DAY OF PENTECOST (B)

Acts 2:1-21 Wind and tongues of fire—the Holy Spirit—spread among all the believers. Are they drunk? "No," says Peter, "it's only nine in the morning. But while I have your attention, let me tell you about Jesus Christ."

or **Ezekiel 37:1-14** The vision of the valley of dry bones. "Preach to the dry bones," Yahweh tells Ezekiel, "that they shall live." So Ezekiel does as commanded. And astonishingly the bones come together and breath comes into them, all by the power of the Word of God.

Romans 8:22-27 All creation groans, as do we who have the firstfruits of the Spirit, for redemption. But we have an advantage: The gift of the Spirit supports our confident hope that we shall be saved. We do not know how to pray, yet the Spirit transforms our weak groanings into prayer. The Spirit pleads with God on our behalf so we may share in the glory which God prepares for those who love him.

or **Acts 2:1-21** *See above.*

John 15:26-27; 16:4b-15 "I," says Jesus, "will send to you from the Father, the Paraclete (the Spirit of truth) who will bear witness to me, as also will you. Now I shall go away to the one who sent me in order that the Paraclete may come to you and convince the world of sin and of righteousness and of judgment. When the Spirit of truth comes, he will guide you into all the truth and he will glorify me."

Psalm 104:24-34
1. Metrical, *O Worship the King All Glorious Above*, HB 26, tune: Lyons
2. Gelineau, *Bless the Lord, My Soul!, GG*, p. 63
3. Gregorian psalm tone, *GP*, Pentecost ABC

Hymns for the Day	HL	HB	WB
Come, Holy Ghost, Our Souls Inspire	–	237	335
Holy Spirit, Truth Divine	208	240	422
O Spirit of the Living God	207	242	528
Come, Thou Almighty King	52	244	343
The Day of Pentecost Arrived	–	–	583
God, Our Father, You Our Maker	–	–	399

Anthems for the Day
Acts 2:1-21 *Whitsunday Canticle*, Erik Routley (*Two for Pentecost*, Hinshaw); SATB (ME)
or **Ezek. 37:1-14** *Holy Spirit, Truth Divine*, Jean Pasquet (Elkan-Vogel); 2-part (E)
Rom. 8:22-27 *Come, Spirit, Divine*, Hugo Distler (Joseph Boonin); SATB (MD)
or **Acts 2:1-21** *(See above)*
John 15:26-27; 16:4b-15 *And They Were Filled with the Holy Spirit*, George Lynn (Golden); SATB (MD)
Ps. 104:24-34 *Descend, O Spirit, Purging Flame* (WB 353)

TRINITY SUNDAY [First Sunday After Pentecost] (B)

Isaiah 6:1-8 Confronted by the immediate presence of the enthroned God and of seraphim singing "Holy, holy, holy," which rocked the very foundations of the Temple, Isaiah feels his hair stand on end, shirt buttons pop, and shoelaces untie as he is denuded of his pretense of worthiness before the Lord. "Woe is me!" cries out Isaiah. "For I am a man of unclean lips, and I dwell in the midst of a people of unclean lips." Astonishingly, one of the seraphim then touches Isaiah's lips with a burning coal from the altar, saying, "Your guilt is taken away, and your sin forgiven." Upon hearing the voice of the Lord say, "Whom shall I send, and who will go for us?" Isaiah's lips now inexplicably respond, "Here am I! Send me."

Romans 8:12-17 An exhortation to live not according to the anxiety and fear of human nature but according to the life-giving Spirit. Though we constantly get tangled in the slavery of our pious self-interest and cravings for acceptance, God's Spirit works among us to bring about a new relationship that enables us to cry out boldly, *"Abba!"*

John 3:1-17 By day, Nicodemus is everything you could want to be; by night, he comes secretly in search of Jesus. By day, Nicodemus controls the affairs of his kingdom; by night, he comes looking for the kingdom of God. Replies Jesus, "Unless one is born of water and the Spirit, he cannot enter the kingdom of God." "How can this be?" asked Nicodemus.

Psalm 29
1. Free paraphrase, *God the Omnipotent!*, Henry F. Chorley and John Ellerton, *HB* 487, tune: Russian Hymn
2. Gelineau, *O Give the Lord, You Sons of God*, 24P&1C, p. 10

Hymns for the Day	HL	HB	WB
God the Omnipotent!	420	487	–
Holy, Holy, Holy	57	11	421
Come, Thou Almighty King	52	244	343
I Sing as I Arise Today	–	–	428

Anthems for the Day
Isa. 6:1-8 *In the Year That King Uzziah Died*, David McK. Williams (H. W. Gray); SATB (D)
Rom. 8:12-17 *Sing and Dance, Children of God*, Michael Bedford (Hinshaw); 2-part (E)
John 3:1-17 *God So Loved the World*, Heinrich Schütz (Concordia); SATB (M)
Ps. 29 *Give Unto the Lord, O Ye Mighty*, Heinrich Schütz (Abingdon); unison (E)

SUNDAY BETWEEN MAY 29 AND JUNE 4
(Proper 4) (B) [use only if after Trinity Sunday]*

1 Samuel 16:1-13 Yahweh commands Samuel to offer a sacrifice at Bethlehem as a ruse to anointing the one whom Yahweh has chosen as king. At the sacrifice, Samuel surveys seven sons of Jesse who are present, but Yahweh selects none of these. The youngest, most inexperienced, least likely son is taking care of the sheep. And Yahweh says, "Arise, anoint him; for this is he."

2 Corinthians 4:5-12 "We don't promote ourselves," says Paul, "we preach Christ as Lord and serve him alone. We are frail, weak human beings, earthenware vessels, in whom God has entrusted the powerful treasure of the gospel of Jesus Christ. Yes, we are often afflicted, perplexed, persecuted, and struck down, but our 'suffering life' reflects Jesus' life. We are not success devotees but suffering disciples."

Mark 2:23–3:6 Two controversy-pronouncement stories about plucking grain and healing on the Sabbath. Jesus counters Pharisaical accusations with questions about the precedence of human need over legalistic restrictions, the priority of humans in the order of creation, and the intention of the Sabbath: to do good or to harm, to save life or to kill. Jesus then affirms his authority by pronouncing that "the Son of man is lord even of the sabbath." Rather than amazement, Jesus' adversaries (religious and political leaders) stare in silence, then conspire to kill him.

Psalm 20
1. Metrical, *In the Day of Need May Your Answer Be the Lord*, PP, p. 77

Hymns for the Day	HL	HB	WB
This Is the Day the Lord Hath Made	23	69	–
Come, You People, Rise and Sing	–	39	345
Let There Be Light, Lord God of Hosts	402	480	451
Break Forth, O Living Light of God	–	–	316
Christ Is the World's True Light	–	492	326

Anthems for the Day
1 Sam. 16:1-13 *Now David Was a Shepherd Boy*, Austin Lovelace (H. W. Gray); unison, children
2 Cor. 4:5-12 *Anthem of Dedication*, Warren Martin (Presser); SATB (ME)
Mark 2:23–3:6 *A Song of the Kingdom*, Austin Lovelace (Triune); SATB (ME)
Ps. 20 *We Will Rejoice*, William Croft (A. Broude); SATB (M)

---

*NOTE: If the Sunday between May 24 and May 28 follows Trinity Sunday, use the Eighth Sunday after the Epiphany on that day.

SUNDAY BETWEEN JUNE 5 AND JUNE 11
(Proper 5) (B) [use only if after Trinity Sunday]

1 Samuel 16:14-23 The Spirit of Yahweh withdraws from the rejected Saul and allows an "evil spirit" to torment him continually. The king's servants believe music will cure their sickly Saul and thus submit letters of recommendation for a lyre-playing, handsome, soldierly, able-speaking son of Jesse whom Yahweh is with. "Send him to me," clamors Saul, who unwittingly unlatches the throne-room doors to his successor. In this manner, David enters Saul's court as his personal attendant and finds favor with him by refreshing Saul with sweet, healing music that prods the evil spirit to depart.

2 Corinthians 4:13–5:1 "I believed, therefore I spoke," says the Septuagint version of Psalm 115:1. Likewise, we and Paul believe in a resurrection faith; therefore we all preach the gospel, knowing that God will raise us all and join us to Christ. Though we may occasionally succumb to despair when we realize we are edging closer to our mortal death, still we fix our eyes not on the ephemeral, material securities of this world but on the eternal, invisible home which God has prepared for us.

Mark 3:20-35 Neighbors and scribes reject Jesus, saying he is insane and demonic, respectively. He counters with a rhetorical question and three "if . . . then" sayings (all about a divided "house" falling), and a pronouncement about the unforgivable sin of blasphemy against the Holy Spirit at work in Jesus. Then Jesus' family show their blindness about Jesus' identity, which elicits another question from Jesus and his pronouncement about the doers of God's will being his true family.

Psalm 57
1. Frank Quinn, *The Dawning of New Hope, MP&E*, p. 81

Hymns for the Day	HL	HB	WB
Jesus, Lead the Way	–	334	441
Thou Hidden Source of Calm Repose	–	423	–
Father, We Greet You	–	285	364
How Sweet the Name of Jesus Sounds	310	130	–

Anthems for the Day
1 Sam. 16:14-23 *When in Our Music God Is Glorified*, C. V. Stanford (*Westminster Praise*, no. 12, Hinshaw); unison (E)
2 Cor. 4:13–5:1 *Open, Lord, My Inward Ear*, Malcolm Williamson (*Ecumenical Praise*, no. 31, Agape); unison (E)
Mark 3:20-35 *In Christ There Is No East or West*, Ned Rorem (*Ecumenical Praise*, no. 86, Agape); unison (E)
Ps. 57 *Psalm 57*, Charles Webb (Choristers Guild); unison (E)

SUNDAY BETWEEN JUNE 12 AND JUNE 18
(Proper 6) (B) [use only if after Trinity Sunday]

2 Samuel 1:1, 17-27 "How are the mighty fallen!" David publicly laments the slaying of Saul and Jonathan—"Israel's glory." This song of raw feelings shall "be taught to the people of Judah" so they will know of David's grief as well as the nation's. The shields of Israel's undivided heroes—"who were swifter than eagles, stronger than lions"—lie in disgrace on Gilboa. Weep, women of Israel, for Saul will no longer clothe you. And Jonathan's deep affection will be but a memory. "How are the mighty fallen!"

2 Corinthians 5:6-10, 14-17 In our earthly life we live by faith, trusting the invisible rather than the visible, hoping for the unseen rather than the seen, and daring to be courageous in the face of death. For our hope is in Jesus Christ; after all, for what more could we ask than a fuller, transformed life at home with the Lord. So we seek to please Christ now and then, for we shall not be judged by human standards but by Christ, the one who died on behalf of us all.

Mark 4:26-34 Two surrealistic parables: Is one about a lazy or pious farmer? No, this is about God's grain growing automatically by stages during the sabbatical year but concluding with a horrid, apocalyptic harvest of the enemies of God (see Joel 3:13). The other is about an unpopular, despised, rejected weed (not a triumphant cedar of Lebanon) where foolish birds find refuge and make their home.

Psalm 46
1. Metrical, *A Mighty Fortress Is Our God* (found in most hymnals)
2. Contemporary setting, *Psalm 46* from *Three Psalms of Celebration*, Arthur Wills (Royal School of Church Music, 1980)
3. Gregorian psalm tone, *GP*, Easter Vigil, Proper 29 C

Hymns for the Day	HL	HB	WB
God Is Our Refuge	91	381	–
Come, You Thankful People, Come	460	525	346
How Firm a Foundation	283	369	425
Love Divine, All Loves Excelling	308	399	471

Anthems for the Day
2 Sam. 1:1, 17-27 *The Lament of David*, Daniel Pinkham (E. C. Schirmer); SATB, electronic tape (D)

2 Cor. 5:6-10, 14-17 *Holy Ghost, Dispel Our Sadness*, Jane Marshall (*Westminster Praise*, no. 38, Hinshaw); (E)

Mark 4:26-34 *Song of the Mustard Seed*, Hal Hopson (G.I.A); unison (E)

Ps. 46 *God Is Our Strength and Refuge*, Philip Landgrave (Hope); unison (E)

SUNDAY BETWEEN JUNE 19 AND JUNE 25
(Proper 7) (B) [use only if after Trinity Sunday]

2 Samuel 5:1-12 All the tribes of Israel gather at the sanctuary in Hebron and affirm David as "bone and flesh." Thus, in fulfillment of the promise (1 Sam. 25:30) and in the presence of Yahweh, the elders anoint David as king over all Israel. David and "his men" then capture the fortress of Jerusalem from the Jebusites by some perplexing tactics against "the blind and the lame." Here David now lives, renaming it the city of David, and becomes greater and greater because "Yahweh was with him."

2 Corinthians 5:18–6:2 God has entrusted us with the ministry of reconciliation and appointed us as ambassadors for Christ. Our message? God tracked down and made up with our rebellious, guilty, frightened world. Instead of tallying up all our sins, God incarnate, Jesus Christ, strode into our world and loved us and forgave us, transforming our world into a new creation. Anyone on earth "in Christ" is already part of that new order. So we say, "Be reconciled; we plead with you on behalf of Christ—now is the hour to be reconciled!"

Mark 4:35-41 Jesus and his disciples enjoy an evening boat ride until a rampaging, howling storm slings their boat from wave to wave. Terrified, helpless disciples scream at the slumbering Jesus, "Teacher, don't you care?" So Jesus puts down the beastly storm by simply saying, "Be quiet!" "Who is this that has such power that the wind and sea obey him?" ask the awestruck disciples. Guess who's really in charge of the world.

Psalm 48
1. Metrical, *Within Thy Temple's Sacred Courts*, HB 438, tune: St. John's Highlands
2. Metrical, *How Great Is God Almighty*, PP, p. 94

Hymns for the Day	HL	HB	WB
Christ, of All My Hopes the Ground	316	314	–
Hope of the World	–	291	–
Give to the Winds Your Fears	294	364	377
Hills of the North, Rejoice	–	478	–

Anthems for the Day
2 Sam. 5:1-12 No setting suggested
2 Cor. 5:18-6:2 *Reconciliation*, Lloyd Pfautsch (Abingdon); SATB (M)
Mark 4:35-41 *Grant Us Thy Peace*, Felix Mendelssohn (Boosey & Hawkes); SATB (E)
Ps. 48 *God Has Gone Up*, Jack Goode (H. W. Gray); SATB (M)

SUNDAY BETWEEN JUNE 26 AND JULY 2
(Proper 8) (B)

2 Samuel 6:1-15 Following victory over the Philistines, David and his "chosen men" jubilantly march back to Jerusalem with the ark of God leading them. On the way the oxen suddenly stumble and the ark appears about to tumble, but Uzzah leaps quickly to steady the ark—God's presence—on the cart. So angry is God about this meddling that he smites Uzzah right there and kills him. David, filled with anger at and fear of Yahweh's impetuosity, abandons the ark at a pagan farmer's home which then is unexpectedly blessed by the presence of the Lord. Regarding this blessing as a sign of the dissolution of Yahweh's anger, David resumes the "ark processional" by offering a solemn sacrifice and dancing with all his might before the Lord.

2 Corinthians 8:7-15 Perhaps more than any other word, "giving" best characterizes the life-style of Christians. We give to neighbors our faith, speech, knowledge, help, love, and now Paul even charges us to give our cash. Surprised? No, for our whole life points to the servant Christ who "though he was rich, yet for our sakes he became poor." He is the self-giver par excellence.

Mark 5:21-43 A story within a story about two desperate yet faithful people. Jairus' faith in Jesus restores his daughter to life, and an unknown woman's flow of faith saves her from an uncurable illness and makes her whole. No wonder everyone is amazed.

Psalm 24
1. Psalm paraphrase, *Lift Up Your Heads, Ye Mighty Gates*, George Weissel, trans. Catherine Winkworth, *HB* 152, *WB* 454, tune: Truro
2. Gelineau, *O Gates, Lift High Your Heads*, *GG*, p. 156
3. Gregorian psalm tone, *GP*, Advent 4 A
4. Mixed medium, *Psalm 24*, Arthur Wills (G. Schirmer)
5. *PS*, p. 16

Hymns for the Day	*HL*	*HB*	*WB*
Lift Up Your Heads, O Mighty Gates	114	152	454
Lord of the Dance	–	–	426
Father, Whose Will Is Life and Good	–	309	368
We Thank You, Lord, for Strength of Arm	–	–	629

Anthems for the Day
2 Sam. 6:1-15 *Sing and Dance, Children of God*, Michael Bedford (Hinshaw); 2-part (E)
2 Cor. 8:7-15 *When God Almighty*, John Maynard (*Ecumenical Praise*, no. 115, Agape); unison (E)
Mark 5:21-43 *Draw Us in the Spirit's Tether*, Harold Friedell (H. W. Gray); SATB (ME)
Ps. 24 *Who Shall Ascend*, Hank Beebe (C. Fisher); 2-part (E)

SUNDAY BETWEEN JULY 3 AND JULY 9
(Proper 9) (B)

2 Samuel 7:1-17 Now that David thinks he has established his power, he observes that "God's tent is not as good as my home." Replies Nathan: "Do what's in your heart, for Yahweh is with you." But that same night the word of the Lord comes to Nathan: "Do not try to contain and control me in a house (temple), for I have been and will be with you all wherever you are. Go tell David that I chose him, I established him, I will build him an enduring house (family dynasty), and I will keep my steadfast love with him forever."

2 Corinthians 12:1-10 "I've had ecstatic spiritual experiences that rival anyone else's," says Paul, "but what ultimately strengthens me is not such visions and revelations but insults, hardships, persecutions, calamities, and 'thorns in the flesh.'" Despite our list of achievements and presumed self-esteem that create in us a false sense of self-sufficiency, ultimately we are completely dependent upon Christ. Yes, faith in him will generate an assortment of suffering cross-experiences, but paradoxically, when we are weak, then we are strong, for God's grace alone is sufficient to sustain us.

Mark 6:1-6 Jesus preaches his homecoming sermon in his boyhood synagogue. His friends and relatives are astonished at his teachings, wondering where this carpenter's son obtained such ideas. So amazed at his wisdom are they that they take offense and reject him. In the midst of such unfaith, such closed-mindedness to the power of God at work, Jesus "could do no mighty work there," so he goes elsewhere to continue his ministry.

Psalm 89:20-37
1. Metrical, *My Song Forever Shall Record*, HB 516, tune: St. Petersburg
2. Gelineau, *With My Chosen One I Have Made a Covenant*, GG, p. 12
3. Gregorian psalm tone, *GP*, Epiphany 1 ABC
4. *Forever I Will Sing—The Son of David*, Howard Hughes (G.I.A.)

Hymns for the Day	HL	HB	WB
Sing Praise to God, Who Reigns Above	–	15	568
God Moves in a Mysterious Way	103	112	391
Make Me a Captive, Lord	247	308	–
God of Compassion, in Mercy Befriend Us	290	122	392

Anthems for the Day
2 Sam. 7:1-17 *Lord, Thou Hast Told Us*, Arnold Bax (*Anthems for Choirs*, vol. 4, Oxford); SATB (E)
2 Cor. 12:1-10 *Open, Lord, My Inward Ear*, Malcolm Williamson (*Ecumenical Praise*, no. 31, Agape); unison (E)
Mark 6:1-6 *They Saw You as the Local Builder's Son*, Verner Ahlberg (*Ecumenical Praise*, no. 105, Agape); unison (E)
Ps. 89:20-37 No setting suggested

SUNDAY BETWEEN JULY 10 AND JULY 16
(Proper 10) (B)

2 Samuel 7:18-29 Following Nathan's oracle in which Yahweh has just signed a blank-check promise to David and his family forever, David enters the tent of Yahweh's presence and prays: "You really shouldn't have promised all that because I am unworthy of all that you've done already. How great you are! But now since you have promised all these things to me and my family, I will depend upon your fulfilling all your promises. And now you can bless my descendants so they will continue to enjoy your favor according to your promises."

Ephesians 1:1-10 In Christ, God blessed us, chose us, adopted us as his children, redeemed us, and revealed to us his will and purpose that all things in heaven and earth might be united in Christ. Thanks be to God for Jesus Christ.

Mark 6:7-13 Unworthy, incomplete, imperfect disciples are commissioned by Jesus and given his authority. "Do not encumber yourself with material goods," charges Jesus. "Stay where you're welcome and leave where you're rebuffed." So they go obediently, untrained and inexperienced though they are: preaching, exorcizing, anointing, and healing in the name of Jesus.

Psalm 132:11-18
1. Metrical, *Arise, O Lord, Our God, Arise*, HB 518, tune: Federal Street
2. Gelineau, *Lord, Go Up to the Place of Your Rest*, GG, p. 164
3. Gregorian psalm tone, *GP*, Advent 4 B

Hymns for the Day	HL	HB	WB
Glorious Things of You Are Spoken	339	434	379
Praise, My Soul, the King of Heaven	14	31	551
O Master, Let Me Walk with Thee	364	304	520
We Greet You, Sure Redeemer from All Strife	–	144	625

Anthems for the Day
2 Sam. 7:18-29 *Cantique de Jean Racine*, Gabriel Fauré (A. Broude); SATB (M)
Eph. 1:1-10 *Messenger to Ephesus*, Eugene Butler (Agape); SATB (M)
Mark 6:7-13 *Good Spirit of God*, Jean van de Canter (*Ecumenical Praise*, no. 82, Agape); unison (E)
Ps. 132:11-18 *I Will Clothe Thy Priests with Salvation*, Johann Peter (Boosey & Hawkes); SATB (ME)

SUNDAY BETWEEN JULY 17 AND JULY 23
(Proper 11) (B)

2 Samuel 11:1-15 David arises from his afternoon nap one day and happens to lay his eyes upon a beautiful woman, Bathsheba, bathing in her home. Overcome, he sends his couriers to fetch her to him, whereupon he indulges in sexual intercourse with her, unexpectedly resulting in her becoming pregnant. David recalls her husband, Uriah the Hittite, from the battlefield for some R&R at home with his wife, but dutiful Uriah keeps watch all night outside the palace. David then plies Uriah with alcohol, but still he sleeps outdoors in the palace compound. So David plots to send Uriah back to the war, to be killed in a retreat ordered by David via Joab.

Ephesians 2:11-22 Remember when we were separated from each other by walls of hostility, accusation, name-calling, hatred? We were strangers to each other. But then Christ's cross rammed our barricades of pride and smashed our fortifications of bitterness and guilt, reconciling us all to him. That's the good news we preach: that we have been re-created as a new people, a new family in union with Christ.

Mark 6:30-34 Jesus urges the disciples to rest after their ministry. He feels compassion for the multitude following him because they are like shepherdless sheep, so he teaches them.

Psalm 53
1. Pointed in *LBW* for psalm tone, p. 240

Hymns for the Day	HL	HB	WB
Christ Is Made the Sure Foundation	336	433	325
Saviour, Like a Shepherd Lead Us	458	380	–
We Are One in the Spirit	–	–	619
Judge Eternal, Throned in Splendor	–	517	447

Anthems for the Day
2 Sam. 11:1-15 *Come, My Soul, Thou Must Be Waking*, F. J. Haydn (*HB* 44); SATB (E)

Eph. 2:11-22 *Come, Peace of God*, Eugene Butler (Sacred Music); SATB (E)

Mark 6:30-34 *O Jesus Christ, to You May Hymns Be Rising*, Daniel Moe (*WB* 509)

Ps. 53 *The Fool Hath Said in His Heart*, Alan Hovhaness (*Four Motets*, no. 4, Associated); SATB (M)

SUNDAY BETWEEN JULY 24 AND JULY 30
(Proper 12) (B)

2 Samuel 12:1-14 Yahweh is outraged by David's adultery with Bathsheba and murder of Uriah, so he sends the prophet Nathan to tell David a story about a rich man commandeering a poor man's precious lamb. Recognizing himself as a sinner, David repents. "You're not going to die," says Nathan, "because the Lord has forgiven you and will work through your brokenness. But the terrible mess you've created still remains, which means the child born to you shall die."

Ephesians 3:14-21 Paul falls on his knees and prays that the Spirit will strengthen us, that Christ will make his home among us so we may understand the incredible breadth, length, height, and depth of his love, and that God will fill us with his nature. To God be the glory!

John 6:1-15 Near the time of the Passover a multitude follow Jesus "into the hills." "How are we to feed so many?" tests Jesus. "Two hundred denarii couldn't buy enough," replies Philip. Andrew spots a boy with merely five loaves and two fish. Jesus says, "Tell everyone to sit" (about 5,000 do so). Then Jesus takes the loaves, gives thanks and distributes to those seated; so also the fish, as much as they want. And the disciples collect an abundant twelve basketfuls of leftovers. The people see this "sign" and identify Jesus as "the prophet who is to come." But Jesus' kingdom is not of this world, so he departs.

Psalm 32
1. Metrical, *How Blest Is He Whose Trespass*, HB 281, tune: Rutherford
2. Gelineau, *Happy the Man Whose Offence Is Forgiven*, GG, p. 86
3. Gregorian psalm tone, *GP*, Epiphany 7 B

Hymns for the Day	HL	HB	WB
Guide Me, O Thou Great Jehovah	104	339	409
Jesus, Thy Boundless Love to Me	314	404	–
Put Forth, O God, Your Spirit's Might	–	477	559
How Blest Is He Whose Trespass	–	281	–
O Love, How Deep, How Broad, How High!	139	–	518

Anthems for the Day
2 Sam. 12:1-14 *Have Mercy on Us, O My Lord*, Aaron Copland (Boosey & Hawkes); SATB (MD)

Eph. 3:14-21 *To Him Be Glory*, Austin Lovelace (H. W. Gray); SATB (ME)

John 6:1-15 *Thou Hast Given Us Bread from Heaven*, Johann Geisler (H. W. Gray); SATB (M)

Ps. 32 *Give Thanks to the Lord*, Erik Satie, arr. Zanielli (Walton); SATB (M)

SUNDAY BETWEEN JULY 31 AND AUGUST 6
(Proper 13) (B)

2 Samuel 12:15b-24 Sure enough, just as Nathan foretold, Yahweh smites the baby created through the adultery of David and Bathsheba. So David prays for the infant's health, fasts, and isolates himself from others. On the seventh day the child dies. For fear of a potential suicidal reaction, no one tells David. But he finds out by himself and puts his paralyzing grief behind him by washing, putting on clean clothes, worshiping in the Lord's house, and returning to the palace to eat. David and Yahweh are reconciled. A sign: David and Bathsheba have another child, Solomon, whom the Lord loves.

Ephesians 4:1-6 We have received as a gift from God a way of life in Christ and therefore are called to exemplify it: humility, gentleness, patience, and tolerance. Above all, preserve (not presume) the fragile unity the Spirit gives to the community, for there is only one Lord, one faith, and one baptism.

John 6:24-35 People searching for Jesus are accused by him of seeking only another free lunch. "Work for imperishable, eternal manna," says Jesus, "which the Son of man will give you." What kind of works must we do? "Believe in the one whom God has sent," says Jesus. Then show us a sign—like the manna in the wilderness—so we will believe. "That bread," retorts Jesus, "came from heaven." That's the bread we want; give it to us. "Simply open your eyes and see," answers Jesus; "I am the bread of life, whoever comes to me shall not hunger, and whoever believes in me shall never thirst."

Psalm 32:11-22
1. Gelineau, *I Will Bless the Lord at All Times*, GG, p. 109
2. Gregorian psalm tone, *GP*, Proper 16 B

Hymns for the Day	HL	HB	WB
Hope of the World	–	291	423
Break Thou the Bread of Life	216	250	317
The Church's One Foundation	333	437	582
Break Forth, O Living Light of God	–	–	316

Anthems for the Day
2 Sam. 12:15b-24 *Lord, We Cry to Thee*, melody and text by Ulrich Zwingli, arr. Dickenson (H. W. Gray); SATB (E)
Eph. 4:1-6 *Verse/Unity*, Richard Hillert (*Verses and Offertories, Lesser Festivals*, Augsburg); unison (E)
John 6:24-35 *The Bread of Life*, Gerhard Krapf (*Seven Seasonal Sentences*, Sacred Music); SAB (E)
Ps. 34:11-22 *Come, Ye Children*, Agostino Steffani (Concordia); 2-part (E)

SUNDAY BETWEEN AUGUST 7 AND AUGUST 13
(Proper 14) (B)

2 Samuel 18:1, 5, 9-15 Intrafamily strife over succession to the throne ignites rape, revenge, fratricide, and Absalom's wide-scale revolt against his father, who flees Jerusalem. When David organizes his army in the forest of Ephraim, he explicitly orders his officers not to harm Absalom. All the troops hear his command. But when Absalom freakishly becomes ensnarled among the branches of a tree while riding his mule, Joab deliberately disobeys David: first, he offers a fat reward to a soldier if he will kill Absalom (but the soldier refuses to transgress David's public command) and, second, he plunges three spears into Absalom's chest, which opens the way for ten armor bearers to kill him.

Ephesians 4:25–5:2 You are one in the Spirit, so do not sin against the Spirit by thriving on slander, bitterness, anger, or divisiveness. Rather, as beloved children of God, imitate God's new life in Christ: speak the truth openly with one another, use words that build up the body, be kind and tenderhearted to each other, and forgive one another, as God in Christ forgave you.

John 6:35, 41-51 How can this son of Joseph, this man from Nazareth, say he is the bread which came down from heaven? "Do not be so disbelieving, so stubborn, so closed-minded," says Jesus, "for belief is a gift from God. I am the living bread which came down from heaven. My flesh is the sustenance, the very stuff of life which God gives. Whoever believes has eternal life."

Psalm 143:1-8
1. Metrical, *When Morning Lights the Eastern Skies, HB* 49, tune: St. Stephen
2. Gregorian psalm tone, *GP*, Easter Vigil ABC

Hymns for the Day	HL	HB	WB
God of Compassion in Mercy Befriend Us	290	122	392
Jesus, Thou Joy of Loving Hearts	354	215	–
Bread of the World	353	445	–
Guide Me, O Thou Great Jehovah	104	339	409

Anthems for the Day
2 Sam. 18:1, 5, 9-15 *Help Me, O Lord*, Thomas Arne (*Oxford Easy Anthem Book*, Oxford); canon in 3 parts (E)
Eph. 4:25–5:2 *Grieve Not the Holy Spirit*, T. T. Noble (H. W. Gray); SATB, soprano or tenor solo (M)
John 6:35, 41-51 *The Living Bread*, Leland Sateren (Augsburg); SATB (E)
Ps. 143:1-8 *I Call to the Lord*, Felix Mendelssohn, arr. Hopson (A. Broude); SATB (ME)

SUNDAY BETWEEN AUGUST 14 AND AUGUST 20
(Proper 15) (B)

2 Samuel 18:24-33 Ahimaaz, son of Zadok, races to David to report the Lord's victory over the rebellious forces. "Is Absalom well?" queries David. "Too much commotion to tell," replies Ahimaaz. A Cushite slave, also a commissioned messenger, arrives to recount the Lord's victory over the rebellious forces. "Is Absalom well?" queries David. Knowing that kings usually react to bad news by thrashing the bearer, the Cushite answers circumspectly, "May what happened to him befall all your enemies." David, overcome with grief, reacts in an unkingly way by retiring to the room above the gateway and weeping uncontrollably over the death of his traitorous son: "O my son Absalom. Would I had died instead of you."

Ephesians 5:15-20 Watch how you walk. You can walk foolishly, hesitatingly, aimlessly, wobbly, fearfully from birth to death. Or you can walk as God's beloved children in Christ who are at home in God's grace and therefore walk wisely, purposefully, joyfully, steadily with each other while singing praise and thanks to God.

John 6:51-58 For two thousand years, many an argument has been generated by the nuances between "believing in Jesus" and "eating his flesh and drinking his blood." Advocates of cognitive and experiential "means of grace" have long battled over the "presence of God" and "the way to eternal life." Now hear Jesus' audacity when he proclaims that only those who "have life in," "abide in," "eat and drink," him—the bread of life—have eternal life.

Psalm 102:1-12
1. Gregorian psalm tone, *GP,* Monday of Holy Week ABC

Hymns for the Day	HL	HB	WB
O Holy City, Seen of John	409	508	505
Come, Ye Disconsolate	293	373	–
Come, You People, Rise and Sing	–	39	345
O Love Divine, That Stooped to Share	–	116	–

Anthems for the Day
2 Sam. 18:24-33 *When David Heard,* Thomas Tompkins (Oxford); SATB (D)
Eph. 5:15-20 *Be Filled with the Spirit,* Ludwig Lenel (Concordia); SATB (ME)
John 6:51-58 *Verily, Verily, I Say Unto You,* Thomas Tallis (Oxford); SATB (M)
Ps. 102:1-12 *Psalm 102,* J. P. Sweelinck (Mercury); SATB (M)

SUNDAY BETWEEN AUGUST 21 AND AUGUST 27
(Proper 16) (B)

2 Samuel 23:1-7 David—the one whom Yahweh was with—sings his last words. "As the anointed one, the Spirit of the Lord speaks his word through my tongue, saying, 'The just ruler beams like the rising sun and makes the grass as richly green as after the early spring rain.' Such is my house (family dynasty), for the Lord has stood by his eternal covenant with me and secured my salvation in him. But the godless people are like wind-blown, prickly tumbleweeds that no one can hold without getting hurt. One must be an iron spear in order to put these thorny enemies to their only use: to burn in the fire."

Ephesians 5:21-33 A difficult text. God chose us to be imitators, proclaimers, "sign-doers" of the New Age inaugurated by Christ. Human relationships, therefore, can no longer tolerate the dominion of one person over the other because that reflects the old order of sin which Christ overcame. The new pattern set for us by Christ is that of feeding, nourishing, caring for one another even to the point of laying down your life for another. Thus, a man leaves his father and mother and is united with his wife. The oneness of this new relationship demands that each partner serve, love, respect the other.

John 6:55-69 Many people grumble at Jesus' hard teachings and "eating his flesh and drinking his blood." Some withdraw and some—like Peter—confess Jesus as "the Holy One of God." It truly is the Spirit that gives life.

Psalm 67
1. Metrical psalm, *Lord, Bless and Pity Us*, from *The Psalter*, 1912, HB 493, WB 456, tune: St. Michael
2. Gelineau, *O God, Be Gracious and Bless Us*, GG, p. 17
3. Gregorian psalm tone, *GP*, Proper 15 A
4. Mixed medium, *Psalm 67*, Arthur Wills (G. Schirmer)
5. *PS*, p. 21

Hymns for the Day	HL	HB	WB
God of Our Fathers, Whose Almighty Hand	414	515	394
He Is the Way	–	–	413
God of Our Life	88	108	395
Lord, Bless and Pity Us	–	493	456
Love Divine, All Loves Excelling	308	399	471

Anthems for the Day

2 Sam. 23:1-7 *The Last Words of David*, Randall Thompson (E. C. Schirmer); SATB (D)

Eph. 5:21-33 *Seek to Serve*, Lloyd Pfautsch (Agape); 2-part (E)

John 6:55-69 *Lord, to Whom Shall We Go?*, Willem Mudde (Augsburg); SATB (ME)

Ps. 67 *Festival Psalm*, Ronald Arnatt (H. W. Gray); SATB, optional trumpets (M)

SUNDAY BETWEEN AUGUST 28 AND SEPTEMBER 3 (Proper 17) (B)

1 Kings 2:1-4, 10-12 David's deathbed instructions to Solomon, his successor to the throne: Be strong and confident. Keep the ways of Yahweh—his statutes, commandments, ordinances, and testimonies—so you may prosper and so Yahweh may keep his word which he promised me concerning my house (family dynasty). Then David died and was buried, and Solomon acceded to the throne of his father.

Ephesians 6:10-20 Much to our surprise, we peace-loving Christians discover that trying to keep the faith in our world is a battle against an unseen foe—the "principalities and powers" which live in our mind and our world. With what shall we defend ourselves? Put on the armor of God: truth, righteousness, peace, faith, and salvation. And one offensive weapon is permitted—the Word of God as your sword. Now pray that you may be bold in proclaiming the gospel message.

Mark 7:1-8, 14-15, 21-23 "Why do your disciples eat ritually unclean food?" demand the Pharisees and scribes. Jesus counters by quoting Isaiah 29:13—"You honor me with your words, but your hearts are far from me." Then he pronounces: "You're obsessed with your own laws and have abrogated God's law. Listen, what makes a person unclean is not by ingesting unclean things but by emitting the evil things in one's heart: theft, envy, slander, pride, and more."

Psalm 121
1. Metrical psalm, *I to the Hills Will Lift My Eyes*, from *The Psalter*, 1912, *HB* 377, *WB* 430, tune: Dundee
2. Metrical psalm, *Unto the Hills I Lift Mine Eyes*, from *The Psalter*, 1912, *MP&E*, p. 90, tune: Dunfermline
3. Gelineau, *I Lift Up My Eyes to the Mountains*, *GG*, p. 127
4. Gregorian psalm tone, *GP*, Proper 24 C
5. *PS*, p. 32

Hymns for the Day	HL	HB	WB
Christ Is the World's Redeemer	–	136	–
A Mighty Fortress Is Our God	266	91	274
I to the Hills Will Lift My Eyes	–	377	430
Glorious Is Your Name, Most Holy	–	–	378

Anthems for the Day
1 Kings 2:1-4, 10-12 *If Thou but Suffer God to Guide Thee*, Jody Lindh (Concordia); 2-part (E)
Eph. 6:10-20 *Soldiers of Christ*, Robert J. Powell (C. Fischer); SATB (ME)
Mark 7:1-8, 14-15, 21-23 *Create in Me a Clean Heart*, Paul Bouman (Concordia); 2-part (E)
Ps. 121 *I Will Lift Up My Eyes*, Lloyd Pfautsch (Hope); SATB (ME)

SUNDAY BETWEEN SEPTEMBER 4 AND SEPTEMBER 10 (Proper 18) (B)

Proverbs 2:1-8 An invitation to obey a tradition, and an assurance of the awaiting outcome for fulfilling the prerequisites. If you diligently look, search, dig for the hidden treasure of wisdom, then you will discover what it means to have reverential awe of the Lord. For it is Yahweh alone who gives such knowledge and who shields, protects, and guards those who walk the paths of Yahweh's *mishpat* (justice).

James 1:17-27 Hearing what we want to hear is nothing new—remember Adam and Eve, who heard what they wanted to hear and did what they wanted to do. So we too hear God's word yet do as we please. We see our broken lives reflected in life's mirror but deny or ignore or forget what we see and continue on our merry way. Now hear this! Blessed are those who peer into God's liberating word and then act upon it in word and deed.

Mark 7:31-37 Hearing and speaking are two interlinked gifts that depend upon each other. Now see a deaf man with a speech impediment. He can neither hear the word of God nor speak it. But Jesus miraculously frees this shackled man to hear and to speak. Now there's just no hiding this good news about Jesus Christ, right? Once again, God astonishingly finds a way to speak to us so we can hear and then speak the word.

Psalm 119:129-136
1. Metrical, *The Will of God to Mark My Way*, PP, p. 128
2. Metrical, *Oh, that the Lord Would Guide My Ways*, LBW 480, tune: *Her vil Ties*
3. Gregorian psalm tone, GP, Proper 12 A

Hymns for the Day	*HL*	*HB*	*WB*
Be Thou My Vision	325	303	304
O for a Thousand Tongues to Sing	199	141	493
Lamp of Our Feet, Whereby We Trace	–	254	–

Anthems for the Day
Prov. 2:1-8 *If You Receive My Words*, Knut Nystedt (Augsburg); SATTBB (MD)
James 1:17-27 *Every Good Gift and Every Perfect Gift*, Rudolf Moser (Concordia); SATB (ME)
Mark 7:31-37 *He Hath Done All Things Well*, Jan Bender (Concordia); SATB (ME)
Ps. 119:129-136 *Thy Word Is a Lantern Unto My Feet*, Leo Sowerby (H. W. Gray); SATB (M)

SUNDAY BETWEEN SEPTEMBER 11 AND SEPTEMBER 17 (Proper 19) (B)

Proverbs 22:1-2, 8-9 If you seek to stockpile riches, ignore the poor, and plant seeds of injustice, disaster will burst up like a death-dealing mushroom cloud. So open your eyes to the rich life in the service of the Lord and experience blessings rather than self-destruction. Share your "bread" with those who have less than you.

James 2:1-5, 8-10, 14-18 Sisters and brothers in Christ, we are charged to live according to the part of the Holiness Code as revealed in Leviticus 19:18. So we hardly conceive of ourselves as practicing partiality, discrimination, snobbishness, or any other degrading human "relationship," or lack thereof. Yet each of us can easily succumb to the irresistible temptation to favor the powerful, the rich, the influential and therefore immediately create unjust distinctions among social groups. So feed, clothe, and shelter all your neighbors as you care for your own family. In this way you will manifest the conjuncture of faith and actions.

Mark 8:27-38 Peter's confession about Christ is immediately corrected, followed by Jesus' first passion prediction: the Son of man must suffer, be rejected, be killed, and rise again. "Oh no," remonstrates Peter, "we don't want a convicted criminal, a societal failure for our leader. We'll never succeed if you do that." Surprisingly, Jesus censures Peter with harsh words, "If you want to play human games of power, success, and triumphalism, then you're demonically inspired. If anyone wants to follow me, then deny yourself and take up your cross. You must be willing to lose your life in this world."

Psalm 125
1. Gelineau, *Those Who Put Their Trust in the Lord*, GG, p. 35
2. Gregorian psalm tone, *GP*, Lent 4 B

Hymns for the Day	HL	HB	WB
Let There Be Light, Lord God of Hosts	402	480	451
Glorious Is Your Name, Most Holy	–	–	378
When I Survey the Wondrous Cross	152	198	635
Lift Up Our Hearts, O King of Kings	–	481	–

Anthems for the Day
Prov. 22:1-2, 8-9 *Poverty*, M. Lee Suitor (Hope); ATB (E)

James 2:1-5, 8-10, 14-18 *Neighbors*, arr. Austin Lovelace (H. W. Gray); SATB (E)

Mark 8:27-38 *Thou Art Jesus, Saviour and Lord*, Heinrich Schütz (Augsburg); SATB (M)

Ps. 125 *All Who with Heart Confiding*, Orlando di Lasso (Elkan-Vogel); SATB (M)

SUNDAY BETWEEN SEPTEMBER 18 AND SEPTEMBER 24 (Proper 20) (B)

Job 28:20-28 Job has been rebuking his friends for their claim to understand the ways of God. Who can know the ways of God? Can any creature see, touch, weigh, measure, test such omniscience? Yet humankind futilely searches for this inaccessible Wisdom in order to control creation and guarantee tomorrow today. Better that we have reverence for the Lord and turn away from evil—a wise thing to do—so the way may be paved for us to hear Yahweh's voice out of the whirlwind.

James 3:13-18 Watch people interact with each other and you'll see either earthly wisdom or wisdom "from above." Worldly wisdom prompts jealousy, bitterness, prejudice, covetousness, self-aggrandizement, and every other vile behavior that polarizes people and ignites demonic disorder. The wisdom of God is sown in peace so the harvest yields peaceful, compassionate, and merciful deeds. Be careful if you claim to be wise; your actions will reveal the source of your wisdom.

Mark 9:30-37 Jesus speaks again of impending suffering, death, and resurrection, but his disciples dream of personal grandeur. So Jesus places a child—the lowest ranking member on society's status list—among the disciples, saying, "True greatness is daring to become 'last of all and the servant of all.'"

Psalm 27:1-6
1. Psalm paraphrase, *God Is Our Strong Salvation*, James Montgomery, *HB* 347, tune: *Mein Leben*
2. Psalm paraphrase, *God Is Our Strong Salvation*, James Montgomery, *WB* 388, tune: Wedlock
3. Gelineau, *The Lord Is My Light and My Help*, GG, p. 59
4. Folk setting, *The Lord Is Near*, Michael Joncas, *OEW*, p. 66 (guitar chords included)

Hymns for the Day	HL	HB	WB
God Is Our Strong Salvation (tune: Aurelia)	92	347	388
Come, Labor On	366	287	–
Be Thou My Vision	–	303	304
O Grant Us Light, That We May Know (vs. 1, 2, tune: Tallis Canon)	210	335	–
Eternal God, Whose Power Upholds	–	485	357

Anthems for the Day
Job 28:20-28 *O Where Shall Wisdom Be Found*, W. Boyce (E. C. Schirmer); SATB (M)

James 3:13-18 *Eternal God, Whose Power Upholds* (WB 357)

Mark 9:30-37 *Let Them Come to Be Blessed*, J. Bert Carlson (AMSI); SATB (E)

Ps. 27:1-6 *The Lord Is My Light and My Strength*, Heinrich Schütz, arr. Wagner (Belwin-Mills); 2-part mixed with optional 2 trumpets (E)

SUNDAY BETWEEN SEPTEMBER 25 AND OCTOBER 1 (Proper 21) (B)

Job 42:1-6 For chapters on end, Job thought he had wisdom enough to criticize, rebuke, challenge, and, ultimately, condemn God's way of running creation. But the overwhelming effect of the theophanic whirlwind, in which he sees what God is really like, results in an immediate repudiation by Job of his former certainty. In dust and ashes, Job finds his rightful place and accepts his vocation as one of God's creatures.

James 4:13-17; 5:7-11 Preoccupation with tomorrow's profit, security, or happiness exposes a presumptuous way to live because your life, a fleeting mist, may vanish today. Try this: Allow God's providence to guide you today and tomorrow and the day after tomorrow. Be patient about the "coming of the Lord"—no need to blame your neighbors for its delay or for your unfulfilled desires. Sow seeds of patience and cultivate your firmness in the faith throughout the rainy seasons. The Lord, full of mercy and compassion, is near.

Mark 9:38-50 Who is marching with Jesus on the way to the cross? Not necessarily those in the visible pilgrimage, for there may be invisible, yet faithful, followers who are passing a cup of water from one neighbor's hand to the next. It is better to be partial, incomplete people than to cause others to sin annd fail to serve God. It is better to stumble through life broken and humble while serving others than to fulfill our own human potential.

Psalm 27:7-14
1. Gelineau, *The Lord Is My Light and My Help, GG*, p. 26
2. Gregorian psalm tone, *GP*, Lent 2 C

Hymns for the Day	HL	HB	WB
We Sing the Mighty Power of God	65	84	628
Sometimes a Light Surprises	296	418	–
I Bow My Forehead to the Dust	282	109	–
Thou Whose Purpose Is to Kindle			
(alt. tune: Austrian Hymn)	–	–	603
Where Charity and Love Prevail	–	–	641
God Is Working His Purpose Out	–	500	389

Anthems for the Day

Job 42:1-6 *Praise the Lord with Joyful Cry*, Lawrence Bartlett (*Ecumenical Praise*, no. 100, Agape); 2-part (E)

James 4:13-17; 5:7-11 *What God Ordains Is Just and Right*, J. S. Bach (*Eight Extended Bach Chorales*, p. 17, Hinshaw); SATB (M)

Mark 9:38-50 *Where Charity and Love Prevail* (WB 641)

Ps. 27:7-14 *Be Strong*, Roger Sherman (G.I.A.); 2-part (E)

SUNDAY BETWEEN OCTOBER 2 AND OCTOBER 8 (Proper 22) (B)

Genesis 2:18-24 The earthling whom Yahweh created from the earth wanders alone in the garden. "This is not good," says Yahweh. "I'll make a suitable companion." Plan A results in beasts of the field and birds of the air whom the earthling names, but none is a fitting companion. So Yahweh puts the earthling to sleep and tries Plan B. Yahweh's creative act produces a woman whom the earthling recognizes as an appropriate companion: "Bone of my bones and flesh of my flesh"—a covenant of trust, respect, *shalom*. The garden exists as a place for male-female union through covenant relationships.

Hebrews 1:1-4; 2:9-11 How do we hear God's word? Through prophets of old and, ultimately, through a Son whom God appointed as heir of all things and who upholds the world by his word. This Son reflects the nature of God and is superior to angels, for he achieved purification of sin. Yet he also reflects the nature of humankind, for he shared our flesh and blood and tasted suffering and death for us. He is the pioneer of salvation who united himself with all humankind.

Mark 10:2-16 Adversaries come to test Jesus on the legality of divorce; instead, they learn about marriage. According to the law books—starting with Moses—divorce is lawful. "But," teaches Jesus, "only as a concession to your stubbornness to accepting God's will for creation." God intended male and female to be joined together as one. But marital relationships do rupture in our broken world. May we all receive the kingdom of God as dependent children who rely on direction, love, forgiveness, and care from above.

Psalm 128
1. Gelineau, *O Blessed Are Those Who Fear the Lord*, GG, p. 16
2. Gregorian psalm tone, *GP*, Proper 22 B

Hymns for the Day	*HL*	*HB*	*WB*
From All That Dwell Below the Skies	388	33	373
For the Beauty of the Earth	71	2	372
Hope of the World	–	291	423
Jesus, Friend, So Kind and Gentle	–	451	–
O God, This Child from You Did Come	–	–	501

Anthems for the Day
Gen. 2:18-24 *O Father, All Creating*, Dietrich Buxtehude (*Wedding Blessings*, Concordia); unison or soprano solo with 2 violins (M)
Heb. 1:1-4; 2:9-11 *The Head That Once Was Crowned with Thorns* (*HB* 211)
Mark 10:2-16 *With Thankful Hearts*, Austin Lovelace (*Two Baptismal Responses*, Augsburg); unison (E)
Ps. 128 *How Blest Are They*, Richard Proulx (Augsburg); unison with flute (E)

SUNDAY BETWEEN OCTOBER 9 AND OCTOBER 15 (Proper 23) (B)

Genesis 3:8-19 The interminable quest of human beings' craving to control creation and, therefore, destiny. But even possessing "knowledge" in excess can neither lock in our future nor lock out our Creator. So in fear of having our real selves exposed by God or neighbors, we search frantically for places to hide—behind lies, laws, violence, flattery—and for people to blame for our predicament—from the weak to the mighty, enemies one and all. The risk in permitting people freedom to love as well as to disobey has resulted in broken relationships between God and humanity, and within humanity itself.

Hebrews 4:1-3, 9-13 If we do not listen to God's word, we shall experience the same fate as our Israelite ancestors who meandered in the wilderness for their remaining days. So heed God's word and strive eagerly to enter God's rest (salvation), for the entryway is still open. Be careful of rejecting or disobeying God's word, for it is two-edged and will expose you to the very depths of your soul.

Mark 10:17-30 What's the price of "eternal life"? Total self-giving to obeying the will of God as exemplified by the suffering messiah, Jesus Christ. Impossible for anyone to do that? Right! You cannot save yourself, but with God all things are possible. Simply respond to Jesus' call to follow him along the way of permanent servanthood, and you may discover that eternal life is God's free gift in Christ.

Psalm 90:1-12
1. Metrical, *Lord, Thou Hast Been Our Dwelling Place*, HB 88, tune: St. Catherine
2. Metrical, *O God, Our Help in Ages Past*, HB 111, tune: St. Anne
3. Gelineau, *You Turn Men Back Into Dust*, GG, p. 113
4. Gregorian psalm tone, *GP*, Proper 23 B
5. *PS*, p. 23

Hymns for the Day	HL	HB	WB
Our God, Our Help in Ages Past	77	111	549
Lord God of Hosts, Whose Purpose	368	288	460
Jesus, I My Cross Have Taken	274	279	–
Lord, Thou Hast Been Our Dwelling Place	–	88	–
God's Word Is like a Flaming Sword	–	–	405

Anthems for the Day
Gen. 3:8-19 *The Apple Tree*, K. Lee Scott (Hinshaw); SATB (E)
Heb. 4:1-3, 9-13 *God's Word Is like a Flaming Sword* (WB 405)
Mark 10:17-30 *Treasures in Heaven*, Joseph Clokey (Summy-Birchard); SATB (ME)
Ps. 90:1-12 *Lord, Thou Hast Been Our Refuge*, R. Vaughan Williams (G. Schirmer); SATB/SATB (D)

SUNDAY BETWEEN OCTOBER 16 AND OCTOBER 22 (Proper 24) (B)

Isaiah 53:7-12 The latter half of the fourth Song of the Servant of Yahweh. The submissive, innocent servant obediently suffers alone as "a lamb that is led to slaughter." With the sanction of the courts of the land, he is put to death because of our sins, and is buried with shame and disgrace. Yet this humiliated servant is the one whom Yahweh endorsed, vindicated, exalted, and restored. This blameless Suffering Servant accepted and "bore the sins of many" by interceding with his life and death for us.

Hebrews 4:14-16 We have a great high priest to represent us to God, a simple human being named Jesus, who lived in the same kind of power-hungry, achievement-oriented, complacently religious, me-first world. But this Jesus was sinless: he never turned away from God; he obeyed God's will even though constantly tempted to win the world for himself. So with Christ as our high priest, let us approach God with confidence, that we may receive mercy and grace.

Mark 10:35-45 A bald request for power. Did ambition ever reach so high? James and John petition Jesus for seats at the right and the left hand of power (seeking to cash in on their devotion to Jesus?). Asks Jesus, "Can you drink the cup I must drink, be baptized in the way I am baptized?" Sure, we can do that! "Then you will drink the cup and be baptized in the same manner as I, and you will endure rejection and suffering and death on the cross. You're going to have to give your whole life as a slave of all."

Psalm 35:17-28
None known to be available

Hymns for the Day	HL	HB	WB
You Servants of God, Your Master Proclaim	198	27	645
The Head That Once Was Crowned with Thorns	195	211	589
Son of God, Eternal Savior	393	–	573
How Sweet the Name of Jesus Sounds (v. 3)	310	130	–
The Lord Ascendeth Up on High	–	212	–

Anthems for the Day
Isa. 53:7-12 *He Opened Not His Mouth,* Joseph Roff (Concordia); SATB (ME)
Heb. 4:14-16 *Seeing That We Have a Great High Priest,* Robert J. Powell (Abingdon); SAB (ME)
Mark 10:35-45 *Whoever Would Be Great Among You,* Ronald A. Nelson (Augsburg); SAB (E)
Ps. 35:17-28 No choral setting suggested

SUNDAY BETWEEN OCTOBER 23 AND OCTOBER 29 (Proper 25) (B)

Jeremiah 31:7-9 Sing and shout for joy because Yahweh has graciously deliv ered Israel from bondage. The Lord will gather his people (including those dependent upon others) from the ends of the earth, and will shepherd them to flowing streams of water and reveal a father's love for his firstborn.

Hebrews 5:1-6 We yearn for someone powerful enough to cure the ills of our world; to redirect our self-destructive urges; to forgive, renew, and comfort us—someone to represent us before God and make God care. Haven't we heard that God already has chosen someone to represent our world, someone weak enough so as to deal gently with the ignorant and the wayward? Someone who is human—one of us—who fills none of our expectations for a superhero? Someone dressed in everyday clothes and is himself victimized by the world? Yet this person represents the world before God and offers his whole life to God for us. Of course, that's what he was called to do as a great high priest—offer gifts and sacrifices on behalf of humankind's sins. His name: Jesus, Son of God.

Mark 10:46-52 A blind beggar, who doesn't look, walk, act, talk, much less see the way we do, sits by the roadside and dares to call for mercy from the "Son of David." Many shun or even rebuke him. But Jesus asks him, "What do you want me to do for you?" "Let me receive my sight," pleads Bartimaeus. "Your faith has made you well," says Jesus. Though Jesus' followers remain blind to his mission, this blind beggar sees well enough to respond to Jesus' call and follow him "on the way."

Psalm 126
1. Gregorian psalm tone, *GP*, Lent 5 C

Hymns for the Day	HL	HB	WB
If You Will Only Let God Guide You	105	344	431
Father Eternal, Ruler of Creation	–	486	362
Father, We Greet You	–	285	364
Father, Whose Will Is Life and Good	–	309	368
God Is Love: Let Heaven Adore Him	–	–	386
The Lord Ascendeth Up on High	–	212	–

Anthems for the Day
Jer. 31:7-9 *By the Springs of Water*, Cecil Effinger (Augsburg); SATB (M)
Heb. 5:1-6 *O Most Merciful*, Münster Gesangbuch, 1677 (Hinshaw); SATB (ME)
Mark 10:46-52 *Thine Arm, O Lord, in Days of Old* (HB 179)
Ps. 126 *He Who with Weeping Soweth*, H. Schütz–R. Shaw (Lawson-Gould); SSATB (MD)

SUNDAY BETWEEN OCTOBER 30 AND NOVEMBER 5 (Proper 26) (B)

Deuteronomy 6:1-9 This daily living confession prayed by Jews announces that Yahweh is one and they shall love and serve Yahweh alone. "Hear, O Israel": Remember these words and let your love of God permeate your whole life.

Hebrews 7:23-28 There is but one (not many) permanent, unchanging, perpetual, eternal officeholder as high priest. His work, therefore, continues today and tomorrow and tomorrow as he constantly intercedes, pleads, and mediates for those who draw near to God. Jesus Christ is the holy, blameless, unstained One who offered one complete, finished, final sacrifice of his life, once for all. In Christ, God has appointed one who has been made perfect forever; in this One alone we can trust.

Mark 12:28b-34 Jesus answers a trick question about the "greatest commandment" by quoting Deuteronomy 6:4: "Love God with all your heart, soul, mind, and strength." Then Jesus unexpectedly adds Leviticus 19:18: "Love your neighbors as your own kin." You cannot love God without loving your neighbor, nor vice versa. "Right you are!" affirms a wise scribe. "Your call to such love far outweighs all else we do." Replies Jesus, "You are not far from the kingdom of God."

Psalm 119:33-48
1. Metrical psalm, *How Shall the Young Direct Their Way?*, from *The Psalter*, 1912, *HB* 258, tune: Preston (Doane)
2. Gregorian psalm tone, *GP*, Proper 18 A

Hymns for the Day	HL	HB	WB
Come, You People, Rise and Sing	–	39	345
The God of Abraham Praise	8	89	587
How Sweet the Name of Jesus Sounds	310	130	–
How Shall the Young Direct Their Way? (alt. tune: Duke Street)	–	258	–

Anthems for the Day
Deut. 6:1-9 *Trust in the Lord*, Jean Berger (Augsburg); SATB (M)
Heb. 7:23-28 *I Will Not Leave You Comfortless*, Ron Nelson (*Four Anthems for Young Choirs*, no. 2, Boosey & Hawkes); unison (E)
Mark 12:28b-34 *The Great Commandment*, Jane Marshall (Broadman); unison (E)
Ps. 119:33-48 *Teach Me, O Lord*, William Byrd (Oxford); SAATB (M)

SUNDAY BETWEEN NOVEMBER 6 AND NOVEMBER 12 (Proper 27) (B)

1 Kings 17:8-16 In a time of dried-up brooks and faith, death-dealing famine, and withering trust and confidence in the Lord, Yahweh sends the prophet Elijah to the home of a poor foreign widow for food. "Feed me," importunes Elijah. "Not with a handful of flour and a vial of oil," responds the widow; "barely enough for me and my son to prepare one last meal before we starve." "Fear not!" counters Elijah. And miraculously the widow trusts this word and obediently risks all she has.

Hebrews 9:24-28 Christ, the eternal high priest, solemnly entered the heavenly, invisible, spiritual sanctuary (not the earthbound temple) only one time and offered his blood, once for all, to put away the sins of many. In Christ, a new age has begun through his act of total self-giving. He will appear again to save those who eagerly await him.

Mark 12:38-44 Jesus boldly cites the scribes as hypocrites—a dirty word in any age—and exposes their greed. Unlike the scribes who calculate their giving according to percentages, a poor widow simply gives her whole life to God in the form of two small coins. She is the model of genuine piety we are called to emulate.

Psalm 146
1. Metrical, *O Praise the Lord, My Soul!*, *MP&E*, p. 39, tune: St. Thomas (A. Williams)
2. Metrical, *Praise We Our Maker While We've Breath*, *WB* 558, tune: Old 113th
3. Metrical (Folk), *Lord, Come and Save Us*, *OEW*, p. 32, music by Michael Joncas
4. Gelineau, *The Lord Is Kind and Full of Compassion*, *GG*, p. 54
5. Gregorian psalm tone, *GP*, Proper 27 B
6. *PS*, p. 36

Hymns for the Day

	HL	HB	WB
Now Thank We All Our God	459	9	481
Praise We Our Maker While We've Breath	–	–	558
Love Divine, All Loves Excelling	308	399	471
Break Forth, O Living Light of God	–	–	316

Anthems for the Day
1 Kings 17:8-16 *O Lord of Life, to Thee We Lift* (*HB* 256)
Heb. 9:24-28 *All for Love*, Robert Young (C. Fischer); SATB (M)
Mark 12:38-44 *We Would Offer Thee This Day*, Jane Marshall (Sacred Music); SATB (M)
Ps. 146 *A Song of Hope*, Raymond Haan (AMSI); unison (E)

SUNDAY BETWEEN NOVEMBER 13 AND NOVEMBER 19 (Proper 28) (B)

Daniel 7:9-14 A vision of the eternal court: The white-haired Ancient of Days takes a seat on the wheeled, fiery throne, surrounded by countless hosts who serve him, and the "books" are opened—court is in session. The divine sentence: the fourth beast is slain and burned in fire; the first three beasts are removed from power but permitted to live a bit longer. And then the Ancient of Days bestowed upon "one like a son of man" who came with the clouds of heaven, dominion over a kingdom that shall never be destroyed. All should serve this one.

Hebrews 10:11-18 With the effective once-for-all self-sacrifice by Christ, the new covenant of forgiveness displaced the old covenant of ineffective repeated sacrifices. Then, having completed the single perfect sacrifice that did away with sin, Christ sat down and rested while awaiting the end when his enemies would serve as his footstool. The fulfillment of Jeremiah 31:33-34 abrogates the need for any further sacrifices, since God will remember their sin no more.

Mark 13:24-32 Good news! God's purposes revealed in the "Son of man" are coming to fulfillment. Scattered wars and catastrophes and persecutions do not signify the end of our tired world. No, when the Son of man comes the whole cosmos will tumble: sun, moon, stars, everything. We will know the time is near when the fig tree's leaves blossom, but only God knows the precise day and hour when the new world will shatter our twelve-month perpetual calendars.

Psalm 145:8-13
1. Metrical, *O Lord, Thou Art My God and King*, HB 5, tune: Duke Street
2. Gelineau, *I Will Give You Glory, O God My King*, GG, p. 131
3. Gregorian psalm tone, *GP*, Proper 9 A

Hymns for the Day	HL	HB	WB
O Worship the King	2	26	533
O Where Are Kings and Empires Now	334	431	530
Come, Thou Almighty King	52	244	343
Lo! He Comes with Clouds Descending	184	234	–

Anthems for the Day
Dan. 7:9-14 *Lo, in the Time Appointed*, Healey Willan (Oxford); SATB (M)
Heb. 10:11-18 *The New Covenant*, David York (Presser); SATB, tenor solo (MD)
Mark 13:24-32 *The King Shall Come*, arr. John Ness Beck (*Two Carols for Advent*, Beckenhorst); SATB (E)
Ps. 145:8-13 *The Lord Is Gracious*, Joseph Roff (Augsburg); SATB (M)

CHRIST THE KING
[Sunday Between November 20 and November 26]
(Proper 29) (B)

Jeremiah 23:1-6 Shepherds (rulers) who neglect their flocks and allow them to scatter over the land will be dealt with harshly by Yahweh. You can count on it! In fact, Yahweh promises to replace such unjust leaders with shepherds who truly care for Yahweh's people. Behold, the days are coming when Yahweh will raise up "a righteous Branch" from David's line who will rule with justice and righteousness.

Revelation 1:4b-8 The prophet John sends greetings to the seven churches: "Remember to whom you belong—not to the Caesars of this world, but solely to Christ. Remember by whose grace and peace you live—not by the Caesars' mercy, but only by God's. Yes, the claims about Christ—he reliably testified that God's promises will be fulfilled, he inaugurated a new age, he rules as the King of kings—all seem preposterous, but one day the whole world will recognize that he is the one who loves us, frees us from our sins, and makes us priests. To him be glory and power, forever."

John 18:33-37 Political and religious leaders obsessed with finding a king who fits their definition cannot hear the truth to which Jesus bears witness. Everyone who listens to his voice will hear the truth. Those possessed by the frenzy to acquire ephemeral, earthly power will be threatened by the truth to which Jesus bears witness.

Psalm 93
1. Metrical, *God, the Lord, a King Remaineth*, HB 90, tune: Bryn Calfaria
2. Metrical, *God, the Lord, Is King For Ever, MP&E*, p. 201, tune: Lauda anima
3. Gelineau, *The Lord Is King, GG*, p. 137
4. Gregorian psalm tone, *GP*, Proper 29 B

Hymns for the Day	HL	HB	WB
Ancient of Days	58	246	297
Hail to the Lord's Anointed	111	146	–
At the Name of Jesus	–	143	303
Of the Father's Love Begotten	–	7	534
God, the Lord, a King Remaineth	61	90	403

Anthems for the Day
Jer. 23:1-6 *Behold, a Branch Is Growing*, Edgar Aufdemberge (Concordia); SAB (ME)
Rev. 1:4b-8 *Unto Him That Loved Us*, R. Vaughan Williams (*Morning Star Choir Book*, Book 1); unison (E)
John 18:33-37 *Arise, the Kingdom Is at Hand*, Gilbert Martin (Flammer); SATB or 2-part (E)
Ps. 93 *The Lord Reigneth*, Paul Manz (Augsburg); SATB (M)

ALL SAINTS' DAY
[November 1 or First Sunday in November] (B)

Revelation 21:1-6a A vision of a new heaven and a new earth. The new Jerusalem descends from God and joins the transformed earth where chaotic waters, tears, death, mourning, crying have all disappeared. Human beings will see God and live in holy fellowship together. Shouts the great voice from the throne, "I make all things new."

Colossians 1:9-14 Intercessory prayers are offered for the community of faith to be filled with the gifts of the knowledge of God's will, the wisdom and understanding wrought by the Spirit, and strength, power, endurance, and patience so they will conduct themselves in a manner pleasing to God. Then the community is exhorted to offer joyful thanks to God for having made them fit to be transferred from the realm of darkness to the kingdom of light made known in Jesus Christ. God authorized them to participate in the deliverance and redemption in Christ; therefore, praise God with thanksgiving.

John 11:32-44 Jesus risks his life in traveling to Bethany to respond to Mary and Martha's call to visit his sick (and now dead) friend Lazarus. Neither Lazarus nor we can raise ourselves out of our own tomb, but when God in Christ sees the death-dealing predicament of our world, he weeps and then calls Lazarus and us out of our tomb, inviting us to share in his victory over death so that we can experience the freedom of new life in Christ.

Psalm 24:1-6
1. Metrical, *The Earth, with All That Dwell Therein*, HB 38, tune: Boardman
2. Gelineau, *The Lord's Is the Earth and Its Fullness*, GG, p. 167
3. Gregorian psalm tone, *GP*, Advent 4 A
4. *PS*, p. 16

Hymns for the Day	*HL*	*HB*	*WB*
For All the Saints	429	425	369
Ye Watchers and Ye Holy Ones	–	34	–
Father, We Praise You	–	43	365
O Lord of Life, Where'er They Be	–	–	513

Anthems for the Day
Rev. 21:1-6a *I Saw a New Heaven and a New Earth*, A. Eugene Ellsworth (Kjos); SATB, 2 trumpets (MD)
Col. 1:9-14 *We Give Thanks*, Jack C. Goode (Abingdon); unison (E)
John 11:32-44 *The Raising of Lazarus*, Adrian Willaert (Ricordi); SATB (M)
Ps. 24:1-6 *The Earth Is the Lord's*, Hank Beebe (C. Fischer); unison (E)

THANKSGIVING DAY (B)*

Joel 2:21-27 The quintessential, purest, most perfect evangelical word everyone wants to hear: "Fear not!" But note that such a word follows verses 1-11, which say, "Fear, fear, fear!" Then, in verse 18, Yahweh notices Israel—"these are my very own people"—and has pity on them. Now there is talk of a new creation. Early rain, grain, wine, oil, eat plenty, be satisfied, never again be put to shame, and you will know that I, Yahweh, am in the midst of you.

1 Timothy 2:1-7 Lift up your hands and hearts and offer intercessions for all people, friends and enemies alike. Pray especially for those with political power, for they are charged with the responsibility of securing and maintaining an orderly life. They need God's word in order to work for God's truth and justice and peace. And above all, remember that there is only one mediator who brings us together and to whom we owe our total allegiance and trust: Christ, who gave himself as a ransom for all.

Matthew 6:25-33 A rigorous text that defies circumvention. Why are you so driven to scramble up the social ladder of success; so wretchedly uptight over accumulating cash, cash, and more cash; so obsessed with getting ahead in life? Why? Surely life is worth more than all these ephemeral pleasures combined. Do you think you can ward off death or buy more life? Stop for a moment and behold how creation simply lives by the grace of God. Now try steering your fretful energy into serving God by serving neighbors. Seek first the kingdom of God—feed the hungry, clothe the naked, shelter the homeless—and you may discover that life is richer when it is leaner.

Psalm 126
1. Gregorian psalm tone, *GP*, Lent 5C

Hymns for the Day	HL	HB	WB
Come, You Thankful People, Come	460	525	346
Lord, by Whose Breath All Souls and Seeds	–	–	457
Sing to the Lord of Harvest	–	–	569
All Things Bright and Beautiful	–	456	–
Sometimes a Light Surprises	296	418	–

Anthems for the Day
Joel 2:21-27 *Fear Not, O Land; Be Glad and Rejoice*, John Goss (G. Schirmer); SATB (M)
1 Tim. 2:1-7 *A Song of Praise and Thanksgiving*, Allen Pote (Hinshaw); 2-part (E)
Matt. 6:25-33 *Sometimes a Light Surprises*, Jane Marshall (*Ecumenical Praise*, no. 42, Agape); unison (E)
Ps. 126 *When the Lord Turned Again*, William Billings (Concordia); SATB (ME)

---

*NOTE: Readings for Thanksgiving Day are not strictly tied to Year A, B, or C.

FIRST SUNDAY OF ADVENT (C)

Jeremiah 33:14-16 Behold, the days are coming when Yahweh will raise up "a righteous Branch" from David's line who will rule with justice and righteousness (cf. Jer. 23:5-6). In the midst of disorder, anguish, desolation, and uncertainty, Yahweh proclaims, "I will fulfill my promise to raise up the legitimate successor to the throne, whose name will be 'The Lord is our righteousness.' "

1 Thessalonians 3:9-13 For your growth in faith and love, writes Paul, I thank God with great joy. Also, I continually pray that God will soon join us together and that, until such time, God will increase our love for one another, as well as for all God's children. In this way we shall be strengthened for the ultimate test at the Parousia (coming) of our Lord Jesus.

Luke 21:25-36 A Chicken Little picture of the end of the world: signs in sun and moon and stars, distress of nations, people fainting, and the Son of man coming. Listen for the word of God in these signs. What's arriving, judgment? No, mercy! So raise your heads, look up and see that your redemption is near. You don't know when, but watch, pray, prepare, live attentively, gladly expecting the coming of the Lord.

Psalm 25:1-10
1. Metrical, *Grace and Truth Shall Mark the Way*, HB 372, tune: Holley
2. Gelineau, *Lord, Make Me Know Your Ways*, GG, p. 22
3. Taizé, *Miserere mei*, MFT, p. 18

Hymns for the Day	*HL*	*HB*	*WB*
Hail to the Lord's Anointed	111	146	–
Savior of the Nations, Come	–	–	565
Grace and Truth Shall Mark the Way	–	372	–
Wake, Awake, for Night Is Flying	–	–	614
The King Shall Come When Morning Dawns	187	232	–
O Where Are Kings and Empires Now	334	431	530

Anthems for the Day
Jer. 33:14-16 *O Word That Goest Forth on High*, Gerald Near (H. W. Gray); SATB (MD)
1 Thess. 3:9-13 *E'en So, Lord Jesus, Quickly Come*, Paul Manz (Concordia); SATB (M)
Luke 21:25-36 *And There Will Be Signs*, Stephen Chatman (*Ecumenical Praise*, no. 15, Agape); 2-part (M)
Ps. 25:1-10 *Show Me Thy Ways*, Walter Pelz (Augsburg); SATB, guitar, oboe (ME)

SECOND SUNDAY OF ADVENT (C)

Malachi 3:1-4 Behold, the Day of Yahweh is coming and will be heralded by a messenger (angel of the Lord? Elijah the prophet? John the Baptist?). This messenger will prepare the way for Yahweh's return to his Temple, from where swift judgment on wrongdoers will be executed. The priesthood and Temple will be purified in a refiner's fire so that acceptable offerings may be made to the Lord.

Philippians 1:3-11 Paul expresses his unbounded joy for the ongoing witness of the Philippian community of faith and thanks God for their partnership with him in the work of the gospel. Further, Paul offers intercessory prayer for their continued growth in *agape* (love), which will lead to knowledge and discernment of human needs to which they can respond. In this manner, they will serve as sign doers of the day of Christ—through whom God is working—and be filled with "the fruits of righteousness."

Luke 3:1-6 During the reign of a powerful Caesar, the word of God comes to John, son of Zechariah, in the wilderness. Result: John cries out, "Repent! Turn around! Orient yourself to God's future. Place your hope not in the powers of this world but in the One who will flatten mountains and raise up valleys, straighten the crooked, and smooth the rough-hewn (in fulfillment of Isaiah 40:3-5)." The whole Bible says this, cover to cover, but John urgently preaches "a baptism of repentance for the forgiveness of sins" because of the imminent arrival of the Messiah, when "all flesh shall see the salvation of God."

Psalm 126
1. Gregorian psalm tone, *GP*, Lent 5 C

Hymns for the Day	HL	HB	WB
God Himself Is with Us	51	13	384
Hark, What a Sound	110	150	–
Come, Thou Long-expected Jesus	113	151	342
The Race That Long in Darkness Pined	–	153	–
Heralds of Christ	–	498	416

Anthems for the Day
Mal. 3:1-4 *Promise*, Leland B. Sateren (*The Redeemer*, Schmitt, Hall & McCreary); SATB (M)
Phil. 1:3-11 *He Which Hath Begun a Good Work in You*, Jan Bender (Concordia); SAB (E)
Luke 3:1-6 *Festive Procession*, Paul Christiansen (Schmitt, Hall & McCreary); SATB (ME)
Advent Message, Martin How (Boosey & Hawkes); variable voicing (E)
Ps. 126 *The Lord Has Done Great Things for Them*, Barry Bobb (Concordia); unison or SATB, congregation (E)

THIRD SUNDAY OF ADVENT (C)

Zephaniah 3:14-20 A psalm of celebration sung by the faithful remnant: Sing, shout, rejoice, and exult, O Israel, because Yahweh has taken away, has cast out the menacing threat, and is "in your midst" reigning as King. Fear not! Yahweh, your God, will renew you. Promises Yahweh, "I will transform the shame of the lame and the outcast into praise, and I will bring you home."

Philippians 4:4-9 The Philippians are told, rejoice and demonstrate to the world gentleness and forbearance. Why? Because the Lord is at hand and the peace of God will guard your hearts and minds from any new threats. So no need to fret over your own well-being: forsake your Sisyphus-like drivenness to secure tomorrow today, and consider practicing the virtues embraced by Paul: truth, honor, justice, purity, agreeableness, excellence, and whatever is praiseworthy.

Luke 3:7-18 See the deluge of people stream toward John, the voice in the wilderness, standing knee-deep in the muddy Jordan and greeting the baptism seekers with these words: "You snakes! Who told you to flee here so you could smugly receive another ritual cleansing while clutching your social status card? Turn away from yourselves and face God." "How?" ask the people. "Share your food and clothing with less fortunate neighbors, and dispose of your greedy, cheating, and intimidating ways." Hearing such words, the people inquire of John, "Are you the Christ?" "No," replies John, "I baptize only with water, but the One who is to come will baptize with the Holy Spirit and with fire, and will winnow the wheat from the chaff."

Isaiah 12:2-6 (Song of Thanksgiving)
None known to be available

Hymns for the Day	HL	HB	WB
The Race That Long in Darkness Pined	–	153	–
Lift Up Your Heads	114	152	454
Come, You Thankful People, Come	460	525	346
Rejoice, the Lord Is King	193	140	562
O for a Thousand Tongues to Sing	199	141	493

Anthems for the Day
Zeph. 3:14-20 *Daughter of Zion*, Joseph Clokey (Presser); SATB (E)
Phil. 4:4-9 *Rejoice in the Lord Always*, Anon., arr. Jeffrey Rickard (Augsburg); SATB (M)
Luke 3:7-18 *Thou Shalt Know Him*, Austin Lovelace (AMSI); SATB (M)
Isa. 12:2-6 *The First Song of Isaiah*, Erik Routley (Hinshaw); unison, congregation (E)

FOURTH SUNDAY OF ADVENT (C)

Micah 5:2-5a Out of an obscure, insignificant clan shall come a future ruler of Israel with genealogical links to a past shepherd king. At the advent of this new ruler, Yahweh promises to start afresh with Israel by returning the remnant home. Then the new shepherd ruler will feed his flock by relying on the strength, majesty, and name of Yahweh. Since the greatness of this ruler will be acknowledged by all, Yahweh's people shall dwell in safety.

Hebrews 10:5-10 The preexistent Christ speaks the words of Psalm 40:6-8 in order to define the purpose of his incarnation. No longer will the old Levitical sacrifices be either necessary or efficacious, for the ultimate sacrifice of Christ's body upon the cross will establish the new covenant. The justification for the incarnation is that Christ will take a human body in order to offer this perfect sacrifice in obedience to the will of God.

Luke 1:39-55 The grand conclusion to Luke's two annunciation stories of John and Jesus. A young single peasant of low estate from Nazareth, a slave of the Lord, is favored by God. Mary's whole being, soul and spirit, offers a canticle of praise to God, for "he has done great things for me, and holy is his name." Mary's words of thanksgiving, recited by her people for centuries (cf. 1 Sam. 2:1-10), testify to her faith in the sovereign God.

Psalm 80:1-7
1. Gelineau, *O Shepherd of Israel, 30P&2C*, p. 23
2. Gregorian psalm tone, *GP*, Advent 1 B

Hymns for the Day	HL	HB	WB
O Come, O Come, Emmanuel	108	147	489
O Little Town of Bethlehem	121	171	511
Come, Thou Long-expected Jesus	113	151	342
Lord God of Hosts, Whose Purpose	368	288	460
Born in the Night, Mary's Child	–	–	312
Come, My Soul, You Must Be Waking	487	44	337

Anthems for the Day
Micah 5:2-5a *O Bethlehem*, Basque Carol, arr. E. Poston (*Penguin Book of Christmas Carols*, Penguin Books); SATB (ME)
Heb. 10:5-10 *The Only Son from Heaven*, J. S. Bach (*Cantata 22*, in *Third Morning Star Choir Book*, Concordia); SATB (E)
Luke 1:39-55 *Magnificat in G*, C. V. Stanford (Stainer & Bell); SATB, soprano solo (MD)
Ps. 80:1-7 *Hear, Thou Shepherd of Israel*, John C. Beckwith (*Sing Joyfully*, vol. 2, Walton); 2-part (E)

CHRISTMAS/EVE DAY (ABC)

Isaiah 9:2-7 Darkness reigns everywhere, yet people have seen a great light: the presence of God. All rejoice, as with joy at the harvest, for the rule of darkness will be lifted. A child shall reign as God's representative on earth, and God's light shall shine without end.

Titus 2:11-14 Jesus, the grace of God, has appeared for the salvation of all and taught us a new way of life. Because we now live in the light of his second coming, we can celebrate his first coming when he gave himself for us and set us free from all wickedness.

Luke 2:1-20 The birth of Jesus in the "city of David," Bethlehem, and the angelic proclamation to shepherds in the same area where David was a shepherd. *Gloria in excelsis!* The shepherds go to Bethlehem. As they return to their fields, they glorify and praise God "for all they had heard and seen." Their listeners are astonished. Mary treasures all these things.

Psalm 96
1. Metrical psalm, *O Sing a New Song to the Lord,* from the *Scottish Psalter,* 1650, *HB* 37, *WB* 525, tune: Song 67
2. Free paraphrase, *Earth and All Stars,* Herbert Brokering, *WB* 354, tune: Earth and All Stars
3. Gelineau, *O Sing a New Song to the Lord, GG,* p. 126
4. Gregorian psalm tone, *GP,* Christmas Day ABC
5. Anglican chant, *O Come, Let Us Sing,* William Boyce, *HB* 586
6. *PS,* p. 28

Hymns for the Day	HL	HB	WB
The Race That Long in Darkness Pined	–	153	–
It Came Upon the Midnight Clear	127	160	438
To Thee with Joy I Sing	–	–	610
Christ Is the World's True Light	–	492	326
While Shepherds Watched Their Flocks	120	169	643
All My Heart This Night Rejoices	125	172	287
Silent Night	132	154	567
Let All Mortal Flesh (Communion)	112	148	449

Anthems for the Day
Isa. 9:2-7 *Break Forth, O Beauteous Heavenly Light,* J. S. Bach (*Christmas Oratorio,* E. C. Schirmer or many other editions); SATB (E)
Titus 2:11-14 *Salvation Is Created,* Paul Tschesnokoff, arr. Becker (G.I.A.); SATTBB (M)
Luke 2:1-20 *As on the Night,* Orlando Gibbons (Oxford); SATB (ME)
Ps. 96 *O Sing Unto the Lord a New Song,* Peter Aston (Hinshaw); SATB (M)

CHRISTMAS DAY: ADDITIONAL LECTIONS 1
(ABC)

Isaiah 62:6-7, 10-12 Remind Yahweh of his promises and plead unceasingly for their fulfillment. Prepare the way, clear it of any obstacles, for Yahweh keeps his promises. "Behold, your salvation comes."

Titus 3:4-7 God our Savior has appeared and has saved us by God's mercy (and not because of any good deeds on our part). Through Jesus Christ our Savior, God has poured out the Holy Spirit on us and transformed us and given us new life in the waters of baptism.

Luke 2:8-20 Jesus is born in the "city of David," Bethlehem, and the angels tell the shepherds in the same area where David was a shepherd. *Gloria in excelsis!* The shepherds go to Bethlehem. As they return to their fields, they glorify and praise God "for all they had heard and seen." Their listeners are astonished. Mary treasures all these things.

Psalm 97
1. Metrical psalm, *The Lord Is King!*, Christopher Idle, *PP*, no. 112, contemporary musical setting by Norman Warren
2. Gelineau, *The Lord Is King, GG*, p. 163
3. Gregorian psalm tone, *GP*, Christmas Day 2 ABC

Hymns for the Day	HL	HB	WB
Joy to the World!	122	161	444
Watchman, Tell Us of the Night	109	149	617
Lo, How a Rose E'er Blooming	–	162	455
Angels We Have Heard on High	–	158	299
On This Day Earth Shall Ring	–	–	538
To Abraham the Promise Came	–	–	608

Anthems for the Day
Isa. 62:6-7, 10-12 *Today Is Salvation Come*, Raymond Haan (G.I.A.); SATB, 4 handbells (E)
Titus 3:4-7 *Let All Together Praise Our God*, setting by Johann Schein (*Church Choir Book*, vol. 2, Concordia); 2-part, SATB (ME)
    Come, Love We God, Daniel Pinkham (E. C. Schirmer); SATB (MD)
Luke 2:8-20 *On Christmas Night All Christians Sing*, Sussex Carol, James Melby (Concordia); SATB, bells (ME)
    Hear the Joyful News This Day, J. S. Bach (*Cantata 141*, Galaxy); SATB (M)
Ps. 97 *Psalm 97*, Heinrich Schütz (Mercury); SATB (M)

CHRISTMAS DAY: ADDITIONAL LECTIONS 2
(ABC)

Isaiah 52:7-10 A messenger is coming across the mountains. Ascending and descending from one hill to the next, he joyously cries out, "Your God reigns!" Let everyone sing together of the "salvation of God."

Hebrews 1:1-12 God has spoken to us through the prophets; now God speaks uniquely to us through the Son, the descending-ascending savior of all. The true image of God is Christ, whose throne is forever and ever. He is of the same flesh and blood as we are, yet greater than all the angels. God's Son is the risen exalted Christ.

John 1:1-14 "In the beginning was the Word, and the Word was with God." All things were made through the Word, and in the Word were life and light. The Word came into the world and to God's own people, but the world rejected the Word as did God's own people. Yet those who received and believed in the Word were given power to announce and to bear witness, as John (the Baptizer) did, to the coming of the Word among us, full of grace and truth.

Psalm 98
1. Metrical psalm, *New Songs of Celebration Render*, Erik Routley, *SOT&P*, p. 2, tune: *Rendez à Dieu*
2. Free paraphrase, *Sing a New Song to the Lord*, Timothy Dudley-Smith, *WII*, p. 245, tune: *Cantate Domino* by David G. Wilson, fresh, contemporary setting
3. Gelineau, *Sing a New Song to the Lord*, *GG*, p. 15
4. Gregorian psalm tone, *GP*, Christmas Day 3 ABC

Hymns for the Day	*HL*	*HB*	*WB*
O Come, All Ye Faithful	116	170	486
Of the Father's Love Begotten	–	7	534
Joy to the World!	122	161	444
O Splendor of God's Glory Bright	32	46	529
Hark! the Herald Angels Sing	117	163	411
Comfort, Comfort You My People	–	–	347

Anthems for the Day
Isa. 52:7-10 *How Beautiful Upon the Mountains*, Daniel Moe (Presser); SAB (M)
Heb. 1:1-12 *Of the Father's Love Begotten*, arr. John Erickson (Choristers Guild); unison, handbells (E)
John 1:1-14 *The Glory of the Father*, Egil Hovland (Walton); SATB (ME)
Ps. 98 *Sing to the Lord a New Song*, Donald Busarow (Augsburg); SATB, congregation, brass (ME)

FIRST SUNDAY AFTER CHRISTMAS (C)

1 Samuel 2:18-20, 26 Every year Hannah weaves a little robe for her son Samuel (who faithfully serves Yahweh at the sanctuary in Shiloh) and personally delivers it to her son when she and her husband, Elkanah, offer their annual sacrifice. Then Eli, the high priest, blesses Elkanah and Hannah, petitioning Yahweh to repay them with seed for children because of the gift of their son Samuel to Yahweh's service. And Samuel continues to grow in stature and in favor with Yahweh and with humankind.

Colossians 3:12-17 You are the chosen, holy, beloved people of God. So put on the freely given garments Christ has offered you and model them to the world. Array yourselves with his example of "compassion, kindness, lowliness, meekness, and patience"—clothe yourselves with concern first for others' needs. Be tolerant with one another, forgive one another as Christ has forgiven you, and wrap yourselves with love which binds you together. Let the peace of Christ and Christ's word govern all you do and say, remembering always to be thankful for what God in Christ has done for you.

Luke 2:41-52 At Passover time, Mary and Joseph take their son Jesus to Jerusalem, where they lose him among the crowd. Their anxious search finds their son in the Temple, listening and asking questions and amazing all with his answers. "Why did you seek all over for me?" queries Jesus. "Didn't you know I must be here, concerned about my Father's things?" Parents simply do not understand such fanciful statements by their children—and Mary and Joseph are no exception. But Jesus goes with them and is "obedient to them; and his mother kept all these things in her heart." And Jesus grew in "wisdom and in stature, and in favor with God and humankind."

Psalm 111
1. Gregorian psalm tone, *GP*, Epiphany 4 B
2. Cantillation (also tones are given for a simpler rendition), Arlo Duba, unpublished

Hymns for the Day	*HL*	*HB*	*WB*
O Sing a Song of Bethlehem	138	177	526
Thou Didst Leave Thy Throne	231	184	–
Ah, Dearest Jesus, Holy Child	118	173	179
Once in Royal David's City	454	462	539
How Dear to Me, O Lord of Hosts	–	440	–
When Stephen, Full of Power and Grace	–	–	638

Anthems for the Day
1 Sam. 2:18-20, 26 *Be Strong in the Lord*, Thomas Matthews (Fitzsimons); SATB (M)
Col. 3:12-17 *You Are the People of God*, Gerhardt Becker (Concordia); unison (E)
Luke 2:41-52 *Son, Why Have You Treated Us So?*, Jan Bender (Concordia); 2-part (E)
Ps. 111 *My Heart Is Full Today*, Richard Proulx (Augsburg); 2-part, handbells (E)

THE NAME OF JESUS [January 1] (ABC)

Numbers 6:22-27 The well-known Aaronic blessing: three simple poetic lines, each petitioning Yahweh to move toward his people through the presence of his protection, favor, and peace. And where the name of Yahweh is put upon his people, he is present in blessing.

Galatians 4:4-7 When God decided the right time had come, he sent his Son, fully human, to release all those under the law so they might be God's children. Then God sent the Spirit of his Son who empowered these adopted children to name God as *"Abba*, Father."

or **Philippians 2:9-13** Part of a primitive Christological hymn in which the name bestowed by God upon Jesus is the name "Lord." At the name of Jesus, may all confess him as Lord and live as his people, for God will support us.

Luke 2:15-21 Shepherds see what the angel of the Lord announced and thus glorify and praise God for all they have heard and seen. After eight days, the infant is circumcised and named "Jesus" in fulfillment of the angel's command at the annunciation.

Psalm 67
1. Metrical psalm, *Lord, Bless and Pity Us*, from *The Psalter*, 1912, HB 493; WB 456, tune: St. Michael
2. Gelineau, *O God, Be Gracious and Bless Us*, GG, p. 17
3. Gregorian psalm tone, *GP*, Proper 15 A
4. Mixed medium, *Psalm 67*, Arthur Wills (G. Schirmer)
5. *PS*, p. 21

Hymns for the Day	HL	HB	WB
At the Name of Jesus	–	143	303
What Child Is This	–	159	630
Gentle Mary Laid Her Child	453	167	375
Ah, Dearest Jesus, Holy Child	118	173	279
How Sweet the Name of Jesus Sounds	310	130	–
Hark! the Herald Angels Sing	117	163	411
All Praise Be Yours	–	–	290

Anthems for the Day
Num. 6:22-27 *The Lord Bless You and Keep You*, John Rutter (Hinshaw); SATB (M)

Gal. 4:4-7 or **Phil. 2:9-13** *Of the Father's Love Begotten*, 4 traditional tunes arr. Robert Lind (Augsburg); SATB, flute (M)

Luke 2:15-21 *What Is This Fragrance?*, French, setting by Werner Grams (Concordia); SATB (ME)

Ps. 67 *Let the People Praise Thee*, William Mathias (Oxford); SATB (M)

JANUARY 1 [When observed as New Year] (C)

Isaiah 49:1-10 Yahweh's chosen servant summons the nations to hear Yahweh's word. The servant publicly announces his prenatal call and his subsequent despondency about performing the task in vain. But now, Yahweh has expanded the call to be a light to all the nations (Gentiles) in order that "salvation may reach to the end of the earth," and Yahweh will raise up the deeply despised servant for all the nations to see and before whom they shall prostrate themselves.

Ephesians 3:1-10 Paul's vocation is the privilege of making known to the Gentiles God's plan of salvation. And his gospel message is that through the sheer grace of God, the Gentiles have been included in God's people. Now all the people of God, Jews and Gentiles, share the same promises revealed in Jesus Christ and receive his Spirit to proclaim God's plan of salvation.

Luke 14:16-24 A man invites many to a great banquet. But all the invited guests are preoccupied with securing future property concerns. Whereupon the man burned white-hot angry and ordered his slave to bring in "the poor and maimed and blind and lame" (an example of vs. 13-14?). In order to fill the banquet hall, the host then sends out his slave to compel the outcasts who dwell in "the highways and hedges" to come to the feast. Do you identify with the excuse makers, the outcasts, or the host who invites outcasts?

Psalm 90:1-12
1. Metrical, *Lord, Thou Hast Been Our Dwelling Place*, HB 88, tune: St. Catherine
2. Metrical, *O God, Our Help in Ages Past*, HB 111, tune: St. Anne
3. Gelineau, *You Turn Men Back Into Dust*, GG, p. 113
4. Gregorian psalm tone, *GP*, Proper 23 B
5. *PS*, p. 23

Hymns for the Day	HL	HB	WB
Christ for the World We Sing	378	489	–
Ah, Dearest Jesus, Holy Child	118	173	279
Christ Is the World's True Light	–	492	326
Ye Christian Heralds, Go Proclaim	381	494	–
God Is Working His Purpose Out	–	500	389
O Holy City, Seen of John	409	508	505
Great God, We Sing That Mighty Hand	470	527	408

Anthems for the Day
Isa. 49:1-10 *By the Springs of Water*, Cecil Effinger (Augsburg); SATB (M)
Eph. 3:1-10 *Give Us Joy for This New Year*, P. H. Erlebach (Marks Music); SATTB (MD)
Luke 14:16-24 *At the Time of the Banquet*, Gerhard Krapf (Concordia); unison (E)
Ps. 90:1-12 *Lord, Thou Hast Been Our Refuge*, John Joubert (Novello); SATB (MD)

SECOND SUNDAY AFTER CHRISTMAS (ABC)

Jeremiah 31:7-14 Shout for joy because the Lord has graciously delivered Israel from bondage. The Lord will gather his people (including those dependent upon others) from the ends of the earth, and he will shepherd his company to flowing streams and reveal a father's love for his firstborn. Declare to the world: "The Lord has repurchased his flock; he will comfort them and bless them with abundant life."

Ephesians 1:3-6, 15-18 Thanks to be you, O God, for blessing our union with Christ by bestowing the gift of the Spirit, and for choosing us as your servants for the purpose of praising your glorious free grace. May the God of our Lord Jesus Christ continually give us discernment regarding our calling and rich inheritance.

John 1:1-18 "In the beginning was the Word, and the Word was with God." All things were made through the Word, and in the Word were life and light. The Word came into the world and to his own people, but the world rejected the Word as did his own people. Yet, those who received and believed in the Word were given power to announce and to bear witness, as John (the Baptizer) did, to the coming of the Word among us, full of grace and truth.

Psalm 147:12-20
1. Metrical psalm, *O Praise Your God, O Zion*, from *The Psalter*, 1912, *MP&E*, p. 69
2. Gregorian psalm tone, *GP*, Christmas 1 ABC

Hymns for the Day	HL	HB	WB
O Splendor of God's Glory Bright	32	45	529
Glorious Things of You Are Spoken	339	434	379
Built on the Rock	–	432	320
Christ Is Made the Sure Foundation	336	433	325
Break Forth, O Living Light of God	–	–	316
The True Light That Enlightens Man	–	–	598

Anthems for the Day
Jer. 31:7-14 *In Thee Is Gladness*, Giovanni Gastoldi, arr. Diane Bish (Hinshaw); SATB (M)
Eph. 1:3-6, 15-18 *Blessed Be the Father*, Paul Christiansen (AMSI); SATB (E)
John 1:1-18 *The Word Became Flesh*, George Brandon (Canyon); unison (E)
Ps. 147:12-20 *Praise the Lord, O Jerusalem*, Malcolm Williamson (*Psalms of the Elements*, Boosey & Hawkes); unison choir, congregation (E)

THE EPIPHANY OF THE LORD (ABC)

Isaiah 60:1-6 Awake, light has overcome the darkness! The glory of the Lord's presence will be reflected in Jerusalem's arising to rebuild the city. Open your eyes and see the caravans from all the nations that shall come of their own free will to your light. Rejoice, for they bring your sons and daughters as well as a multitude of treasures and herds of animals.

Ephesians 3:1-12 Paul's vocation is the privilege of making known to the Gentiles God's plan of salvation. And his gospel message is that, through the sheer grace of God, the Gentiles have been included in God's people. Now all the people of God, Jews and Gentiles, share the same promises revealed in Jesus Christ and receive his Spirit to proclaim God's plan of salvation.

Matthew 2:1-12 Magi from the East come to Jerusalem in search of the King of the Jews. King Herod, out of fear, also wants to know where this threatening challenger can be found. So Herod offers the magi a deal they can't refuse. But when the magi arrive in the presence of the child, they fall down on their knees and worship him and give him everything they have. They return home another way, other than through Herod's palace.

Psalm 72:1-14
1. Metrical psalm, *Hail to the Lord's Anointed*, James Montgomery, *LBW* 87, tune: *Freut euch, ihr lieben*
2. Gelineau, *O God, Give Your Judgement*, *30P&2C*, p. 22
3. Gregorian psalm tone, *GP*, Advent 2 A

Hymns for the Day	HL	HB	WB
O Morning Star, How Fair and Bright	321	415	521
Christ, Whose Glory Fills the Skies	26	47	332
Christ Is the World's True Light	–	492	326
We Three Kings	–	176	–
Break Forth, O Living Light of God	–	–	316
What Star Is This	–	–	632
Brightest and Best	136	175	318

Anthems for the Day
Isa. 60:1-6 *Arise, Shine, for Thy Light Is Come*, Healey Willan (Concordia); SATB (E)
Eph. 3:1-12 *The Only Son from Heaven*, J. S. Bach (*Cantata 22*, in *Third Morning Star Choir Book*, Concordia); SATB (E)
Matt. 2:1-12 *The Three Kings*, Healey Willan (Oxford); SSATBB (MD)
   We Have Seen His Star, Everett Titcomb (C. Fischer); SATB (E)
Ps. 72:1-14 *Jesus Shall Reign*, setting by Carl Schalk (Concordia); SATB (E)

BAPTISM OF THE LORD
[First Sunday after the Epiphany] (C)

Isaiah 61:1-4 The prophet announces his calling through God's Spirit. He has been anointed to proclaim the season of Yahweh's favor when the afflicted, the disenfranchised, the oppressed, the tormented, the grieving, the imprisoned shall be restored, and they shall raise up ancient ruins.

Acts 8:14-17 The gospel is preached in Samaria; the people receive the word of God and are baptized in the name of the Lord Jesus. When the apostles at Jerusalem hear about this, they send Peter and John to pray for the believers to receive the divine gift of the Holy Spirit. They lay their hands upon the people, who receive the divine gift of the Spirit and can now discern the difference between truth and illusion.

Luke 3:15-17, 21-22 Upon hearing jolting words from John, the people inquire, "Are you the Christ?" "No," replies John, "I baptize only with water, but the One who is to come will baptize with the Holy Spirit and with fire, and will winnow the wheat from the chaff." After all are baptized, including Jesus who is now praying, the heavens open, the Holy Spirit descends like a dove upon Jesus, and a voice proclaims, "You are my beloved Son, with you I am well pleased."

Psalm 29
1. Free paraphrase, *God the Omnipotent!*, Henry F. Chorley and John Ellerton, HB 487, tune: Russian Hymn
2. Gelineau, *O Give the Lord, You Sons of God*, 24P&1C, p. 10

Hymns for the Day	HL	HB	WB
Guide Me, O Thou Great Jehovah	104	339	409
Here, O Lord, Your Servants Gather	–	–	417
The Lone, Wild Bird	496	540	591
Descend, O Spirit, Purging Flame	–	–	353
Take My Life, and Let It Be Consecrated	242	310	–
Come Down, O Love Divine	–	–	334
I Sing as I Arise Today	–	–	428

Anthems for the Day
Isa. 61:1-4 *The Spirit of the Lord Is Upon Me*, Edward Elgar (Novello); SATB (M)

Acts 8:14-17 *O Lord, Give Thy Holy Spirit*, Thomas Tallis (*Second Concord Anthem Book*, E. C. Schirmer); SATB (M)

Luke 3:15-17, 21-22 *Jesus! Name of Wondrous Love*, Robert J. Powell (Abingdon); 2-part mixed (E)

Ps. 29 *Festal Anthem*, Robert Leaf (Augsburg); SATB, trumpet (M)

SECOND SUNDAY AFTER THE EPIPHANY

Isaiah 62:1-5 A promise by the prophetic community to intercede without ceasing for Jerusalem—forsaken and desolate—until she is saved and newly named by Yahweh. Then her light (glory) shall dawn like the morning brightness, a burning torch, a gleaming jewel, and her children shall farm once again the land promised to the faithful.

1 Corinthians 12:1-11 Though every congregation is a fragile group, one spiritual gift bonds all together: profession of Jesus as Lord. In addition there are varieties of gifts, services, and working, but it is the same Spirit, Lord, and God operating in all. So Paul's partial list of spiritual gifts to each person—knowledge, faith, healing, miracle-working, prophecy, preaching, speaking or interpreting in tongues—are all from one and the same Spirit and, therefore, must serve the common good.

John 2:1-11 A grand wedding feast is about to come to an embarrassing end because the supply of wine is dwindling. What an opportune hour for Jesus to change miraculously some water in Jewish purification jars into premium wine. Instead, what a marvelous story pointing to the new way of Christ's mercy toward us. Water transformed into new wine, guilt into free grace, accusation and retaliation into justification, judgment into forgiveness—all this happened when the time came for Jesus' "hour" on Calvary. Surely God works in mysterious ways.

Psalm 36:5-10
1. Metrical, *Thy Mercy and Thy Truth, O Lord*, HB 82, tune: sing to Dundee
2. Gregorian psalm tone, *GP*, Monday of Holy Week ABC

Hymns for the Day	HL	HB	WB
We Are One in the Spirit	–	–	619
When All Thy Mercies, O My God	81	119	–
Thy Mercy and Thy Truth, O Lord	–	82	–
Son of God, Eternal Savior	393	–	573
Put Forth, O God, Your Spirit's Might	–	477	559
Lord God of Hosts, Whose Purpose	368	288	460

Anthems for the Day
Isa. 62:1-5 *King of Glory, King of Peace*, Harold Friedell (H. W. Gray); SATB (M)
1 Cor. 12:1-11 *Draw Us in the Spirit's Tether*, Harold Friedell (H. W. Gray); SATB (ME)
John 2:1-11 *Let Us Ever Walk with Jesus*, setting by Paul Manz (Concordia); unison (E)
Ps. 36:5-10 *O How Precious*, Raymond Haan (Hinshaw); 2-part (E)

THIRD SUNDAY AFTER THE EPIPHANY (C)

Nehemiah 8:1-4a, 5-6, 8-10 All the people gather as one when Ezra the scribe brings forth the book of the law of Moses, which Yahweh gave to Israel. Ezra reads from it. All ears listen. All eyes watch. Everybody stands. All hands are lifted, and all mouths respond, "Amen." All heads are bowed, and all worship Yahweh. Levites explain the law so that all minds understand. And all eyes shed tears when they discern Yahweh's incredible care for all humanity. So all the people celebrate Yahweh's saving presence among them.

1 Corinthians 12:12-30 Conventional wisdom believes in the precedence of the individual who decides to associate with others and thereby form a group to which each member may contribute prized talents according to the reigning hierarchy. The biblical vision, however, believes in the precedence of the body (of Christ) in which baptized members (a foot, hand, ear, eye) may discern their God-given, essential gifts for contributing to the care of the body.

Luke 4:14-21 Jesus returns home to open his public ministry in Galilee by reading Isaiah 61:1-2 and a modified 58:6. These words not only begin but foreshadow Jesus' entire ministry, for he is the one anointed by the Spirit at his baptism "to preach good news to the poor and to proclaim release to the captives."

Psalm 19:7-14
1. Metrical, *Most Perfect Is the Law of God*, from *The Psalter*, 1912, HB 257, tune: Glasgow
2. Gelineau, *The Law of the Lord Is Perfect, GG*, p. 121
3. Gregorian psalm tone, *GP*, Proper 21 B

Hymns for the Day	HL	HB	WB
Most Perfect Is the Law of God	–	257	–
Hark! the Glad Sound, the Savior Comes	–	–	410
Christ Is Made the Sure Foundation	336	433	325
Christ Is the World's True Light	–	492	326
We Are Living, We Are Dwelling	374	356	618

Anthems for the Day
Neh. 8:1-4a, 5-6, 8-10 *Praise the Lord*, Heinz Werner Zimmerman (*Five Hymns*, Concordia); SATB (ME)
1 Cor. 12:12-30 *The Church of Christ Is One*, Stanley Tagg (*Westminster Praise*, Hinshaw); unison (E)
Luke 4:14-21 *Good News*, Jane Marshall (C. Fischer); SATB (ME)
Ps. 19:7-14 *Silent Devotion and Response*, Ernest Bloch (A. Broude); SATB (M)

FOURTH SUNDAY AFTER THE EPIPHANY (C)

Jeremiah 1:4-10 Jeremiah's vision, in which Yahweh anoints him to be a "prophet to the nations." "But I do not know how to speak," laments Jeremiah. "Fear not," answers Yahweh, "I am with you. What I command, you shall speak." Yahweh then touches Jeremiah's mouth, saying, "I have put my words into your mouth so that you shall speak the double-edged word of judgment and salvation that uproots and smashes, and builds and plants."

1 Corinthians 13:1-13 What is love? Love is action, not a feeling. Love is self-giving, even unto death, in the manner of Christ's self-giving. Love maintains all faithfulness, all hope, all steadfastness. Love is eternal because it is the purpose and nature of God. Today we see that dimly, but someday we shall see clearly and understand fully.

Luke 4:21-30 Everyone is aglow the day the hometown boy, Joseph's son, returns to preach his inaugural sermon. All speak well of him and marvel at his words, until he speaks about the favoring of outsiders—Gentiles by name. Then the crowd's admiration turns to rejection, and they seek to execute vigilante justice on the brow of a hill outside the city. Yet Jesus passes through the midst of this frenzied crowd and goes away.

Psalm 71:1-6
1. Metrical, *O Gracious God, Forsake Me Not, HB* 396, tune: Martyrdom
2. Gelineau, *In You, O Lord, I Take Refuge, GG,* p. 159
3. Gregorian psalm tone, *GP,* Tuesday of Holy Week ABC

Hymns for the Day	HL	HB	WB
Where Charity and Love Prevail	–	–	641
Who Trusts in God, a Strong Abode	–	375	–
O Thou, in All Thy Might So Far	176	219	–
God of the Prophets!	481	520	398
Beloved, Let Us Love	500	–	–
Behold the Amazing Gift of Love	–	120	–

Anthems for the Day
Jer. 1:4-10 *O Thou Whose Power,* Gilbert Martin (H. W. Gray); SATB (M)
1 Cor. 13:1-13 *Where Charity and Love Prevail,* Paul Benoit (*WB* 641); unison (E)
Luke 4:21-30 *Insult and Reproach,* Gaudenzio Battistini (*Sing Joyfully,* vol. 4, Walton); SATB (M)
Ps. 71:1-6 *In Thee, O Lord,* Joseph Haydn (Sam Fox); SATB (M)

FIFTH SUNDAY AFTER THE EPIPHANY (C)

Isaiah 6:1-8 (9-13) Confronted by the immediate presence of the enthroned God and by seraphim singing "Holy, holy, holy," which rocked the very foundations of the Temple, Isaiah feels his hair stand on end, shirt buttons pop, and shoelaces untie as he is denuded of his pretense of worthiness before the Lord. "Woe is me!" cries out Isaiah. "For I am a man of unclean lips and I dwell in the midst of a people of unclean lips." One of the seraphim then touches Isaiah's lips with a burning coal from the altar, saying, "Your guilt is taken away, and your sin forgiven." Upon hearing the voice of the Lord say, "Whom shall I send, and who will go for us?" Isaiah's lips now inexplicably respond, "Here am I! Send me."

1 Corinthians 15:1-11 This is the good news in which we stand: Christ died for our sins according to the Scriptures, was buried, raised on the third day, and appeared to Peter, to the Twelve, and to many faithful witnesses. Finally, he appeared to me, Paul, the least of all apostles.

Luke 5:1-11 A crowd presses upon Jesus, who gets into a boat and teaches from it. He then tells Simon to catch fish on a day when all-night labor had yielded empty nets. But Peter obeys Jesus' word and, behold, hauls in such a great catch that the boat begins to sink. So Peter falls down at Jesus' feet, confessing, "I am a sinner, Lord." "Fear not," replies Jesus. "From now on you will be catching people alive." Then Simon and his partners leave their successful catch of fish behind and follow Jesus.

Psalm 138
1. Gelineau, *I Thank You, Lord, with All My Heart, GG,* p. 73
2. Gregorian psalm tone, *GP,* Proper 16 A

Hymns for the Day	HL	HB	WB
Holy, Holy, Holy!	57	11	421
God, the Lord, a King Remaineth	61	–	403
Spread, O Spread the Mighty Word	–	–	577
They Cast Their Nets in Galilee	–	421	–
Lord God of Hosts, Whose Purpose	368	288	460
Come, Labor On	366	287	–

Anthems for the Day

Isa. 6:1-8 (9-13) *In the Year That King Uzziah Died,* David McK. Williams (H. W. Gray); SATB (MD)

1 Cor. 15:1-11 *We Know That Christ Is Raised,* C. V. Stanford (Augsburg); SATB (E)

Luke 5:1-11 *How Lovely Are the Messengers,* Felix Mendelssohn (*St. Paul,* G. Schirmer); SATB (M)

Ps. 138 *With Songs of Rejoicing,* J. S. Bach, arr. by Hal Hopson (C. Fischer); 2-part mixed (E)

SIXTH SUNDAY AFTER THE EPIPHANY
(Proper 1) (C)

Jeremiah 17:5-10 In whom do you trust? Trust any human being or human-created social structure or institution (even a church denomination), and you are guaranteed to end up a lonely shrub in the desert—isolated, parched, anxious, helpless, wilting, dying a slow death—in a word, cursed. Trust in the Lord, and you are certain to be rooted by the living waters—drinking as needed in times of anguish, pain, distress—and therefore always bearing fruit—in a word, blessed. Are you unsure about whom you trust? Yahweh already knows, because your actions reveal in whom your heart trusts, and therefore you live accordingly.

1 Corinthians 15:12-20 Writes Paul, "If there is no resurrection, then Christ wasn't raised, you're locked into your sins forever, and your faith is futile. But," continues Paul, "Christ has been raised from the dead." An irrational and unconvincing deduction. Yet it worked. How? Hint: churches open to the power of the Spirit experience the presence of the risen Christ in their life together.

Luke 6:17-26 Jesus' opening words in his Sermon on the Plain describe the life of a healed community. "Blessings to you who are poor, hungry, weeping, and despised. Woe to you who are rich, full, laughing and respected." Jesus has a way of turning our values upside down, doesn't he? He also makes us squirm.

Psalm 1
1. Metrical, *That Man Hath Perfect Blessedness*, *MP&E*, p. 182, tune: Dunfermline
2. Metrical, *That Man Is Ever Blessed*, *LW*, p. 388, tune: St. Michael
3. Gelineau, *Happy Indeed Is the Man*, *GG*, p. 76
4. Gregorian psalm tone, *GP*, Epiphany 6 C

Hymns for the Day	HL	HB	WB
Blest Are the Pure in Heart	–	226	–
Christ, of All My Hopes the Ground	316	314	–
Give to the Winds Your Fears	294	364	377
Father, in Your Mysterious Presence	256	384	363
The Lord I Will at All Times Bless	–	412	–

Anthems for the Day
Jer. 17:5-10 *Blessed the People*, Johann Geisler (Boosey & Hawkes); SATB (E)
1 Cor. 15:12-20 *Christ Is Risen*, John Joubert (Novello); SATB (MD)
Luke 6:17-26 *The Beatitudes*, Lawson Lunde (A. Broude); SATB (M)
Ps. 1 *Blessed Is the Man*, Jane Marshall (Abingdon); SATB (E)

SEVENTH SUNDAY AFTER THE EPIPHANY
(Proper 2) (C)

Genesis 45:3-11,15 The simple, self-disclosing words, "I am Joseph," send waves of alarm, shock, dismay through his brothers because their cunning and deceptive past now jeopardizes their future. But, instead of revenge, Joseph breaks with the past and offers a gift of a new future. Why? Because "God sent me to preserve life." God's will for life is at work in spite of all resistant human efforts. Make haste, therefore, in telling the world that God mysteriously works for life in the midst of our leanness.

1 Corinthians 15:35-38, 42-50 Paul undermines our obsession with preserving our earthly body as well as our Greek notions of immortality. Our physical body that has been sown will die and be raised as a spiritual body. Death will end our earthly life, but we shall experience the new creation of resurrected life. We shall be changed people.

Luke 6:27-38 More injunctions from Jesus' Sermon on the Plain that invert our conventional wisdom: "Do not take any retaliatory action against those who do physical violence to you, extract forced labor from you, or make demands for gifts and loans. But love and serve your enemies, and pray for them as a sign of the age to come."

Psalm 37:1-11
1. Psalm paraphrase, *The Steps of Those Whom He Approves*, from *The Psalter*, 1912, *HB* 422, tune: Downs
2. Psalm paraphrase, *Give to the Winds Your Fears*, Paul Gerhardt, trans. John Wesley, tune: St. Bride, *HB* 364, *WB* 377
3. Gregorian psalm tone, *GP*, Epiphany 4 A

Hymns for the Day	HL	HB	WB
The Steps of Those Whom He Approves	–	422	–
"Am I My Brother's Keeper?"	–	–	295
O God of Every Nation	–	–	498
Let There Be Light, Lord God of Hosts	402	480	451
Father, We Greet You	–	285	364

Anthems for the Day

Gen. 45:3-11, 15 *In Adam We Have All Been One* (*Westminster Praise*, Hinshaw); SATB (E)

1 Cor. 15:35-38, 42-50 *Praise to the Holiest*, arr. Erik Routley (*Westminster Praise*, Hinshaw); SATB (E)

Luke 6:27-38 *On Love of One's Enemies*, Virgil Ford (Broadman); SATB (E)

Ps. 37:1-11 *O Rest in the Lord*, Felix Mendelssohn (*Elijah*, any edition); unison or solo (E)

EIGHTH SUNDAY AFTER THE EPIPHANY
(Proper 3) (C)

Isaiah 55:10-13 God's intentions for human history may be delayed, but they are not nullified. God's full promises still stand, for the word of God abides forever, and surrounds (cf. Isa. 40:6-8 and 55:11) God's people. Sooner or later, God's rule will be visible among all. Which means that instead of "thorns and thistles" (cf. Gen. 3:18), "the fall" shall end and "the homecoming" shall begin a new, everlasting creation in which relationships among all exiles are fully restored. You can count on God's promises.

1 Corinthians 15:51-58 A mystery: all of us may not die before the eschaton, but all of us shall be changed. At the last trumpet, all shall put on the imperishable, immortal heavenly garment, and thus death itself shall lose its sting, die, and be swallowed up in victory through our Lord Jesus Christ. Thanks be to God! Therefore, confident of this ultimate victory, let us now "be steadfast, immovable, always abounding in the work of the Lord."

Luke 6:39-49 We are all so blind, which is why we lead each other into ditches. Worse, we trust our own obstructed sight, condemning ourselves to the pit—after all, "thorns and thistles" do not produce "figs and grapes." So those who hear and obey Christ's words are like those who build stone houses on a rock base, and those who do not hear and obey are like those who build mud houses in an arroyo.

Psalm 92:1-4, 12-15
1. Metrical, *It Is Good to Sing Thy Praises,* from *The Psalter,* 1912, *HB* 20, tune: Elleside
2. Gelineau, *It Is Good to Give Thanks to the Lord, GG,* p. 80
3. Gregorian psalm tone, *GP,* Epiphany 8 C
4. Frank Quinn, *Song of Those Who Are Right with God, MP&E,* p. 52

Hymns for the Day	HL	HB	WB
It Is Good to Sing Thy Praises	–	20	–
The Strife Is O'er, the Battle Done	164	203	597
How Firm a Foundation	283	369	425
How Blest Is He Whose Trespass	–	281	–
O Love of God Most Full	84	118	–
"Take Up Thy Cross," the Saviour Said	–	293	–

Anthems for the Day
Isa. 55:10-13 *For as the Rain Cometh Down,* Sven Lekberg (G. Schirmer); SATB
1 Cor. 15:51-58 *Lo! I Tell You a Mystery,* Don McAfee (Canyon); SATB (M)
Luke 6:39-49 *Be Merciful, Even as Your Father Is Merciful,* Gerhard Krapf (Concordia); unison (M)
Ps. 92:1-4, 12-15 *The Just Man Shall Flourish,* Richard Proulx (Augsburg); unison, flute, oboe (E)

TRANSFIGURATION OF THE LORD
[Last Sunday After the Epiphany] (C)

Exodus 34:29-35 Moses makes his final descent from Mt. Sinai, only this time with a shining face. Immediately the Israelites and their leaders see the glory of God shining in the uncovered face of Moses, "and they were afraid to come near him." But, insofar as Moses was human and not divine, they could behold him and receive the commandments that Yahweh had given Moses. Whenever Moses spoke with Yahweh or mediated Yahweh's guidance to the people, Moses' radiant face was unveiled. And when he wasn't performing his mediatorial task, his face was veiled.

2 Corinthians 3:12–4:2 When we turn to Christ, we behold the unveiled glory of God in Christ and are, surprisingly, transformed into Christ's likeness. Lest we think our turning to Christ is solely by our choice, remember that it is the Holy Spirit who frees us to turn and to follow Christ.

Luke 9:28-36 Eight days after speaking to his disciples about "taking up the cross," Jesus ascends a mountain with Peter, James, and John. As Jesus is praying, the external appearance of his face becomes different, his clothing becomes dazzling white, and Moses and Elijah talk with him about his exodus from Jerusalem. Peter and the others "saw his glory" and want to set up the festival tents right there. But a cloud overshadows them, and a voice proclaims words that recall Jesus' baptism—"This is my Son, my chosen (or Beloved)"–and then adds this charge: "Listen to him!" The disciples open their eyes and see only Jesus, so they keep silent about what they have heard.

Psalm 99
1. Pointed in *LBW* for psalm tone, p. 262
2. Gregorian psalm tone, *GP*, Epiphany A

Hymns for the Day	HL	HB	WB
At the Name of Jesus	–	143	303
Father, We Greet You	–	285	364
Light of the World, We Hail Thee	422	138	–
O Light, Whose Beams Illumine All	180	145	–
O Wondrous Type, O Vision Fair	142	182	531
O Love, How Deep, How Broad, How High!	139	–	518

Anthems for the Day

Ex. 34:29-35 *Open Thou Mine Eyes*, John Rutter (Hinshaw); SATB, soprano solo (M)

2 Cor. 3:12–4:2 *Christ, Upon the Mountain Peak*, Peter Cutts (*Ecumenical Praise*, Agape); unison (E)

Luke 9:28-36 *This Is My Beloved Son*, Knut Nystedt (Concordia); SAB (E)

Ps. 99 *The Lord God Reigneth*, Johann Pachelbel (Concordia); SATB/SATB (M)

ASH WEDNESDAY (ABC)

Joel 2:1-2, 12-17a Blow the trumpet, for the Day of Yahweh is coming! Yahweh's judgment is near! Turn back to Yahweh with all your heart. Fast, weep, mourn. Return to Yahweh who manifests *hesed* (steadfast love). Perhaps Yahweh will forgive you and bless you. Gather together all the people and turn back to Yahweh.

2 Corinthians 5:20b–6:2 (3-10) Do you remember what God in Christ has done for you all? Then accept the reconciliation that God offers you in Christ. Let God transform you! Christ shared our human estrangement from God so that we sinners might be joined with Christ and reconciled with God. So work with God today, for the day of salvation is now.

Matthew 6:1-6, 16-21 Three acts of personal piety (charity, private prayer, and fasting) and a note on treasuring God's will—all are signs of the age to come. Don't broadcast your acts of personal piety to the world. God sees what you do and therefore will give to you from the future. What you value in life is where you will devote your time, energy, emotional commitment, everything.

Psalm 51:1-12
1. Metrical, *God, Be Merciful to Me*, from *The Psalter*, 1912, *HB* 282, tune: Redhead, No. 76
2. Gelineau, *Have Mercy on Me, God, GG*, p. 34
3. Gregorian psalm tone, *GP*, Lent 5 B
4. David Isele, *Have Mercy on Me, O God, Praise God in Song*, p. 28
5. *PS*, p. 18

Hymns for the Day	HL	HB	WB
God, Be Merciful to Me	–	282	–
O God of Bethel, by Whose Hand	98	342	496
Ah, Holy Jesus	158	191	280
Lead Us, Heavenly Father, Lead Us	304	343	–
God of Compassion, in Mercy Befriend Us	290	122	392

Anthems for the Day
Joel 2:1-2, 12-17a *Judgment*, Alec Wyton (*Two Choral Hymns*, H. W. Gray); SSATB (M)

2 Cor. 5:20b–6:2 (3-10) *Lord, for Thy Tender Mercies' Sake*, Richard Farrant (H. W. Gray); SATB (E)

Matt. 6:1-6, 16-21 *Treasures in Heaven*, Joseph Clokey (Summy-Birchard); SATB, soprano solo (E)

Ps. 51:1-12 *Cast Me Not Away from Thy Presence*, S. S. Wesley (Novello); SSATTB (MD)

FIRST SUNDAY IN LENT (C)

Deuteronomy 26:1-11 Instructions on offering firstfruits of the land to the Lord so you will not succumb to the temptation to believe you achieved the harvest which the Lord has given you. First, recite the ancient creedal story of Yahweh's actions for his people—hearing their distress, delivering them from affliction, and guiding them to the promised land. Then offer the firstfruits of your God-given gifts to the Lord. Why all this ritual? So you will remember how Yahweh took care of your refugee ancestors, rejoice in such unmerited love, and therefore care for the outsiders who live among you.

Romans 10:8b-13 When your lips confess "Jesus is Lord" because your heart trusts "God raised him from the dead," you acknowledge the nearness of Christ and his salvation offered to all, which Isaiah said will not be transitory. Therefore the Lord of all bestows such enduring riches upon everyone who calls upon the name of the Lord.

Luke 4:1-13 Jesus has just been "ordained" in baptism and is full of the Holy Spirit which leads him into the wilderness for forty days, where he is tempted by the devil to become three different kinds of messiah: prosperity giver, political leader, or miracle worker. Jesus, however, repudiates each temptation with a quote from Deuteronomy, indicating he will let God define his ministry. The devil then departs until an opportune time.

Psalm 91:9-16
1. Gelineau, *He Who Dwells in the Shelter of the Most High, GG*, p. 23
2. Gregorian psalm tone, *GP*, Proper 24 B
3. *PS*, p. 24

Hymns for the Day	*HL*	*HB*	*WB*
Lord, Who Throughout These Forty Days	144	181	470
Thou Hidden Source of Calm Repose	–	423	–
Call Jehovah Your Salvation	292	123	322
O Love, How Deep, How Broad, How High!	139	–	518

Anthems for the Day
Deut. 26:1-11 *Thanks to God the Lord,* Heinrich Schütz (Concordia); SATB (E)

Rom. 10:8b-13 *Lenten Litany,* Martin How (Boosey & Hawkes); unison, baritone solo (E)

Luke 4:1-13 *O Love, How Deep, How Broad, How High,* Philip Dietterich (Sacred Music); 2-part (E)

Ps. 91:9-16 *Happy Are You,* Jane Marshall (Augsburg); SATB, baritone solo (ME)

SECOND SUNDAY IN LENT (C)

Genesis 15:1-12, 17-18 Yahweh promises through Abram to be our shield and that our gifts shall be great. But like Abram we protest: "We live in the 'real world' where human ambition breeds carelessness and unfulfilled divine promises are trusted less than a falling star." Yahweh's response: the same promise is pledged and a sign—the countless fixed stars—given. Miraculously, Abram surrenders his craving for control and "believes Yahweh." Yahweh then seals the covenant with Abram.

Philippians 3:17–4:1 Paul's exhortation to imitate him in pressing on toward the goal of true righteousness which God has already given in Christ. Abandon earthly pleasure-seeking which makes you "enemies of the cross of Christ," and follow the example of the citizens of heaven, whose lowly bodies will be transformed to be like Christ's glorious body.

Luke 13:31-35 Jesus so passionately yearns to shield God's people under his protective wings that neither warnings nor threats could possibly deter his urgent passion-journey to Jerusalem. In his three-day ministry he laments "Jerusalem's" continual resistance to God's unremitting grace.

or **Luke 9:28-36** The transfiguration of Jesus.

Psalm 127
1. Gelineau, *If the Lord Does Not Build the House*, 24P&1C, p. 34
2. Pointed in *LBW* for psalm tone, p. 280

Hymns for the Day	HL	HB	WB
Faith of Our Fathers!	267	348	361
The God of Abraham Praise	8	89	587
Give to the Winds Your Fears	294	364	377
How Firm a Foundation	283	369	425
Who Trusts in God, a Strong Abode	–	375	–
If You Will Only Let God Guide You	105	344	431

Anthems for the Day
Gen. 15:1-12, 17-18 *Show Me Thy Ways*, Walter Pelz (Augsburg); SATB, guitar, oboe (ME)
Phil. 3:17-4:1 *Open Thou Mine Eyes*, John Rutter (Hinshaw); SATB, soprano solo (M)
Luke 13:31-35 or **Luke 9:28-36** *Jerusalem, Thou That Killed the Prophets*, Christoph Bernhard (Concordia); SSB, 2 violins (M)
Ps. 127 *Put Thou Thy Trust in God*, Philip Tomblings (Oxford); SATB (ME)

THIRD SUNDAY IN LENT (C)

Exodus 3:1-15 Yahweh freely chooses to reveal himself to Moses in a burning bush in the desert. "I will save my people by sending you to lead them out of Egypt." "But," protests Moses, "I am a nobody." So God gives Moses a sign: "When you lead my people out of Egypt, you shall serve God upon this mountain." Still Moses balks: "But whom shall I say sent me?" "Tell them," replies God, "I AM WHO I AM. The God of Abraham and Isaac and Jacob."

1 Corinthians 10:1-13 Paul recalls the exodus-wilderness events. Those who were under the protection of the cloud, led through the sea, given manna to eat and water to drink presumed they could live as they pleased. But God was not pleased with them, so they were destroyed. But know also that God faithfully struggles with us against these seductive forces—idolatry, immorality, testing God, grumbling—that threaten to drive a wedge between us and God.

Luke 13:1-9 Were the Galileans destroyed during the sacrificial worship in the Temple because they were worse sinners than all other Galileans? Were the eighteen Jerusalemites killed in the catastrophic collapse of the Siloam tower because they were worse offenders than all other Jerusalemites? Do bad things happen only to bad people? No! But we all are ultimately judged by our fruits. Meanwhile, all barren fig trees will be given a little more time to bear fruit. Only by God's sheer grace and good patience are we given time to repent (but not forever).

Psalm 103:1-13
1. Metrical, *Bless, O My Soul! the Living God, HB* 8, tune: Park Street
2. Gelineau, *My Soul, Give Thanks to the Lord, GG,* p. 77
3. Gregorian psalm tone, *GP,* Lent 3 C

Hymns for the Day	*HL*	*HB*	*WB*
Amazing Grace!	–	275	296
There's a Wideness in God's Mercy	93	110	601
God of Compassion, in Mercy Befriend Us	290	122	392
O My Soul, Bless God, the Father	–	–	523

Anthems for the Day
Ex. 3:1-15 *Let Your Eye Be to the Lord,* Daniel Moe (Augsburg); SATB (M)
1 Cor. 10:1-13 *Our Soul Waits for the Lord,* Jane Marshall (*Two Quiet Psalms,* Sacred Music); SATB (ME)
Luke 13:1-9 *We Are a Garden,* Alice Parker (E. C. Schirmer); SATB, harp, organ, triangle (MD)
Ps. 103:1-13 *Bless the Lord, My Soul,* J. S. Bach, arr. Hal Hopson (Flammer); 2-part (E)

FOURTH SUNDAY IN LENT (C)

Joshua 5:9-12 Yahweh has liberated the people of Israel from the disgrace of slavery in Egypt and brought them to Gilgal, where they solemnly celebrate the first Passover in the Promised Land. Down drops the curtain on forty years of wilderness wanderings and sustenance by miraculous manna from the heavens, and up rises the curtain on Yahweh's nourishment of Israel by the produce and fruit of the land.

2 Corinthians 5:16-21 God has entrusted us with the ministry of reconciliation and appointed us as ambassadors for Christ. Our message? God tracked down and made up with our rebellious, guilty, frightened world. Instead of tallying up all our sins, God incarnate, Jesus Christ, strode into our world and loved us and forgave us, transforming our world into a new creation.

Luke 15:1-3, 11-32 The younger of two sons requests his share of property from his father, who foolishly gives away his life. The younger son then sqaunders everything in wild living in a foreign country and tumbles to the depths of pig herder. Realizing there is fresh bread on the table back home, he seeks to earn his food by working as his father's hired servant. But the father has compassion, embraces and kisses him, and throws an extravagant homecoming party, completely restoring him. Meanwhile, the obedient, hardworking elder son becomes angry and, though his father pleads with him, keeps his distance from the party. Declares the father, "Child, everything of mine is yours." No repentance, no conversion, but lots of unconditional love.

Psalm 34:1-8
1. Metrical, *The Lord I Will at All Times Bless*, *HB* 412, tune: Ames
2. Gelineau, *I Will Bless the Lord at All Times*, *GG*, p. 104
3. Gregorian psalm tone, *GP*, Proper 14 B

Hymns for the Day	HL	HB	WB
Give to the Winds Your Fears	294	364	377
Your Love, O God	–	–	646
Behold the Amazing Gift of Love	–	120	–
How Gentle God's Commands	279	105	–
There's a Wideness in God's Mercy	93	110	601

Anthems for the Day
Josh. 5:9-12 *O Taste and See*, R. Vaughan Williams (Oxford); SATB, soprano solo (M)
2 Cor. 5:16-21 *God Loved the World*, Melchior Vulpius (*Church Choir Book*, vol. 2, Concordia); SATB (E)
Luke 15:1-3, 11-32 *See What Love Hath the Father*, Felix Mendelssohn (*St. Paul*, G. Schirmer); SATB (M)
Ps. 34:1-8 *I Will Always Give Thanks*, Maurice Greene (*Sing Joyfully*, vol. 3, Walton); SAB (MD)

FIFTH SUNDAY IN LENT (C)

Isaiah 43:16-21 "Behold, I am doing a new thing," proclaims Yahweh. Yes, the exodus from Egypt was dramatic and formative for Israel's existence, but now Yahweh is bringing about a new exodus by making a straight road in the wilderness and creating thirst-quenching rivers in the desert so that Yahweh's chosen people may sing their praise to the Lord.

Philippians 3:8-14 Paul has discarded all that was precious to him—achievements, respectability, reputation, moral uprightness, obeying the law—for the sake of something far more valuable: knowledge of Christ Jesus as his Lord and being in union with him. In order to know the power of Christ's resurrection, Paul and those "in Christ" must model their life on Christ's sufferings and death. For though Christ Jesus has made Paul and us his own, we still must paradoxically "press on" and "strain forward" to make the prize of the upward call of God our own.

John 12:1-8 Irrepressible Mary gets carried away at dinner and shocks everyone by pouring thousands of dollars' worth of perfume on Jesus' feet. "An extravagant waste," cries the morally upright Judas, "the money could have been given to the poor." Replies Jesus, "You'll always have the opportunity to serve the poor; so leave her alone, for you'll not always have me. She has saved her perfume for my burial." Mary anoints her only Lord and Savior.

Psalm 126
1. Gelineau, *When the Lord Delivered Sion from Bondage*, GG, p. 7
2. Gregorian psalm tone, *GP*, Lent 5 C

Hymns for the Day	*HL*	*HB*	*WB*
Let Us with a Gladsome Mind	64	28	453
Jesus, Priceless Treasure	–	414	442
Be Thou My Vision	325	303	304
O Jesus, We Adore Thee	156	200	–
Awake, My Soul, Stretch Every Nerve	278	346	–
Master, No Offering, Costly and Sweet	407	299	–

Anthems for the Day
Isa. 43:16-21 *By the Springs of Water*, Cecil Effinger (Augsburg); SATB (M)
Phil. 3:8-14 *The True Glory*, Peter Aston (Hinshaw); SATB (M)
John 12:1-8 *Worthy Is the Lamb (Dignus est Agnus)*, Malcolm Williamson (Piedmont Music); SATB, soprano solo (MD)
Ps. 126 *The Lord Has Done Great Things for Them*, Barry Bobb (Concordia); unison or SATB, congregation (E)

PASSION SUNDAY [Sixth Sunday in Lent] (C)

Isaiah 50:4-9a The third of the four Songs of the Servant of Yahweh: Each day Yahweh wakens me and opens my ears to his word, which sustains me. Though I have suffered ridicule, insults, hostility, and physical abuse, I have not turned from my task. I trust Yahweh's help; Yahweh will vindicate me. So who will declare me guilty?

Philippians 2:5-11 A primitive Christological hymn about the descent and ascent of a divine savior. By divesting himself of divine glory, he voluntarily assumed the form of a human servant who impoverished himself and "became obedient unto death, even death on a cross." That's why God raised him up and gave him the name above every other name: Lord.

Luke 22:14–23:56 The passion narrative according to Luke.

or Luke 23:1-49 The Sanhedrin brings Jesus before Pilate and accuses him of proclaiming himself a king and of inciting the people to riot. "Are you," inquires Pilate, "the king of the Jews?" "So you say," replies Jesus. Announces Pilate, "I find no crime in this man." But since Jesus is a Galilean, he is taken before Herod, who asks numerous questions to which Jesus gives no answers. So they mock him and send him back to Pilate, who still contends that he and Herod find Jesus not guilty. But the frenzied multitude shouts down Pilate three times, demanding Jesus be crucified and Barabbas be freed. Then Simon of Cyrene is seized and forced to carry the cross. The innocent yet condemned Jesus laments over the judgment coming to guilty Jerusalem and calls for repentance. Still, he is crucified between two criminals, while mockers tempt him to save himself and one criminal proclaims Jesus has done nothing wrong. Since he united himself to us in our guilt and shared our death, surely we can trust his promise that we will be with him "in Paradise."

Psalm 31:9-16
1. Gelineau, *In You, O Lord, I Take Refuge*, GG, p. 37

Hymns for the Day	HL	HB	WB
All Praise Be Yours	–	–	290
Ride On! Ride On in Majesty!	150	188	563
At the Name of Jesus	–	143	303
Lord Jesus, Think on Me	239	270	–
In the Cross of Christ I Glory	154	195	437
Lord, from the Depths to You I Cry	240	277	459

Anthems for the Day
Isa. 50:4-9a *Lord, to Thee We Turn (Inimici Autem)*, Orlando di Lasso (*Second Concord Anthem Book*, E. C. Schirmer); SATB (ME)
Phil. 2:5-11 *Let This Mind Be in You*, Lee Hoiby (Presser); SATB (D)
Luke 22:14–23:56 or Luke 23:1-49 *Ride On! Ride On!*, Graham George (H. W. Gray); SATB (E)
Ps. 31:9-16 *Out of the Depths*, Marc-Antoine Charpentier (Concordia); SATB (ME)

PALM SUNDAY [Sixth Sunday in Lent] (C)

Isaiah 50:4-9a The third of the four Songs of the Servant of Yahweh: Each day Yahweh wakens me and opens my ears to his word, which sustains me. Though I have suffered ridicule, insults, hostility, and physical abuse, I have not turned from my task. I trust Yahweh's help; Yahweh will vindicate me. So who will declare me guilty?

Philippians 2:5-11 A primitive Christological hymn about the descent and ascent of a divine savior. By divesting himself of divine glory, he voluntarily assumed the form of a human servant who impoverished himself and "became obedient unto death, even death on a cross." That's why God raised him up and gave him the name above every other name: Lord.

Luke 19:28-40 Jesus instructs two of his disciples to fetch a colt on which no one has ever sat. So they do everything according to Jesus' plan, and all goes well. They then set Jesus upon the colt, and spread their garments in his path as if this were a royal procession. As Jesus draws near to Jerusalem, the whole multitude of disciples praises God for all the mighty works of Jesus they had witnessed. But not everyone is jubilant over this regal parade. Some killjoy Pharisees demand that Jesus curb his noisy disciples. Replies Jesus, "Even if they were silent, the very stones would cry out" (because heaven is about to establish its peace on earth).

Psalm 118:19-29
1. Metrical, *The Glorious Gates of Righteousness*, HB 71, tune: Zerah
2. Gelineau, *Give Thanks to the Lord for He Is Good*, GG, p. 46
3. Gregorian psalm tone, *GP*, Passion (Palm) Sunday ABC

Hymns for the Day	HL	HB	WB
All Glory, Laud, and Honor	146	187	284
When, His Salvation Bringing	149	186	–
O How Shall We Receive You	–	–	506
So Lowly Does the Savior Ride	–	–	571
Hosanna, Loud Hosanna	147	185	424
Ride On! Ride On in Majesty!	150	188	563
Draw Nigh to Thy Jerusalem	148	–	–

Anthems for the Day
Isa. 50:4-9a *Lord, to Thee We Turn (Inimici Autem)*, Orlando di Lasso (*Second Concord Anthem Book*, E. C. Schirmer); SATB (ME)
Phil. 2:5-11 *Let This Mind Be in You*, Austin Lovelace (J. Fischer); SATB, alto solo (M)
Luke 19:28-40 *Thy Glory Dawns, Jerusalem, Awake*, John Davye (World Library); SATB (MD)
Ps. 118:19-29 *Lift Up Your Heads, Ye Gates*, Andreas Hammerschmidt (Concordia); SSATBB (ME)

MONDAY OF HOLY WEEK (ABC)

Isaiah 42:1-9 The first of the four Songs of the Servant of Yahweh (vs. 1-4) and the response to it (vs. 5-9). Yahweh officially presents his chosen servant, upon whom he has put his Spirit, who is to perform the task of bringing forth *mishpat* (justice) to the nations by his own suffering. Yahweh gives his servant as a light to the people who live in darkness. Verses 8-9 affirm that Yahweh will give no glory or praise to any idol, and that Yahweh declares in advance new things of the future.

Hebrews 9:11-15 Christ enters not the earthly Holy of Holies, offering a ritual sacrifice, but he enters once for all the holy dwelling place of God, offering a sacrifice of himself—his own life-giving blood. In his sacrifice Christ attains what none other ever could—eternal redemption for his people. Christ is truly the high priest of the "good things that have come."

John 12:1-11 Irrepressible Mary gets carried away at dinner and shocks everyone by pouring thousands of dollars' worth of perfume on Jesus' feet. "An extravagant waste," cries the morally upright Judas, "the money could have been given to the poor." Replies Jesus, "You'll always have the opportunity to serve the poor; so leave her alone, for you'll not always have me. She has saved her perfume for my burial." Mary anoints her only Lord and Savior.

Psalm 36:5-10
1. Metrical, *Thy Mercy and Thy Truth, O Lord, HB* 82, tune: Dundee
2. Gregorian psalm tone, *GP*, Monday of Holy Week ABC

Hymns for the Day	HL	HB	WB
Thy Mercy and Thy Truth, O Lord	–	82	–
Cross of Jesus, Cross of Sorrow	155	196	–
Master, No Offering Costly and Sweet	407	299	–
Behold the Amazing Gift of Love	–	120	–
O Christ, Whose Love Has Sought Us Out	–	–	485
There's a Wideness in God's Mercy	93	110	601

Anthems for the Day
Isa. 42:1-9 *Behold the Savior of Mankind*, Christopher Tye (*A First Motet Book*, Concordia); SATB (E)
Heb. 9:11-15 *The Promise of Eternal Inheritance*, Rudolf Moser (Concordia); unison (E)
John 12:1-11 *Worthy Is the Lamb (Dignus est Agnus)*, Malcolm Williamson (Piedmont Music); SATB, soprano solo (MD)
Ps. 36:5-10 *O How Precious*, Raymond Haan (Hinshaw); 2-part (E)

TUESDAY OF HOLY WEEK (ABC)

Isaiah 49:1-7 The second of the four Songs of the Servant of Yahweh. Yahweh's chosen servant summons the nations to hear Yahweh's word. The servant publicly announces his prenatal call and his subsequent despondency about performing the task in vain. But now Yahweh has expanded the call to be a light to all the nations (Gentiles), in order that "salvation may reach the ends of the earth."

1 Corinthians 1:18-31 The gospel always seems to turn our world upside down. Here worldly wisdom and strength are characterized as foolish and weak, and the nonsense and weakness of the crucifixion are labeled as wise and strong. The epitome of God's love for us is revealed in the offensiveness of the cross.

John 12:20-36 Some Gentiles seek to see Jesus. "The hour has come . . . ," says Jesus, "for when a single grain of wheat falls into the earth and dies, it produces many grains." Jesus then wrestles with the full import of "the hour" and decides to submit obediently to the Father's will. An affirming voice from heaven accepts the Son's obedience and promises the Son his own glorification. In fact, Jesus' decision to die will open the possibility for others to be liberated from the ruler of this world. Jesus' hour of glory, his death, brings forth life for Jesus and for all those who follow him and serve him.

Psalm 71:1-12
1. Metrical, *O Gracious God, Forsake Me Not, HB* 396, tune: Martyrdom
2. Gelineau, *In You, O Lord, I Take Refuge, GG,* p. 159
3. Gregorian psalm tone, *GP,* Tuesday of Holy Week ABC

Hymns for the Day	HL	HB	WB
Who Trusts in God, a Strong Abode	–	375	–
O Light, Whose Beams Illumine All	180	145	–
O Jesus, I Have Promised	268	307	–
When I Survey the Wondrous Cross	152	198	635
God Is Love; His Mercy Brightens	80	103	–
Christ Is the World's True Light	–	492	326

Anthems for the Day
Isa. 49:1-7 *O Send Thy Light,* M. A. Balakireff (J. Fischer); SATB (E)
1 Cor. 1:18-31 *Almighty God, the Fountain of All Wisdom,* Ernest Farrar (*Anthems for Choirs,* vol. 1, Oxford); SATB (ME)
John 12:20-36 *The Promise Which Was Made,* Edward Bairstow (Novello); SATB (M)
Ps. 71:1-12 *In Thee, O Lord,* Jane Marshall (Augsburg); SATB (E)

WEDNESDAY OF HOLY WEEK (ABC)

Isaiah 50:4-9a The third of the four Songs of the Servant of Yahweh: Each day Yahweh wakens me and opens my ears to his word which sustains me. Though I have suffered ridicule, insults, hostility, physical abuse, I have not turned from my task. I trust Yahweh's help; Yahweh will vindicate me. So who will declare me guilty?

Hebrews 12:1-3 A lifelong marathon race: that's what you're in for when you join the crowd trying to keep pace with Jesus. So strip off your warm-up suit, throw away your pride, scrap your blueprints for success and any other sins that weigh you down. To endure in this race, you've got to be lean. And you've got to be determined and tenacious in keeping your eyes fixed on Jesus. He didn't become discouraged or give up because of hostility from sinners or even death on the cross. So persevere in following the pacesetter Jesus. And remember, you're not alone—all the racers from the past are cheering you on.

John 13:21-30 Following the act of footwashing, Jesus announces that one who is present will betray him. Such a disclosure perks up the disciples' conversation and introduces the unknown Beloved Disciple. Jesus then dips some bread in the sauce and gives it to Judas, presumably to indicate him as the betrayer. Then, at Jesus' request, Judas leaves "to do what he has to do."

Psalm 70
1. Gelineau, *O God, Make Haste to My Rescue*, 30P&2C, p. 21
2. Gregorian psalm tone, *GP*, Proper 27 A

Hymns for the Day	HL	HB	WB
Christ, Above All Glory Seated	–	–	324
Ah, Holy Jesus	158	191	280
Make Me a Captive, Lord	247	308	–
Who Trusts in God, a Strong Abode	–	375	–
I Look to Thee in Every Need	79	114	–

Anthems for the Day

Isa. 50:4-9a *Lord, to Thee We Turn (Inimici Autem)*, Orlando di Lasso (*Second Concord Anthem Book*, E. C. Schirmer); SATB (ME)

Heb. 12:1-3 *He That Shall Endure*, Felix Mendelssohn (*Elijah*, G. Schirmer); SATB (ME)

John 13:21-30 *Ah, Holy Jesus (Choral Variations on Herzliebster Jesu)*, Roger Petrich (*Anthems for Choirs*, vol. 4, Oxford); SATB (D)

Ps. 70 *Haste Thee, O God*, Adrian Batten (*Anthems for Choirs*, vol. 1, Oxford); SATB (M)

MAUNDY THURSDAY (C)

Jeremiah 31:31-34 Yahweh is going to make a new covenant with his people. This new covenant will not be like the old Sinai one which his people adulterated, even though he was their faithful husband; this time Yahweh will cut his new covenant into his people's hearts, minds, and will. They will be his people, he will be their God. Everyone will know Yahweh—no need to teach one another about Yahweh—for he will forgive their iniquity and no longer remember their sin.

Hebrews 10:16-25 The fulfillment of Jeremiah 31:33-34 abrogates the need for any further sacrifices, since God will no longer remember our sin. Christ's sacrifice truly is once and for all. Now that all guilt is lifted from us, we may freely and confidently respond to God's love offered in Jesus Christ by encouraging one another to trust God's faithful promises. Such trust may lead to a caring, supportive, loving community of faith.

Luke 22:7-20 On the Day of Unleavened Bread, Jesus dispatches Peter and John to prepare the Passover by following a man carrying a pitcher of water into a house where they are to tell the householder to show them a large upper room. Jesus earnestly desires to eat this Passover with his apostles because his impending death will preclude future observances with them. Instead, Jesus commands all to share in the cup from which he drinks, and the loaf of bread broken for them—"This is my body."

Psalm 116:12-19
1. Metrical, *What Shall I Render to the Lord, HB* 32, tune: Lambeth
2. Gelineau, *I Trusted Even When I Said, GG,* p. 25
3. Gregorian psalm tone, *GP,* Easter 3 B

Hymns for the Day	HL	HB	WB
Where Charity and Love Prevail	–	–	641
Go to Dark Gethsemane	–	193	–
When We Are Tempted to Deny Your Son	–	–	640
Jesus, Lead the Way	–	334	441
Lead Us, O Father, in the Paths of Peace	262	341	–
'Twas on That Night	360	448	–
'Tis Midnight; and on Olive's Brow	–	189	–
O Sacred Head, Now Wounded	151	194	524

Anthems for the Day
Jer. 31:31-34 *This Is the Covenant,* Jean Berger (Augsburg); SATB
Heb. 10:16-25 *Thou Wilt Keep Him in Perfect Peace,* Herbert Sumsion (Royal School of Church Music); SATB (M)
Luke 22:7-20 *An Upper Room Did Our Lord Prepare,* arr. John Wilson (*Hymnal Supplement,* Agape); unison (E)
Ps. 116:12-19 *Offertory/Lent II (Verses and Offertories—Lent),* Kevin Norris (Augsburg); unison (E)

GOOD FRIDAY (ABC)

Isaiah 52:13–53·12 The fourth of the four Songs of the Servant of Yahweh. Yahweh promises the coming vindication of his servant. Thus many are shocked to see an afflicted, disfigured, marred servant. Has God smitten him for past sins? No, the servant has participated in our human brokenness. He has "borne our griefs and carried our sorrows" according to God's will. This humiliated servant is the one whom Yahweh will vindicate.

Hebrews 4:14-16; 5:7-9 We have a great high priest to represent us to God. A simple human being named Jesus who lived in the same kind of power-hungry, achievement-oriented, complacently religious, me-first world. But this Jesus was sinless. He is the perfect one who is the source of salvation and now reigns with God.

John 18:1–19:42 The passion narrative according to John.

or **John 19:17-30** The crucifixion and death of Jesus.

Psalm 22:1-18
1. Gelineau, *My God, My God, Why Have You Forsaken Me?*, 30P&2C, p. 5
2. Gregorian psalm tone, *GP*, Good Friday ABC
3. Howard Hughes, *My God, My God, Why Have You Abandoned Me?* (G.I.A.)

Hymns for the Day	HL	HB	WB
Throned Upon the Awful Tree	–	197	605
Behold the Lamb of God!	153	–	307
Ah, Holy Jesus	158	191	280
O Sacred Head, Now Wounded	151	194	524
There Is a Green Hill Far Away	157	202	–
When I Survey the Wondrous Cross	152	198	635
Alone You Journey Forth, O Lord	–	–	294

Anthems for the Day
Isa. 52:13–53:12 *Saw Ye My Savior*, David Johnson (Augsburg); unison, flute (E)
Heb. 4:14-16; 5:7-9 *Christus Factus Est*, Juan B. Comes (Leeds Music); SATB (ME)
John 18:1–19:42 or **John 19:17-30** *O Vos Omnes*, Carlos Correa (*Anthems for Choirs*, vol. 1, Oxford); SATB (E)
Ps. 22:1-18 *My God, My God, Why Hast Thou Forsaken Me?*, Gerald Near (H. W. Gray); SATB (M)

EASTER VIGIL (ABC)

Genesis 1:1–2:2 All was dark upon the formless, chaotic, unordered waters of creation. God spoke a word, and there was light. When God speaks, action occurs. God spoke again and again and there was firmament-dome-sky, dry land, vegetation, lights (sun, moon, and stars), living beings, animal life, and finally human beings—a community of male and female. And God saw that all of creation was very good. Chaos is transformed into cosmos by the majesty and mystery of God, whose will for creation is unity and harmony.

Psalm 33
1. Vs. 1-22: *LBW*, p. 230, suggested tone—9
2. Vs. 18-22: Gelineau, *Ring Out Your Joy to the Lord*, *GG*, p. 105
3. Vs. 18-22: Gregorian psalm tone, *GP*, Lent 2 A

Genesis 7:1-5, 11-18; 8:6-18; 9:8-13 Both J and P sources are interwoven to form an abridged version of the flood narrative. The rebellion against God (sin) by God's creatures leads creation to disorder, disharmony, and disunity. Yahweh therefore decides to destroy all except Noah and his family. So the death-dealing power of water is unleashed as Yahweh fulfills his promise. Yet God mysteriously makes a unilateral covenant with Noah and his descendants and all living beings: Never again will I destroy creation by flood. As a sign of God's eternal promise to all creation, God lays down his bow in the sky.

Psalm 46
1. Metrical, *A Mighty Fortress Is Our God* (found in most hymnals)
2. Contemporary setting, *Psalm 46* from *Three Psalms of Celebration*, Arthur Wills (Royal School of Church Music, 1980)
3. Gregorian psalm tone, *GP*, Easter Vigil, Proper 29 C

Genesis 22:1-18 God tests Abraham in order to find out whether Abraham trusts only God's promise: "Give up your only son." A repugnant, disturbing test, yet Abraham faithfully obeys. Asks Isaac, "Where is the lamb?" "God will provide," replies Abraham, and an angel of the Lord cries out, "Now I know you trust only God's promise because you have not withheld from God that which is most precious to you." Miraculously, God provides a ram for the offering and again blesses Abraham.

Psalm 16
1. *LBW*, p. 220, suggested tone—9
2. Gelineau, *Preserve Me, God, I Take Refuge in You*, *GG*, p. 91
3. Gregorian psalm tone, *GP*, Easter Vigil ABC

Exodus 14:10–15:1 Moses' prebattle motivational speech to the Israelites: "Fear not, stand firm, keep still, for Yahweh will fight for you." Yahweh commands Moses to raise his walking stick over the waters so they will divide. An angel of God and the pillar of cloud move to the rear of the Israelites and veil them from the Egyptians. And all comes to fulfillment according to the word of God. Yahweh drives back the sea by a strong east wind, throws the Egyptians into panic, causes their wheels to become mired in mud, and tosses them into the sea. Thus Yahweh saves Israel from the Egyptians, and Israel believes in Yahweh and his servant Moses. So Moses and the people sing a song to Yahweh.

Exodus 15:1-6, 11-13, 17-18
1. Gelineau, *I Will Sing to the Lord*, GG, p. 41

Isaiah 54:5-14 "For a brief moment," repents Yahweh, "I cast off my unfaithful bride Israel. In an outburst of wrath, I hid my face from her. But with great compassion I will take her back forever. As I swore an oath to Noah never again to destroy creation by flood, so I have sworn an oath to you, O Israel, never again to withdraw my love for you. My covenant of peace is more firm than seemingly immovable mountains. O afflicted one, I will build you a new city of precious stones where you shall be secure and your children shall learn my ways, and peace and prosperity shall reign."

Psalm 30
1. *LBW*, p. 228, suggested tone—8
2. Gelineau, *I Will Praise You, Lord*, GG, p. 42
3. Gregorian psalm tone, *GP*, Easter Vigil ABC

Isaiah 55:1-11 An imperative invitation to the eschatological banquet. Come! Buy! Eat! Free wine and milk. Why futilely try to buy your way into the banquet or purchase unsatisfying pleasures? Heed my word and you shall eat well. Summon your neighbors while Yahweh is near. And return to the Lord, our God, who is merciful and quick to forgive, for Yahweh's ways are not our ways. When God speaks, action occurs. Does rain fall from the skies and return there before fulfilling its purpose of watering the earth? Neither does God's word. It shall accomplish that which God intends.

Isaiah 12:2-6
1. Gelineau, *Truly, God Is My Salvation*, GG, p. 43

Baruch 3:9-15, 32–4:4 Why, O Israel, are you in exile, alienated from God? Because you have forsaken the fountain of wisdom, you are growing old in a foreign land. If you had walked in God's way (Torah), then you would be living forever in peace. Turn away from all seductive ephemeral pleasures, and walk toward God's enduring gift of wisdom's shining light. Happy indeed are those who know what is pleasing to God.

Psalm 19
1. Vs. 1-14, *LBW*, pp. 223, 224, suggested tone—9
2. Vs. 7-14, Metrical, *Most Perfect Is the Law of God*, from *The Psalter*, 1912, HB 257, tune: Glasgow
3. Vs. 7-14, Gelineau, *The Law of the Lord Is Perfect*, GG, p. 121
4. Vs. 7-14, Gregorian psalm tone, *GP*, Proper 21 B

Ezekiel 36:24-28 Thus says the Lord God: "I will gather together you exiles and bring you home. I will sprinkle you with clean water and therefore forgive you and cleanse you from all that has defiled you. I will renew you by taking away your stubborn heart and giving you a new heart and a new mind. And I will empower you by putting my spirit among you so that you can walk in my ways. Then you shall live in the land I gave your ancestors; and you shall be my people, and I shall be your God. We shall be inseparable."

Psalm 42
1. Metrical, *My Soul Is like the Deer*, MP&E, p. 197, tune: Hosmer
2. Metrical, *As Pants the Hart for Cooling Streams*, HB 322, tune: Spohr
3. Gelineau, *My Soul Is Thirsting for God*, GG, p. 44
4. Gregorian psalm tone, *GP*, Easter Vigil ABC
5. *PS*, p. 11

Ezekiel 37:1-14 The vision of the valley of dry bones, dead dry bones of Israel everywhere. Asks Yahweh, "Can these bones live?" "Perhaps you know," replies Ezekiel. "Preach to the dry bones," commands Yahweh, "that they shall live." So Ezekiel does as commanded. And astonishingly the bones come together and breath comes into them, all by the power of the Word of God.

Psalm 143
1. Metrical, *When Morning Lights the Eastern Skies*, HB 49, tune: St. Stephen
2. Gregorian psalm tone, *GP*, Easter Vigil ABC

Zephaniah 3:14-20 A psalm of celebration sung by the faithful remnant: Sing, shout, rejoice, and exult, O Israel, because Yahweh has taken away, has cast out the menacing threat, and is "in your midst" reigning as King. Fear not! Yahweh, your God, will renew you. Promises Yahweh, "I will transform the shame of the lame and the outcast into praise, and I will bring you home."

Psalm 98
1. Metrical psalm, *New Songs of Celebration Render*, Erik Routley, SOT&P, p. 2, tune: *Rendez à Dieu*
2. Psalm paraphrase, *Sing a New Song to the Lord*, Timothy Dudley-Smith, WII, p. 245, tune: *Cantate Domino* by David G. Wilson, fresh, contemporary setting
3. Gelineau, *Sing a New Song to the Lord*, GG, p. 15
4. Gregorian psalm tone, *GP*, Christmas Day 3 ABC

Romans 6:3-11 Why not continue in sin so God's grace and glory may overflow? Responds Paul, "How can we who died to sin still live in it? When we were baptized into union with Christ, we became one with him in death and were set free from the power of sin, and then we were raised with Christ to new life. So our old being is dead to sin, and we now have a new life in Christ."

Psalm 114
1. Gregorian psalm tone, *GP*, Proper 12 B

Year A: Matthew 28:1-10 Two women at Jesus' tomb encounter God's power in the form of an earthquake and an angel. They hurriedly leave the tomb in fear and great joy.

Year B: Mark 16:1-8 Three women go to Jesus' tomb to anoint his body. Instead they find the tomb unsealed and a young man in a white robe sitting on the right side who says, "Jesus has risen. Go, tell his disciples that he is going before you to Galilee." The women flee from the tomb, for they are afraid.

Year C: Luke 24:1-12 The message of the two men to the women at the empty tomb, who then relay this good news to the apostles, who disbelieve such idle tales.

Hymns for the Day	HL	HB	WB
O God of Bethel, by Whose Hand	98	342	496
God Is Our Refuge and Our Strength	91	381	–
Come, Ye Disconsolate	293	373	–
Give to the Winds Your Fears	294	364	377
At the Name of Jesus	–	143	303
The Day of Resurrection!	166	208	584
The Strife Is O'er, the Battle Done	164	203	597

	HL	HB	WB
Come, We That Love the Lord	–	408	–
All Glory Be to God on High	–	–	283

Anthems for the Day

Gen. 1:1–2:2 *In the Beginning of Creation*, Daniel Pinkham (E. C. Schirmer); SATB, tape (ME)

Ps. 33 *Our Soul Waits for the Lord*, Jane Marshall (*Two Quiet Psalms*, Sacred Music); SATB (ME)

Sing, Ye Righteous, Lodovico Viadana (Concordia); SATB (M)

Gen. 7:1-5, 11-18; 8:6-18; 9:8-13 *If Thou but Suffer God to Guide Thee*, Jody Lindh (Concordia); SATB (E)

Ps. 46 *Psalm 46*, Arthur Wills (*Three Psalms of Celebration*, Royal School of Church Music); unison (E)

Gen. 22:1-18 *On God and Not on Human Trust*, Johann Pachelbel (Concordia); SATB (M)

Ps. 16 *Preserve Me, O Lord*, Benedetto Marcello (Concordia); SATB (E)

Ex. 14:10–15:1 *Thanks Be to Thee, O Lord*, G. F. Handel, arr. Saar (E. C. Schirmer); SATB, alto solo (E)

Ex. 15:1-6, 11-13, 17-18 *I Will Sing to the Lord*, Alec Wyton (Hinshaw); unison (E)

A Song of Exaltation, Samuel Adler (Abingdon); SATB (MD)

Isa. 54:5-14 *Blessed the People*, Johann Geisler (Boosey & Hawkes); SSAB or SATB (E)

Ps. 30 *I Will Greatly Rejoice*, Donald Rotermund (Concordia); SATB (M)

Isa. 55:1-11 *The Second Song of Isaiah*, Erik Routley (Hinshaw); unison, congregation (E)

Seek Ye the Lord, Austin Lovelace (Augsburg); SATB (E)

Isa. 12:2-6 *The First Song of Isaiah*, Erik Routley (Hinshaw); unison, congregation (E)

O Lord, I Will Praise Thee, Gordon Jacob (*Oxford Easy Anthem Book*, Oxford); SATB (ME)

Baruch 3:9-15, 32–4:4 *Hear Ye, Israel!*, Felix Mendelssohn (*Elijah*, G. Schirmer); soprano solo (M)

Ps. 19 *The Heavens Are Telling*, Ludwig van Beethoven (E. C. Schirmer); SATB (E)

Ezek. 36:24-28 *Behold, the Tabernacle of God*, W. H. Harris (Hinshaw); SATB (M)

Ps. 42 *As a Hart Longs for the Brooklet*, Claude Goudimel (Mercury); SATB (ME)

Ezek. 37:1-14 *Ezekiel Saw the Wheel*, Spiritual, arr. Gilbert Martin (Hinshaw); SATB (M)

Ps. 143 *Hear My Prayer*, Alan Hovhaness (Peters); SSATBB (MD)

Zeph. 3:14-20 *Offertory/Advent IV* (*Verses and Offertories—Advent*), Robert Wetzler (Augsburg); SATB or unison (E)

Ps. 98 *Rejoice in the Lord*, Raymond Haan (Augsburg); SATB (E)

Rom. 6:3-11 *Let Us Ever Walk with Jesus*, Paul Manz (Concordia); unison (E)

Ps. 114 *When Israel Went Out of Egypt*, Hans Leo Hassler (Lawson-Gould); SATB (M)

Year A: Matt. 28:1-10 *Mary Magdalene*, Johannes Brahms (H. W. Gray); SATB (E)

Year B: Mark 16:1-8 *Who Rolls Away the Stone*, Andreas Hammerschmidt (Concordia); SSATB, 2 violins (M)

Year C: Luke 24:1-12 *Magdalen, Cease from Sobs and Sighs*, Peter Hurford (Oxford); SATB (ME)

EASTER DAY (C)

Acts 10:34-43 At Cornelius' house in Caesarea, Peter recounts how his own life has been transformed by the power of the risen Lord, and everyone else (Jews and Gentiles) also can be transformed by that power.

or **Isaiah 65:17-25** Behold, Yahweh creates new heavens and a new earth where all may truly rejoice.

1 Corinthians 15:19-26 Christ has been raised from death; all who belong to him will rise also.

or **Acts 10:34-43** *See above.*

John 20:1-18 Peter and the Beloved Disciple seek the truth about the empty tomb. Mary engages the "gardener" in conversation, who says, "Tell them I am ascending."

or **Luke 24:1-12** The message of the two men to the women at the empty tomb, who then relay this good news to the apostles, who disbelieve such idle tales.

Psalm 118:14-24
1. Metrical, *This Is the Day the Lord Hath Made, HB* 69, tune: Arlington
2. Gelineau, *This Is the Day the Lord Has Made, GG,* p. 46
3. Gregorian psalm tone, *GP,* Easter Day ABC
4. Richard Proulx, *Processional Psalm for a Festival* (G.I.A.)

Hymns for the Day	HL	HB	WB
Jesus Christ Is Risen Today	163	204	440
The Strife Is O'er, the Battle Done	164	203	597
Come, You Faithful, Raise the Strain	168	205	344
"Welcome, Happy Morning"	169	207	–
The Day of Resurrection!	166	208	584
Christ the Lord Is Risen Again	–	–	328
This Is the Day the Lord Hath Made	23	69	–

Anthems for the Day

Acts 10:34-43 *Good Christian Friends, Rejoice and Sing!,* Melchior Vulpius, arr. Bisbee (Augsburg); SA, SAB, or SATB, instruments (M)

or **Isa. 65:17-25** *Salvation Is Created,* Paul Tschesnokoff, arr. Becker (G.I.A.); SATTBB (M)

1 Cor. 15:19-26 or **Acts 10:34-43** *Christ Is Risen,* John Joubert (Novello); SATB (MD)

John 20:1-18 *Christ the Lord Is Risen Again,* Richard Proulx (G.I.A.); SATB, brass, tympani (MD)

or **Luke 24:1-12** *Magdalen, Cease from Sobs and Sighs,* Peter Hurford (Oxford); SATB (ME)

Ps. 118:14-24 *This Is the Day,* Richard Proulx (G.I.A.); cantor, congregation, descant, bells, percussion (E)

EASTER EVENING (ABC)

Acts 5:29-32 The apostles' response to the Sanhedrin's prohibition of teaching "in the name of Jesus": We must obey God rather than men in giving witness to God's raising of Jesus from death.

or **Daniel 12:1-3** A vision of the archangel Michael ushering in the day of resurrection for Israel and consummating God's plan for all of creation.

1 Corinthians 5:6-8 You are the new people of God by God's gracious act of salvation through the sacrifice of his Son, the true paschal lamb.

or **Acts 5:29-32** *See above.*

Luke 24:13-49 Two of Jesus' followers walking from Jerusalem to Emmaus are joined by the risen Jesus, but they fail to recognize him. Astounded at his unawareness of events in Jerusalem, the two travelers relate their hopes concerning Jesus of Nazareth, whom they thought was the one to redeem Israel, and their disillusionment upon his death on the cross. Jesus responds to their despair by interpreting the scriptures to them. Then they go into a home where at the table "Jesus took the bread and blessed, and broke it, and gave it to them. And their eyes were opened and they recognized him." The travelers immediately return to Jerusalem to tell others that "the Lord has risen." Then Jesus suddenly appears to his disciples. They are terrified. He shows them his hands and feet, eats some fish, and opens their minds about how the scriptures have been fulfilled.

Psalm 150
1. Metrical, *Praise the Lord, His Glories Show*, HB 4, tune: Llanfair
2. Metrical, *Bless'd Be the Lord Our God!*, P&E, tune: Diademata
3. Gregorian psalm tone, GP, Trinity Sunday A
4. *PS*, pp. 39, 40

Hymns for the Day	HL	HB	WB
Rejoice, the Lord Is King	193	140	562
O Sons and Daughters, Let Us Sing!	167	206	527
Thine Is the Glory	–	209	–
Praise the Lord, Who Reigns Above	–	–	553

Anthems for the Day
Acts 5:29-32 *Easter Carol*, Malcolm Williamson (Weinberger); SATB (M)

or **Dan. 12:1-3** *Then Shall the Righteous Shine Forth*, Felix Mendelssohn (*Elijah*, G. Schirmer); tenor solo (M)

1 Cor. 5:6-8 *Christ, Our Passover*, Healey Willan (*A First Motet Book*, Concordia); SATB (E)

or **Acts 5:29-32** *(See above)*

Luke 24:13-49 *This Joyful Eastertide*, Alec Wyton (H. W. Gray); SATB, optional brass (ME)

Ps. 150 *Psalm 150*, John Harper (Oxford); 2-part (E)

SECOND SUNDAY OF EASTER (C)

Acts 5:27-32 The apostles' response to the Sanhedrin's prohibition of teaching "in the name of Jesus": We must obey God rather than men in giving witness to God's raising of Jesus from death.

Revelation 1:4-8 The prophet John sends greetings to the seven churches: "Remember to whom you belong—not to the Caesars of this world but solely to Christ. Remember by whose grace and peace you live—not by the Caesars' mercy but only by God's. Yes, the claims about Christ—he reliably testified that God's promises will be fulfilled, he inaugurated a new age, he rules as the King of kings—all seem preposterous, but one day the whole world will recognize that he is the one who loves us, frees us from our sins, and makes us priests. To him be glory and power, forever."

John 20:19-31 Verses 19-23 are a series of symbolic episodes: The risen Jesus appears to his frightened disciples and says, "Peace." Then he shows them his hands and his side (which fills the disciples with joy) and again says, "Peace." He gives them the Holy Spirit by breathing on them and concludes with an eschatological saying about resisting forgiveness. In verses 24-31, Thomas says he must see with his eyes before he will believe. So again Jesus appears. He tells Thomas to touch his side. Thomas confesses. Blessed are those who believe solely on the basis of the word alone.

Psalm 2
1. Gelineau, *Why This Tumult Among Nations*, 24P&1C

Hymns for the Day	HL	HB	WB
O for a Thousand Tongues to Sing	199	141	493
O Sons and Daughters, Let Us Sing!	167	206	527
Strong Son of God, Immortal Love	175	228	578
Rejoice, the Lord Is King	193	140	562
Ask Ye What Great Thing I Know	312	371	–

Anthems for the Day

Acts 5:27-32 *Sing, Men and Angels, Sing*, Gerald Near (Augsburg); unison or SATB (E)

Rev. 1:4-8 *Unto Him That Loved Us*, R. Vaughan Williams (*Morning Star Choir Book*, Book 1, Concordia); unison (E)

John 20:19-31 *Because You Have Seen Me, Thomas*, Luca Marenzio (Concordia); SATB (M)

Second Sunday of Easter, Nancy Maeker (Augsburg); unison, speech choir, Orff instruments (E)

Ps. 2 *O God, Whose Will Is Life and Peace*, Thomas Tallis, arr. Busarow (Concordia); SATB, flute (E)

THIRD SUNDAY OF EASTER (C)

Acts 9:1-20 When Saul of Tarsus sets out on his way to Damascus, he bears the reputation of a feared, zealous persecutor of those who acknowledge Jesus as the Way. But when Saul departs from Damascus, he is an ardent advocate for the risen Christ. What happens to Saul on the way? Suddenly blinded by the light, he falls to the roadside, hears and obeys a voice, experiences the touch of Ananias' hands, regains his sight, and is baptized. The tormentor of Christ has been miraculously transformed into a Spirit-filled propagator who publicly proclaims Jesus as the Son of God, and who will suffer for the sake of the name of the Way.

Revelation 5:11-14 The prophet John weeps because there is no one worthy to open the seven-sealed scroll containing the proclamation of God's plan. But then he sees a lamb, a leader of the flock, apparently slain yet living. A slaughtered lamb who suffered for our sake and rose for our sake is worthy to open the scroll. No wonder the living creatures, elders, angels, and the myriads burst forth in song.

John 21:1-19 or **John 21:15-19** A fish tale (vs. 1-8) about seven disciples who fish all night and catch nothing. At dawn a stranger standing on the beach tells them to cast their net on the other side of the boat. They obey. Presto! Their net bulges with fish. Then Peter, whom Jesus loved, exclaims, "It is the Lord!" A eucharistic story (vs. 9-14) about the risen Christ taking bread and fish and giving it to the disciples while they were standing around a charcoal fire; the place of the ultimate denial of Jesus by Peter becomes the place at which Jesus forgives and feeds his disciples (cf. 18:18). A commissioning (vs. 15-19) in which Jesus asks Peter three times if he loves him. Following each of three affirmations by Peter, Jesus commissions him to feed his sheep.

Psalm 30:4-12
1. Gelineau, *I Will Praise You, Lord, GG*, p. 42
2. Gregorian psalm tone, *GP*, Proper 5 C

Hymns for the Day	HL	HB	WB
Blessing and Honor and Glory and Power	196	137	311
Praise to the Lord, the Almighty	6	1	557
Come, Let Us to the Lord Our God	–	125	–
Hark, My Soul, It Is the Lord!	224	263	–
All Ye That Fear God's Holy Name	–	35	–

Anthems for the Day
Acts 9:1-20 *Saul*, Egil Hovland (Walton); SATB, narrator (D)
Rev. 5:11-14 *To the Lamb Be Glory*, Paul Weber (Concordia); unison, congregation, optional brass (E)
John 21:1-19 or **John 21:15-19** *Feed My Lambs*, Natalie Sleeth (C. Fischer); unison, 2 flutes (E)
Ps. 30:4-12 *Praise Ye*, Heinrich Schütz (Belwin-Mills); 2-part (ME)

FOURTH SUNDAY OF EASTER (C)

Acts 13:15-16, 26-33 In the second half of Paul's sermon in the synagogue in Antioch of Pisidia in Asia Minor, he retells the story of the innocent Jesus who was crucified because of the ignorance of the Jews and their unwitting fulfillment of the prophecies (manifested in Ps. 2:2). But God reverses their mistaken judgment by raising him from the dead. Therefore Paul brings all hearers the good news that what God promised our ancestors has now been fulfilled.

Revelation 7:9-17 A vision of the glory and joy of the faithful in the New Age. A countless multitude comprised of all peoples, tongues, nations, races, and tribes stands before the throne and before the Lamb. Clothed in white robes (because they have been washed in the blood of the Lamb) and waving palm branches in their hands, the numberless throng and angels sing and shout acclamations. They serve God day and night. They experience the life of salvation where there is no more hunger, no more thirst, no more enervating heat, no more tears, no more pain, for Christ their shepherd guides them to springs of eternal living water.

John 10:22-30 The Jews (the opposition) want a crystal-clear answer from Jesus to their question: "Are you the Christ?" Jesus seems to respond opaquely. "I told you. The works I do in my Father's name bear witness to me. My sheep hear me and follow me, and I give them eternal life." What Jesus reall˙ does is ask a plain counter-question: "Do you belong to my flock?"

Psalm 23
1. Metrical, *The Lord's My Shepherd*, from the *Scottish Psalter*, 1650, *HB* 104, tune: Crimond
2. Gelineau, *The Lord Is My Shepherd*, *GG*, p. 136
3. Gregorian psalm tone, *GP*, Proper 23 A
4. Frank Quinn, *The Lord Is My Shepherd*, *MP&E*, p. 196
5. *PS*, p. 14

Hymns for the Day	HL	HB	WB
We Greet You, Sure Redeemer from All Strife	–	144	625
The King of Love My Shepherd Is	99	106	590
You Servants of God, Your Master Proclaim	198	27	645
Praise the Lord! You Heavens, Adore Him	10	3	554

Anthems for the Day
Acts 13:15-16, 26-33 *Lord That Descendedst*, Eric Gritton (*Anthems for Choirs*, vol. 1, Oxford); SATB (ME)
Rev. 7:9-17 *Amen, Praise Ye the Lord*, C. Hasse (C. Fischer); SATB, bass solo (E)
John 10:22-30 *Very Bread, Good Shepherd, Tend Us*, Charles Talmadge (H. W. Gray); SATB (E)
Ps. 23 *The Lord Is My Shepherd*, John Rutter (Oxford); SATB, oboe (M)

FIFTH SUNDAY OF EASTER (C)

Acts 14:8-18 In Lystra a crippled man, unable to use his feet from the day he was born, listens to Paul speaking. Paul sees that he has faith, so he says loudly, "Stand up on your feet!" And he leaps up and walks. The "pagan" crowd deduces that Paul and Barnabas possess divine powers; they lift up their voices in praise of the "gods come down to earth" and begin to offer sacrifices. Horrified by the crowd's response, Paul and Barnabas cry out, "We are of the same nature as you. We bring you good news that you can turn from such vain idols to the living God who made heaven and earth."

Revelation 21:1-6 A vision of a new heaven and a new earth. The new Jerusalem descends from God and joins the transformed earth where chaotic waters, tears, mourning, crying, death have all disappeared. Human beings will see God and live in holy fellowship together. Shouts the great voice from the throne, "I make all things new."

John 13:31-35 Christ gives God glory by living a life of simple, obedient love: seeking out the lost, the hurt, the suffering, the oppressed, the outcast. He lives a life of poverty and concern for others which ultimately earns him death on the cross. When he is lifted up on the cross to die for us, he gives God glory. He gives away himself in love for us, and commands us to love one another.

Psalm 145:13b-21
1. Metrical, *O Lord, Thou Art My God and King*, HB 5, tune: Duke Street
2. Metrical, *O Lord, You Are Our God and King*, HB 517, tune: Duke Street
3. Gelineau, *The Lord Is Kind and Full of Compassion*, GG, p. 102

Hymns for the Day	HL	HB	WB
O Holy City, Seen of John	409	508	505
O Love Divine, That Stooped to Share	–	116	–
Of the Father's Love Begotten	–	7	534
Open Now the Gates of Beauty	–	40	544
I Know Not How that Bethlehem's Babe	181	224	–

Anthems for the Day
Acts 14:8-18 *Not Unto Us, O Lord*, William Byrd (*A First Motet Book*, Concordia); 3-part canon (E)
Rev. 21:1-6 *And I Saw a New Heaven*, Edgar Bainton (Novello); SATB (M)
John 13:31-35 *Most Glorious Lord of Life*, W. H. Harris (Oxford); STB (ME)
Ps. 145:13b-21 *The Eyes of All Wait Upon Thee*, Jean Berger (Augsburg); SATB (MD)

SIXTH SUNDAY OF EASTER (C)

Acts 15:1-2, 22-29 The potential fracturing of the early church over the osten-
sible issue of circumcision necessitates the first apostolic council in Jerusalem.
After deliberation, "it seemed good to the Holy Spirit and to the apostles and
elders" to lift not only the legal requirement of circumcision of Gentiles but,
in effect, to lay the cornerstone for "salvation by grace" and, therefore,
approve the Gentile mission.

Revelation 21:10, 22-27 John gets a glimpse of the holy city Jerusalem coming
down out of heaven from God. He sees no temple, no natural light (sun),
and no closed gates. Rather, the only necessary temple is the one of the Lord
God Almighty and the Lamb; the glory of God and the lamp of the Lamb
provide sufficient light; and the open-gated city admits friends and foes
around the world who are now reconciled. Nothing unclean or profane
enters, but only those whose names are inscribed in the Lamb's book of life.

John 14:23-29 Says Jesus, "If you love me, then do (keep) my words (which
are God's will)." When Jesus departs, God sends the Paraclete (companion
interpreter) to teach us and remind us of the same words Jesus spoke.

Psalm 67
1. Metrical psalm, *Lord, Bless and Pity Us*, from *The Psalter*, 1912, HB 493, WB
   456, tune: St. Michael
2. Gelineau, *O God, Be Gracious and Bless Us*, GG, p. 17
3. Gregorian psalm tone, *GP*, Proper 15 A
4. Mixed medium, *Psalm 67*, Arthur Wills (G. Schirmer)
5. *PS*, p. 21

Hymns for the Day	HL	HB	WB
O Holy City, Seen of John	409	508	505
"Thy Kingdom Come"	363	484	–
Walk Tall, Christian	–	–	616
This Is the Day of Light	20	72	–
Lord of All Being, Throned Afar	87	87	463

Anthems for the Day
Acts 15:1-2, 22-29 *Tarry No Longer*, W. H. Harris (*Oxford Easy Anthem Book*,
   Oxford); unison (ME)
Rev. 21:10, 22-27 *O Holy City, Seen of John* (HL 409, HB 508, WB 505)
John 14:23-29 *Peace I Leave with You*, Knut Nystedt (Augsburg); SSATB (M)
Ps. 67 *Let the People Praise Thee*, William Mathias (Oxford); SATB (M)

THE ASCENSION OF OUR LORD (ABC)

Acts 1:1-11 Jesus charges the apostles to wait in Jerusalem for "the promise of the Father" which is the gift of the Holy Spirit. The apostles ask the risen Jesus if he will now restore the kingdom to Israel. "That's not your worry but God's," replies Jesus. "You'll receive power when the Holy Spirit comes, and then you shall be my witnesses proclaiming the gospel everywhere." Then Jesus is lifted up and departs on a cloud.

Ephesians 1:15-23 May God give you the Spirit who will make you wise and understanding in the knowledge of Christ. In this way you will know the hope to which Christ has called you (the kind of New Age that is coming), and to recognize God's power among us, especially his power in raising Christ to a position above all earthly powers.

Luke 24:46-53 Jesus preaches a kerygmatic sermon on Christ as Lord and the message of repentance and forgiveness. He then constitutes his disciples as the New Israel, promises them the gift of the Spirit, and ascends.

or **Mark 16:9-16, 19-20** Jesus appears to Mary Magdalene, two disciples, and then to eleven disciples: "Go and preach the gospel!" He then ascends to the right hand of God.

Psalm 47
1. Metrical, *O Clap Your Hands, All Ye People, NSC*, p. 5, tune by Eric Reid
2. Gelineau, *All Peoples, Clap Your Hands, GG*, p. 58
3. Gregorian psalm tone, *GP*, Ascension Day ABC

Hymns for the Day	HL	HB	WB
The Head That Once Was Crowned with Thorns	195	211	589
The Lord Ascendeth Up on High	172	212	–
A Hymn of Glory Let Us Sing	–	–	273
Christ, Above All Glory Seated	–	–	324
Crown Him with Many Crowns	190	213	349
Christ, Whose Glory Fills the Skies	26	47	332

Anthems for the Day
Acts 1:1-11 *O for a Shout of Sacred Joy*, Alice Parker (E. C. Schirmer); SATB, snare drum (ME)

Eph. 1:15-23 *Look, Ye Saints, the Sight Is Glorious*, Henry Purcell (*Westminster Praise*, Hinshaw); SATB (E)

Luke 24:46-53 or **Mark 16:9-16, 19-20** *O God the King of Glory*, Henry Purcell (*Anthems for Choirs*, vol. 1, Oxford); SATB (M)

Ps. 47 *Alleluia, Ascendit Deus*, William Byrd (Stainer & Bell); SSATB (MD)

SEVENTH SUNDAY OF EASTER (C)

Acts 16:16-34 In the thoroughly Roman city of Philippi in Macedonia, Paul and Silas are stripped, whipped, and imprisoned on trumped-up charges because when they restored a soothsayer to health, they deprived some local owners of further exploitative economic gain. But an earthquake (divine intervention?) turns the city upside down and allows the jailer and his household to hear the gospel and to be baptized. The story of defeat transformed into victory continues.

Revelation 22:12-14, 16-17, 20 "Behold, I am coming soon. I am the Alpha and the Omega. Blessed are those who wash their robes in preparation for entry into the city and for partaking of the tree of life." The Spirit and the Bride say, "Come." And those who are thirsty for the water of life may say, "Come." Amen. Come, Lord Jesus!

John 17:20-26 Right there in the upper room, Jesus concludes his great prayer by praying for us and all others in all times and places who believe in him, so that we may all be one in the same way the Father and Son are one. Such union with Christ and with each other will manifest to the world the mission and work of Christ which the Father sent him to do.

Psalm 97
1. Metrical psalm, *The Lord Is King!*, Christopher Idle, *PP*, no. 112, contemporary musical setting by Norman Warren
2. Gelineau, *The Lord Is King, GG*, p. 163
3. Gregorian psalm tone, *GP*, Christmas 2 ABC

Hymns for the Day	HL	HB	WB
Put Forth O God, Your Spirit's Might	–	477	559
Rejoice, the Lord Is King	193	140	562
The Lord Is King!	–	83	–
All Praise Be Yours	–	–	290
Look, Ye Saints, the Sight Is Glorious	201	133	–
Where High the Heavenly Temple	–	389	–
Forgive, O Lord, Our Severing Ways	344	476	–

Anthems for the Day
Acts 16:16-34 *All That Christians Have in Life*, C. Young (*Hymnal Supplement*, Agape); unison (E)
Rev. 22:12-14, 16-17, 20 *E'en So, Lord Jesus, Quickly Come*, Paul Manz (Concordia); SATB (M)
John 17:20-26 *Rejoice with Us in God the Trinity*, John Wilson (*Westminster Praise*, Hinshaw); SATB (E)
Ps. 97 *The Lord Is King O'er Land and Sea*, Heinrich Schütz (*Four Psalms*, Mercury); SATB (E)

THE DAY OF PENTECOST (C)

Acts 2:1-21 Wind and tongues of fire—the Holy Spirit—spread among all the believers. Are they drunk? "No," says Peter, "it's only nine in the morning. But while I have your attention, let me tell you about Jesus Christ."

or **Genesis 11:1-9** The inflammable combination of the fear of loss of control and pretentious "possibility thinking" ignites a drivenness to make a name and a place for ourselves, in the name of religion. Such foolish self-reliant crusades always end in babbling chaos.

Romans 8:14-17 An exhortation to live not according to the anxiety and fear of human nature but in harmony with the life-giving Spirit. Though we constantly get tangled in the slavery of our pious self-interest and cravings for acceptance, God's Spirit works among us to create a new relationship that enables us to cry out boldly, "*Abba!*"

or **Acts 2:1-21** *See above.*

John 14:8-17, 25-27 All of Jesus' life was a revelation of God—his words and deeds were ultimately God's. So whoever believes in and loves God and Jesus will speak and do the words and deeds of Jesus. How? God sends the Paraclete (companion interpreter) to teach and remind us of Jesus' words and deeds so we can speak them and live them.

Psalm 104:24-34
1. Metrical, *O Worship the King All Glorious Above, HB* 26, tune: Lyons
2. Gelineau, *Bless the Lord, My Soul!, GG*, p. 63
3. Gregorian psalm tone, *GP*, Pentecost ABC

Hymns for the Day	HL	HB	WB
Come, Holy Ghost, Our Souls Inspire	–	237	335
O Spirit of the Living God	207	242	528
Spirit Divine, Attend Our Prayers	212	243	574
Gracious Spirit, Dwell with Me	214	241	–
The Day of Pentecost Arrived	–	–	583
Our Blest Redeemer	205	–	–

Anthems for the Day
Acts 2:1-21 *The Day of Pentecost*, John A. Nickson (Kjos); SATB, narrator (M)
or **Gen. 11:1-9** *The Spirit of the Lord*, Healey Willian (*A Second Motet Book*, Concordia), SATB (ME)
Rom. 8:14-17 or **Acts 2:1-21** *Come, Mighty Father, Mighty Lord*, G. F. Handel (Edward Marks); SATB (M)
John 14:8-17, 25-27 *Come, Holy Spirit (Veni Creator)*, arr. John Erickson (G.I.A.); unison, handbells (E)
Ps. 104:24-34 *O Lord, How Manifold Are Thy Works*, Martin Shaw (Novello); unison (ME)

TRINITY SUNDAY [First Sunday After Pentecost] (C)

Proverbs 8:22-31 I, Wisdom, was present at the ordering of creation, when Yahweh had yet to shape the springs of water, mountains, hills, and fields; when the sky and horizon were positioned; when clouds were placed in the sky above and seas were opened below; when boundaries were set for ocean tides. At that time, I was beside Yahweh like an architect and a firstborn child, constantly rejoicing in creation and delighting in the human race.

Romans 5:1-5 Whether we know it or not, our social world unceasingly tempts us to seek acceptance by being someone, owning something, or living somewhere. Futilely striving to prove our worth, we are hemmed in, restricted, hampered, overburdened, and eventually entrapped by "one thing more to achieve," and therefore we submit to a crinkled-up squatting position in order to survive. Good news! We can stand up straight and rejoice because we are justified by faith and have peace with God through Jesus Christ. God who came to us in Jesus Christ totally accepts us—even our hate and our guilt.

John 16:12-15 "When the Spirit of truth comes, he will guide you into all the truth. He will glorify me," says Jesus in his farewell discourse. The same word and work of God will continue to be disclosed by the Spirit of truth, who will instruct you on a way of life that conforms to Jesus Christ.

Psalm 8
1. Metrical, *O Lord, Our Lord, in All the Earth, HB* 95, tune: Dunfermline
2. Metrical, *O Lord, Our Lord, in All the Earth, MP&E*, p. 5, tune: St. Bernard
3. Gelineau, *When I See the Heavens, GG*, p. 14
4. Gregorian psalm tone, *GP*, Holy Name ABC

Hymns for the Day	HL	HB	WB
Come, Thou Almighty King	52	244	343
Holy, Holy, Holy!	57	11	421
O Word of God Incarnate	215	251	532
O Lord, Our Lord, in All the Earth	–	95	515
Holy Spirit, Truth Divine	208	240	422
Holy Ghost, Dispel Our Sadness	–	–	419

Anthems for the Day
Prov. 8:22-31 *Break Forth in Praise to God*, Johann Franck (*Church Choir Book*, vol. 2, Concordia); SATB (E)

Rom. 5:1-5 *Lord, Grant Grace*, Orlando Gibbons (Concordia); SATB/SATB (M)

John 16:12-15 *O Most Merciful*, Münster Gesangbuch, 1677 (RSCM/Hinshaw); SATB (E)

Trinity, Alec Wyton (*Two Choral Hymns*, H. W. Gray); SATB (M)

Ps. 8 *How Excellent Thy Name*, Howard Hanson (C. Fischer); SATB (MD)

SUNDAY BETWEEN MAY 29 AND JUNE 4
(Proper 4) (C) [use only if after Trinity Sunday]*

1 Kings 8:22-23, 41-43 Solomon stands before the altar of the newly constructed Temple, raises his outstretched arms, and offers the dedicatory
prayer: "Yahweh, God of Israel, you are incomparable to all above and
below. You keep covenant and show *hesed* (steadfast love) to your people.
When a foreigner (who hears about your mighty hand of deliverance of your
people from Egypt) offers prayer to you, hear him and do what he asks so
that all people may know your name and obey you, as do your people Israel."

Galatians 1:1-10 A letter from Paul, an apostle chosen by God through Jesus
Christ, to the churches of Galatia: Grace and peace to you. So much for
greetings; on to the harangue proper. "I am shocked that you Galatians are
so quickly deserting Christ (who called you by sheer grace) and turning your
allegiance to the false teachings of seductive agitators. Let an anathema come
upon any who pervert the gospel of Christ."

Luke 7:1-10 Town leaders pressure Jesus to heal a deserving centurion's
slave. But the centurion says to Jesus, "Lord, I am not worthy; I am a sinner.
But say the word and my servant will be healed, for I understand the power
of real authority." And Jesus marvels that "not even in Israel, God's chosen
people, have I found such faith."

Psalm 100
1. Metrical, *All People That on Earth Do Dwell*, HB 24, tune: Old Hundredth;
   WB 288, tune: Old Hundredth
2. Metrical, *O Be Joyful in the Lord!* WB 482, tune: Rock of Ages
3. Metrical, *Sing, All Creation*, MP&E, p. 50, tune: Iste Confessor (Rouen)
4. Gelineau, *Cry Out with Joy to the Lord*, GG, p. 51
5. Gregorian psalm tone, *GP*, Easter 4 B
6. *PS*, p. 29

Hymns for the Day	HL	HB	WB
All People That on Earth Do Dwell	1	24	288
God of Our Life	88	108	395
At the Name of Jesus	–	143	303
God Himself Is with Us	51	13	384
From All That Dwell Below the Skies	388	33	373

Anthems for the Day
1 Kings 8:22-23, 41-43 *O Lord, My God,* John Rush (G. Schirmer); SATB (ME)
Gal. 1:1-10 *Close in My Breast Thy Perfect Love,* David Lord (*Anthems for Choirs,*
   vol. 2, Oxford); 2-part (ME)
Luke 7:1-10 *O Lord, I Am Not Worthy,* Melchior Franck (Concordia); SATB (M)
Ps. 100 *Jubilate Deo,* Benjamin Britten (Oxford); SATB (M)

---

*NOTE: If the Sunday between May 24 and May 28 follows Trinity Sunday, use the
Eighth Sunday after the Epiphany on that day.

SUNDAY BETWEEN JUNE 5 AND JUNE 11
(Proper 5) (C) [use only if after Trinity Sunday]

1 Kings 17:17-24 An astonishing tale. When a widow's son falls deathly ill, she flies into an anguished dither of accusatory finger-pointing. So Elijah cradles the hollow-eyed son, cries out to Yahweh, and the unexpected, the unforeseen, the unpredictable occurs. In the midst of uncertainty, turmoil, dejection, desolation, hopelessness, fear, or death, life comes by God's word through ordinary human beings. The stunning result: The widow confesses Elijah's authority—"Now I know the word of Yahweh in your mouth is truth."

Galatians 1:11-24 Opponents of Paul have questioned his dubious credentials, for everyone knows Paul's reputation as a persecutor of Christians. Paul's rebuttal: "I was a faithful, law-abiding Jew who zealously obeyed the traditions of my people. But when the risen Christ revealed himself to me through his grace, then by his authority I pursued a different path, preaching to Gentiles the faith that I once tried to destroy. And now others glorify God because of me."

Luke 7:11-17 Jesus sees a funeral procession in Nain—a widow burying her only son, her only source of support. He has compassion for her but says, astoundingly, "Do not weep." He then jolts everyone by breaking the law when he touches the bier and commands the young man to arise. Thus Jesus restores the relationship between mother and son; he heals separation caused even by death.

Psalm 113
1. Metrical, *Praise God, Ye Servants of the Lord, HB* 19, tune: Andre
2. Metrical, *Praise God You Servants of the Lord, MP&E,* p. 60, tune: Eisenach
3. Gelineau, *Praise, O Servants of the Lord, GG,* p. 119
4. Gregorian psalm tone, *GP,* Epiphany 3 C
5. *PS,* p. 30

Hymns for the Day	HL	HB	WB
Rejoice, the Lord Is King	193	140	562
Praise God, Ye Servants of the Lord	–	19	–
We Greet You, Sure Redeemer from All Strife	–	144	625
I Know Not How that Bethlehem's Babe	181	224	–
Thine Arm, O Lord, in Days of Old	–	179	
Father, Whose Will Is Life and Good	–	309	368

Anthems for the Day
1 King 17:17-24 *A Sun, a Shield,* Alice Parker (E. C. Schirmer); 2-part, autoharp, electric bass, percussion (ME)
Gal. 1:11-24 *I Am Content!,* Paul Weber (Concordia); SATB or SAB (E)
Luke 7:11-17 *He Hath Done All Things Well,* Jan Bender (*A First Motet Book,* Concordia); SATB (ME)
Ps. 113, *Ye Children Who Do Serve the Lord,* Scottish Psalter (E. C. Schirmer); SATB (ME)
Praise the Lord, Heinz Werner Zimmermann (*Five Hymns,* Concordia); SATB (ME)

SUNDAY BETWEEN JUNE 12 AND JUNE 18
(Proper 6) (C) [use only if after Trinity Sunday]

1 Kings 19:1-8 By relying on the power of Yahweh, Elijah has gained victory over the established power of the Baal priests. But Queen Jezebel, feeling her power threatened, ruthlessly seeks revenge against Elijah, who flees into the wilderness. "Take my life, Lord," Elijah laments, "victory has turned into defeat, life into death." Here's how Yahweh responds to such a plea: An inexplicable angel unaccountably feeds and cares for Elijah until he is restored and able to walk forty days into the Sinai. Such a gift is truly a sign of God's presence.

Galatians 2:15-21 "Peter," says Paul, "you and I are Jews by birth, so we learned to keep the obligations of the law. Yet we know a person receives God's favorable judgment not by human achievements but by faith in Jesus Christ. So why should Gentiles, who were never under the law, be compelled to obey it? Because the law is from God? Don't you remember that Christ, who died to the law, redeemed us from its curse? Why then try to rebuild it? We have been put to death with Christ on his cross and now live in Christ."

Luke 7:36–8:3 Simon the Pharisee invites Jesus to an elegant dinner party at which a "woman of the streets" washes Jesus' feet with her tears, wipes them with her hair, kisses them, and pours costly perfume on them. Simon is appalled that Jesus allows such a sinner to touch him. So Jesus tells a story about a creditor who forgave two bankrupt debtors. Which debtor will love him more? Replies Simon, "The one who was forgiven more." Right! Have we and Simon forgotten how much we've been forgiven?

Psalm 42
1. Metrical, *My Soul Is like the Deer*, MP&E, p. 197, tune: Hosmer
2. Metrical, *As Pants the Hart for Cooling Streams*, HB 322, tune: Spohr
3. Gelineau, *My Soul Is Thirsting for God*, GG, p. 44
4. Gregorian psalm tone, GP, Easter Vigil ABC
5. PS, p. 11

Hymns for the Day	HL	HB	WB
As Pants the Hart for Cooling Streams	317	322	–
Master, No Offering Costly and Sweet	407	299	–
Love Divine, All Loves Excelling	308	399	471
There's a Wideness in God's Mercy	93	110	601
Jesus, Thy Boundless Love to Me	314	404	–

Anthems for the Day
1 Kings 19:1-8 *Where Do I Go*, Ronald A. Nelson (Augsburg); SAB, baritone solo, flute (M)
Gal. 2:15-21 *I Trust in Thee, Lord Jesus*, Giovanni Bononcini (Concordia); unison, violin (E)
Luke 7:36–8:3 *A Litany*, William Walton (*Anthems for Choirs*, vol. 4, Oxford); SATB (M)
Ps. 42 *As a Hart Longs for the Brooklet*, Claude Goudimel (Mercury); SATB (ME)

SUNDAY BETWEEN JUNE 19 AND JUNE 25
(Proper 7) (C) [use only if after Trinity Sunday]

1 Kings 19:9-14 Elijah escapes the death clutches of Jezebel by hiding out in a cave in the wilderness. Asks Yahweh, "What are you doing here?" "I'm the only faithful one left," responds Elijah self-righteously. So Yahweh commands him to stand upon the mount and then sends a shattering wind, rumbling earthquake, and raging fire—spectacular phenomena but no presence of Yahweh—followed by a majestic "still small voice," causing Elijah to wrap his cloak around his face. Yahweh again asks, "What are you doing here?" Still, Elijah offers his identical complaint, "It's me against the world."

Galatians 3:23-29 Paul tells the Galatians: Law was an intermediate guardian for us minors in order to keep us in line while God's purposes were coming to maturity. But now that the full revelation has taken place in the coming of Christ, you all are freed from such a custodian, for in Christ you all are heirs, through faith. As you were baptized into union with Christ, you became new people clothed in Christ's way of living. Regardless of human categories of cultural or religious heritage, socioeconomic class, or gender, "You are all one in Christ," which qualifies you as Abraham's descendants.

Luke 9:18-24 As Jesus was praying with his disciples, he asked, "Who do people say I am?" Numerous popular views were offered. "Then who do you say I am?" he probed further. Peter responded, "The Christ of God." Charging them to tell this to no one, Jesus announced that the Son of Man must suffer, be rejected by religious leaders, killed, and raised on the third day. "Any of you who want to come after me, simply deny yourself, take up your cross each day, and follow me."

Psalm 43
1. Gelineau, *My Soul Is Thirsting for God*, GG, p. 44
2. Gregorian psalm tone, *GP*, Maundy Thursday A
3. Gregorian, *Defend Me, O God*, setting by Frank Quinn, *MP&E*, p. 66

Hymns for the Day	HL	HB	WB
All Ye That Fear God's Holy Name	–	35	–
In Christ There Is No East or West	341	479	435
Christ Is Made the Sure Foundation	336	433	325
The Church's One Foundation	333	437	582
O Jesus, I Have Promised	268	307	–

Anthems for the Day
1 Kings 19:9-14 *It Is Enough*, Felix Mendelssohn (*Elijah*, any edition); baritone solo
Gal. 3:23-29 *Divided Our Pathways*, Christopher Coelho (*Hymnal Supplement*, Agape); unison (E)
Luke 9:18-24 *He Who Would Valiant Be*, arr. Gerald Near (Augsburg); SATB (E)
Ps. 43 *Psalm 43*, Alan Luff (*Psalms and Hymns*, Agape); unison, congregation (E)

SUNDAY BETWEEN JUNE 26 AND JULY 2
(Proper 8) (C)

1 Kings 19:15-21 Yahweh charges Elijah to stop running away and to return to his ministry: "Cease your self-serving despair and get on with your mission. And by the way, you're hardly the only faithful one left; at least 6,999 others have not bowed to the false gods." So Elijah abandons his hideout and finds Elisha plowing some fields. As Elijah passes by, he casts his cloak upon Elisha, thereby investing him as a prophet of Yahweh. Elisha breaks with his old life by symbolically preparing a sacrificial meal and giving it to the people. Then he follows Elijah and ministers to him.

Galatians 5:1, 13-25 Paul tells the Galatians: Christ freed you from the slavery of law in order to set you free to be "servants of one another," to love your neighbor as yourself. If you abuse your freedom by producing works of the flesh, then you destroy others as well as yourself and shall not inherit the kingdom of God. But those who belong to Christ Jesus have crucified the flesh and therefore can freely produce fruits of the Spirit.

Luke 9:51-62 As the days draw near when Jesus is "to be received up," he sets his face firmly toward Jerusalem. But as he passes through a village of Samaritans, they will not receive him because of this. The disciples want to punish them, but Jesus rebukes his disciples for considering such destructive force. As they travel toward Jerusalem, they meet some people who want to follow Jesus wherever he is going. "Follow me," invites Jesus, "proclaim the kingdom of God in which we are going to live." Such single-minded commitment, however, presents a problem. Many are tempted to cling to family, job, socioeconomic responsibilities. Are these simply pretenses to avoid complete loyalty to Jesus by constantly looking over one's shoulder for more rewarding possibilities?

Psalm 44:1-8
None known to be available

Hymns for the Day	HL	HB	WB
God of the Prophets!	481	520	398
We Come Unto Our Fathers' God	342	16	623
O Master, Let Me Walk with Thee	364	304	520
Spirit of God, Descend Upon My Heart	204	236	575
God Gives His People Strength	–	–	381

Anthems for the Day
1 Kings 19:15-21 *Let Your Eye Be to the Lord*, Daniel Moe (Augsburg); SATB (M)
Gal. 5:1, 13-25 *The Fruit of the Spirit Is Love*, Johann Geisler (Boosey & Hawkes); SATB, flute (M)
Luke 9:51-62 *The King's Highway*, David McK. Williams (H. W. Gray); SATB (M)
Ps. 44:1-8 *We Have Heard with Our Ears*, Herbert Howells (Oxford); SATB (M)

SUNDAY BETWEEN JULY 3 AND JULY 9
(Proper 9) (C)

1 Kings 21:1-3, 17-21 In expropriating Naboth's vineyard, King Ahab and Queen Jezebel did everything right and nothing wrong, according to the law. But they did everything wrong and nothing right, according to God's ethics; they are guilty of insidious murder and acquisitive land-grabbing, announces Yahweh's speaker, Elijah. Now Ahab will have to live with the consequences of his killing and seizing—his dynasty will end.

Galatians 6:7-18 Paul's final words to the Galatians: "Don't kid yourselves; God is not mocked. You are accountable for what you do and say. What you sow, you shall reap. Remember, the only thing you may glory in is the cross—the sign of the powers of the old order who humiliated and seemingly defeated our Lord Jesus Christ. Yet by the cross Christ transforms those who constitute God's people into a new creation of mercy and peace."

Luke 10:1-12, 17-20 Jesus appoints seventy others to go out into the world and harvest a ripe crop before it spoils in the field. He sends them ahead of himself, as lambs in the midst of wolves, to announce that "the kingdom of God has come near to you." In the face of adversity, the Seventy discover the incredible power of their Lord's words, but their real joy is in learning that God embraces them forever.

Psalm 5:1-8
1. *PS*, p. 13

Hymns for the Day	HL	HB	WB
Hear My Words, O Gracious Lord	–	48	–
When I Survey the Wondrous Cross	152	198	635
In the Cross of Christ I Glory	154	195	437
Go, Labor On: Spend and Be Spent	376	283	–
Put Forth, O God, Your Spirit's Might	–	477	559
Beneath the Cross of Jesus	162	190	308

Anthems for the Day
1 Kings 21:1-3, 17-21 *Wash Me Thoroughly from My Wickedness*, G. F. Handel (Hinshaw); 2-part (E)
Gal. 6:7-18 *Of All the Spirit's Gifts to Me*, Norman Cocker (*Hymnal Supplement*, Agape); SATB (E)
Luke 10:1-12, 17-20 *O Jesus, King Most Wonderful*, Christopher Tye (Concordia); SATB (E)
Ps. 5:1-8 *Keep Me Faithfully in Thy Paths*, G. F. Handel (G.I.A.); 2-part (E)

SUNDAY BETWEEN JULY 10 AND JULY 16
(Proper 10) (C)

2 Kings 2:1, 6-14 Elijah, on his last journey, tests his disciple Elisha three times concerning his loyalty, but each time Elisha vows lifelong commitment. Even the prophets' guilds fail to deter Elisha from following Elijah to the very end. Upon reaching the Jordan River, Elijah parts the waters with his mantle in Moses-like fashion. After crossing to dry ground, Elijah says to Elisha, "What shall I do for you, before I am taken from you?" Elisha asks for a "double share of your *ruach* (spirit, wind)." He asks for the creative power of Yahweh which liberates. Then fire and wind whisk away Elijah while Elisha laments. But then he takes up the mantle of Elijah and parts the Jordan in Moses-like fashion.

Colossians 1:1-14 Intercessory prayers are offered for the community of faith to be filled with the gifts of the knowledge of God's will, the wisdom and understanding wrought by the Spirit, and strength, power, endurance, and patience, so the people will conduct themselves in a manner pleasing to God. Then the community is exhorted to offer joyful thanks to God for having made them fit to be transferred from the realm of darkness to "the saints in light" (or the kingdom of light made known in Jesus Christ). God authorizes them to participate in the deliverance and redemption in Christ; therefore, praise God with thanksgiving.

Luke 10:25-37 A lawyer seeks to test Jesus' ability as a teacher but ends up reciting the commandment to love God and neighbor. So then he asks, "Who is my neighbor?" Whereupon Jesus tells a story about a traveler victimized by some robbers. Well-intentioned, concerned people are unable to help the injured pilgrim because they have to fulfill their responsibilities. But an irreligious, despicable, villainous Samaritan sees the needy, broken person and shows neighborly compassion and mercy. Scandalous! God sends grace to us in neighbors whom we reject.

Psalm 139:1-12
1. Metrical, *There Is No Moment of My Life, Hymns III* (Church Hymnal Corp.), 240, tune: Burford
2. Gelineau, *O Lord, You Search Me, GG*, p. 160

Hymns for the Day	HL	HB	WB
O Lord, My Inmost Heart and Thought	–	129	–
Lord God of Hosts, Whose Purpose	368	288	460
So Let Our Lips and Lives Express	–	289	–
Jesus, Joy of Loving Hearts	354	215	510
O for a Thousand Tongues to Sing	199	141	493
Ancient of Days	58	246	297

Anthems for the Day
2 Kings 2:1, 6-14 *Then Round About the Starry Throne*, G. F. Handel (*Second Concord Anthem Book*, E. C. Schirmer); SATB (M)
Col. 1:1-14 *You That Know the Lord Is Gracious*, Cyril Taylor (*Westminster Praise*, Hinshaw); SATB (E)
Luke 10:25-37 *The Greatest of These*, Jane Marshall (Agape); SATB, congregation (E)
Ps. 139:1-12 *Lord, Thou Hast Searched Me Out*, Healey Willan (Flammer); SATB (E)

SUNDAY BETWEEN JULY 17 AND JULY 23
(Proper 11) (C)

2 Kings 4:8-17 A wealthy woman shows hospitality by providing lodging and food for Elisha. When Elisha offers to show his thanks to her by putting in a good word with the civil or military powers, she graciously declines such favors. So Elisha promises a son to this barren woman and her elderly husband. She doesn't believe it possible (cf. Sarah in Genesis 18), but within a year she's embracing a son.

Colossians 1:21-29 Paul tells the Colossians: You unlikely people (remember, you were once estranged from and actively hostile toward God) are part of what God has done in Christ: reconciled you through his death so that you are now radically new, provided you continue in steadfast faith and do not shift from the hope of the gospel to every other creature under the sun. Now I rejoice in my sufferings for the sake of the body of Christ. Commissioned by the hand of God, I became a minister to make the word of God fully known, for what was mysterious is now made clear in Jesus Christ.

Luke 10:38-42 On the way to Jerusalem, Jesus is offered hospitality by a woman named Martha. While she busily prepares food for the guest, her sister, Mary, sits at the Lord's feet and listens attentively to his teaching. So Martha complains, "Lord, don't you care that Mary neglects her duty while I alone serve? Tell her to help me." But he, surprisingly, replies, "Martha, you're so preoccupied with arranging, cleaning, cooking, preparing, and producing things for this world that you're not ready to receive the grace-filled hospitality of the kingdom."

Psalm 139:13-18
1. Metrical, *There Is No Moment of My Life, Hymns III* (Church Hymnal Corp.), 240, tune: Burford
2. Gelineau, *O Lord, You Search Me, GG*, p. 160

Hymns for the Day	HL	HB	WB
When All Thy Mercies, O My God	81	119	–
Christ, of All My Hopes the Ground	316	314	–
Christ Is the World's True Light	–	492	326
We Love Your Kingdom, Lord	337	435	626
A Charge to Keep I Have	–	301	–
Call Jehovah Your Salvation	292	123	322

Anthems for the Day
2 Kings 4:8-17 *What God Ordains Is Always Good*, Johann Pachelbel (*Morning Star Choir Book*, vol. 1, Concordia); unison (E)

Col. 1:21-29 *Jesus, Thy Blood and Righteousness*, J. S. Bach (Concordia); SATB (E)

Luke 10:38-42 *The Best of Rooms*, Randall Thompson (E. C. Schirmer); SATB (MD)

Ps. 139:13-18 *O Lord, Thou Hast Formed Mine Every Part*, J. S. Bach (*Red Concord Anthem Book*, E. C. Schirmer); SATB (E)

SUNDAY BETWEEN JULY 24 AND JULY 30
(Proper 12) (C)

2 Kings 5:1-15ab (". . . in Israel") Naaman, a Syrian military commander, suffers from leprosy. Hearing that healing is possible in Israel, he packs his bags, empties out several bank accounts, and sets off to see the wizard. But the only thing he receives from the king of Israel is the royal run-around treatment—the king is impotent to heal Naaman and knows it. But Elisha, the simple man of God, instructs Naaman to wash himself in the Jordan. This makes no sense to Naaman, for he could have done that back home; so he goes away in a rage. At the insistence of his servants, however, Naaman does wash and miraculously is made clean. He almost misses this experience because of his preconceived expectations of God's healing word.

Colossians 2:6-15 Paul tells the Colossians: You began in Christ; therefore, root yourself, stand fast, live in union with Christ and no other, abounding in thanksgiving. Resist religious sampling, for it can erode faith in Jesus Christ; cults play on your primal fears and guilts and desires for influence and wealth and thus promise self-fulfillment. But Christ disarmed such principalities and powers and delivered you from evil and self-preoccupation. It is with Christ that you were buried and raised, through faith in the working of God, and therefore find the fullness of life.

Luke 11:1-13 Jesus teaches his disciples a simple prayer—five petitions for the reign of God's kingdom. Friends and family may need to be importuned to respond to our needs, but God is always waiting to hear our prayers, serve us, and give us the gift of the Holy Spirit. Simply ask, seek, and knock.

Psalm 21:1-7
None known to be available

Hymns for the Day	HL	HB	WB
Lord of All Being, Throned Afar	87	87	463
Christ, of All My Hopes the Ground	316	314	–
At the Name of Jesus	–	143	303
Christ Is Made the Sure Foundation	336	433	325
I Look to Thee in Every Need	79	114	–
God Is Our Strong Salvation	92	347	388

Anthems for the Day
2 Kings 5:1-15ab *I Have Longed for Thy Saving Health*, William Byrd (H. W. Gray); SATB (ME)
Col. 2:6-15 *To Our Redeemer's Glorious Name*, Christopher Tye (Concordia), SATB (E)
Luke 11:1-13 *The Lord's Prayer*, Maurice Duruflé (Durand); SATB (M)
   The Lord's Prayer, Gregorian, setting by Healey Willan (*Third Morning Star Choir Book*, Concordia); unison (E)
   Ask . . . Using My Name, Bob Burroughs (Hinshaw); SATB (ME)
Psalm 21:1-7 *Be Thou Exalted, Lord My God*, Heinrich Schütz (Shawnee); SATB (M)

SUNDAY BETWEEN JULY 31 AND AUGUST 6
(Proper 13) (C)

2 Kings 13:14-20a As Elisha lies dying, King Joash weeps before him, crying, "My father, my father! The chariots of Israel and its horsemen!" (cf. Elisha's acclamation of Elijah in 2 Kings 2:12). In order to obtain Yahweh's word, Joash is then curiously instructed by Elisha to shoot an arrow to the east and to strike the ground with the remaining arrows, which Elisha then interprets as partial victory over the Syrians. Who's in charge here? Clearly not the king, who is dependent on the nonrational and enigmatic ways of a prophet, and a dying one at that.

Colossians 3:1-11 Paul tells the Colossians: You have been baptized and therefore raised by Christ to new life. So put to death the practices of your old past way which has died. Set your mind and heart on things above—on Christ alone, following in his way. Because you're raised to new life in Christ, get rid of all these evil practices in which you once walked. Seek your obedience "in Christ" who set you free from all these binding laws and earthly things so that you may be freed for love of God and neighbors in the way of Jesus Christ.

Luke 12:13-21 Someone said to Jesus, "Teacher, I want my share of property to which I am entitled. Tell my brother to give it to me." Replied Jesus, "Beware of and guard against all covetousness." A rich man sought to guarantee tomorrow today by building bigger storehouses to hoard his goods. He wanted to ensure a secure future for himself but forgot that the future—life and death—is in God's hands. So be "rich toward God": give away your "self" to neighbors rather than foolishly trying to secure your "self" for yourself.

Psalm 28
None known to be available

Hymns for the Day	HL	HB	WB
You Servants of God, Your Master Proclaim	198	27	645
Fight the Good Fight	270	359	–
Strong Son of God, Immortal Love	175	228	578
Rise, My Soul, and Stretch Thy Wings	264	330	–
Ask Ye What Great Thing I Know	312	371	–

Anthems for the Day
2 Kings 13:14-20a *God Be in My Head*, John Rutter (Oxford); SATB (M)
Col. 3:1-11 *Fight the Good Fight*, John Gardner (Oxford); SATB (M)
Luke 12:13-21 *Treasures in Heaven*, Joseph Clokey (Summy-Birchard); SATB, soprano solo (E)
Ps. 28 *Hear Us, O Lord*, Jacob Obrecht (G.I.A.); SAB (M)

SUNDAY BETWEEN AUGUST 7 AND AUGUST 13
(Proper 14) (C)

Jeremiah 18:1-11 At Yahweh's command, Jeremiah visits a potter's house where he sees some clay resisting being molded into the intended shape by deft hands of the potter. So the potter patiently reworks the stubborn clay into another shape "as it seemed good to the potter to do so." Then Jeremiah hears the words of Yahweh, "I, too, judge and forgive, pluck up and plant, destroy and build according to the quality of the clay in my hands. Behold, I am shaping evil against you; so repent, turn around, and return from your evil ways."

Hebrews 11:1-3, 8-19 Faith is belief in God's promises, the only thing upon which to rest one's faith. For example, by faith, Abraham obeyed the call to enter a strange land. By faith, he looked forward to the city of permanent foundations designed and built by God. By faith, barren Sarah received power to conceive. Thus from one aged couple came descendants as plentiful as the "stars in heaven" or "grains of sand." They died before receiving the things God had promised, but they saw them from afar and acknowledged themselves as strangers and sojourners on earth. By faith, Abraham offered to God that which was most precious to him, believing in God's promises.

Luke 12:32-40 "Fear not, little flock," to give you the kingdom pleases God. Likewise, your almsgiving to neighbors in need also pleases God. So keep your lamps burning brightly and wait patiently for the arrival of the bridegroom at an unexpected hour; you may be surprised to discover that he will serve you at table.

Psalm 14
None known to be available

Hymns for the Day	HL	HB	WB
Guide Me, O Thou Great Jehovah	104	339	409
Faith of Our Fathers!	267	348	361
Children of the Heavenly King	347	340	–
The God of Abraham Praise	8	89	587
Lord, from the Depths to You I Cry	240	277	459
My Faith Looks Up to Thee	285	378	–

Anthems for the Day
Jer. 18:1-11 *Turn Ye, Turn Ye*, Charles Ives (Presser); SATB (ME)

Heb. 11:1-3, 8-19 *O Lord God, You Have Called Your Servants*, Carl Schalk (Concordia); SATB (E)

Luke 12:32-40 *Have No Fear, Little Flock*, Heinz Werner Zimmermann (*Five Hymns*, Concordia); SATB (M)

Ps. 14 *O Lord God, Unto Whom Vengeance Belongeth*, Robert Baker (H. W. Gray); SATB, baritone solo (M)

SUNDAY BETWEEN AUGUST 14 AND AUGUST 20
(Proper 15) (C)

Jeremiah 20:7-13 A depressed Jeremiah prays to God (or should we say assaults God?) by offering his rage, hostility, and anguish that God has deceived him, which is costly to Jeremiah. "When I speak your word, people make fun of me; I am an object of reproach and derision, but I can't stop speaking. Terror surrounds me; friends watch for my fall. But you are with me. Thus, it is these human adversaries who will stumble and be shamed. So 'sing to the LORD; praise the LORD!' " Admitting and submitting to God one's rage and hunger for vengeance is an act of profound faith, and also mysteriously creates new possibilities.

Hebrews 12:1-2, 12-17 A lifelong marathon race, that's what you're in for when you become part of the crowd trying to keep pace with Jesus. So keep your eyes fixed on him, lift your drooping hands, strengthen your weak knees, and run a straight path. Strive for peace with all people. See to it that no one falls from the grace of God by your allowing an idolatrous "root of bitterness" to spring up and defile the whole community. And see to it that no one rejects the "Esau-like birthright," for there is no second chance to repent.

Luke 12:49-56 Do you think Christ came to give peace on earth, harmony, tranquillity, serenity, comfort? Think! No wonder we're shocked to hear him say he "came to cast fire upon the earth." His baptism demands unflinching allegiance and may therefore divide families and separate friends. We can accurately forecast what western rain clouds and southern winds will bring us, but we're unable to foretell that the fiery Spirit of Christ will sear our self-love and ignite our love for neighbors.

Psalm 10:12-18
None known to be available

Hymns for the Day	HL	HB	WB
Judge Eternal, Throned in Splendor	417	517	447
Awake, My Soul, Stretch Every Nerve	278	346	–
Christ, Above All Glory Seated	–	–	324
Jesus, Lead the Way	–	334	441
Jesus Calls Us	223	269	439
Give to the Winds Your Fears	294	364	377

Anthems for the Day
Jer. 20:7-13 *Why Art Thou Cast Down,* Daniel Pinkham (Peters); SATB (M)
Heb. 12:1-2, 12-17 *How Firm a Foundation,* arr. John Rutter (Hinshaw); SATB (E)
Luke 12:49-56 *Grant Me True Courage, Lord,* J. S. Bach (*Red Concord Anthem Book,* E. C. Schirmer); SATB (E)
Ps. 10:12-18 *Be Unto Me, O Lord,* William Byrd (*Two Sacred Songs in Four Parts,* Music Press); SATB (M)

SUNDAY BETWEEN AUGUST 21 AND AUGUST 27
(Proper 16) (C)

Jeremiah 28:1-9 Soon after the first citizens of Judah have been deported to Babylon (ca. 598 B.C.), the prophet Hananiah announces the solution to the problem of desolation: "Yahweh has broken the yoke of Babylon, and within two years will bring back the king and all the exiles." Then the prophet Jeremiah speaks. "Amen! May your words of prophecy come true. But there are no quick fixes to anguish, suffering, wretchedness, or misery because they are not problems to be solved. Yesterday's true prophecies are not today's guarantees; first you must acknowledge the reality of pain and live with it."

Hebrews 12:18-29 Remember Sinai when the first covenant was given: fire, darkness, gloom, whirlwind, trumpet sound, and frightening voice of words. No wonder Moses "trembled with fear." But you have come to Mt. Zion, the city of the living God, where angels and others who lived in faith now gather together in praise and joy. All meet God, who is judge of all, and also Jesus, mediator of the new covenant, whose blood cries out in mercy and forgiveness. Caution: do not refuse this joy-filled, merciful gift. Listen to this heaven-and-earth-shaking voice and pay heed to what you hear, for the Israelites did not listen and were refused entry to the promised land.

Luke 13:22-30 Will the saved be few in number? Well, the door is narrow; you may enter only through confession and ethical obedience. But the table is large enough to accommodate many from east, west, north, and south. So don't miss this banquet.

Psalm 84
1. Metrical, *Lord of the Worlds Above*, HB 14, tune: Darwall's 148th
2. Gelineau, *My Soul Is Longing and Yearning*, 30P&2C, p. 25
3. Gregorian psalm tone, *GP*, Proper 25
4. Tone and antiphon by Frank Quinn, *How Lovely Is Your Dwelling Place*, *MP&E*, p. 199
5. *PS*, p. 22

Hymns for the Day	HL	HB	WB
Rise, My Soul, and Stretch Thy Wings	264	330	–
Lord of the Worlds Above	50	14	–
Be Thou My Vision	325	303	304
Open Now the Gates of Beauty	–	40	544
Lead On, O King Eternal	371	332	448
We Are Living, We Are Dwelling	374	356	618

Anthems for the Day
Jer. 28:1-9 *O Lord, in Thee Have I Trusted*, G. F. Handel (*Dettingen Te Deum*, Belwin-Mills); SSATB (M)

Heb. 12:18-29 *Christ the Glory*, J. F. Lallouette (G.I.A.); 2-part (E)

Luke 13:22-30 *Let My Heart Be Pure*, Merrill Bradshaw (Sonos Music Resources); SATB (E)

Ps. 84 *Psalm 84*, Richard Proulx (G.I.A.); SATB (ME)

SUNDAY BETWEEN AUGUST 28 AND SEPTEMBER 3
(Proper 17) (C)

Ezekiel 18:1-9, 25-29 Two typical rationalizations for our current plight are to blame others and to point the finger at God's unjust ways. Yes, we are shaped by multiple influences, but we still can't explain our present condition by bad genes or a capricious God—both excuses are self-destructive alibis to evade our responsibility for living according to God's just ways. Despite our self-justifying unjust ways, God constantly invites us to look at ourselves, to turn from self-interest to concern for neighbors, and therefore to live

Hebrews 13:1-8 "Let brotherly love continue": open your home to strangers (you might be entertaining angels), care for the imprisoned and ill-treated, honor marriage, resist love of money—be content with what you have. Not exactly conventional or popular ways to love one another, but no wonder the writer quotes Psalm 118:6, because God is your support and will take care of you. Remember and imitate the fidelity of your leaders, those who spoke the word of God to the community. And, most important, imitate Jesus Christ, the one who is always the same—yesterday, today, and forever.

Luke 14:1, 7-14 When you are invited to a marriage feast, resist taking the exalted seat of honor, for you will be covered with shame when a more eminent one arrives and sits in your chair. Rather, sit at a humble place so you may be invited to a seat of honor. Moreover, don't invite friends to your dinner parties; they will simply invite you to theirs. Rather, "invite the poor and the maimed," and you will discover that Christ is present with you too.

Psalm 15
1. Metrical, *Blest Are the Pure in Heart, HB* 226, tune: Franconia
2. Gelineau, *He Who Walks Without Fault, GG,* p. 98
3. Gregorian psalm tone, *GP,* Proper 11 ⌣

Hymns for the Day	HL	HB	WB
Whate'er Our God Ordains Is Right	291	366	633
Blest Are the Pure in Heart	–	226	–
O Holy City, Seen of John	409	508	505
Immortal Love, Forever Full	178	229	434
The Lord Will Come and Not Be Slow	185	230	–

Anthems for the Day
Ezek. 18:1-9, 25-29 *Put Thou Thy Trust in God,* Philip Tomblings (Oxford); SATB (ME)
Heb. 13:1-8 *Let Love Continue,* Eugene Butler (Hinshaw); SATB (ME)
Luke 14:1, 7-14 *He That Is Down Needs Fear No Fall,* John Dowland (*Oxford Easy Anthem Book,* Oxford); SATB (M)
Ps. 15 *Who Shall Abide,* Walter Pelz (Augsburg); SAB, flute, guitar (M)

SUNDAY BETWEEN SEPTEMBER 4 AND SEPTEMBER 10 (Proper 18) (C)

Ezekiel 33:1-11 The awesome responsibility of serving as a sentry is often underestimated, so consider the following: While people sleep, work, play, eat, and stroll through life, who must constantly stay awake, on guard, alert, watching for approaching danger? Who must sound the alarm when judgment time nears? Who must boldly speak the word of the Lord to those who turn away from God's protected path? Who bears full responsibility for your welfare? Who must unceasingly try to convince you that your seeming enemy, God, desires life for you? No wonder Ezekiel—or anyone else— shrinks back when called by God to serve as sentry.

Philemon 1-20 Paul appeals to his friend Philemon, in whose home the Colossian church met, to accept back a runaway slave, Onesimus, who met Paul while in prison and became a Christian. Keep in mind that punishment for runaway slaves in first-century Colossae was not much different from nineteenth-century America. So to ask Philemon to treat a fugitive slave "no longer as a slave, but as a beloved brother" is indeed bold. "Receive him as you would me." Paul simply trusts God to set free from sin Philemon and all of us captives.

Luke 14:25-33 "In order to be my disciples," declares Jesus, "you must love everyone and everything less than me. You must be willing to bear your own cross and come after me: dedicating yourself to going where I go, associating with outcasts, reaching out your hands to the dependent or helpless, renouncing all that you treasure (including family loyalties) in order to be my disciples. Count the cost of discipleship before committing yourself, otherwise you will fall short and be mocked by others." Isn't that how you would construct towers, wage war, or sue for peace? Tally the cost before committing yourself; otherwise it would be foolish even to begin, for others would laugh at your unfinished, bankrupt venture.

Psalm 94:12-22
1. Pointed in *LBW* for psalm tone, p. 260

Hymns for the Day	HL	HB	WB
My Soul, Be on Thy Guard	–	363	–
Be Thou My Vision	325	303	304
Our God, Our Help in Ages Past	77	111	549
How Firm a Foundation	283	369	425
"Take Up Thy Cross," the Saviour Said	–	293	–

Anthems for the Day
Ezek. 33:1-11 *Turn Ye, Turn Ye,* Charles Ives (Presser); SATB (ME)
Philemon 1-20 *O Brother Man,* Malcolm Williamson (*Dove Chorales,* Agape); SATB (E)
Luke 14:25-33 *Seasons of Time,* Samuel Adler (Hinshaw); SATB (M)
Ps. 94:12-22 *O Lord, Save Thy People,* Anton Bruckner, ed. Peek (Augsburg); SATB (ME)

SUNDAY BETWEEN SEPTEMBER 11 AND SEPTEMBER 17 (Proper 19) (C)

Hosea 4:1-3; 5:15–6:6 Hear the word of Yahweh, for Yahweh has a legal suit against you people. The charges: no faithfulness, no devotion, no knowledge of God in the land. Rather, cursing, lying, killing, stealing, and adultery abound. You have broken the covenant. Yahweh is still your God, but are you still the people of Yahweh? The land shall wither and you all shall languish. Yahweh will return home and wait for you until you all acknowledge your guilt. Come, let's return to Yahweh, who has torn and who will heal us. Replies Yahweh, "What am I to do with you broken people, for your faith is as solid as the morning mist and as lasting as the evaporating dew. Yet I desire *hesed* (steadfast love) from you."

1 Timothy 1:12-17 Thanks to Christ Jesus, who has appointed me to serve him and given me strength for his work. I formerly spoke evil of him and persecuted his people. I didn't know who I was or what I was doing. Fortunately, Christ came to save sinners, and I am the foremost. So the Lord worked through a wretch like me as an example; he poured out his abundant grace on me and gave me faith and love in him. Now as an apostle I spread his good news everywhere. To the eternal King—glory and honor forever!

Luke 15:1-10 Is anyone fool-headed enough to risk the safety of ninety-nine sheep in order to look for a single lost sheep? Yet here is a shepherd forsaking the greatest good for the most sheep and seeking a lost sheep "until he finds it," at which time he rejoices with friends and neighbors. Likewise, it's incredible that a woman would turn a home inside out "until she finds" one lost coin, and then throw a party with friends and neighbors to celebrate its recovery. It's amazing how much joy there is in heaven over the finding of a single lost sinner.

Psalm 77:11-20
None known to be available

Hymns for the Day	HL	HB	WB
Immortal, Invisible, God Only Wise	66	85	433
God Moves in a Mysterious Way	103	112	391
There's a Wideness in God's Mercy	93	110	601
When All Thy Mercies, O My God	81	119	–
Amazing Grace!	–	275	296

Anthems for the Day
Hos. 4:1-3; 5:15–6:6 *Look Down, O Lord*, Clement Janequin (Schmitt, Hall & McCreary); SATB (ME)
1 Tim. 1:12-17 *Amazing Grace*, Lena J. McLin (Kjos); SATB (ME)
Luke 15:1-10 *O Christ Whose Love Has Sought Us Out*, Lee Hastings Bristol, Jr. (*Westminster Praise*, Hinshaw); SATB (E)
Ps. 77:11-20 *Lord, in Thee Have I Trusted*, Tomás Luis de Victoria, ed. Klein (Kjos); SATB (ME)

SUNDAY BETWEEN SEPTEMBER 18 AND SEPTEMBER 24 (Proper 20) (C)

Hosea 11:1-11 I loved you as a child, but the more I called you near me, the more you withdrew from me. I taught you how to walk, cradled you in my arms, healed you when you were sick, bent down and fed you. Bah! Return to the land of destruction, where the sword will rage against you. Because you are determined to turn away from me, you will bear your earned yoke which no one shall remove. But how can I give up on you? My heart recoils. I will not execute my fierce anger or destroy you, for I am God, the Holy One present among you. I will return you to your homes.

1 Timothy 2:1-7 Lift up your hands and hearts and offer intercessions for all people—friends and enemies alike. Pray especially for those with political power, for they are charged with the responsibility of securing and maintaining an orderly life. They need God's word in order to work for God's truth and justice and peace. And above all, remember there is only one mediator who brings us together and to whom we owe our total allegiance and trust: Christ, who gave himself as a ransom for all.

Luke 16:1-13 A strange story: Jesus praises a crooked steward who cheated his employer and gouged his customers. Only when his boss barked the word "audit" did this slimy steward realize the day of reckoning was at hand for his dishonest dealings. Only then did he desperately seek to save his own neck by performing good deeds for others and righting the wrongs he had done, but which ironically resulted in his doing justly. Thank God we don't need to be threatened to do God's will, because we know about free grace handed out by Christ on the cross. No need to delay another moment in giving away ourselves to neighbors, is there?

Psalm 107:1-9
1. Metrical, *Praise the Lord, for He Is Good, HB* 115, tune: Halle
2. Gregorian psalm tone, *GP,* Proper 7 B

Hymns for the Day	HL	HB	WB
God of Our Life	88	108	395
Now Thank We All Our God	459	9	481
O Love That Wilt Not Let Me Go	307	400	519
You Servants of God, Your Master Proclaim	198	27	645
At the Name of Jesus	–	143	303

Anthems for the Day

Hos. 11:1-11 *Like as a Father,* Luigi Cherubini, arr. Lovelace (Choristers Guild); 3-part canon (E)

1 Tim. 2:1-7 *He's the Lily of the Valley,* arr. Alice Parker (*Two Negro Spirituals,* Lawson-Gould); SATB, baritone solo (ME)

Luke 16:1-13 *The Canticle of the Rock,* Alan Luff (*Psalms and Hymns,* Agape); unison, congregation (E)

Ps. 107:1-9 *O Give Thanks to the Lord,* Emma Lou Diemer (Franco Columbo); SATB (M)

SUNDAY BETWEEN SEPTEMBER 25 AND OCTOBER 1 (Proper 21) (C)

Joel 2:23-30 Lots of talk about new creation: "early rain, plentiful grain, wine, oil, eat in plenty, be satisfied, never again be put to shame, and you will know that I, Yahweh, am in the midst of you." Afterward, Yahweh's spirit/ wind will make everybody open to this new creation. Everybody's going to dream and have visions and hope and turn loose of the way things are now organized, because God is establishing a whole new creation.

1 Timothy 6:6-19 Resist the temptation to desire riches, for love of money will lure you into ruin and destruction. Remember, you entered the world with nothing and you will depart with nothing. Recall your baptism, for, as a new creature "in Christ," God called you to pursue the rich life of "righteousness, godliness, faith, love, steadfastness, and gentleness." Run, run, run on this path of life until the day when our Lord Jesus Christ appears.

Luke 16:19-31 Jesus retells an old familiar Egyptian folktale about a rich man and a poor man. But Jesus' version isn't very funny: we are shocked, outraged, offended to discover that the ostensibly cursed poor Lazarus rests in the bosom of Abraham and the seemingly blessed, righteous rich man sizzles in a frying pan of a place, seeking cool relief from Lazarus and pleading for someone to get the word to his brothers that God's judgments reverse everything. But Lazarus isn't running any more errands for the rich man, especially when we already have all we need in the Law and the Prophets and in Jesus Christ. Listen to God's word and repent, turn around now.

Psalm 107:1, 33-43
1. Pointed in *LBW* for psalm tone, p. 268

Hymns for the Day	HL	HB	WB
We Sing the Mighty Power of God	65	84	628
O Spirit of the Living God	207	242	528
Fight the Good Fight	270	359	–
Faith of Our Fathers!	267	348	361
For the Beauty of the Earth	71	2	372

Anthems for the Day
Joel 2:23-30 *God Is One, Unique and Holy*, Peter Cutts (Agape); SATB (ME)
1 Tim. 6:6-19 *Fight the Good Fight*, John Gardner (Oxford); SATB (M)
Luke 16:19-31 *Father Abraham, Have Mercy on Me*, Gerhard Krapf (Concordia); unison (ME)
Ps. 107:1, 33-43 *Thou Visitest the Earth*, Maurice Greene (*Church Anthem Book*, Oxford); SATB, tenor solo (M). (Also a 2-part arrangement in *Morning Star Choir Book*, Concordia)

SUNDAY BETWEEN OCTOBER 2 AND OCTOBER 8 (Proper 22) (C)

Amos 5:6-7, 10-15 Seek Yahweh and live, lest his wrath roar like devouring fire. Woe to you who twist justice into wormwood and discard righteousness. You abhor anyone who speaks the truth. Because you trample on the poor and extract grain from them, you will not dwell in your comfortable homes or sip wine from your vineyards, for I know your myriad crimes. You pervert the legal system, take bribes, spurn the poor, and pressure neighbors to keep silent in such an evil time. Seek good, not evil, that you may live, and so Yahweh may be with you.

2 Timothy 1:1-14 You have been called to be speakers of the gospel, and in our world that's not what people want to hear. So you will have to accept your share of suffering. God saved you, chose you, and will give you strength to spread the good news that the love of God was revealed to us in Jesus Christ. But the only way you are going to do that without being afraid or ashamed is by trusting in God. For the sake of this gospel, I suffer, but I am not ashamed because I know whom I've trusted. Keep on telling the gospel, no matter what the cost, because God wants everyone to hear it and be liberated. That's why God came to us in Jesus Christ: to set us all free.

Luke 17:5-10 Do you invite your letter carrier in for gourmet luncheons, prepare six-course dinners for your trash collector, or serve elegant hors d'oeuvres to your street sweeper? After all, who's serving whom? We expect such workers to serve us and thereby earn their pay. Likewise, we expect God to do his job: take care of us, protect us from any harm, listen to our prayer requests, forgive us for the wrongs we have committed. Stop! Who's serving whom? We are God's servants in the world. So "when you have done all that is commanded you, say, 'We are unworthy servants; we have done only what was our [joyful] duty.'"

Psalm 101
None known to be available

Hymns for the Day	HL	HB	WB
God of Our Life	88	108	395
I'm Not Ashamed to Own My Lord	–	292	–
O for a Heart to Praise My God!	260	325	–
Immortal, Invisible, God Only Wise	66	85	433
Christ, of All My Hopes the Ground	316	314	–

Anthems for the Day
Amos 5:6-7, 10-15 *Hide Not Thou Thy Face from Us*, Richard Farrant (Oxford); SATB (ME)
2 Tim. 1:1-14 *Kindle the Gift of God*, Gerre Hancock (H. W. Gray); SATB (M)
Luke 17:5-10 *O Lord, Increase My Faith*, Orlando Gibbons (*Concord Anthem Book*, E. C. Schirmer); SATB (M)
Ps. 101 *I Will Sing of Mercy and Judgment*, Emma Lou Diemer (C. Fischer); SATB (M)

SUNDAY BETWEEN OCTOBER 9 AND OCTOBER 15 (Proper 23) (C)

Micah 1:2; 2:1-10 All peoples of the earth, hear Yahweh's testimony against you. "Woe to you who stay awake at night scheming ways to seize more property when the morning dawns. You oppress people." Therefore, Yahweh says, "Against you I am devising an unremovable yoke for your necks: your property shall be divided among your captors, for it shall be an evil time." Hearing such scathing words, the people angrily shout, "Shut up! Don't preach! Is Israel under a curse? Is Yahweh impatient? Would Yahweh really do such things?" Answer: "You attack my people like enemies. Look at what you've done. You drive away my women and rob my children of my blessings. Your sins have made this an unholy land."

2 Timothy 2:8-15 Remember Christ, risen from the dead, as preached in the gospel for which I am suffering. Indeed, I am even chained like a criminal. But God's word is never shackled, so I endure everything for the sake of God's chosen people in order that they too may obtain salvation through Jesus Christ. "If we have died with him, we shall also live with him; if we endure, we shall also reign with him." Remind your people of this so they do not quibble with each other over trivialities—bureaucratic structures, management techniques, budgeting procedures. All this squabbling will only ruin the hearers of the gospel.

Luke 17:11-19 Ten lepers cry out to Jesus for pity. "Go!" commands Jesus (no comfort here), "Show yourselves to the priests." They obey. They do what Jesus tells them to do—that's faith—and they are healed. But one leper, a despised outsider, turns back to give thanks, glorifying God. He obeys and worships. No wonder Jesus says to him, "Your faith has made you whole."

Psalm 26
1. Gregorian psalm tone, *GP*, Proper 17 A
2. Pointed in *LBW* for psalm tone, p. 226

Hymns for the Day	HL	HB	WB
Lord, from the Depths to You I Cry	240	277	459
Jesus, Thy Boundless Love to Me	314	404	–
O Master, Let Me Walk with Thee	364	304	520
Christian, Dost Thou See Them	275	360	–
Behold the Amazing Gift of Love	–	120	–

Anthems for the Day

Micah 1:2; 2:1-10 *In Adam We Have All Been One* (*Westminster Praise*, Hinshaw); SATB (E)

2 Tim. 2:8-15 *Offertory/Lent V* (*Verses and Offertories—Lent*), Kevin Norris (Augsburg); unison (E)

Luke 17:11-19 *Ten Lepers*, Sister Miriam Therese, arr. Roff (Vanguard); SATB (ME)

Ps. 26 *Lord, Thou Hast Told Us*, Arnold Bax (*Anthems for Choirs*, vol. 4, Oxford); SATB (E)

SUNDAY BETWEEN OCTOBER 16 AND OCTOBER 22 (Proper 24) (C)

Habakkuk 1:1-3; 2:1-4 We live in an unjust world where the odds seem to favor wickedness, violence, and terrorism. Why doesn't God do something? Doesn't God want a peaceful world? So Habakkuk laments, "How long, O Yahweh, must I see indiscriminate evil sweep across the earth, making no distinctions between the righteous and the wicked? How could chaotic forces arrayed against your purposes be an instrument of your judgment?" Then he climbs his watchtower to look for God's answer, given in plain but cryptic terms. "Behold, the vision tarries," says Yahweh, "it may seem slow, but you must wait." In the meantime, when faith is put to the test, the just shall live by faith, confident that God is in control.

2 Timothy 3:14–4:5 Remember what you learned as a child, for all scripture is useful for teaching the truth and giving instructions for right living. Now, in the presence of God and of Christ Jesus, I charge you to preach the word (regardless of the time). Many will not listen to sound teaching but prefer to follow their own desires and therefore gather at the feet of teachers who tell them what their egos are itching to hear. Stand firm, endure suffering, and preach the gospel as a servant of God.

Luke 18:1-8 A parable about an "unrighteous" judge and a relentless widow who keeps pleading this judge to "vindicate me against my adversary." But the judge keeps refusing. So the woman keeps on hounding him. Finally the judge caves in to her bothersome importuning and grants her what she needs. Whew! Isn't it great that the God revealed in Jesus Christ isn't a God you have to bug all the time? We can depend on God; can God depend on our persistence in faith? "When the Son of man comes, will he find faith [not religion, but faith] on earth?"

Psalm 119:137-144
1. Pointed in *LBW* for psalm tone, pp. 277–278

Hymns for the Day	HL	HB	WB
Lord of All Being, Throned Afar	87	87	463
There's a Wideness in God's Mercy	93	110	601
O Word of God Incarnate	215	251	532
A Charge to Keep I Have	–	301	–
Lord God of Hosts, Whose Purpose	368	288	460

Anthems for the Day

Hab. 1:1-3; 2:1-4 *Our Father, Whose Creative Will,* Marvin David Levy (Ricordi); SATB (MD). (Also in a unison setting by Alec Wyton in *Ecumenical Praise,* Agape)

2 Tim. 3:14–4:5 *Be Strong in the Lord,* Thomas Matthews (Fitzsimons); SATB (M)

Luke 18:1-8 *We Do Not Know How to Pray,* Erik Routley (*Ecumenical Praise,* Agape); unison (E)

Ps. 119:137-144 *Righteous, O Lord, Art Thou,* Antonio Vivaldi, arr. Ehret (Elkan-Vogel); SATB, soprano solo (M)

SUNDAY BETWEEN OCTOBER 23 AND OCTOBER 29 (Proper 25) (C)

Zephaniah 3:1-9 The ration does not trust in Yahweh. Officials are roaring lions, judges are hungry wolves, preachers are wanton, faithless people who profane what is sacred. Even though every morning Yahweh faithfully shows righteousness, the unjust still know no shame. Says Yahweh, "I have destroyed nations, laid waste their streets, desolated their cities, so surely Israel will fear me and accept correction. But no, she is all the more eager to make all her deeds corrupt. Therefore, wait for me, for the day when I arise to pour out all the heat of my anger. At that time I will transform her speech so that all may call on my name and serve me with one accord."

2 Timothy 4:6-8, 16-18 The time is near for me to offer my life as a witness to the gospel. I rejoice that "I have fought the good fight and finished the race." Now the crown of righteousness awaits me which the Lord will award to me and to all who have loved his coming on that Day. At my first trial, all deserted me; may God forgive them. But the Lord stood by me and gave me strength to proclaim the word fully that all might hear it. So I was rescued from "the lion's mouth" of death. I am confident the Lord will save me from all evil and deliver me safely into his heavenly kingdom. To him be the glory, forever.

Luke 18:9-14 A Pharisee offers a typical prayer of thanksgiving that he has been blessed and is not like those who are beyond redemption but is able to do what the law requires—fast twice weekly and tithe of his income. He is the ideal model of a pious Jew and therefore must be righteous. A tax collector who knows his outsider's place in the Temple—for he is a sinner—offers a plea acknowledging what everyone knows is true: "I'm no good." But Jesus announces, "I, not the Temple, will determine who is holy. This publican 'beyond redemption' is justified." Free grace boggles our minds every time.

Psalm 3
None known to be available

Hymns for the Day	HL	HB	WB
Guide Me, O Thou Great Jehovah	104	339	409
I Look to Thee in Every Need	79	114	–
God, Be Merciful to Me	–	282	–
God Gives His People Strength	–	–	381
Father Eternal, Ruler of Creation	–	486	362
God of Compassion, in Mercy Befriend Us	290	122	392

Anthems for the Day
Zeph. 3:1-9 *Commit Your Life to the Lord*, Liebhold (*A Second Motet Book*, Concordia); SATB (ME)
2 Tim. 4:6-8, 16-18 *Offertory/26th Sunday After Pentecost*, Donald Busarow (*Verses and Offertories—Pentecost 21—Christ the King*, Augsburg); unison (E)
Luke 18:9-14 *The Pharisee and the Publican*, Heinrich Schütz (G. Schirmer); SATB, tenor, bass solos (M)
Ps. 3 *How Are My Foes Increased, Lord?*, John Joubert (Novello); SATB (M)

SUNDAY BETWEEN OCTOBER 30 AND NOVEMBER 5 (Proper 26) (C)

Haggai 2:1-9 Yahweh speaks to us through Haggai's voice: "Remember how splendid our Temple looked in the good old days? Today it seems in sad shape, nearly in ruins. Don't despair. Get on with the rebuilding. Do the work for which you've been called, for I am with you. When you came out of Egypt, I promised I would stay with you, and I am still with you, so fear not. Sometime soon I will shake heaven and earth, land and sea, and all nations, and bring their treasures here to the new Temple, which will be far more splendid than the old one, for I will give my people *shalom.*"

2 Thessalonians 1:5-12 Here's an oddity: the Thessalonian church grows in faithfulness at the very moment of its affliction. The text offers essentially a reassuring, comforting word to persecuted people. That's the rub, isn't it? The comforting word to oppressed, harassed, aggrieved, suffering people is like cool water that strengthens them to carry on the task: "May God complete your work of faith." But a reassuring word to an unafflicted, comfortable church provides what, threatening judgment? No wonder we struggle with this kind of passage.

Luke 19:1-10 One day the word travels through Jericho that Jesus is approaching. So the chief tax collector, Zacchaeus—a traitorous crook who has sold out to Rome and constantly cheated his neighbors—perches in a tree to see Jesus. Lo and behold, of all people in Jericho, Jesus invites himself in to Zacchaeus' home. When the crowd witnesses Jesus' irreligious behavior, they murmur—outraged that Jesus has entered a sinner's home. But Zacchaeus—miraculously set free—gives half his goods to the poor and restores past fraudulent deals fourfold. On that day salvation comes to his house, for he is a son of Abraham ("a keeper of the law").

Psalm 65:1-8
1. Metrical, *Thy Might Sets Fast the Mountains*, HB 99, tune: Webb
2. Gelineau, *You Care for the Earth*, GG, p. 94

Hymns for the Day	HL	HB	WB
Come, Thou Long-expected Jesus	113	151	342
Thy Might Sets Fast the Mountains	–	99	–
How Firm a Foundation	283	369	425
God Is Our Strong Salvation	92	347	388
Father, We Praise You	24	43	365

Anthems for the Day
Hag. 2:1-9 *How Firm a Foundation*, arr. Alice Parker (Lawson-Gould); SATB (ME)
2 Thess. 1:5-12 *Put Thou Thy Trust in God*, Philip Tomblings (Oxford); SATB (ME)
Luke 19:1-10 *The Best of Rooms*, Randall Thompson (E. C. Schirmer); SATB (MD)
Ps. 65:1-8 *Thou Art Praised in Sion*, Malcolm Williamson (Boosey & Hawkes); unison and congregation (ME)
Thou, O God, Art Praised in Zion, Ian Hare (*Anthems for Choirs*, vol. 4, Oxford); SATB (M)

SUNDAY BETWEEN NOVEMBER 6 AND NOVEMBER 12 (Proper 27) (C)

Zechariah 7:1-10 "Because of the Temple's destruction, should we continue to mourn by following all the jots and tittles of prescribed rituals for fasting?" Replies Yahweh, "That's nice, but I'd rather you'd show justice toward neighbors. When you fasted and mourned, was it for me? And when you fill your bellies with food and drink, isn't it for your own satisfaction? That's why I sent my word through the voices of many prophets: show kindness and mercy to each other; do not oppress widows, orphans, refugees, or anyone else in need; and do not devise ways of doing evil to one another."

2 Thessalonians 2:13–3:5 We thank you, God, for your prior grace in choosing servants to be saved by the power of the Spirit, for calling them through the gospel we preached to them. May they stand firm and hold on to "the traditions" we taught. May our Lord and you encourage and strengthen them so their work for you may be increased. Finally, sisters and brothers, pray for us that the Lord's word may continue to spread rapidly and be received, as it was among you, and that we may be delivered from the wicked and the evil. The Lord is faithful; he will strengthen and keep you safe. May he lead you into greater understanding of God's love.

Luke 20:27-38 Some Sadducees try to discredit Jesus and expose resurrection as an absurdity. So they ask a whole soap opera of trick questions about to whom we will be married when resurrected (our myopic questions too?). "For heaven's sake," Jesus declares, "resurrection is a whole new order where there is a unity among all who serve each other's needs! You can't project the patterns of this present order on the next. Resurrected life has abolished death, and therefore marriage as the means to propagate life or assure legal succession becomes irrelevant." Thank God, because the present order is not so hot. But 'tis troubling how we cling to the present order.

Psalm 9:11-20
1. Pointed in *LBW* for psalm tone, p. 218

Hymns for the Day	HL	HB	WB
Sing Praise to God, Who Reigns Above	–	15	568
O Lord Most High, with All My Heart	–	388	–
O Love of God Most Full	84	118	–
God Is Love; His Mercy Brightens	80	103	–
Blessing and Honor and Glory and Power	196	137	311
God of Our Life	88	108	395

Anthems for the Day

Zech. 7:1-10 *When the Pious Prayers We Make*, Davbid S. Goodall (*Ecumenical Praise*, Agape); unison (E)

2 Thess. 2:13–3:5 *O Lord, Support Us All the Day Long*, Carl Schalk (Concordia); SAB (E)

Luke 20:27-38 *Easter Flowering*, Alan Luff (*Psalms and Hymns*, Agape); unison (E)

Ps. 9:11-20 *Exsurge Domine (Arise, O Lord)*, Alessandro Scarlatti (Plymouth Music); SATB (M)

SUNDAY BETWEEN NOVEMBER 13 AND NOVEMBER 19 (Proper 28) (C)

Malachi 4:1-6 (3:19-24 in Hebrew text) The Day of the Lord is coming when all evildoers and those who seek to be like God will burn like dried grass, including the roots. But you who honor my name and obey me, my saving power shall arise on you like the dawning sun, bringing light to you in darkness, and therefore healing and restoration. You will frolic like calves freed from a stall, and tread on the wicked under your feet. Remember the law of my servant Moses. Behold, I will send you Elijah the prophet before the great and terrible day. And he will turn the hearts of your generations toward each other, lest I come and smite the land with a curse.

2 Thessalonians 3:6-13 Some sisters and brothers in Christ have quit witnessing to the gospel and are preoccupied only with waiting for the Lord's future coming. They are no longer workers in the vineyard but indolent sloths obsessed with heavenly matters. How to deal with these shirkers? Stay away from idle folk who disobey the word. They will hold you back, because they have ceased carrying out Christ's present work. You know how to imitate us; we toiled night and day so as not to be a burden to you, but an example for you to follow. Persist in doing well.

Luke 21:5-19 "All that glistens is not gold." Hard for some people to hear that, especially when they are captivated by the gleaming splendor of the power and the majesty of the Temple. But the days will come when it shall be razed. When? What will be the signs? Stay away from the misguided who predict "the time is at hand." Rather, focus on the time now when creatures and creation futilely seek to control their destiny and turn their rage and frustration upon you. A time to despair? No! A great time to preach the gospel revealed by Christ, who will give words and wisdom to speak so that not even one hair of the heads of the faithful can be separated from God.

Psalm 82
1. Metrical, *The Lord Will Come and Not Be Slow*, HB 230, tune: Old 107th
2. Gregorian psalm tone, *GP*, Proper 15 C

Hymns for the Day	HL	HB	WB
Judge Eternal, Throned in Splendor	417	517	447
Go, Labor On; Spend and Be Spent	376	283	–
Strong Son of God, Immortal Love	175	228	578
Hope of the World	–	291	423

Anthems for the Day
Mal. 4:1-6 (3:19-24 in Hebrew text) *O, How My Heart Is Sore*, Guillaume Costeley (Mercury); SATB (E)

2 Thess. 3:6-13 *The True Glory*, Peter Aston (Hinshaw); SATB (M)

Luke 21:5-19 *He That Shall Endure*, Felix Mendelssohn (*Elijah*, G. Schirmer or other editions); SATB (ME)

Ps. 82 *O God, Whose Will Is Life and Peace*, Thomas Tallis, arr. Busarow (Concordia); SATB, flute (E)

CHRIST THE KING
[Sunday Between November 20 and November 26]
(Proper 29) (C)

2 Samuel 5:1-5 All the tribes of Israel gather at the sanctuary in Hebron and affirm David as "bone and flesh" (shades of Genesis 2:23—a covenant of peace, trust, confidence, respect, *shalom*). Thus, in fulfillment of the promise (1 Sam. 25:30) and in the presence of Yahweh, the elders anoint David as king over all Israel.

Colossians 1:11-20 One sentence in the Greek text encompasses intercessions for the Colossian church, a thanksgiving, and two strophes of a Christological hymn. Praise God for transferring Christ's followers from the realm of darkness to "the saints in light" and thus authorizing them to participate in the deliverance and redemption in Christ, the firstborn of creation and from the dead who was the agent by whom creation originated and therefore could accomplish the redemption of that creation.

John 12:9-19 Because Lazarus was raised from the dead, a great crowd flocks to Bethany to see him and Jesus. Panicked religious leaders decide to kill Lazarus so as to dispel spectacle-seeking people from believing in Jesus. The next day a great crowd in Jerusalem goes out to acclaim Jesus as messianic king and to pay him homage with palm branches. Jesus finds a young ass and sits upon it in fulfillment of Zechariah 9:9 (but noticeably omitting all reference to military triumph and humility). His disciples do not understand all this until he is "glorified." Pharisees observing this people's parade realize their impotence.

Psalm 95
1. **Metrical,** *O Come and Sing Unto the Lord,* from *The Psalter,* 1912, HB 29, tune: Irish
2. Metrical, *To God with Gladness Sing, MP&E,* tune: Darwall's 148th
3. Gelineau, *Come, Ring Out Our Joy to the Lord,* 24P&1C, p. 22
4. Gregorian psalm tone, *GP,* Lent 3 A
5. *PS,* pp. 25, 26

Hymns for the Day	HL	HB	WB
Rejoice, the Lord Is King	193	140	562
Crown Him with Many Crowns	190	213	349
You Servants of God, Your Master Proclaim	198	27	645
O Come and Sing Unto the Lord	49	29	488
O for a Thousand Tongues to Sing	199	141	493

Anthems for the Day
2 Sam. 5:1-5 *The Last Words of David,* Randall Thompson (E. C. Schirmer); SATB (M)

Col. 1:11-20 *Creator of the Stars of Night,* Richard Wienhorst (Concordia); unison, handbells, flute (E)

John 12:9-19 *Christ Is the King,* Lloyd Pfautsch (Agape); SATB (M)

Ps. 95 *Come, Let Us to the Lord Shout Joyfully,* Ross Lee Finney (C. Fischer); SATB (M)

ALL SAINTS' DAY
[November 1 or First Sunday in November] (C)

Daniel 7:1-3, 15-18 Daniel experiences a night vision in which the four winds of heaven churn up the great sea, allowing four successive great beasts to emerge. Perplexed by this dream, Daniel seeks an angelic interpreter, who explains that the four great beasts are kings/kingdoms which arise out of the earth but shall be replaced by "the saints of the Most High," who shall receive and possess the kingdom forever.

Ephesians 1:11-23 May God give you the Spirit who will make you wise and understanding in the knowledge of Christ. In this way you will know the hope to which Christ has called you (the kind of New Age that is coming) and recognize God's power among us, especially his power in raising Christ to a position above all earthly powers.

Luke 6:20-36 Jesus' opening injunctions of his Sermon on the Plain describe the life of a healed community. "Blessings to you who are poor, hungry, weeping, and despised. Woe to you who are rich, full, laughing, and respected. Do not take any retaliatory action against those who do physical violence to you, extract forced labor from you, or make demands for gifts and loans. But as a sign of the age to come, love and serve your enemies, and pray for them." Jesus has a way of turning our values upside down, doesn't he? Also makes us squirm.

Psalm 149
1. Pointed in *LBW* for psalm tone, p. 288
2. *PS*, p. 38

Hymns for the Day	HL	HB	WB
For All the Saints	429	425	369
O What Their Joy and Their Glory Must Be	430	424	–
We Come Unto Our Fathers' God	342	16	623
God of the Living, in Whose Eyes	–	–	397
O Lord of Life, Where'er They Be	–	–	513
Jerusalem the Golden	435	428	–

Anthems for the Day
Dan. 7:1-3, 15-18 *I Heard a Voice from Heaven*, John Goss (*Second Concord Anthem Book*, E. C. Schirmer); SATB (E)

Eph. 1:11-23 *O How Glorious*, Healey Willan (H. W. Gray); SATB (ME)

Luke 6:20-36 *Happy and Blest Are They*, Felix Mendelssohn (*St. Paul*, G. Schirmer); SATB (ME)
Remember Thy Servants, Lord, from Russian Orthodox Liturgy (*Ecumenical Praise*, Agape); unison (E)

Ps. 149 *Praise Ye the Lord*, Emma Lou Diemer (Flammer); SATB (ME)

THANKSGIVING DAY (C)*

Deuteronomy 26:1-11 Instructions on offering firstfruits of the land to the Lord so you will not succumb to the temptation to believe you achieved the harvest which the Lord has given you. First, recite the ancient creedal story of Yahweh's actions for his people—hearing their distress, delivering them from affliction, and guiding them to the promised land. Then offer the firstfruits of your God-given gifts to the Lord. Why all this ritual? So you can always remember how Yahweh took care of your refugee ancestors, rejoice in such unmerited love, and care for the outsiders who live among you.

Philippians 4:4-9 The Philippians are told: Rejoice and demonstrate to the world gentleness and forbearance. Why? Because the Lord is at hand and the peace of God will guard your hearts and minds from any new threats. So no need to fret over your own well-being: forsake your Sisyphus-like drivenness to secure tomorrow today, and consider practicing the virtues embraced by Paul: truth, honor, justice, purity, agreeableness, excellence, and whatever is praiseworthy.

John 6:25-35 People searching for Jesus are accused by him of seeking only another free lunch—an ephemeral nutritional boost. "Work for imperishable, eternal manna," says Jesus, "which the Son of man will give you." What kind of works must we do? "Believe in the one whom God has sent," says Jesus. Then show us a sign—like the manna in the wilderness—so we will believe. "That bread," retorts Jesus, "came from heaven." That's the bread we want; give it to us. "Simply open your eyes and see," answers Jesus; "I am the bread of life, whoever comes to me shall not hunger, and whoever believes in me shall never thirst."

Psalm 100
1. Metrical, *All People That on Earth Do Dwell*, HB 24, tune: Old Hundredth; WB 288, tune: Old Hundredth
2. Metrical, *O Be Joyful in the Lord!* WB 482, tune: Rock of Ages
3. Metrical, *Sing, All Creation*, MP&E, p. 50, tune: Iste Confessor (Rouen)
4. Gelineau, *Cry Out with Joy to the Lord*, GG, p. 51
5. Gregorian psalm tone, *GP*, Easter 4 B
6. *PS*, p. 29

Hymns for the Day	HL	HB	WB
All People That on Earth Do Dwell	1	24	288
Before the Lord Jehovah's Throne	63	81	306
Rejoice, O Pure in Heart	297	407	561
Now Thank We All Our God	459	9	481
For the Beauty of the Earth	71	2	372
Let Us with a Gladsome Mind	64	28	453

Anthems for the Day
Deut. 26:1-11 *Every Good Gift*, Richard Monaco (H. W. Gray); SATB (MD)
Phil. 4:4-9 *Rejoice in the Lord Alway*, Henry Purcell (Concordia); SATB (MD)
John 6:25-35 *Very Bread, Good Shepherd, Tend Us*, Charles Talmadge (H. W. Gray); SATB (E)
Ps. 100 *The Hundredth Psalm*, Richard T. Gore (Chantry); SATB (M)
  All People That on Earth Do Dwell, J. P. Sweelinck (E. C. Schirmer); SATB (M)

---

*NOTE: Readings for Thanksgiving Day are not strictly tied to Year A, B, or C.

ANNUNCIATION [March 25] (ABC)

Isaiah 7:10-14 Isaiah offers the disbelieving King Ahaz of Judah a sign of God's care, but the king piously refuses to test the Lord for a sign. "Well then," says Isaiah, "the Lord will give you a sign: a young woman shall conceive and bear a son, and shall call his name Immanuel, for God is with his people."

Hebrews 10:4-10 The preexistent Christ speaks the words of Psalm 40:6-8 in order to define the purpose of his incarnation. No longer will the old Levitical sacrifices be either necessary or efficacious, for the ultimate sacrifice of Christ's body upon the cross will establish the new covenant. The justification for the incarnation is that Christ will take a human body in order to offer this perfect sacrifice in obedience to the will of God.

Luke 1:26-38 The angel Gabriel announces to an ordinary peasant girl that she will be impregnated by the invisible power of God and give birth to a son who "will be called the Son of the Most High; and of his kingdom there will be no end." "Preposterous!" you say. Consider this: From the beginning of time God has been at work in bringing forth Jesus Christ so he could be one with his people. Now, in this final annunciation story in the Bible, God's purpose will be fulfilled. God will act to save his people. This child is to be born to this woman for the saving of the world. Shall we join our voice with Mary in saying, "Let it be according to your word; let it happen through our lives."

Psalm 45
1. Gelineau, *On Your Right Stands the Queen, GG*, p. 165

or **Psalm 40:6-10**
1. Gelineau, *I Waited, I Waited for the Lord, GG*, p. 64
2. Gregorian psalm tone, *GP*, Good Friday ABC

Hymns for the Day	HL	HB	WB
Come, Thou Fount of Every Blessing	235	379	341
Come, Thou Long-expected Jesus	113	151	342
Fairest Lord Jesus	194	135	360
Lo, How a Rose E'er Blooming	–	162	455
O Come, O Come, Emmanuel	108	147	489

Anthems for the Day

Isa. 7:10-14 *Behold, a Virgin Shall Conceive* (recitative) and *O Thou That Tellest Good Tidings to Zion* (air and chorus), G. F. Handel (*Messiah*, ed. Watkins Shaw, Novello); alto (M)

Heb. 10:4-10 *Lo, in the Time Appointed*, Healey Willan (Oxford); SATB (M)

Luke 1:26-38 *Righteous Joseph*, Richard Peek (E. C. Kirby); SATB (E)

Ps. 45 or 40:6-10 *Beautiful Savior*, arr. F. Melius Christiansen (Augsburg); SATB divisi (E)

VISITATION [May 31] (ABC)

1 Samuel 2:1-10 After years of childlessness, Hannah gives birth to a son named Samuel, whom she now presents at the sanctuary in Shiloh. Here she offers praise to Yahweh, who can bring a child out of barrenness, abundance out of poverty, princes out of the needy, life out of death, something out of nothing. Yahweh is in charge of this world. His political purposes, economic ways, and social plans will come to fruition.

Romans 12:9-16b Paul's catalog of conduct within the Christian community: hate evil, love one another, be constant in prayer, practice hospitality, bless those who persecute you (noted twice so we'll know he means what he says), weep with those who weep, associate with the lowly, and more.

Luke 1:39-57 The grand conclusion to the two annunciation stories of John and Jesus. Here Mary's whole being, soul and spirit, offers a canticle of praise to God for "he has done great things for me, and holy is his name."

Psalm 113
1. Metrical, *Praise God, Ye Servants of the Lord*, HB 19, tune: Andre
2. Metrical, *Praise God, You Servants of the Lord*, MP&E, p. 60, tune: Eisenach
3. Gelineau, *Praise, O Servants of the Lord*, GG, p. 119
4. Gregorian psalm tone, *GP*, Epiphany 3 C
5. *PS*, p. 30

Hymns for the Day

	HL	HB	WB
At the Name of Jesus	–	143	303
Love Divine, All Loves Excelling	308	399	471
O Love, How Deep, How Broad, How High!	139	–	518
O Love of God Most Full	84	118	–
Praise God, Ye Servants of the Lord	–	19	–
The King of Love My Shepherd Is	99	106	590

Anthems for the Day
1 Sam. 2:1-10 *Lo! How a Rose E'er Blooming*, Hugo Distler (Concordia); SATB (M)

Rom. 12:9-16b *Love Divine, All Loves Excelling*, J. S. Bach (G. Schirmer); unison (E)

Luke 1:39-57 *Magnificat*, Harold Friedell (*Magnificat and Nunc Dimittis in F Major*, H. W. Gray); SATB with brass quartet, timpani, and organ (M)
Song of Mary, Harold Friedell (H. W. Gray); SATB (E)

Ps. 113 *Praise the Lord, Ye Servants*, Richard Peek (Ars Nova [Brodt]); unison (E)

PRESENTATION [February 2] (ABC)

Malachi 3:1-4 Behold, the Day of Yahweh is coming and will be heralded by a "messenger" (angel of the Lord? Elijah the prophet? John the Baptist?). This messenger will prepare the way for Yahweh's return to his Temple, from where swift judgment on wrongdoers will be executed. The priesthood and Temple will be purified in a refiner's fire so that acceptable offerings may be made to the Lord.

Hebrews 2:14-18 Jesus shared our flesh and blood, our nature and life, our suffering and temptation, in order to serve as God's high priest and atone for our sins.

Luke 2:22-40 Parents who fulfill the law and prophets who break into song and utterances of thanksgiving frame this narrative of the presentation of Jesus. Simeon the watchman has now seen the Lord's salvation, a light to the nations, and Anna begins telling everyone that the redemption of Jerusalem is at hand.

Psalm 84
1. Metrical, *Lord of the Worlds Above*, HB 14, tune: Darwall's 148th
2. Gelineau, *My Soul Is Longing and Yearning*, 30P&2C, p. 25
3. Gregorian psalm tone, *GP*, Proper 25 C
4. Tone and antiphon by Frank Quinn, *How Lovely Is Your Dwelling Place*, *MP&E* p. 199
5. *PS*, p. 22

or Psalm 24:7-10
1. Metrical, *Lift Up Your Heads, Ye Mighty Gates*, HB 152, tune: Truro
2. Gelineau, *O Gates, Lift High Your Heads*, GG, p. 156
3. Gregorian psalm tone, *GP*, Advent 4 A
4. *PS*, p. 16

Hymns for the Day	HL	HB	WB
How Dear to Me, O Lord of Hosts	–	440	–
Lord of the Worlds Above	50	14	–
Praise to the Lord, the Almighty	6	1	557
The Head That Once Was Crowned with Thorns	195	211	589
The True Light That Enlightens Man	–	–	598

Anthems for the Day
Mal. 3:1-4 *Thus Saith the Lord* and *But Who May Abide the Day of His Coming?*, G. F. Handel (*Messiah*, ed. Watkins Shaw, Novello); bass solo (M)

Heb. 2:14-18 *The Word Became Flesh*, George Brandon (E. C. Kirby); unison (E)

Luke 2:22-40 *Nunc Dimittis*, Harold Friedell (*Magnificat and Nunc Dimittis in F Major*, H. W. Gray); SATB (E)

Ps. 84 or Ps. 24:7-10 *Praise to the Lord*, Hugo Distler (*A First Motet Book*, Concordia); SATB (M)

HOLY CROSS [September 14] (ABC)

Numbers 21:4b-9 Impatient Israel wanders in the wilderness murmuring (i.e., complaining) and speaking against God and Moses and the food and water. Yahweh has had enough of this murmuring, so he sends judgment in the form of fiery serpents that bite the people so that many die. Result: Israel confesses her sin and prays that the serpents be removed. Yahweh instructs Moses to "make an image of a serpent, and set it on a pole; and every one who is bitten, when he sees it, shall live." And it was so. Judgment was and is the means of God's redemption.

1 Corinthians 1:18-24 The gospel always seems to turn our world upside down. Here worldly wisdom and strength are characterized as foolish and weak, and the nonsense and weakness of the crucifixion are labeled as wise and strong.

John 3:13-17 The possibility of new life "from above" is available only through Christ, the one who was publicly lifted up on the cross so that all might see and believe and therefore "have eternal life."

Psalm 98:1-5
1. Metrical psalm, *New Songs of Celebration Render*, Erik Routley, *SOT&P*, p. 2, tune: *Rendez à Dieu*
2. Psalm paraphrase, *Sing a New Song to the Lord*, Timothy Dudley-Smith, *WII*, p. 245, tune: *Cantate Domino* by David G. Wilson, fresh, contemporary setting
3. Gelineau, *Sing a New Song to the Lord*, GG, p. 15
4. Gregorian psalm tone, *GP*, Christmas Day 3 ABC

or Psalm 78:1-2, 34-38
1. Metrical, *O Come, My People, to My Law*, HB 255, tune: Heber (Kingsley)
2. Gelineau, *The Things We Have*, GG, p. 103
3. Gregorian psalm tone, *GP*, Proper 13 A

Hymns for the Day	HL	HB	WB
Christ Is the World's True Light	–	492	326
Let All Together Praise Our God	–	–	450
The Great Creator of the Worlds	–	–	588
The Strife Is O'er, the Battle Done	164	203	597
When I Survey the Wondrous Cross	152	198	635

Anthems for the Day
Num. 21:4b-9 *Bow Down Thine Ear, O Lord*, Anton Arensky (*Church Anthem Book*, Oxford); SATB (E)
1 Cor. 1:18-24 *Christus Factus Est* (And Being Found in Human Form), Anton Bruckner (Summy-Birchard); SATB (M)
John 3:13-17 *For God So Loved the World*, Heinrich Schütz (*A Second Motet Book*, Concordia); SATB (M)
Ps. 98:1-5 or Ps. 78:1-2, 34-38 *Cantate Domino*, David McK. Williams (H. W. Gray); SATB with organ and optional brass and timpani (MD)

SOURCES
FOR THE PSALM SETTINGS

GG   *The Gelineau Gradual* (1969, 1975, 1977), Joseph Gelineau (G-2124). G.I.A. Publications, 7404 South Mason Avenue, Chicago, IL 60638.

GP   *Gradual Psalms.* Church Hymnal Series VI, in three volumes— Year A, Year B, Year C (1980, 1981, 1982). Church Hymnal Corp., 800 Second Avenue, New York, NY 10017.

HB   *The Hymnbook* (1955), published by Presbyterian Church in the United States, The United Presbyterian Church in the U.S.A., Reformed Church in America. Westminster Press, 925 Chestnut Street, Philadelphia, PA 19107.

LBW   *Lutheran Book of Worship* (1978). Augsburg Publishing House, 426 South Fifth Street, Minneapolis, MN 55440.

LW   *Lutheran Worship.* Concordia Publishing House, 3558 South Jefferson Avenue, St. Louis, MO 63118.

MFT   *Music from Taizé,* Jacques Berthier, G-2433. G.I.A. Publications.

MP&E   *Morning Praise and Evensong,* ed. and arr. by William G. Storey, D.M.S., Frank C. Quinn, O.P., and David F. Wright, O.P. Fides Publishers.

NHAS   *New Hymns for All Seasons,* James Quinn. Fowler Wright Books Ltd., Leominster, Herefordshire, England.

NSC   *New Songs for the Church,* Book 1, Galliard Press.

OEW   *On Eagle's Wings,* Michael Joncas. Epoch Universal Publications, North American Liturgy Resources, Phoenix, AZ 85029.

PFTD   *The Psalmody for the Day,* Series A. Fortress Press, 2900 Queen Lane, Philadelphia, PA 19129.

PP   *Psalm Praise.* G.I.A. Publications.

PS   *A Psalm Sampler* (1986), Psalter Task Force, Office of Worship, Presbyterian Church (U.S.A.). Westminster Press.

SOT&P   *Songs of Thanks and Praise.* Hinshaw Music, P.O. Box 470, Chapel Hill, NC 27514.

WB   *The Worshipbook* (1972), prepared by The Joint Committee on Worship for Cumberland Presbyterian Church, Presbyterian Church in the United States, The United Presbyterian Church in the United States of America. Westminster Press.

WII   *Worship II.* G.I.A. Publications.

24P&1C   *Twenty-four Psalms and a Canticle,* Joseph Gelineau (G-1424). G.I.A. Publications.

30P&2C   *Thirty Psalms and Two Canticles,* Joseph Gelineau (G-1430). G.I.A. Publications.

BIBLIOGRAPHY
ON LECTIONARIES

Abba, Raymond. "The Ministry of the Word," *Principles of Christian Worship.* New York: Oxford University Press, 1960. Pp. 45–84.

Achtemeier, Elizabeth. "Aids and Resources for the Interpretation of Lectionary Texts," *Interpretation: A Journal of Bible and Theology,* vol. 31, no. 2 (April 1977), pp. 154–164.

Allen, Horace T., Jr. Introduction to *Common Lectionary: The Lectionary Proposed by the Consultation on Common Texts.* New York: Church Hymnal Corp., 1983. Pp. 7–27.

———. "Understanding the Lectionary," *A Handbook for the Lectionary.* Philadelphia: Geneva Press, 1980. Pp. 11–44.

———. "Using the Consensus Lectionary: A Response." In *Social Themes of the Christian Year: A Commentary on the Lectionary,* ed. Dieter T. Hessel. Philadelphia: Geneva Press, 1983. Pp. 264–268.

Anglican Church of Canada. *The Lectionary.* Toronto: Anglican Book Center, 1980.

Babin, David E. *Week In—Week Out: A New Look at Liturgical Preaching.* New York: Seabury Press, 1976.

Bailey, Lloyd R. "The Lectionary in Critical Perspective," *Interpretation: A Journal of Bible and Theology,* vol. 31, no. 2 (April 1977), pp. 139–153.

———. "Lectionary Preaching," *Duke Divinity School Review,* Winter 1976, pp. 25–35.

Bass, George M. *The Renewal of Liturgical Preaching.* Minneapolis: Augsburg Publishing House, 1967.

Briner, Lewis A. "Bibliography on the Lectionary and the Church Year," *Reformed Liturgy & Music,* vol. 9, no. 4 (Fall 1975), pp. 19–25.

———. "A Look at New Proposals for the Lectionary," *Worship,* vol. 53, no. 2, pp. 83–87; reprinted by permission in *Reformed Liturgy & Music,* vol. 17, no. 3 (Summer 1983), pp. 126–129.

———. "Preaching the Lectionary," *Reformed Liturgy & Music,* vol. 13, no. 2 (Spring 1979), pp. 5–12.

———. "Using the Lectionary," *Reformed Liturgy & Music,* vol. 9, no. 4 (Fall 1975), pp. 13–17.

Büchler, Adolf. "The Reading of the Law and Prophets in a Triennial Cycle," *Jewish Quarterly Review,* vol. 5 (1893), pp. 420–468; vol. 6 (1894), pp. 1–73.

Carl, William J., III. "Doctrine and the Bible." In *Preaching Christian Doctrine.* Philadelphia: Fortress Press, 1984. Pp. 33–57.

———. "Planning Your Preaching: A Look at the Lectionary," *Journal for Preachers,* vol. 4, no. 3 (Easter 1981), pp. 13–17.

Carrington, Philip. *The Primitive Christian Calendar: A Study in the Making of the Marcan Gospel,* vol. 1: *Introduction and Text.* New York: Cambridge University Press, 1952.

The Church of South India. "The 'Christian Year' Lectionary and Collects," in *The Book of Common Worship*. Madras: Oxford University Press, 1963. Pp. 23–68.

Clarke, W. K. Lowther, and Charles Harris. "The Lectionary." In *Liturgy and Worship*. New York: Macmillan Co., 1946. Pp. 296–301.

Commission on Worship of the Consultation on Church Union. *A Lectionary*. Princeton: Consultation on Church Union, 1974.

Crockett, Larrimore. "Luke 4:16–30 and the Jewish Lectionary Cycle: A Word of Caution," *Journal of Jewish Studies*, vol. 17 (1966), pp. 13–45.

Davies, J. G., ed. *The New Westminster Dictionary of Liturgy and Worship*. Philadelphia: Westminster Press, 1986.

Davies, W. D. "Reflections on Archbishop Carrington's *The Primitive Christian Calendar*." In W. D. Davies and D. Daube, eds., *The Background of the New Testament and Its Eschatology: In Honour of C. H. Dodd*. New York: Cambridge University Press, 1956. Pp. 124–152. Reprinted in Davies' *Christian Origins and Judaism*. Philadelphia: Westminster Press, 1962. Pp. 67–95.

Delling, Gerhard. *Worship in the New Testament*. Tr. Percy Scott. Philadelphia: Westminster Press, 1962.

Directory for the Service of God, *The Constitution of the Presbyterian Church (U.S.A.), Part II: Book of Order*, 1986–87. New York and Atlanta: The Office of the General Assembly of the Presbyterian Church (U.S.A.), 1986.

Finch, Rowland G. *The Synagogue Lectionary and the New Testament: A Study of the Three-Year Cycle of Readings from the Law and the Prophets as a Contribution to New Testament Chronology*. London: S.P.C.K., 1939.

Fuller, Reginald H. *Preaching the New Lectionary: The Word of God for the Church Today*. Rev. and exp. 2nd ed. Collegeville, Minn.: Liturgical Press, 1986.

———. *What Is Liturgical Preaching?* London: SCM Press, 1957.

Gonzalez, Justo and Catherine. *Liberation Preaching*. Nashville: Abingdon Press, 1980.

Goulder, M. D. *Midrash and Lection in Matthew*. London: S.P.C.K., 1974.

Grisbrooke, W. J. "A Contemporary Liturgical Problem: The Divine Office and Public Worship," *Studia Liturgica*, vol. 9, no. 3 (1973), pp. 81–106.

Guilbert, Charles Mortimer, Custodian of the Standard Book of Common Prayer of the Protestant Episcopal Church in the United States. *The Book of Common Prayer and Administration of the Sacraments and Other Rites and Ceremonies of the Church*. New York: Church Hymnal Corp. and Seabury Press, 1979.

Guilding, Aileen. *The Fourth Gospel and Jewish Worship: A Study of the Relation of St. John's Gospel to the Ancient Jewish Lectionary System*. Oxford: Clarendon Press, 1960.

Gunstone, John. *Commentary on the New Lectionary*, vol. 1. Rev. ed. London: S.P.C.K., 1979.

———. "Contemporary Problems of Liturgical Time: Calendar and Lectionary," *Studia Liturgica*, vol. 14, nos. 2, 3, 4 (1982), pp. 74–89.

Hageman, Howard G. "A Brief Study of the British Lectionary," *Worship*, vol. 56, no. 4 (July 1982), pp. 356–364.

Heinemann, Joseph. "The Triennial Lectionary Cycle," *Journal of Jewish Studies*, vol. 19 (1968), pp. 41–48.

Huxtable, John; John Marsh; Romilly Micklem; and James Todd. "Lectionary," comp. for the use of Congregationalists in *A Book of Public Worship*. London: Oxford University Press, 1959. Pp. 212–222.

Inter-Lutheran Commission on Worship. *The Church Year: Calendar and Lectionary, Contemporary Worship No. 6*. Minneapolis: Augsburg Publishing House; Philadelphia: Board of Publication, Lutheran Church in America; and St. Louis: Concordia Publishing House, 1973.

————. "Propers," *Lutheran Book of Worship*, Ministers Edition. Minneapolis: Augsburg Publishing House; Philadelphia: Board of Publication, Lutheran Church in America, 1978. Pp. 121–195.

The Joint Committee on Worship for Cumberland Presbyterian Church, Presbyterian Church in the United States, and The United Presbyterian Church in the United States of America. *The Worshipbook—Services and Hymns.* Philadelphia: Westminster Press, 1970, 1972.

————. Ronald C. D. Jasper, ed. *The Calendar and Lectionary: A Reconsideration.* London: Oxford University Press, 1967.

The Joint Liturgical Group, *The Calendar and Lessons for the Church Year.* London: S.P.C.K., 1969.

Jones, Cheslyn; Geoffrey Wainwright; and Edward Yarnold, eds. *The Study of Liturgy.* New York: Oxford University Press, 1978.

Lamb, J. A. "The Place of the Bible in the Liturgy," *The Cambridge History of the Bible*, vol. 1: *From the Beginnings to Jerome.* New York: Cambridge University Press, 1970. Pp. 572ff.

Lengling, E. J. "Pericopes," *New Catholic Encyclopedia*, vol. II. New York: McGraw-Hill Book Co., 1967. Pp. 130–138.

Mann, Jacob. *The Bible as Read and Preached in the Old Synagogue*, vol. 1: *The Palestinian Triennial Cycle: Genesis and Exodus.* Cincinnati: Hebrew Union College—Jewish Institute of Religion, 1940. Reprinted in "The Library of Biblical Studies," New York: KTAV Publishing House, 1971. Jacob Mann with Isaiah Sonne, vol. 2: *Leviticus and Numbers to Seder 106.* Cincinnati: Hebrew Union College—Jewish Institute of Religion, 1966.

McArthur, A. Allan. *The Christian Year and Lectionary Reform.* London: SCM Press, 1958.

————. *The Evolution of the Christian Year.* London: SCM Press, 1953.

Melton, Julius. *Presbyterian Worship in America.* Atlanta: John Knox Press, 1967.

Minutes of the Consultation on Common Texts. Washington, D.C., March 29–31, 1978.

Morris, Leon. *The New Testament and the Jewish Lectionaries.* London: Tyndale Press, 1964.

Nesper, Paul. *Biblical Texts* (A Collection of Lectionaries). Columbus, Ohio: Wartburg Press, 1952.

Nichols, James Hastings. *Corporate Worship in the Reformed Tradition.* Philadelphia: Westminster Press, 1968.

Old, Hughes Oliphant, "The Ministry of the Word," *Worship That Is Reformed According to Scripture.* In John H. Leith and John W. Kuykendall, series eds., *Guides to the Reformed Tradition.* Atlanta: John Knox Press, 1984. Pp. 57–85.

————. *The Patristic Roots of Reformed Worship.* Zurich: Theologischer Verlag Zurich, 1975.

————. Book review of *A Handbook for the Lectionary*, by Horace T. Allen, Jr., *Worship*, vol. 56, no. 1 (January 1982), pp. 85, 86.

Porter, J. R. "The Pentateuch and the Triennial Lectionary Cycle: An Examination of a Recent Theory" In F. F. Bruce, ed., *Promise and Fulfillment: Essays Presented to Professor S. H. Hooke.* Edinburgh: T. & T. Clark, 1963. Pp. 163–174.

Reed, Luther D. *The Lutheran Liturgy.* Rev. ed. Philadelphia: Muhlenberg Press, 1960. Pp. 460–462.

Reumann, John. "A History of Lectionaries: From the Synagogue at Nazareth to Post-Vatican II," *Interpretation: A Journal of Bible and Theology*, vol. 31, no. 2 (April 1977), pp. 116–130.

Rordorf, Willy. *Sunday: The History of the Day of Rest and Worship in the Earliest*

Centuries of the Christian Church. Tr. A. A. K. Graham. Philadelphia: Westminster Press, 1968.

Sacred Congregation for Divine Worship. *Ordo Lectionum Missae.* Rome: Vatican Polyglot Press, 25 May 1969.

Sacred Congregation for the Sacraments and Divine Worship. *Lectionary for Mass*, Introduction (*Second Editio Typica*, 1981), no. 4, tr. International Commission on English in the Liturgy, *Lectionary*, I (London: Collins Liturgical Publications and Cassell Ltd.; Dublin: Veritas Publications; Sydney: E. J. Dwyer Ltd., 1981), and *Liturgy Documentary Series*, 1 (Washington, D.C.: Office of Publishing Services, United States Catholic Conference, 1982).

Sanders, James A. "Canon and Calendar: An Alternative Lectionary Proposal." In *Social Themes of the Christian Year: A Commentary on the Lectionary*, ed. Dieter T. Hessel. Philadelphia: Geneva Press, 1983. Pp. 257–263.

Section on Worship of the Board of Discipleship of The United Methodist Church. *Seasons of the Gospel: Resources for the Christian Year.* Nashville: Abingdon Press, 1979.

———. *Word and Table: A Basic Pattern of Sunday Worship for United Methodists.* Nashville: Abingdon Press, 1976. Pp. 50–57.

Shepherd, Massey H., Jr. "The Lectionary," *The Oxford American Prayer Book Commentary.* New York: Oxford University Press, 1963. Pp. xi–xlv.

Skudlarek, William. "The Structure and Use of the Lectionary," and "The Pastoral Use of the Lectionary." In *The Word in Worship: Preaching in a Liturgical Context.* Nashville: Abingdon Press, 1981. Pp. 31–44 and pp. 45–64.

Sloyan, Gerard S. *A Commentary on the New Lectionary.* Mahwah, N.J.:Paulist Press, 1975.

———. "The Lectionary as a Context for Interpretation," *Interpretation: A Journal of Bible and Theology*, vol. 31, no. 2 (April 1977), pp. 131–138.

Trotter, J. Irwin. "Are We Preaching a 'Subversive' Lectionary?" *School of Theology at Claremont Bulletin: Occasional Paper Number 7*, vol. 28, no. 2 (December 1985).

Vatican Council II. Constitution on the Liturgy, *Sacrosanctum Concilium*, December 4, 1963, tr. International Commission on English in the Liturgy, *Documents on the Liturgy, 1963–1979: Conciliar, Papal, and Curial Texts.* Collegeville, Minn.: Liturgical Press, 1982.

Von Allmen, Jean-Jacques. *Preaching and Congregation.* Tr. B. L. Nicholas. Atlanta: John Knox Press, 1962.

Werner, Eric. *The Sacred Bridge: Liturgical Parallels in Synagogue and Early Church.* New York: Columbia University Press, 1959.

White, James F. *Christian Worship in Transition.* Nashville: Abingdon Press, 1976.

———. *Introduction to Christian Worship.* Nashville: Abingdon Press, 1980.

Wikgren, Allen P. "Chicago Studies in the Greek Lectionary of the New Testament." In J. N. Birdsall and R. W. Thomson, eds., *Biblical and Patristic Studies in Memory of Robert Pierce Casey.* Freiburg: Herder & Co., 1963. Pp. 96–121.

Willis, G. G. *St. Augustine's Lectionary*, Alcuin Club Collection, 44. London: S.P.C.K., 1962.

RESOURCES
FOR LECTIONARY USE

Catalogue of Choral Music Listed in Biblical Order by James Laster. Metuchen, N.J.: Scarecrow Press, 1983.

A very complete and most eclectic catalog of choral music for worship. Contains thousands of listings, ranging from standard choral literature to the newest publications in contemporary styles, thus reflecting many traditions of choral music.

Celebrating Liturgy: The Book for the Liturgy of the Word

A weekly workbook for a whole year—Year A, B, or C—according to the Roman Catholic lectionary. Contains notes on the seasons, two translations of each scripture lesson, suggestions for reading each text, pronunciation guide, seasonal responsorial psalms with original music, and homiletical notes—for use by lectors, musicians, liturgy planners, and preachers. Available from Liturgy Training Publications, 1800 North Hermitage Avenue, Chicago, IL 60622-1101.

Celebration—A Creative Worship Service

A monthly packet of ecumenically designed resource materials based on the Common Lectionary: scripture commentaries, homiletical aids, music suggestions, general intercessions, prayer responses, bulletin art. Available from P.O. Box 414293, Kansas City, MO 64141.

Church Dogmatics: An Index Volume with Aids for the Preacher by Karl Barth. Ed. G. W. Bromiley and T. F. Torrance. Edinburgh: T. & T. Clark, 1977.

An index to all scripture references in Karl Barth's *Church Dogmatics*, providing theological and homiletical insights when cross-referenced with a lectionary.

Commentaries on the Readings of the Lectionary by Robert Crotty and Gregory Manley. New York: Pueblo Publishing Co., 1975.

Contains an introduction that presents the theology and interpretative principles used by the authors (including essays on the nature of the Bible, of revelation, of the church, of the life of the Word in the church, and of the liturgical year); theological reflections on all lessons of the Roman Catholic lectionary; and an index of principal biblical-theological subjects and themes, with cross-references.

A Commentary on the New Lectionary by Gerard S. Sloyan. Mahwah, N.J.: Paulist Press, 1975.

A one-volume commentary on all three years of the Roman Catholic lectionary.

Commentary on the Sunday Lectionary, Cycle A, Cycle B, and Cycle C, by Peter Coughlan and Peter Purdue. Collegeville, Minn.: Liturgical Press, 1986.
A three-volume set which gives explanatory comments, an exposition of themes, and suggestions for a homily on each reading in the Roman Catholic lectionary.

Emphasis: A Preaching Journal for the Parish Pastor
A monthly journal that lists scripture lessons from three different lectionaries; supplies four illustrations for each of those biblical texts, and three sermon outlines for every Sunday in the month. Available from C.S.S. of Ohio, 628 South Main Street, Lima, OH 45804.

An English-Speaking Hymnal Guide by Erik Routley. Collegeville, Minn.: Liturgical Press, 1979.
Copious notes on 888 hymns in the English language: metrical form, rhyme scheme, historical data on the original source and first appearance of the hymn, biographical information on the author, and usually a description of the author's reason for composing it.

Homily Service: An Ecumenical Resource for Sharing the Word
A monthly journal offering exegetical and homiletical notes on each pericope for the day according to the Roman Catholic lectionary, with cross-references to the Common Lectionary. Available from Liturgical Conference, 810 Rhode Island Avenue, N.E., Washington, DC 20018.

Lectionary Preaching Workbook by John R. Brokhoff. Lima, Ohio: C.S.S. of Ohio. A rev. 1986, B 1984, C rev. 1985.
A series of notebooks providing brief liturgical, exegetical, theological, and homiletical suggestions for each Sunday of the year, according to the Lutheran, Common, and Roman Catholic lectionaries.

Looseleaf Lectionary
As entitled, a "looseleaf" collection of the scriptural texts for the day (according to the Roman Catholic lectionary) on a dated basis, a reflective introduction to each day's readings, "Homily Hints," and prayers. Available from Liturgical Press, St. John's Abbey, Collegeville, MN 56321.

"An Organist's Companion to *The Worshipbook*" by Erik Routley, in *Reformed Liturgy & Music,* vol. 9, no. 2 (Spring 1975), pp. 7-78.
Comments on playing each of the hymns in *The Worshipbook;* notes may be technical, or historical, or merely a pointer toward the mood in which the hymn should be approached. Available from *RL&M* Administration Office, The Office of Worship, 1044 Alta Vista Road, Louisville, KY 40205.

Preaching the New Common Lectionary by Fred. B. Craddock, John H. Hayes, Carl R. Holladay, and Gene M. Tucker. Abingdon Press, 1985, 1986.
A series of commentaries on the Common Lectionary texts. Two volumes for each year are devoted to the texts for Advent, Christmas, Epiphany and Lent, Holy Week, Easter.

Preaching the New Lectionary: The Word of God for the Church Today by Reginald H. Fuller. Rev. and exp. 2nd ed. Collegeville, Minn.: Liturgical Press, 1986.
A one-volume commentary on all three years of the Roman Catholic lectionary.

Proclamation 1 (1973–76), *2* (1979–82), and *3* (1984–87): *Aids for Interpreting the Lessons of the Church Year*. 24 vols. in each set. Philadelphia: Fortress Press.
An ongoing series of exegetical and homiletical paperback commentaries on the weekly lessons "used by most denominations on any given Sunday." In *Proclamation 3* each volume is written by a single author and is devoted to a particular time of the church year.

Psalms and Prayers for Congregational Participation: Appropriate for Use with the Common Lectionary, Series A, Series B, and Series C, by B. David Hostetter. Lima, Ohio: C.S.S. of Ohio, 1983, 1984, 1985.
A worship resource book containing models for all elements for every Sunday.

Pulpit Resources
Homiletical aids for preachers. Available from 5016 Double Point Way, Byron, CA 94514.

Respond & Acclaim: Responsorial Psalms and Gospel Acclamations, Cycle A, 1986; Cycle B, 1984; and Cycle C, 1985, by Owen Alstott.
Arrangements written to help congregations respond in song to the reading of the biblical texts according to the Roman Catholic lectionary. Arranged for choir and congregation, with organ or guitar accompaniment. Available from Oregon Catholic Press, P.O. Box 14809, Portland, OR 97214.

Scripture Notes by Norman A. Beck. A rev. 1986, B 1984, C 1985. Lima, Ohio: C.S.S. of Ohio.
Provides an overview of tone and theme for each Sunday. Gives concise background information for the Lutheran, Common, and Roman Catholic lectionary readings for every Sunday.

Sharing Our Biblical Story: A Guide to Using Liturgical Readings as the Core of Church and Family Education by Joseph P. Russell. San Francisco: Harper & Row, Winston Press, 1979.
Shows how to use Bible stories to form the central focus of Christian education in the home or in a school setting, placing special emphasis on stories which appear in the Episcopalian, Roman Catholic, and Lutheran lectionaries, including a commentary on those lections.

Social Themes of the Christian Year: A Commentary on the Lectionary ed. Dieter T. Hessel. Philadelphia: Geneva Press, 1983.
A broad range of writers highlight basic biblical themes, develop a brief interpretation of each seasonal cluster of texts, and show how congregational worship-education-action can manifest the story line of each season.

We Pray to the Lord: General Intercessions Based on the Scriptural Readings for Sundays and Holy Days by Richard Mazziotta. Notre Dame, Ind.: Ave Maria Press, 1984.
Provides models for offering suitable intercessions based upon the scriptural readings for the day according to the Roman Catholic lectionary.

When We Gather: A Book of Prayers for Worship, Year A, Year B, and Year C, by James G. Kirk. Philadelphia: Geneva Press, 1983, 1984, 1985.
Three separate volumes of worship aids—calls to worship, prayers of confession, assurances of pardon, prayers of dedication, and prayers of

praise and petition—based on the Common Lectionary prepared for trial use by the North American Committee on Calendar and Lectionary.

Word and Witness
A bimonthly, four-page leaflet for each Sunday in the year, plus occasional supplements for special days or topics. Available from Sunday Publications, 193 10th Avenue, N., Lake Worth, FL 33461.

The Year of the Lord's Favor: Preaching the Three-Year Lectionary by Sherman E. Johnson. San Francisco: Harper & Row, Winston-Seabury, 1983.
A one-volume commentary on the lectionary, noted for its grouping of various texts around common theological themes.

INDEX
OF SCRIPTURE READINGS

Dates refer to Sundays after Pentecost (e.g., Sunday between October 2 and October 8)

54:5-14	Easter Vigil ABC
55:1-11	Easter Vigil ABC
55:10-13	Epiphany 8 (Proper 3) C
58:3-9a	Epiphany 5 A
60:1-6	Epiphany ABC
61:1-4	Baptism of the Lord (Epiphany 1) C
61:1-4,8-11	Advent 3 B
61:10–62:3	Christmas 1 B
62:1-5	Epiphany 2 C
62:6-7,10-12	Christmas Day: Additional Lections 1 ABC
63:7-9	Christmas 1 A
63:16–64:8	Advent 1 B
65:17-25	Easter Day C (2nd option)

Jeremiah

1:4-10	Epiphany 4 C
17:5-10	Epiphany 6 (Proper 1) C
18:1-11	Aug. 7–13 (Proper 14) C
20:7-13	Aug. 14–20 (Proper 15) C
23:1-6	Christ the King (Nov. 20–26) (Proper 29) B
28:1-9	Aug. 21–27 (Proper 16) C
31:1-6	Easter A (2nd option)
31:7-9	Oct. 23–29 (Proper 25) B
31:7-14	Christmas 2 ABC
31:31-34	Lent 5 B
	Maundy Thursday C
33:14-16	Advent 1 C

Baruch

3:9-15,32-4:4	Easter Vigil ABC

Ezekiel

18:1-9,25-29	Aug. 28–Sept. 3 (Proper 17) C
33:1-11	Sept. 4–10 (Proper 18) C
34:11-16,20-24	Christ the King (Nov. 20–26) (Proper 29) A
36:24-28	Easter Vigil ABC
37:1-14	Lent 5 A
	Easter Vigil ABC
	Pentecost B (2nd option)

Daniel

7:1-3,15-18	All Saints' Day (Nov. 1) C
7:9-14	Nov. 13–19 (Proper 28) B
12:1-3	Easter Evening ABC (2nd option)

Hosea

2:14-20	Epiphany 8 (Proper 3) B
4:1-3;5:15–6:6	Sept. 11–17 (Proper 19) C

11:1-11	Sept. 18–24 (Proper 20) C

Joel

2:1-2,12-17a	Ash Wednesday ABC
2:21-27	Thanksgiving Day B
2:23-30	Sept. 25–Oct. 1 (Proper 21) C

Amos

5:6-7,10-15	Oct. 2–8 (Proper 22) C
5:18-24	Nov. 6–12 (Proper 27) A

Jonah

3:1-5,10	Epiphany 3 B

Micah

1:2; 2:1-10	Oct. 9–15 (Proper 23) C
5:2-5a	Advent 4 C
6:1-8	Epiphany 4 A

Habakkuk

1:1-3; 2:1-4	Oct. 16–22 (Proper 24) C

Zephaniah

1:7,12-18	Nov. 13–19 (Proper 28) A
3:1-9	Oct. 23–29 (Proper 25) C
3:14-20	Advent 3 C
	Easter Vigil ABC

Haggai

2:1-9	Oct. 30–Nov. 5 (Proper 26) C

Zechariah

7:1-10	Nov. 6–12 (Proper 27) C

Malachi

3:1-4	Advent 2 C
	Presentation (Feb. 2) ABC
4:1-6	(3:19-24 in Hebrew text) Nov. 13–19 (Proper 28) C

Matthew

1:18-25	Advent 4 A
2:1-12	Epiphany ABC
2:13-15,19-23	Christmas 1 A
3:1-12	Advent 2 A
3:13-17	Baptism of the Lord (Epiphany 1) A
4:1-11	Lent 1 A
4:12-23	Epiphany 3 A
5:1-12	Epiphany 4 A
	All Saints' Day (Nov. 1) A
5:13-16	Epiphany 5 A
5:17-26	Epiphany 6 (Proper 1) A
5:27-37	Epiphany 7 (Proper 2) A
5:38-48	Epiphany 8 (Proper 3) A

6:1-6,16-21	Ash Wednesday ABC
6:25-33	Thanksgiving Day B
7:21-29	May 29–June 4 (Proper 4) A
9:9-13	June 5–11 (Proper 5) A
9:14-17	January 1 (New Year) B
9:35–10:8	June 12–18 (Proper 6) A
10:24-33	June 19–25 (Proper 7) A
10:34-42	June 26–July 2 (Proper 8) A
11:2-11	Advent 3 A
11:25-30	July 3–9 (Proper 9) A
13:1-9,18-23	July 10–16 (Proper 10) A
13:24-30,36-43	July 17–23 (Proper 11) A
13:44-52	July 24–30 (Proper 12) A
14:13-21	July 31–Aug. 6 (Proper 13) A
14:22-33	Aug. 7–13 (Proper 14) A
15:21-28	Aug. 14–20 (Proper 15) A
16:13-20	Aug. 21–27 (Proper 16) A
16:21-28	Aug. 28–Sept. 3 (Proper 17) A
17:1-9	Lent 2 A (2nd option) Transfiguration (Last Sunday After Epiphany) A
18:15-20	Sept. 4–10 (Proper 18) A
18:21-35	Sept. 11–17 (Proper 19) A
20:1-16	Sept. 18–24 (Proper 20) A
21:1-11	Palm Sunday (Lent 6)
21:28-32	Sept. 25–Oct. 1 (Proper 21) A
21:33-43	Oct. 2–8 (Proper 22) A
22:1-14	Oct. 9–15 (Proper 23) A
22:15-22	Oct. 16–22 (Proper 24) A
22:34-46	Oct. 23–29 (Proper 25) A
23:1-12	Oct. 30–Nov. 5 (Proper 26) A
24:36-44	Advent 1 A
25:1-13	Nov. 6–12 (Proper 27) A
25:14-30	Nov. 13–19 (Proper 28) A
25:31-46	January 1 (New Year) A Christ the King (Nov. 20–26) (Proper 29) A
26:14–27:66	Passion Sunday (Lent 6) A (1st option)
27:11-54	Passion Sunday (Lent 6) A (2nd option)
28:1-10	Easter Vigil ABC Easter A (2nd option)
28:16-20	Trinity Sunday (Pentecost 1) A

Mark

1:1-8	Advent 2 B
1:4-11	Baptism of the Lord (Epiphany 1) B
1:9-15	Lent 1 B
1:14-20	Epiphany 3 B
1:21-28	Epiphany 4 B
1:29-39	Epiphany 5 B
1:40-45	Epiphany 6 (Proper 1) B
2:1-12	Epiphany 7 (Proper 2) B
2:18-22	Epiphany 8 (Proper 3) B
2:23–3:6	May 29–June 4 (Proper 4) B
3:20-35	June 5–11 (Proper 5) B
4:26-34	June 12–18 (Proper 6) B
4:35-41	June 19–25 (Proper 7) B
5:21-43	June 26–July 2 (Proper 8) B
6:1-6	July 3–9 (Proper 9) B
6:7-13	July 10–16 (Proper 10) B
6:30-34	July 17–23 (Proper 11) B
7:1-8,14-15, 21-23	Aug. 28–Sept. 3 (Proper 17) B
7:31-37	Sept. 4–10 (Proper 18) B
8:27-38	Sept. 11–17 (Proper 19) B
8:31-38	Lent 2 B (1st option)
9:1-9	Lent 2 B (2nd option)
9:2-9	Transfiguration (Last Sunday After Epiphany) B
9:30-37	Sept. 18–24 (Proper 20) B
9:38-50	Sept. 25–Oct. 1 (Proper 21) B
10:2-16	Oct. 2–8 (Proper 22) B
10:17-30	Oct. 9–15 (Proper 23) B
10:35-45	Oct. 16–22 (Proper 24) B
10:46-52	Oct. 23–29 (Proper 25) B
11:1-11	Palm Sunday (Lent 6)
12:28b-34	Oct. 30–Nov. 5 (Proper 26) B
12:38-44	Nov. 6–12 (Proper 27) B
13:24-32	Nov. 13–19 (Proper 28) B
13:32-37	Advent 1 B
14:1–15:47	Passion Sunday (Lent 6) B (1st option)
14:12-26	Maundy Thursday B
15:1-39	Passion Sunday (Lent 6) B (2nd option)
16:1-8	Easter Vigil ABC Easter B (2nd option)
16:9-16,19-20	Ascension ABC (2nd option)

Luke

1:26-38	Advent 4 B Annunciation (March 25) ABC
1:39-55	Advent 4 C Visitation (May 31) ABC
1:39-57	Visitation (May 31) ABC
1:46b-55	(Canticle in lieu of psalm) Advent 3 B
2:1-20	Christmas Eve/Day ABC
2:8-20	Christmas Day: Additional Lections 1 ABC

INDEX
OF PSALMS

Dates refer to Sundays after Pentecost (e.g., Sunday between October 23 and October 29)

119:33-40	Epiphany 8 (Proper 3) A	133	Easter 2 B
119:33-48	Oct. 30–Nov. 5	135:1-14	Oct. 9–15 (Proper 23) A
	(Proper 26) B	137:1-6	Lent 4 B
119:129-136	Sept. 4–10 (Proper 18) B	138	Epiphany 5 C
119:137-144	Oct. 16–22 (Proper 24) C	139:1-12	July 10–16 (Proper 10) C
121	Aug. 28–Sept. 3	139:13-18	July 17–23 (Proper 11) C
	(Proper 17) B	143	Easter Vigil ABC
122	Advent 1 A	143:1-8	Aug. 7–13 (Proper 14) B
124	July 3–9 (Proper 9) A	143:1-10	July 31–Aug. 6
125	Sept. 11–17 (Proper 19) B		(Proper 13) A
126	Advent 2 C	145:8-13a	Nov. 13–19 (Proper 28) B
	Lent 5 C	145:13b-21	Easter 5 C
	Oct. 23–29 (Proper 25) B	146	Oct. 16–22 (Proper 24) A
	Thanksgiving Day B		Nov. 6–12 (Proper 27) B
127	Lent 2 C	146:5-10	Advent 3 A
	Oct. 30–Nov. 5	147:1-11	Epiphany 5 B
	(Proper 26) A	147:12-20	Christmas 2 ABC
128	Oct. 2–8 (Proper 22) B	149	All Saints' Day
	Oct. 23–29 (Proper 25) A		(Nov. 1) C
130	Lent 1 A	150	Easter Evening ABC
132:11-18	July 10–16 (Proper 10) B		